Women in the Holocaust

Women in the Holocaust

Edited by Dalia Ofer and Lenore J. Weitzman

Yale University Press　　*New Haven and London*

Designed by Sonia Scanlon.
Set in Bulmer type by à la page, New Haven, Conn.
Printed in the United States of America by Vail-
Ballou Press, Binghamton, New York.

Library of Congress Cataloging-in-Publication Data

Women in the Holocaust / [edited by] Dalia Ofer
    and Lenore J. Weitzman.
        p.   cm.
    Includes bibliographical references and index.
    ISBN 0-300-07354-2 (cl. : alk. paper)
    1. Jewish women in the Holocaust.   I. Ofer,
Dalia.   II. Weitzman, Lenore J.
D804.47.W66   1998
940.53′18′082—dc21   97-46011
                            CIP

A catalogue record for this book is available from the
British Library.

The paper in this book meets the guidelines for per-
manence and durability of the Committee on Production Guidelines for Book Longevity of the
Council on Library Resources.

10 9 8 7 6 5 4 3 2 1

Contents

Women in the Holocaust

Introduction
The Role of Gender in the Holocaust

Lenore J. Weitzman and Dalia Ofer

hy women? Why should a book on the Holocaust—which targeted all Jews for annihilation irrespective of their sex or age or any other social characteristic—focus on women?

This book shows how questions about gender lead us to a richer and more finely nuanced understanding of the Holocaust. They help us envision the specificity of everyday life and the different ways in which men and women responded to the Nazi onslaught. The discussion of women's unique experiences provides a missing element of what we must now see as an incomplete picture of Jewish life during the Holocaust.

In the first section of this introduction we discuss four structural sources of gender differences during the Holocaust: (1) the culturally defined gender roles of Jewish men and women before the war, which endowed the two sexes with different skills, knowledge, and expertise; (2) the Jews' "anticipatory reactions" to what they believed the Nazis were going to do to Jewish men (but not to women and children); (3) the differences in the nature and degree of harassment, work requirements, arrests, and regulations that the Nazis imposed on Jewish men and women—even though they were equally destined for death; and (4) the different reactions of Jewish men and women in their everyday lives in the ghettos, the forests, and the camps as they tried to cope with the destruction they were facing.

In the second section of this introduction we look at the larger ramifications of focusing on gender and examine the resistance of some Holocaust survivors and Holocaust scholars to gender-based research. One such concern is that a focus on gender will distract us from the unity of the Nazi assault on all Jews and "make the Holocaust secondary to feminism." Others fear that it might add to the popularization and banalization of the Holocaust, or lead to invidious comparisons among victims. On the other hand, however, feminist scholars have criticized the "Holocaust establishment" for ignoring the distinctive voice of women survivors.

Although the chapters in this book represent cutting-edge scholarship in an emerging field, the book departs from traditional academic norms by including personal testimonies from survivors of the Holocaust. As the last generation of scholars to have the privilege of listening to survivors speak about their experiences, we are honored to have several survivors join us as colleagues in this endeavor. Their voices are the starting point for our analysis.

The Structural Sources of Gender Differences

We use the term *gender* to refer to the social and cultural construction of the roles and positions of men and women in society. (In contrast, *sex* refers to the biological differences between men and women.) To use gender as a framework for analysis is simply to become more attentive to the possible consequences of one of the major axes of all social organization—along with age, class, race, and religion. Just as all societies make distinctions between children and adults, between rich and poor, and between members of different racial and religious groups, every known society—modern or ancient, big or small—creates different roles and different expectations for men and women. When we undertake a gender analysis, we typically look at the relative positions of men and women in the social structure (their occupations, wealth, or political power, for example); the cultural definitions and expectations of the two sexes; and the differences in how men and women experience their lives. As the chapters in this book illustrate, once we are alert to and begin to ask questions about the social expectations and behaviors of men and women, a variety of assumptions, decisions, and social patterns become more noticeable and take on added meaning.

We are not asserting that women's experiences during the Holocaust were totally different from those of men. That would be as false and misleading as to argue that their experiences were identical to men's. Nazi policy targeted all Jews as Jews, and the primary status of Jews was their "race," not their gender. Nevertheless, scholars studying Jewish responses to Nazi persecution must be attentive to the differences between men and women just as we must be attentive to other social differences among Jews, such as those between religious and secular Jews, or those among Jews of different social classes. (Nor can we generalize without specifying the dates and stages of Nazi policy.)

Thus even though our inquiry focuses on gender, it is clear that gender is only one component of the survivors' total experiences. As Sara Horowitz (Chapter 21) concludes, it is the bringing together of the two sets of details—those particular to women and those relevant to all Jewish survivors—that enables us to provide a more complex and more complete account of what happened during the Holocaust. We begin this task by examining the four structural sources of gender differences during the Holocaust that we identified above.

Prewar Roles and Responsibilities

The prewar lives of most Jewish men and women in Europe followed traditional gender patterns. In the 1920s and 1930s, in both Eastern and Western Europe, men and women lived in gender-specific worlds. In most Jewish families, as in most non-Jewish families, married men were responsible for the economic support of their families, while women, even if they had learned a trade or were helping in the family business, were responsible for the home and the children. Although the specific family patterns of Jews depended on their class and the cultural and sociopolitical milieu in which they lived, Paula Hyman (Chapter 1) shows that by the middle of the nineteenth century, Jewish men and women in Western Europe had adapted to the prevailing bourgeois model, which conferred responsibility for the physical survival of the family on men but placed its psychological and spiritual well-being in the hands of women.

The prewar roles of Jewish men and women thus exposed the two sexes to different experiences, social milieus, and social networks, and endowed them with different spheres of knowledge, expertise, and skills with which to face the Nazi onslaught. As Marion Kaplan (Chapter 2) observes, for example, when Jewish families in Germany faced worsening living conditions after the Nuremberg Laws of 1935 were passed, it was the women who were supposed to "make things work" by coping with ever-shrinking resources for running their households. Women also took responsibility for the psychological work of raising their family's spirits. Children who faced Nazi teachers and hostile classmates at school needed understanding and encouragement. Husbands who faced the loss of customers, patients, clients, and jobs needed a haven from the daily assaults. As late as February 1938, an article in a Jewish newspaper reminded Jewish women that they had to brighten their homes with cheer.

One consequence of the cultural norm of separate spheres was that women in Western Europe were generally excluded from the world of business, higher education, and politics. They were therefore less assimilated than Jewish men and were less likely to have Gentile business partners, professional colleagues, close friends, or extended Christian families to protect them during the years of Nazi persecution.

In Poland and the countries of Eastern Europe, the gender differences in assimilation were reversed. There Jewish women assumed more responsibility for contributing to the support of the household. Most Jews did not attain middle-class status, and because of economic necessity, women participated more actively in small family businesses or worked in the textile industry.

They were also more familiar with the world of culture. In fact, in many families, especially middle-class families, it was the women who were the "engines of acculturation," bringing Polish culture into the home.[1] Because Jewish girls were more likely than Jewish boys to attend regular Polish schools, learn the Polish language, become involved in secular activities, and grow up enjoying Polish literature and culture, they were the ones to introduce these interests to their children. As Lenore Weitzman shows (Chapter 11), Jewish women's prewar involvement in economic and secular activities in Poland provided them with important networks for securing false papers, with resources for locating jobs, and with friends to help them find a place to hide or live (illegally) outside the ghetto. Their ability to speak Polish and their knowledge of Polish customs were tremendous assets in helping them escape from the ghettos and pass on the "Aryan" side.

In other countries (and periods) women's traditional roles inhibited their possibilities for escape. In the mid-1930s, for example, young and middle-aged German women were reluctant to abandon their aging parents and take advantage of opportunities to emigrate. In contrast, during the war years, especially in the early days of the Polish ghettos, women's caretaking, homemaking, food-stretching, and coping skills greatly enhanced their chances of survival.

While there were many continuities between women's prewar roles and their subsequent behavior, it is important to note that the war also brought disjunctures and changes, such as the need for many more Jewish women to seek regular jobs. Nevertheless they continued to shoulder their traditional (and increasingly difficult) tasks of shopping, cooking, housekeeping, and caring for their husbands, parents, and children.

Anticipatory Reactions

The second source of gender differences during the Holocaust arises from the Jews' anticipatory reactions to what they believed the Germans were going to do. Most Jews believed—at least in the beginning—that the Germans were "civilized" and would honor traditional gender norms and would not harm women and children. Because the Jews believed that only men were in real danger, they responded with gender-specific plans to protect and save their men. Thus, in formulating their strategies for migration, hiding, and escape, they typically decided that men should leave first and should have priority for exit visas.

In Paris, for example, before the Black Thursday of July 16, 1942, when 12,884 French Jews were arrested, many Jewish men had been warned of the impending roundups by the hundreds of policemen, bureaucrats, and office workers who were organizing the schedules.[2] Because it was assumed that women and children were safe, they remained at home—and hence they turned out to be the disproportionate victims of the sweeping arrests. On that day 5,802 women and 4,051 children were arrested (compared with only 3,031 men). These women and children were also the disproportionate victims of the subsequent deportations to Auschwitz.

Similarly, in Eastern Europe, anticipation of what the Germans would do spurred different behavior among men and women. There, too, everyone assumed that men would receive harsher treatment from the Germans and that only men were in real danger. That belief led to gender-specific plans to keep the men off the streets and to help them escape to the East in the early days of the German invasion. As a result of the male exodus from Poland, women were a majority of the Jewish population in many ghettos.

Testimonies and ghetto diaries also attest to the ways in which the anticipation of German behavior shaped everyday life in the cities and ghettos in Eastern Europe. Because Jewish men, especially those with long beards, earlocks, and traditional Orthodox clothing, were easy to identify and target for harassment, many families decided that it was safer for the women to go out in the streets—even before the ghettos were formed. As Emmanuel Ringelblum noted in his diary in 1940 (before the ghetto period): "Men don't go out. . . . She stands on the long line. . . . The women are everywhere."[3] Thus family strategies for daily life—from who should wait in line for bread to who should go to the Nazi authorities—were forged in response to the perception and anticipation of how the Germans would treat men and women.

German Policy and Treatment of Men and Women

Although men and women were equally targeted for death, their paths— especially in the early years of the war—were paved with different regulations, work requirements, opportunities, and constraints. One difference in the Germans' treatment of men and women was their consistent pattern of delegating the leadership roles to men. Ruth Bondy (Chapter 17), Felicja Karay (Chapter 16), and Yehuda Bauer (Chapter 14) point to the overwhelming predominance of men in German-organized Jewish Councils and administrative positions. In Theresienstadt all twelve members of the Judenrat were men during its entire three-and-a-half years of existence; in the Skarżysko-Kamienna camp, all but one of the internal administrative officials were men. What is remarkable about Gisi Fleischmann of Slovakia is that she was the only woman to serve in a leadership role in a Jewish community in occupied Europe or in a satellite country of Germany.

A second German policy in the early years of the war (although this policy was not universally applied) was the perpetuation of the traditional division of labor and the assignment of heavy manual labor to men. Jewish workers were rarely paid wages for their forced labor, but in those places where they were paid (or where the Jewish Council was paid for ghetto workers in, for example, German factories), there were always systematic wage differentials between men and women. Women were typically paid two-thirds to three-quarters of men's wages, even if they were doing the same work (see Bondy, Chapter 17; Karay, Chapter 16; and Unger, Chapter 8).

A third difference was the initial focus on Jewish men for arrest and incarceration in both Western and Eastern Europe. In Germany, for example, in the November 1938 Kristallnacht pogrom only Jewish men—thirty thousand of them—were arrested and sent to concentration camps (see Kaplan, Chapter

2). Similarly, in the early days of the war in Poland, Jewish men were much more likely than women to be beaten, arrested, and imprisoned. They were also more likely to be executed in the systematic targeting of community leaders (because men were more likely to be community leaders). In addition, in the early ghetto period, men were much more likely to be picked up for a day of hard physical labor (accompanied by arbitrary beatings and abuse on the part of German or Polish supervisors) and for deportation to a forced-labor camp outside the ghetto.

The most infamous distinction between the sexes was the German treatment of pregnant women. It is important to distinguish what happened in the ghettos from what happened in the labor camps and concentration camps, even though considerable variation existed within each of these three spheres, depending on the location (and on the month and year). In many ghettos the Germans instituted a policy of compulsory abortion. In Theresienstadt, for example, an order for compulsory abortion was issued in July 1943. After that any woman who rejected an abortion or gave birth was sent on the next transport to the concentration camps in the East (see Bondy, Chapter 17).

In many forced-labor camps, however, abortion was not an option: pregnancy automatically condemned a woman to death. Felicja Karay, for example, writes about the "bunk romances" among the Jewish population of the Skarżysko labor camp and the different consequences they had for women and men (see Chapter 16). Only the women took the real risk—the danger of becoming pregnant—because pregnant women were singled out for death in every selection.

Pregnancy was also a life-threatening event in the concentration camps. There, too, visibly pregnant women (and women with small children) were selected for immediate killing (see Goldenberg, Chapter 18; and Horowitz, Chapter 21). Testimonies from survivors are filled with heart-wrenching accounts of mothers in the prime of life who were sent to the gas chambers because they were holding the hands of their young children.

The last distinction in the German treatment of men and women—ironically, a clear violation of German policy—was that Jewish women were more likely than men to be subjected to sexual harassment and rape. Although the incidence of rape by the Nazis appears to have been rare—or at least that is our impression, based on the diaries and testimonies we have read—it is clear that many Jewish women were terrorized by rumors of rape. This fear of sexual assault was also experienced by women in hiding.

In addition, a number of testimonies report systematic sexual assaults on Jewish women in specific localities. Survivors of the Skarżysko camp, for example, reported several sexual assaults and brutal rapes by German commanders even though Germans were prohibited from such "racial shame" (Karay, Chapter 16).

Responses of Jewish Men and Women

Although the Nazis imposed harsh edicts on all Jews, and although all Jews faced the same ultimate fate, as Mary Felstiner concluded, "along the stations toward extinction . . . each gender lived its own journey."[4] In the early years of the war, Ruth Bondy observes, men and women in Prague responded differently because they experienced opposite crises. The men lost their jobs, their economic security, and their status: they felt degraded because they were compelled to be idle or to shovel snow or build roads in forced-labor squads. Women, in contrast, faced an increase in their traditional workload because most middle-class Jewish families in Prague could no longer afford (and were forbidden to employ) their Czech housekeepers. The women took on the work of stoking the coal fires, washing the clothes, preparing the meals from increasingly scarce rations, and recycling old materials into clothing for their families (Bondy, Chapter 17).

As we follow these men and women into the ghettos and camps, we see the two sexes responding differently to each new setting. In Theresienstadt, where the men and women from Prague lived in separate barracks, the women tried to convert their places on the three-tiered bunks into surrogate homes, by covering the mattress with a colored sheet, hanging photographs on the back wall, or laying a napkin on the plank housing their possessions (Bondy, Chapter 17).

In 1943–1944 the men and women from Prague were transferred from Theresienstadt to Auschwitz-Birkenau. Here Bondy points to the differences in their appearance although their clothes were distributed to them at random (actually, the clothes were thrown at them without regard to size or fit or appropriateness):

> Only a day after their arrival, the differences between the sexes was already striking. The men, in hats with cut-off brims and in trousers

and coats thrown to them at random—too short, too long, too wide, too small—looked like sad black storks. The women, also wearing garments that had been distributed to them at random, had somehow succeeded in only twenty-four hours in adjusting them to their bodies and sewing up the holes, using needles made out of wooden splinters and threads pulled out of the one blanket allocated to them. . . . [The women] carried the heavy wooden soup barrels, three women on each side, for the privilege of scraping whatever stuck to the sides and bottom after distribution—most of it for their children, husbands, or brothers. In the same conditions, with the same scarce nourishment, they could bear hunger more easily, and deteriorated more slowly, than the men. (Bondy, Chapter 17)

In the Polish ghettos of Lodz and Warsaw we find a similar gender-based division of labor (see Unger, Chapter 8; and Ofer, Chapter 9). Women remained responsible for what was left of cooking, cleaning, and child care even though their occupational roles had changed dramatically. The most dramatic shift in women's occupational roles occurred in the city of Lodz. Before the war about one-third of the Jewish women were employed. As Michal Unger notes in Chapter 8, however, ghetto conditions forced women to find work when having a job became a prerequisite for survival. From 1942 on, anyone who was not working was regarded as "superfluous" and was deported. By 1944, when the final census was taken in the Lodz ghetto, virtually all the women were working (and 60 percent of all workers were women).

Whereas Lodz became a working ghetto, in which virtually all the women and men were employed, jobs were much more limited in Warsaw. There both men and women suffered from unemployment. Women had a harder time finding jobs (owing to both the scarcity of jobs and their lack of experience), but large numbers of men were also unable to work to provide for their families. In fact, in September 1941, about half the inhabitants of the Warsaw ghetto (200,000–250,000 people) had no regular income and were essentially starving to death. Most of them were women and children. Especially vulnerable were the single mothers and their children, who constituted a sizable portion of the ghetto's poor population.

Dalia Ofer (Chapter 9) writes of the ingenuity and adaptability of many women in the Warsaw ghetto in finding ways to feed their children. Many of them took great risks, and some even turned to the dangerous occupation of smuggling to support their families. Whereas most of these women explained their coping strategies as natural extensions of their traditional roles, with today's hindsight we see them taking on new roles in their fight for survival.

In fact, we are shown portraits of women in both Lodz and Warsaw who faced overwhelming forces with incredible resourcefulness, courage, and persistence. Seeing their children and husbands endangered filled them with a sense of mission and superhuman strength—to spend long days at exhausting work, to piece together resources and contacts for trade and barter, to try to ignore their own hunger while sharing their meager rations, and to cope with rampant sickness (Unger, Chapter 8; Ofer, Chapter 9).

A recurrent theme in the ghetto diaries was the desperate sacrifice of mothers who tried to keep their children alive by depriving themselves of food. As diarist Dawid Sierakowiak wrote, his "tiny, emaciated mother" had surrendered her life to others by giving away her food. She had valued her family more than herself.[5]

We also find many examples of young women who sacrificed themselves for their mothers. One of the most difficult choices that Jewish families faced occurred when one member of the family was selected for a transport. Many memoirs and testimonies tell of women who refused to abandon their mothers and instead chose to face the unknown with them, even when it became evident that the transports and selections were likely to lead to death (see Karay, Chapter 16).

Another sphere of gender-differentiated patterns of behavior during the war was in activities that involved rescue and resistance. Women took on special roles in the French Resistance (Poznanski, Chapter 13), among the forest partisans (Tec, Chapter 12), and within the Jewish underground in Poland. For example, the testimonies of Liza Chapnik (Chapter 6) and Bronka Klibansky (Chapter 10) dramatically illustrate the unique and vital role that women played as couriers for the resistance in Poland.

In the camps women and men faced both similar and different threats and challenges. On the arrival ramp at Auschwitz the orders were for all children to remain with the women; the Nazis thus linked the destiny of women and children. It is well known that some of the Jews who worked on the arrival ramp walked among the women lining up for the selection and told the young women to "give their children to the grandmother." The workers, who knew that the grandmothers—and the children—were already destined for the gas chambers, were trying to save the lives of the young mothers. The new arrivals, however, did not know what was happening—and certainly did not understand the true meaning of the instruction. Naturally most women clung to their children (and many young girls to their mothers) and were sent to the gas chambers with them. (See Lidia Vago's vivid account in Chapter 15.)

Those men and women who survived the initial selection were put to work, typically at harsh physical labor. In analyzing three Auschwitz testimonies, Myrna Goldenberg (Chapter 18) notes some gender-specific coping skills, such as the formation of surrogate families and "camp sister" relationships for mutual aid and nurturance; and the sharing of recipes, cooking techniques, and memories of holiday meals to help cope with hunger.

Along similar lines, Felicja Karay (Chapter 16) points to the strategies that the women in the Skarżysko labor camp used in order to avoid personal deterioration. Although many men stopped washing and shaving, the women continued to pay attention to personal hygiene; they kept their bodies and hair clean, mended their clothing, and maintained a human and even feminine appearance. Their nearly normal appearance induced their overseers to give them more assistance, to subject them to fewer beatings, and, most important, to treat them more humanely.

Throughout this introduction we have referred to the Nazis' practice of immediately sending young mothers and children to the gas chambers. Because the Nazis disguised the gas chambers as showers and assured everyone that they were about to undergo disinfection, most of the women were not aware of what was happening when they and their children were put on the line for the gas chambers. Thus the women did not intentionally choose to die with their children. It was the Nazis who sentenced these women to death because they were mothers.

In contrast to this general pattern, however, one group of women knowingly chose to die in order to be with their children until the end. When the women of Theresienstadt were sent to the family camp in Auschwitz-Birkenau, they were allowed to live with their children. In June 1944 it became clear that the family camp was going to be liquidated and that the children would be sent to the gas chambers. But the mothers had a choice: because the Nazis needed workers, the mothers could opt to present themselves for a selection in which they might be chosen as workers, or they could go to the gas chambers with their children. This was a choice that men did not have to face, because the men were segregated from the women and children as soon as they arrived at Auschwitz. As Ruth Bondy observed, all but two women of the six hundred who were given the choice decided that they could not abandon their children. They were at their side to the end.

Before we conclude this section on the structural sources of gender differences, we should note that raising questions about gender differences does not inevitably lead to the conclusion that such differences exist. As Gisela Bock notes, asking questions about gender must open our eyes to gender similarities as well as to gender differences. In fact, several chapters in this book, such as those by Bock (Chapter 5) and by Lawrence L. Langer (Chapter 20), conclude that gender differences were not significant or were not as significant as other factors. Clearly, we are still in the early stages of gender-based analyses in the field of Holocaust studies, and many areas remain to be explored. That is why most of the contributors to this volume—especially Gershon Bacon, Daniel Blatman, and Joan Ringelheim—raise so many questions for future research.

Why Is There Resistance to Research on Gender in the Holocaust?

In putting together this book and in organizing the conference that preceded it, we encountered considerable resistance to the study of gender in the Holocaust. This resistance—sometimes, outright hostility—arose from several concerns. One concern that was expressed was that any differentiation of the victims of the Holocaust by gender could distract us from the fact that the Nazis defined their targets as Jews—not as men or women or children—and systematically planned to murder all of them. Others voiced the concern that by raising the question of gender we were imposing today's concerns on the past—allowing a feminist agenda, which may be appropriate to our era, to "take over the Holocaust." Still others were fearful that a focus on gender could diminish the importance of the Holocaust as a singular cataclysmic event and thereby add to the banalization and trivialization of the Holocaust. Finally, some were reluctant to make any distinctions among victims that could lead to invidious comparisons and deflect attention from Nazi policy.

Among those who expressed these concerns were many survivors who said, at first, that being a woman was only rarely meaningful in their war experience. The strict rules and regulations, the limitations on activities, and the denial of personal freedom, which applied to all Jews, were much more critical in their everyday lives than any distinctions between men and women. Some said that they never thought about what it meant to be a woman at that time. And few thought that being a woman or a man made them more or less capable of surviving, or changed the course of events.

Ruth Bondy, for instance, begins her portrait of the role of gender in Theresienstadt by stating that she was offended by the idea of "dividing the Holocaust and its suffering by gender" (Chapter 17). It was only because she did not want the story of the women of Theresienstadt to be left out of the book that she decided to examine whether and in what ways the lives of the women in the ghetto differed from those of the men. Her reflections led to a richly textured analysis that shows the usefulness of these questions.

In the course of writing their chapters, other survivors and Holocaust scholars were surprised by the new insights they gained when they began to raise questions about gender in their analyses. Not everyone, however, was convinced. A few retained their initial skepticism about a focus on gender. Nevertheless, everyone was interested in the answers to the substantive questions that were raised about the lives of women, their plight in the ghettos and the camps, and how they coped with the crises they faced. The chapters in this book illuminate these issues. Rather than distracting us from the Nazi brutality against all Jews, they enhance our understanding of it by locating it in the specificity of individual experiences.

It is also evident that questions about gender and everyday life are not just today's questions imposed on the past. Rather, they are closely linked to the central and most important questions asked by the ghetto historians at that time. Jewish archival sources from the ghettos, especially the Ringelblum archives (the underground archives of the Warsaw ghetto), provide rich accounts of daily Jewish life during the ghetto period. The ghetto historians initiated and collected diaries and personal accounts to find out what was happening to ordinary people, to families, to relationships between husbands and wives, and to relationships between parents and children. They saw these personal accounts, which often discussed gender issues, as the history they wanted to preserve for posterity.

Another indication of the importance attached to these issues during the Holocaust is the separate study of women that Emmanuel Ringelblum commissioned (see Ofer, Chapter 9). It examined women's prewar lives, the German occupation, everyday life in the ghetto, and the struggle for survival. Awareness of the unique position of Jewish women is also recorded for posterity in the famous quotation from Ringelblum's own diary: "The future historian would have to dedicate a proper page to the Jewish woman during this war. She will capture an important part in this Jewish history for her courage and ability to survive. Because of her, many families were able to get over the terrors of these days."[6]

Even without this authoritative documentation from the time of the Holocaust, we would argue that revisiting the past is the mission of historians and social scientists. New perspectives enrich our understanding of the past. As long as we do not bend the facts to current fashions, and as long as we maintain the appropriate historical context, we enrich our analysis of the past when we can benefit from the perspective of time. New questions occur to us because of changes in conventions. Current trends in the study of history, and the shift from political history to social history—which place the individual at the center of our studies—clearly resonate with the themes of this book.

What, then, of the fear that a focus on gender will trivialize or banalize the Holocaust? When one is confronted by the unimaginable suffering of the victims at every stage of Nazi occupation and by their ultimate annihilation, the argument goes, discussions of the minutiae of day-to-day interaction between husband and wife, or of the struggle to find jobs, or of the exchange of recipes in the camps, seem to pale in comparison and rob the victims of the honor and dignity they deserve. But the opposite is true. It is the details of everyday life— the portrait of a woman who saved her single ration of bread for her children, or that of a man who volunteered for forced labor because his wages were promised to his family—that restore individuality and humanity to the victims.

Both survivors and Holocaust scholars are concerned about banalization because of the growing interest in the Holocaust in popular culture, especially in the United States, during the 1980s and 1990s. When the Holocaust is removed from the exclusive domain of serious scholars and made the subject of television mini-series, popular novels, plays, art, films, theater, and literature, the historical record is likely to be simplified and diluted. It may also be distorted or changed—either knowingly or unintentionally—for dramatic impact, or to meet "family viewing" standards or educational needs, or for a better story line (in which the main characters manage to survive). Understandable motives—such as the need to find meaning in the events of the Holocaust, the need to shield the audience from the worst horror of the Holocaust, and the need to comfort ourselves with some "redeeming" message—lead to both popularization and banalization. Nevertheless, concerns about banalization and trivialization of the Holocaust are not appropriately directed at the scholarly essays in this book.

A fourth concern is that any distinctions among victims may lead to invidious comparisons and distract us from the real cause of Jewish suffering, which was the murderous policy of the Nazis. If we begin to look at the differences among victims, some critics maintain, we shall see that some victims were better off. Then, it is claimed, one might conclude that some victims should be praised for their coping skills (or blamed for their lack of them), instead of focusing the blame on the Germans. In other words, if women coped better in the ghettos or men coped better in the camps, we could end up blaming those who did not cope as well for their own suffering rather than blaming the inhuman policies of the Nazis.

Once again, our response to this concern is rooted in the increased understanding that comes from the kind of detailed analyses undertaken by the authors of this book. Invidious comparisons are impossible when one is aware of the full context of constraints under which both men and women lived in the ghettos and the camps. By undertaking studies of specific ghettos, labor camps, and concentration camps, we enlarge our understanding of the impossible choices most Jews faced.

A very different set of concerns has been expressed by feminist scholars who criticize the "Holocaust establishment" for ignoring the role and experiences of women for so long.[7] They point to the lack of serious attention to gender in the academic literature on the Holocaust as well as in the newly established Holocaust memorials and museums (see Ringelheim, Chapter 19). These concerns are legitimate. Scholars and researchers have been reluctant to address many of the issues raised in this book. As Myrna Goldenberg notes (Chapter 18), by assuming that the universal Holocaust experience was the male experience, scholars have simply ignored the different voices of women survivors.[8] Until now works by women survivors have been cited less frequently in scholarly studies, and the indexes of major monographs on the Holocaust have rarely included entries for women. As Sara Horowitz (Chapter 21) notes, although many women survivors have written memoirs and left diaries and letters, women's experiences are assumed not to represent a "typical" Holocaust narrative.

While it is important to stress the distinctiveness of gendered experiences during the Holocaust, it is essential that women's experiences not be discussed exclusively in terms of motherhood or sexuality. To do so marginalizes women and, ironically, reinforces the male experience as the "master narrative." Rather, it is important to pay attention to the particularity of gendered wounding that both sexes experienced.

It is our hope that this book will be the impetus for renewed interest in the totality of women's experiences during the Holocaust, as well as the impetus for future research. Our generation is privileged to still have the opportunity to hear and record the voices of women survivors, which will greatly enhance our understanding of the diversity and complexity of experiences during the Holocaust. This book demonstrates the importance of asking questions about what happened to women in the Holocaust, without in any way minimizing the horror of what the Nazis did to all Jews. Rather, an analysis that includes gender helps us to better understand the impact that the Holocaust had on all its Jewish victims.

The book is organized chronologically. We begin with the decades before the Holocaust: Part I provides an overview of the developments and diversity in Jewish life in Western and Eastern Europe between World War I and World War II. This overview sets the stage for the next three sections of the book, which deal directly with aspects of the Holocaust: life in the ghettos (Part II), rescue and resistance (Part III), and the labor and concentration camps (Part IV). The last four chapters in Part IV address both the specificity of the camps and the more general issue of the role of gender in the Holocaust.

Next, a few notes on style. In the three personal narratives, names are given according to the recollection of the author; first names are not always available and the spellings could not always be verified. Throughout the book, quotations from non-English sources have been translated by the author of the chapter in which the quotation appears, unless otherwise noted. Although we have generally used transliterations for words in Hebrew and Yiddish, where a non-English word has entered the standard English dictionaries, we have used that form rather than a direct transliteration.

Finally, we would like to thank the people and organizations who helped us. Our first expression of gratitude is to the Kaplan-Kushlick Foundation, and especially to Jill Kaplan, who said yes to Lenore J. Weitzman's initial idea and launched this project. The crucial vision and support that Jill Kaplan and Dorothy Pantanowitz of the C. G. Foundation provided made everything else possible.

For additional financial support for the international workshop that we co-chaired in 1995 we are indebted to Hebrew University, our host, and to a variety of individual departments for their generous contributions: The Lafer Center for Women's Studies, the Melton Center for Jewish Education in the Diaspora, the Rosita and Esteban Herczeg Program on Sex Differences in Society, the Avraham Harman Institute of Contemporary Jewry, and the Division of Development and Public Relations.

We are also grateful for the support we received from Yad Vashem, the Martyrs and Heroes' Remembrance Authority in Israel, and the Research Institute of the United States Holocaust Memorial Museum. Michael Berenbaum, who was then director of the Research Institute, played a visionary role, from the beginning, in facilitating our work and the creation of this book.

For the past two years we have had the good fortune to be guided by Gladys Topkis, senior editor at Yale University Press. Her keen judgment, sharp editorial pen, and worldly wisdom have had a transformative impact on every chapter in this book.

We are also indebted to our manuscript editor, Jenya Weinreb, for her diligence in ferreting out mistakes and for her ingenious solutions in correcting them with good humor and endless patience.

Our gratitude to William J. Goode is for both his culinary masterpieces and sage editorial advice. He nourished our bodies and souls while the two of us worked on the manuscript for some eighteen hours a day. His thesaurus-like talent for suggesting the precise phrase, and ruthless willingness to cut, had a beneficial impact on the entire manuscript.

Dalia Ofer would also like to acknowledge her debt to the Max and Rita Haber Chair for Holocaust Studies and to the staff of the Institute for Contemporary Jewry. Lenore J. Weitzman is grateful to the U.S.-Israel Fulbright Commission and to Yad Vashem for hosting her Fulbright year in Israel, and to the Wenner-Gren Foundation for Anthropological Research, the Memorial Foundation for Jewish Culture, and the Harvard University Clark-Tozier Award for financial support. We would both like to thank the Avraham Harman Institute for helping us with the pre-publication costs of preparing the manuscript.

This book has been a truly collaborative project and a source of personal enrichment for both of us. Our different backgrounds and our different initial perspectives led us through many disagreements, agreements, and compromises as we planned first the workshop and then the book. The endless questions we have posed for each other, about the role and importance of gender, the events of the Holocaust, and the interpretations of what we think we know, have given us new insights and have stimulated new research interests for each of us. We thank each other for the privilege of working together and for the personal and intellectual growth—and enjoyment—that this collaboration has provided.

Notes

1. Celia S. Heller, *On the Edge of Destruction: Jews of Poland between the Two World Wars* (Detroit: Wayne State University Press, 1977). See also Chapter 3 in this book.

2. Susan Zuccotti, *The Holocaust, the French and the Jews* (New York: Basic Books, 1993), p. 107.

3. Emmanuel Ringelblum, *Diary and Notes from the Warsaw Ghetto, September 1939–December 1942,* ed. and intro. Yisrael Gutman, Yosef Kermisz, and Israel Sham (Hebrew) (Jerusalem: Yad Vashem, 1992). (This is a complete edition of Ringelblum's diary, unlike the earlier English translations.)

4. Mary Felstiner, *To Paint Her Life: Charlotte Salomon in the Nazi Era* (New York: Harper-Collins, 1994), pp. 205–206.

5. Dawid Sierakowiak, *The Diary of Dawid Sierakowiak: Five Notebooks from the Lodz Ghetto,* ed. Alan Adelson (New York: Oxford, 1996), pp. 219–220, as cited in Unger, Chapter 8 of this book.

6. Ringelblum, *Diary and Notes from the Warsaw Ghetto,* p. 380.

7. Esther Katz and Joan Miriam Ringelheim (eds.), *Proceedings of the Conference, Women Surviving the Holocaust* (New York: Institute for Research in History, 1983).

8. Because we scholars are products of our own cultures and because many of us are women who identify strongly with the victims of the Holocaust, it may be difficult for us (and for other scholars) to face the humiliation and denigration of Jewish women during the Holocaust. As Joan Ringelheim (Chapter 19) points out, the silence that has surrounded women's experiences during the Holocaust may also reflect the fact that researchers have wanted to avoid the pain of hearing about the gender-specific suffering that women endured.

Before the War

The Jews of Europe believed that they had achieved complete emancipation in the various peace agreements following World War I. Notwithstanding the great differences among countries, Jews were becoming integrated into economic and social life. The 1930s, however, shattered their hopes. The economic crises that accompanied the Depression brought serious setbacks in the postwar trends toward Jewish integration, and a persistent undercurrent of exclusion culminated in vicious antisemitic movements.

In Germany, Romania, Poland, and the Baltic states, the Jews became prey to nationalistic propaganda and practical measures that pushed them out of both their traditional vocations and the more recent occupations they had begun to practice. After the rise of Nazism, anti-Jewish measures were stepped up. In 1935, German Jews lost their emancipation. In the countries of Eastern Europe, *numerus clausus* (Jewish quotas) restricted the number of Jewish students admitted to the universities, and Jews were excluded from many occupations and professions.

Part I of this book is set in this general historical context, beginning with Paula Hyman's exploration of the family patterns and status of women in Jewish communities in Western and Eastern Europe. In such countries as France and Germany, where many Jews had attained middle-class status, they followed the prevailing bourgeois pattern of assigning responsibility for the physical survival of the family to men; women were responsible for the home and the family's psychological and spiritual well-being.

In the Jewish communities in Eastern Europe, in contrast, the cultural ideal of male learning and female labor legitimated the presence of women in the world of commerce, and owing to economic necessity, many Jewish women contributed to the support of their households and participated in secular public life. Hyman suggests that this involvement in the world outside the home may have provided the Jewish women of Eastern Europe with important networks and resources for escape and rescue during the Holocaust.

In "Keeping Calm and Weathering the Storm," Marion Kaplan offers a fascinating analysis of Jewish women's responses to daily life in Nazi Germany between 1933 and 1939. Kaplan shows how the Nazi rise to power strengthened many traditional gender norms while disrupting others. The traditional roles of middle-class Jewish women, for example, became even more important in the 1930s, when their families were faced with progressively worsening living conditions. It was women who were supposed to run the household with fewer resources, shop for food in stores owned by hostile non-Jews, soothe children who were harassed at school, and create a haven for their husbands. At the same time, the severity and immediacy of the crisis that most Jewish families faced propelled many women to take on new roles and responsibilities. As men were dismissed from their jobs and lost their businesses, many Jewish women suddenly needed to help support the family. They took on new roles as partner, breadwinner, and even family protector, as they defended their husbands, fathers, and brothers.

Turning next to the prewar period in Eastern Europe, we focus on Poland, home to 3.5 million Jews. In the 1920s and 1930s, the role and status of Jewish women in Poland underwent sweeping changes. Jewish women, especially those of the urban middle classes, were caught up in the modernization processes that swept Poland and were increasingly influenced by Polish culture and language.

In Chapter 3, Gershon Bacon laments the lack of attention paid to women in the historical literature of the prewar period. Pointing to the potential insights to be gained from taking gender issues into account, he urges a re-analysis of traditional sources—for example, census data, election polls, publications of political organizations, autobiographies, and memoirs—in order to re-examine the conclusions that were based on data solely from Jewish men.

In the 1930s, one of the most important Jewish political organizations in Poland was the Bund, the political party of the Jewish labor movement. Daniel Blatman (Chapter 4) demonstrates that the Bund, unlike other Jewish political movements, made an effort to integrate as many women as possible in party activity. Nevertheless, and despite the Bund's strong socialist ideology of equality, Blatman shows that women did not play a major role as either rank-and-file activists or political leaders. Only a limited number of women joined the Bund, and few of them managed to attain positions of power. This may seem surprising, considering that women accounted for 44.5 percent of the Jewish wage earners in Poland in 1931. Women's working conditions, however, were far inferior to those of men (their wages were only 50–60 percent of men's), and they were still seen—by both themselves and their families—as wives and mothers and only secondarily as providers.

In the final chapter in Part I, Gisela Bock takes us back to Germany to show how "ordinary" (non-Jewish) German women were mobilized to implement Nazi policies—not primarily as women but as workers. Bock concludes that most German women, like most German men, participated in the anti-Jewish policies by performing the innumerable tasks that enabled the bureaucracy and war machinery to function. Bock stresses the similarities between the German men and women who carried out the jobs that fueled the Nazi crimes. More than half the women in Germany were employed, and their aid to the Nazi cause was, like that of most men, a function of their employment and their wish to succeed in their jobs and careers. Bock does point to some gender differences, however. She argues, for example, that the ratio of "active" to "passive" participants was different for women and men: fewer women were involved in direct and violent killing operations. Nevertheless, most German women, including women from all walks of life, participated in racist and genocidal policies—as did most German men. Bock concludes by reminding us that using gender as a category of analysis must open our eyes not just to gender differences but also to similarities. In the case of Nazi Germany, she finds the similarities much stronger than the differences.

CHAPTER ONE

Gender and the Jewish Family in Modern Europe

Paula E. Hyman

I t is impossible to speak about *the* Jewish family in modern Europe because the family patterns of Jews in the modern period varied dramatically, depending on their class and the cultural and sociopolitical milieu in which they lived. By the last quarter of the nineteenth century in Western and Central Europe, expanding industrial economies enabled large numbers of Jews to situate themselves securely in the bourgeoisie. Economic prosperity, combined with the achievement—or the tantalizing prospect—of civic emancipation, spurred Jews to embrace secular education and the standards of the urban middle classes. The practice of traditional Judaism declined, and modernized versions of Judaism appeared. In such cities as Paris, Berlin, Frankfurt, Prague, and Vienna, middle-class Jewish families adopted the vision of bourgeois domesticity that conferred upon men the public world of business and politics and upon women the domain of the home.

In the countries of Eastern Europe and the eastern part of Central Europe, whose economic development was retarded in comparison with the West and where Jewish population growth was considerable, Jews were located primarily among the urban working classes and the poor. Bourgeois domesticity may have been the ideal, but most Polish and Russian Jews could not realize that ideal. Although secularization touched a substantial minority of Eastern European Jews by the beginning of the twentieth century, the institutions and leadership of traditional religious culture remained relatively vigorous.[1]

Within these blocs of "Eastern" and "Western" European Jewry, which I have presented as ideal types, many variations existed. Not all Western European Jews were comfortably middle class, nor were all Eastern European Jews members of the working poor. Amsterdam Jewry, for example, was heavily proletarian,[2] whereas prosperous Jewish merchants and professionals could be found in Warsaw and Minsk. Viennese Jewry included both the most splendid examples of the Jewish bourgeoisie and Yiddish-speaking working-class newcomers from Galicia.[3] Substantial numbers of Eastern European immigrant Jews, struggling to establish themselves, could be found in all the major cities of Western Europe in the first decades of the twentieth century. Finally, within each geocultural bloc, changes over time transformed the demography and culture of Jewish families. With these caveats in mind, I shall discuss in turn the development of the Western and Eastern European Jewish families, with a focus on changing gender roles.

The Bourgeois Jewish Families of Western Europe

From the beginning of the nineteenth century the urban Jewish elites of Western and Central Europe sought to adapt to the culture of the larger society and to achieve the material comfort associated with the urban middle class. Although the Jews of France were alone in enjoying civic equality until the last third of the century, a variety of factors—including state policy, economic development, and the emergence of a modernizing lay leadership—enabled increasing numbers of Jews to make their way into the middle class. Even in small towns and villages (where many German and French Jews lived until the end of the nineteenth century), Jews belonged to the rural bourgeoisie and were more likely than their peasant neighbors to be influenced by the standards of the modern city's elite.[4]

Jews had a particular affinity for the values of the European bourgeoisie, whose economic roots were in commerce and whose cultural attributes depended on education. Their historic experience with a market economy enabled Jews in the countries of Western and Central Europe to take advantage of new economic opportunities. As Jacob Toury's and Avraham Barkai's studies of tax records of the German states show, Jews were poorer than their Gentile neighbors at the beginning of the nineteenth century but were more wealthy some two generations later.[5] Although the extent of the socioeconomic mobility of Jews in France was less striking than in Germany, in Paris by the end of the nineteenth century most native-born Jews, and particularly those born in the capital itself, were comfortably middle class.[6] Vienna and Prague, too, boasted substantial populations of middle-class Jews. The economic success of many Jews in the West and some in the East provided monetary resources essential for their survival in the early years of World War II.

Modern bourgeois culture prescribed distinct gender roles. Men were responsible for work in the public sphere, be it earning a living or governing society; women were slated for work in the domestic sphere, primarily the management of the household and the rearing of children. Men confronted the stresses of the marketplace; women created a sheltering environment ideally free from stress. Men and women were considered temperamentally suited for their different roles, with men endowed by nature with rationality and physical and mental strength and women with tenderness and spirituality. A French prayerbook, written for private prayer by Rabbi Arnaud Aron of Strasbourg in 1848 (and subsequently translated into several languages and reprinted as late as the twentieth century), reflected the acceptance, by modern Jewish leaders and their followers, of the European bourgeois gender differentiation. A prayer to be recited by a husband included the following lines:

> May I never forget that if might and reason are the perquisite of my sex, hers is subject to bodily weakness and to spiritual sensitivity; do not permit me, Oh Lord, to be unjust to her or to demand from her qualities that are not of her nature.[7]

In her prayer a wife articulated her complementary and subordinate role:

> Lord, you have given me a husband as the companion of my life. . . . It is from him that I receive my subsistence. . . . May I never forget that man's work taxes his soul . . . with cares . . . and that it is his wife's duty . . . to restore calm and serenity to her husband's heart through her . . . submission, her indulgent character.[8]

By the middle of the nineteenth century, then, Jewish men and women in Western and Central Europe had adapted themselves to the prevailing bourgeois model that conferred responsibility for the physical survival of the family on men but placed its psychological and spiritual well-being in the hands of women. Despite bourgeois presumptions, middle-class women also worked as "helpers" in family businesses or quietly performed money-earning tasks within the home, particularly in the years when families struggled to attain prosperity. But their work was not formally recognized: the attainment of full bourgeois security involved the elimination of women's economic participation outside the home as distinct from management within it.

In the peaceful home environment they created, mothers were expected to preserve and transmit traditional morality. Bourgeois culture linked religious expression, which drew on emotion, to the familial sentiment that fell within women's domain. The bourgeois division of labor between the sexes also held women responsible for religiously based "good works," including the basic religious education of children. Because so much of Jewish religious ritual is performed at home, it was relatively easy for women to meet bourgeois norms. By retaining some domestic aspects of Jewish tradition, including customary foods, and transforming others into ostensibly secular family celebrations, such as dinner on Friday evening rather than Sunday, Jewish women fulfilled their prescriptive role.[9] Women were also the ones who maintained family connections, taking charge of family visits and managing vacations that brought eligible young people together for the informal meetings that gradually replaced formally arranged marriages.[10] One may speculate that the bourgeois reinforcement of the linkage between women and children could have played a role in women's activity during the Holocaust regarding the rescue of children.

Middle-class Jewish women, because of their general exclusion from the world of business, higher education, and politics, had only limited opportunities for radical assimilation. Statistics on the most extreme manifestations of assimilation throughout the Western world reveal that until contemporary times Jewish women were less likely than their brothers to intermarry or convert.[11] In Germany between 1873 and 1882, to give one example, women composed only 7 percent of all Jewish converts. Only as lower-middle-class Jewish women entered the workforce in increasing numbers at the beginning of the twentieth century, and thereby had increasing contact both with non-Jews and with antisemitism, did their proportion among Jewish converts rise. As for marriages between Jews and Christians, a gender gap was also noticeable, though less so than in the case of conversion. Because of this disparity, during the years of Nazi persecution Jewish women were less likely to have Gentile spouses or close Christian kin to protect them.

Although they subscribed to the prevailing bourgeois ideal of their societies, middle-class Jewish families in Western and Central Europe differed from their class compatriots not only in their religious affiliation but also in their size. Jews took the lead by as much as a generation in limiting the number of their children. In fact, Jewish birth rates declined throughout the nineteenth century in all the countries of Western and Central Europe. Only in France, which had the lowest overall fertility rate in Western Europe, did Jews match their fellow citizens. Between 1860 and 1910 Jews in Prussia had succeeded in reducing their fertility by more than 50 percent. Available data on the age of mothers at the birth of their last child reveal that Jews made effective use of birth control. As Marion Kaplan has noted, middle-class German Jews were pioneers of the two-child family. The decline in Jewish fertility was accompanied in the West by postponement of marriage and a rise in the number of Jews who never married.[12]

The smaller size of their families enabled women to devote more of their time to charitable activity than had been the case in traditional communities. The gender ideal of the nineteenth-century European bourgeoisie had relegated philanthropic good works to women as a component of their religious sensibilities. Like other women of the European bourgeoisie, middle- and upper-middle-class Jewish women expanded their charitable activity into social welfare and educational work. Articulating a version of what historians have called social feminism, they established organizations that addressed issues of social and political concern on the grounds that women should bring their particular sensibilities to bear on the larger society, which was merely the household writ large. The most significant of these women's organizations was the German Jüdischer Frauenbund, established in 1904, which attained a membership of thirty-five thousand within a decade and fifty thousand by the end of the 1920s. It assumed responsibility for ameliorating the condition of poor Jewish women and children—who were perceived as the organization's natural constituency—through a variety of programs.[13]

Jewish women's organizations asserted a distinct role for women as sustainers of Jewish communal life and as guardians against defection from Judaism. Without challenging the primacy of home and domestic responsibilities, they reconfigured the boundaries between the domestic and public spheres. The social welfare activities of Jewish women, both within their own organizations and as individual volunteers in nonsectarian groups, brought them increasingly in the twentieth century into contact with Gentile women working on similar issues. Ironically, then, bourgeois Jewish women, supposedly limited to the domestic sphere and perhaps to their extended kin networks, may have been better integrated with non-Jews socially than were their husbands, whose relationships with Gentiles occurred in the context of their professional lives.[14] It would be of interest to explore what happened to these social connections during the Holocaust. Did they facilitate efforts to emigrate, escape, or hide?

The decision to limit family size enabled Jewish families to invest heavily in the education of their children. In addition to the bourgeois concern for education as a marker of class standing and an instrument of social mobility, Jews demonstrated a particular respect for learning that was, in all likelihood, at least in part a secularization of the religious tradition of Torah study. By the second half of the nineteenth century young Jewish men thronged to secondary schools and to universities in the countries of the West. In the German states in the decades around the turn of the century, for example, Jewish males were twice as likely (after controlling for social class and urbanization) to receive gymnasium and university education than were Christians.[15]

In spite of the disproportionate representation of Jewish men in universities, such an elite education was an option for only a minority of Jews. Throughout Jewish communities in the West, social mobility occurred primarily and initially within the world of commerce, and Jewish families selected schools that prepared their sons for careers in business. Nevertheless, Jews continued to be disproportionately represented among university students as well as among the middle and upper middle classes through the early decades of the twentieth century. The impact of World War I, however, and of postwar inflation and depression, affected the wealth and status of Jews along with the rest of the population.

The opening of opportunities previously considered off-limits to women joined with economic and demographic changes to subvert the middle class ideal that women should be free from the world of wage work. By the beginning of the twentieth century university education was available to women throughout Western and Central Europe, and both native-born and immigrant Jewish women, like Jewish men, were disproportionately represented in institutions of higher education.[16] Their access to higher education enabled Jewish women to enter into such professions as medicine, science, and the highest levels of secondary school teaching. During the 1930s the language and professional skills that women acquired at the university may have provided resources upon which they could draw in planning emigration.

The growth in the proportion of women working outside the home, however, reflected socioeconomic changes more all-encompassing than the entry of women into the universities. Whereas some German Jewish families even before World War I depended upon the employment of their daughters in order to retain their middle-class income, the difficult economic conditions of the interwar years impelled many more women into the workforce. Although Jewish women, like Jewish men, concentrated in commerce and industry, they held jobs of far lower status than did their brothers and were far less likely to be "independent," that is, self-employed. Many Jewish women secured positions as clerical employees, but few became professionals. Because so few Gentile women studied for the professions, however, Jewish women comprised a significant segment of female professionals.[17] Along with men, then, women were accustomed to contributing to the family economy, primarily as commercial employees and helpers in family enterprises, and occasionally as professionals. As yet, there has been no assessment of the impact of their changing occupational roles on their responses to the conditions imposed on them by the Nazis.

The Traditional Jewish Families of Eastern Europe

In the countries of Eastern Europe most Jews did not attain middle-class status, although they may have dreamed of doing so. Therefore, male and female roles were less rigidly divided than among middle-class Jews living in Western and Central Europe. Most Jews in Eastern Europe of the nineteenth and early twentieth centuries grew to maturity in a society that did not facilitate the division between the public and domestic realms that was essential for the emergence of the middle-class man and his genteel wife. Jewish women, of necessity, participated actively in secular public and economic life. Although they were excluded from voting or holding positions of leadership within the *kehilla* (the Jewish community) and from public roles within the synagogue, they were responsible for contributing to the economic support of their households.

In Eastern Europe a small elite of learned families realized the Ashkenazi cultural ideal of full-time Torah study for men; the primary obligation for the family's economic support thus fell on their wives.[18] The overwhelming majority of Eastern European Jewish males, however, had neither the talent, nor the education, nor the resources to become Torah scholars. They worked as small-scale merchants or artisans. Nevertheless, the existence of the cultural ideal of male learning, and female labor, legitimated the presence of women in the world of commerce and artisanry and also legitimated their cultivation of character traits that would ensure the survival of the family. Memoirs of Eastern European Jews and unpublished autobiographies of Polish Jewish youth from the 1930s are replete with references to mothers whose work as seamstresses, storekeepers, peddlers, or even sellers of whiskey kept food on their families' tables.[19]

The dominant cultural ideal was the strong, capable working woman, rather than the creator of a domestic haven who prevailed in the bourgeois West. Middle- and upper-class Eastern European Jewish men may have sought a purely domestic role for their wives, as did their compatriots to the west, but the presence of a large proportion of adult Jewish females in the public economic sphere conferred upon women a greater measure of independence and a more extensive variety of social contacts than were common in Western and Central Europe, at least until after World War I. To be sure, by the second half of the nineteenth century the modernizing intelligentsia of the *Haskalah* (the Jewish Enlightenment) aspired to a social situation in which women would retire from the world of commerce to devote themselves to the middle-class female tasks of caring for their homes and children. Economic necessity, however, proved more formidable than *Haskalah* ideology. How women's economic skills and contacts were mobilized during the Holocaust demands further research.

Although Jewish women in the West were less likely than men to manifest signs of radical assimilation, the gender division was reversed among segments of the traditional Jewish population of the Russian and Austro-Hungarian Empires: women predominated in some aspects of assimilation. Most important, the gendered division of education within the traditional Jewish community seems to have facilitated a higher degree of secularization among women than among men in some traditional Jewish families. Traditional Eastern European Jews continued to provide a classical Torah-based education for their sons in *cheders* and *yeshivas,* although with increasing frequency Orthodox parents chose to enroll their sons in modern Jewish private schools. In 1898–1899, almost 54 percent of Jewish boys still attended cheders.[20] However, the same families that chose for their sons various forms of private Jewish education, whether of traditional or modernized curriculum, often sent their daughters to public primary schools, where they were introduced to secular culture. In Galicia, for example, Shaul Stampfer has estimated on the basis of governmental statistics that in 1890 about 40 percent of Jewish girls, but only 25 percent of Jewish boys, were enrolled in public primary schools.[21] Ita Kalish, rebel daughter of a Hasidic rebbe, noted with some surprise in her memoirs that in Warsaw immediately after World War I, even Hasidic families mixed traditional Judaism with assimilation, in a highly gendered fashion: "The sons went to a *shtibl* and learned *gemora*—and the girls studied in foreign schools and were educated in the purity of Polish culture."[22] Those women who received a secular education and were therefore more likely to speak the local language well had advantages in passing as Aryans during the Holocaust.

Some two dozen memoirs in which Eastern European Jews describe their childhoods, from the last third of the nineteenth century through World War I, demonstrate a consistent pattern about the secular education of girls. Although parents in learned and wealthy families generally provided some Jewish education for their daughters, ranging from study in a cheder to private tutoring, their religious education was always less substantial than their brothers'. It also paled in comparison with the secular instruction the girls received in a public school, a private Jewish school, or from private tutors. In several cases mothers or grandmothers, perhaps compensating for their own missed opportunities for education, made sure that their daughters received the instruction that they sought. Shoshana Lishensky's mother and grandmother favored sending her and her sister to learn Russian with a tutor who had been brought to their town to teach the Jewish boys (so that they would be able to get along if drafted into the army). Her grandfather, a rabbi, was opposed to the plan, however. Her older sister had briefly studied at a gymnasium without her grandfather's knowledge, but she had to withdraw when he found out. Her grandmother also secretly funded the girls' membership in the local lending library. Bilha Dinur relates that her mother supported her desire to study in a gymnasium, while her father opposed it, in part because it would expose her to a foreign world she might seek to enter (as, indeed, she later did).[23] Although some critics within the Jewish community chastised the gender division in the education of Jewish youth, the greater exposure of some women to secular education may have conferred upon them an advantage in confronting the dangers of the Holocaust.[24]

Even though most Jewish families in Eastern Europe never attained middle-class status or income, demographic changes similar to those that had occurred among Jews in the West changed the shape of Jewish families in the East. The situation that Puah Rakowski described in the first sentence of her autobiography—"I was born in 1865 to a fifteen-year-old mother and a seventeen-year-old father"—became a phenomenon of the past.[25] As Shaul Stampfer has demonstrated with careful attention to regional variations, by 1921 almost no teenage marriages took place among Polish Jews, and the small percentage of married eighteen- and nineteen-year-olds virtually disappeared in the subsequent decade.[26] Moreover, in the interwar period, because of extremely difficult economic conditions, Polish Jews, and particularly men, postponed marriage. Whereas in the nineteenth century Jews had generally attained universal marriage by age thirty, in 1931 peak marriage rates were not reached until Jews were in their late thirties, and a growing proportion of them never married. Because the age difference between husbands and wives was not large, Jewish women were less likely than Christian women to be widowed in early middle age. In addition to their changed marriage patterns, and related to them, Polish Jews also reduced their fertility strikingly between the end of the nineteenth century and the mid-1930s.[27]

The family lives of Polish Jews in the interwar years were marked not by the problems of adolescent marriage but by the economic deprivation of the country and by the impact of growing official and popular antisemitism. The small numbers of middle-class Jews struggled to preserve their status while most Jews struggled even more fiercely simply to survive. Poverty was the lot of Jewish workers, who still composed between a quarter and a third of the population of many of Poland's major cities and an even larger proportion of its towns.

The murder of 90 percent of Polish Jewry in the Holocaust has overshadowed historical investigation of their lives in the years before the war, for much documentation was destroyed. Moreover, memoirs of survivors have naturally focused on the horrors experienced in the Holocaust and have tended to romanticize prewar childhoods. One source of prewar accounts, which permits us to comment on Jewish families as they were experienced and presented by adolescents at the time, consists of about 350 autobiographies written (in Yiddish, Polish, and Hebrew) by Polish Jewish youth for three autobiography contests conducted by YIVO (the Institute for Jewish Research) in 1932, 1934, and 1939. Although these autobiographies are not scientifically representative of Polish Jewish youth, they are an unparalleled resource.

What emerges from these autobiographies is the portrait of a youth that perceived it had no future. Most of the writers had received at least an elementary education, in cheder or in Polish primary schools or in a combination of both, but they earned a meager living as workers—as tailors or furriers or dressmakers or shoemakers. Those who managed to graduate from gymnasium were often unable to find employment.[28] The families in which they grew up were often unhappy and relatively large: one youth from a Hasidic family had twelve siblings, and another eleven; six or eight children were common.[29] Everyone in the family was mobilized to contribute to collective survival. Many of the adolescents describe families that were characterized by economic deprivation, fighting and sometimes cursing between parents, and lack of understanding between parents and their children.[30] One young woman from a traditionally observant family wrote of her father who had died: "Yes, it is true that he was a strict father but he did not mean to harm me, nor was it his fault that he did not understand me. He did not see the irony in his desire for me to be happy, and at the same time, to be like him."[31] A less generous young man, a maker of shoes for babies, wrote that he and his widowed father, with whom he worked, lived in two separate worlds. "All we have in common is our struggle for a living," he concluded.[32]

The most important phenomenon in the lives of these young Jews was the political movements with which they were affiliated, often against their parents' wishes. The autobiographies testify to the role that the youth movements played in providing an explanation for the adolescents' suffering, a program for the future—whether through Communist or socialist revolution or through settlement in Palestine—and escape from their ineffective or dysfunctional families. In such disparate youth movements as those associated with the Communist Party, the Bund, Poalei Zion, Hechalutz, and Betar, young Jews acknowledged that they had found a community, purposeful activity, and an opportunity to continue their truncated education.[33] One male teenager lamented his need to leave his group in 1936 when he became the main breadwinner in his family: "It is a great loss, as the group was very dear to me."[34] Another writer, a twenty-one-year-old woman who grew up in the most difficult circumstances and became a factory worker as a young teenager, was reluctant to provide details about what she called the three most interesting and important years of her life and her (obviously illegal) work in the Party. But she did affirm that "the organization was the holiest thing in my life."[35] Their prewar experience in political youth groups prepared some Jews for resistance activities during the Holocaust.

In roughly the century and a half that stands between the debate about Jewish emancipation during the French Revolution and the brutal murder of the Jews during the Holocaust, Jews throughout Europe had experienced massive dislocation—in terms of economic stratification, education, urbanization, and acculturation to, at the very least, the language and dress of the larger society. Their geographic mobility had partially eroded the extended kinship networks that Jews had traditionally called upon in times of distress. As Jews experienced social mobility, the gendered roles of men and women within the family were transformed to reflect the class standing and cultural norms appropriate to their situation, whether in the West or in the East. Although the political and economic conditions of modernity were difficult for many families in Europe, Jews faced particular obstacles because of social and governmental discrimination. Despite their belief in the progress of history, Jews in both Western and Eastern Europe found themselves more vulnerable in the interwar years than they would have had reason to anticipate a generation before.

Notes

1. For a discussion of gender roles among middle-class Western European Jews and non-middle-class Jews of Eastern Europe, see Paula E. Hyman, *Gender and Assimilation in Modern Jewish History* (Seattle: University of Washington Press, 1995).

2. See Selma Leydesdorff, *We Lived in Dignity: The Jewish Proletariat of Amsterdam, 1900–1940* (trans. Frank Heny) (Detroit: Wayne State University Press, 1994).

3. On Viennese Jewry, see Marsha Rozenblit, *The Jews of Vienna, 1867–1914* (Albany: State University of New York Press, 1983).

4. On village Jews in France, see Paula E. Hyman, *The Emancipation of the Jews of Alsace* (New Haven: Yale University Press, 1991), and on Germany, see Steven M. Lowenstein, "The Rural Community and the Urbanization of German Jewry," *Central European History* 13, no. 3 (September 1980), pp. 218–236.

5. Jacob Toury, *Soziale und politische Geschichte der Juden in Deutschland, 1847–1871* (Düsseldorf: Droste Verlag, 1977), pp. 113–114; Avraham Barkai, "The German Jews at the Start of Industrialization: Structural Change and Mobility, 1835–1860," in *Revolution and Evolution,* ed. Werner Mosse, Arnold Paucker, and Reinhard Rürup (Tübingen: Mohr, 1981), pp. 133–139.

6. Doris Ben Simon-Donath, *Socio-démographie des juifs de France et d'Algérie:1867–1907* (Paris: Publications orientalistes de France, 1976), pp. 141–201.

7. Arnaud Aron, *Prières d'un coeur israélite* (Strasbourg: Société consistoriale des bons livres, 1848), p. 263.

8. Ibid., pp. 264–265.

9. Marion Kaplan, *The Making of the Jewish Middle Class* (New York: Oxford University Press, 1991), pp. 64–84.

10. Ibid., pp. 108–112, 123–126, and Antoine Halff, "Lieux d'assimilation, lieux d'identité: Les communautés juives et l'essor des stations thermales et balnéaires à la Belle Epoque," *Pardès* 8 (1988), pp. 41–57.

11. Todd M. Endelman, "Introduction," in *Jewish Apostasy in the Modern World,* ed. Todd M. Endelman (New York: Holmes and Meier, 1987), p. 13.

12. See Paula E. Hyman, "Jewish Fertility in Nineteenth Century France," in *Modern Jewish Fertility,* ed. Paul Ritterband (Leiden: Brill, 1981), pp. 79–93; Steven M. Lowenstein, "Voluntary and Involuntary Limitation of Fertility in Nineteenth Century Bavarian Jewry," in ibid., pp. 94–111; Kaplan, *Making of the Jewish Middle Class,* pp. 42–45; and Lawrence Schofer, "Emancipation and Population Change," in *Revolution and Evolution,* pp. 79–81.

13. Marion Kaplan, *The Jewish Feminist Movement in Germany* (Westport, Conn.: Greenwood Press, 1979), pp. 10–11.

14. For the German example, see Kaplan, *Making of the Jewish Middle Class,* pp. 199–227.

15. Calvin Goldscheider and Alan S. Zuckerman, *The Transformation of the Jews* (Chicago: University of Chicago Press, 1984), pp. 85–86.

16. *Zeitschrift für Demographie und Statistik der Juden,* June 1914, pp. 86–87; July–September, 1915, p. 83; ser. 2, no. 2 (1925), p. 33; Nancy Green, "L'émigration comme émancipation: Les femmes juives d'Europe de l'Est à Paris, 1881–1914," *Pluriel,* no. 27 (1981), pp. 56–58.

17. Kaplan, *Making of the Jewish Middle Class,* pp. 158–168, 172–174, 178.

18. For the stresses on family life that resulted, see Immanuel Etkes, "Marriage and Torah Study among the *Lomdim* in Lithuania in the Nineteenth Century," in *The Jewish Family,* ed. David Kraemer (New York: Oxford University Press, 1989), pp. 153–178.

19. See Hyman, *Gender and Assimilation,* pp. 64–65, 67–68.

20. Steven Zipperstein, *The Jews of Odessa* (Stanford: Stanford University Press, 1985), p. 130.

21. Shaul Stampfer, "Gender Differentiation and Education of the Jewish Woman in Nineteenth-Century Eastern Europe," *Polin* 7 (1992), p. 79.

22. Ita Kalish, *Etmoli* (Tel-Aviv: Hakibutz Hameuhad), pp. 99–101. The quotation is from p. 101.

23. Shoshana Lishensky, *Mizror zikhronotai* (Jerusalem, 1942), pp. 21, 23, 25; Bilha Dinur, *Lenechdotai* (arr. and ed. Ben-Zion Dinur) (Jerusalem: privately printed, 1972), p. 32.

24. Puah Rakowski, *Zikhroynes fun a yiddisher revolutsionerin* (Buenos Aires, 1954), p. 19.

25. Ibid., p. 11.

26. Shaul Stampfer, "Marital Patterns in Interwar Poland," in *The Jews of Poland between Two World Wars,* ed. Yisrael Gutman, Ezra Mendelsohn, Jehuda Reinharz, and Chone Shmeruk (Hanover, N.H.: University Press of New England, 1989), pp. 173–197.

27. For the census data, see Lucjan Dobroszycki, "The Fertility of Modern Polish Jewry," in *Modern Jewish Fertility,* pp. 68–69.

28. Autobiography #3792, YIVO Autobiography collection. I would like to thank Rachel Wizner, who is editing a selection of English translations of the autobiographies, for providing me with material from the collection and for her insight into the lives of the writers.

29. See, for example, autobiographies #3582, #3779, #3752, #3514, #3539, #3548, #3772, and #3801, YIVO Autobiography collection. These large families were probably atypical of Polish Jews as a whole.

30. See, for example, autobiographies #3514, #3610, #3690, #3770, #3739, #3779, and #3682, YIVO Autobiography collection.

31. "Esther" [pseud.], autobiography #3559, p. 25 in English translation, YIVO Autobiography collection.

32. Abram, written in Polish, p. 6 in English translation, YIVO Autobiography collection.

33. See, for example, autobiographies #3720, #3514, #3749, #3819A, #3801, #3816, #3804, and #3873, YIVO Autobiography collection.

34. Autobiography #3779, p. 32 in English translation, YIVO Autobiography collection.

35. Autobiography #3610, YIVO Autobiography collection. The quotation is from p. 49 of the Yiddish original.

CHAPTER TWO

Keeping Calm and Weathering the Storm
Jewish Women's Responses to Daily Life in Nazi Germany, 1933–1939

Marion Kaplan

I t was through the dozens of daily tasks that ground their lives that most Jews, particularly women, suffered and assessed their situation under the Nazis. Daily life in Nazi Germany consisted not only of the commonplace—activities and beliefs that continued at least until November 1938—but, increasingly, of the unexpected.[1] Lawlessness, ostracism, and a loss of rights took their toll on Jews of all sexes and ages. As Jews tried to make a living, maintain their previously middle-class economic and cultural standards, nurture their families, and succeed at school, they became more and more aware of the growth of hostility and danger around them.

Daily Privation

In spite of the apparent ordinariness with which Jewish women continued their daily existence, their internal equilibrium was shattered. Jews became vigilant in public and no longer felt safe even in their homes. They were afraid that the Gestapo would search their houses and find or plant incriminating evidence against them. While the Nazis burned books in public, many Jews burned portions of their libraries and their papers in private. Moreover, Jews could no longer take their homes for granted. Many faced eviction by landlords to whom Jewish tenants had become dangerous or undesirable. Food purchases were also limited, either by decree or by the hostility of shopkeepers. For Orthodox families, the prohibition against kosher butchering, which began as early as April 21, 1933, caused great hardship. Yet, as troublesome as renting and shopping had become, the most important indicator of how the Nazi takeover affected Jewish daily life was the interaction that Jews had with non-Jewish strangers, friends, and neighbors.

Absolute strangers became steadily more hostile toward Jews in public. This coarsening of attitudes was part of a more widespread lack of sympathy toward other purported enemies, such as Communists, Jehovah's Witnesses, and oppositional Social Democrats. In fact, such animosity was characteristic of the everyday behavior of many Germans toward one another. Long before Jews were forced to wear a yellow star in order to facilitate their identification, strangers on trams, in stores, and even on the street targeted those who "looked Jewish" and made their victims feel ill at ease. Some Germans literally used their noses to identify Jews. In particular, Germans drew on their long-standing and still common aversion to garlic, really an aversion to things foreign, to torment Jews. The streetcar seemed to be a favored locus of bad temper and ill will, where "Germans" accused "Jews" of smelling of garlic or simply of smelling "like Jews."[2]

The government intended to isolate Jews completely through intimidation and bribery of the "Aryan" populace. And the Nazis could count on grassroots enthusiasm. Well before the Nazis prohibited friendly contact with Jews, denunciation and gossip discouraged such associations. Historian Robert Gellately found "an extraordinary degree and variety of accommodation . . . to the regime's doctrines on race. Friendships and business relationships going back many years were broken off."[3] Of interest here is not only the fear of the authorities but the often zealous restrictions imposed by Germans themselves. Some exceptional Germans remained loyal, but most either avoided Jews or were hostile toward them.

In my reading of the memoirs and interviews of middle-class Jewish women, I observed that the loss of friends and the decline of sociability in the neighborhood evidently affected Jewish women more than men, because women were more integrated into and dependent upon the community and more accustomed to neighborly exchanges and courtesies. Their lives bridged the gap between family and community. Those who had been active in communal, volunteer, or women's groups suffered when they were ostracized. Moreover, women probably had more frequent contacts with state officials—

postal and and railroad clerks, social workers, and, for mothers in particular, teachers. Men saw less of neighbors to begin with and had less time to engage in communal or volunteer activities. Also, although men now suffered the loss of even a modicum of courtesy at work, they were more used to competition and a certain degree of conflict in their everyday work life.

Along with social isolation, unemployment began to plague the Jewish community. With the disappearance of many Jewish firms, joblessness became rampant. Even as the German economy improved and German unemployment dropped, Jewish unemployment climbed, emigration notwithstanding. Because more than half of employed Jewish women worked in business and commerce, many lost their jobs as family businesses and shops closed down. Jewish sources estimated that three-quarters of Jewish women in business and trade were affected by the discriminatory laws and the early anti-Jewish boycotts.[4] By April 1938, more than 60 percent of businesses that Jews had owned before 1933 no longer existed, and Jewish social workers were trying to help sixty thousand unemployed Jews.

In spite of their limited options on the job market, many Jewish women who had never worked outside the home suddenly needed employment. While some sought jobs with strangers, many began to work for their husbands, who could no longer afford to pay employees. One article in a Jewish newspaper praised women's flexibility and versatility, commenting that "we find relatively few families in which the wife does not work in some way to earn a living," and women were the sole support for many a family.[5]

Memoirs and statistics indicate that women trained for new jobs and then retrained when they lost newly acquired jobs. One woman took a speed course in becoming a corsetiere. Although Jews could no longer be licensed by the time she finished, she quickly developed private customers and supported herself. Many women trained for several jobs at once. A mother and daughter took courses in Spanish, English, baking, and fine cookery. Then they asked their laundress to accept them as apprentices. This role not only was new for them but was also a reversal of their previous class position.[6]

According to observers, women seemed "more accommodating and adaptable" than men, had "fewer inhibitions," and were willing to enter retraining programs at older ages. Leaders of the Berlin community noted that retraining for women was less costly and also took less time. Women already had some of the skills necessary for new jobs as, for example, seamstresses, milliners, or domestics.[7]

Young people faced particular employment problems. The exclusion of Jews from German universities, vocational schools, and institutions of higher learning restricted future job possibilities. But certain jobs were available for young women. Even though many had lost jobs in commercial fields, women under the age of thirty-five could still find jobs as other Jews began to emigrate. Also, the demand for Jewish help quickly picked up in the expanding Jewish social service sector. In addition, after the Nuremberg Laws were passed, forbidding Jews from hiring female Aryans under the age of forty-five as household help, Jewish households needed help, too. In Berlin, for example, although the majority of Jewish applicants remained jobless, Jewish employment services were more successful in placing women than men.[8]

Private Responses

In the face of worsening living conditions, it was women who were supposed to "make things work" in the family. The Nuremberg Laws left Jewish women to their own devices in running a household with greater problems, shopping for food in stores staffed by increasingly unfriendly personnel, and performing all these tasks with ever-shrinking resources. Moreover, they had to soothe frightened children who faced harassment at school and on the streets.

Women's organizations, urging their members to preserve the "moral strength to survive," looked to biblical heroines as role models. But it became increasingly apparent that biblical role models would not suffice to provide Jewish women with the courage or the help they needed. Jewish newspapers began to deal more openly (and perhaps more honestly) with the issues plaguing families, particularly women. Cooking seemed to take a preeminent role among stress-causing issues because of tight budgets, limited household help, and the difficulties of acquiring kosher meat. Articles in Jewish newspapers advised housewives to cook vegetarian menus because they were cheaper and healthier, even if they took longer to prepare. The papers urged housewives to organize, streamline, and cut back on their tasks to lighten their load. Husbands were expected to pitch in only minimally but were requested to limit their expectations: "We demand no sacrifices from husbands—only some consideration and . . . adjusting to the changed circumstances!"[9]

Women frequently took responsibility not only for the greater physical burden but also for the psychological work necessary to raise their family's spirits and tide the family over until better times. Children facing Nazi teachers and hostile classmates at school needed understanding and encouragement. Husbands facing unaccustomed mistreatment also needed a comforting haven. In sum, women were to be cheerful when gloom was all about. As late as February 1938, one woman titled her article in a Jewish newspaper "Why So Solemn?" Reminding Jewish women that they had traditionally been the ones to light the candles, she urged them once again to brighten their homes with cheer.[10]

Even when women could no longer "light candles" of joy, they often managed a kind of denial about their immediate hardships (while nevertheless pushing for emigration). Although, in some cases, their efforts to distract themselves and their families may have kept the others from realizing the danger sooner, some denial was necessary in order to preserve their own and their family's stability. They accomplished this through what psychologists call the "adoption of temporary frames of security"—for example, by focusing on the practical tasks of cooking or language training.[11] Some women may have even taken solace from their additional burdens, finding safety in the routine of housework. Other women joined voluntary organizations in an effort to help the community and take their minds off the issues plaguing them. Alice Baerwald distracted herself by setting up a Zionist youth emigration program in Danzig. She was so busy with it that she "forgot to dismantle my own life."[12]

Role Reversals among Jewish Women and Men

Jewish families, with their normal middle-class lives and expectations overturned, embarked on new paths and embraced new strategies that they would never have entertained in ordinary times. For women, this meant new roles as partner, breadwinner, family protector, and defender of the business or practice. These roles were often strange to them. Increasingly, women found themselves representing or defending their husbands, fathers, brothers, or sons. Many accounts have been recorded of women who saved family members from the arbitrary demands of the state or from the Gestapo. In these cases, the Jews always assumed that the Nazis would not disrupt gender norms: they might arrest or torture Jewish men but would not harm women. Thus women at first felt that they had greater freedom than men and were able to manipulate the system to some slight extent. Consequently they took on a more assertive role in the public sphere than ever before. In one small town, a Jewish family sent two of its women to the city hall to ask that part of their house not be used as a meeting place for the Nazi party. Other women interceded for family members with German emigration or finance officials. In some cases they not only broke gender barriers but also bypassed normal standards of legality. Many memoirs report that women, quickly recovering from their shock at discovering that Nazi officials had to be bribed, handed them the necessary goods or money without delay.[13]

Some women took responsibility for the entire family's safety. One woman traveled to Palestine to assess the situation there. Her husband, who in other circumstances had been the decision maker, could not leave his practice and simply told her, "If you decide you would like to live in Palestine, I will like it too." She chose to live in Greece, and her husband agreed. Another woman went to England to negotiate her family's emigration with British officials and medical colleagues. Her daughter noted, "It was thanks to her pertinacity and determination that we were able to leave Germany as soon as we did, and it was always to be a great source of pride to her that it was she who obtained the permit allowing us to come to England."[14]

Women often found themselves in threatening situations, in which they exhibited bravery and benefited from luck. Twenty-year-old Ruth Abraham urged her parents to move to Berlin to escape the hostility of their small town and then regularly accompanied her father to Gestapo headquarters for his weekly interrogation. When her uncle was arrested in Düsseldorf, she hurried from jail to jail until she located him. Then she appealed to a judge, who released him.[15]

Women's new roles may have increased stress in some cases, but in general both women and men appreciated the importance of the new behavior. Women forced themselves to behave in "unwomanly" ways, such as putting up a strong front when men could no longer cope. One woman retained her composure for the sake of her children as her husband sank into a deep depression.

The testimonies of both men and women emphasize women's calm, dry-eyed state in the midst of turmoil. One woman, remembering how painful it had been to give up prized family heirlooms to the Nazis, reflected on the dignity and self-control of Jews around her: "I was glad that the Jews I saw behaved well, they didn't show any excitement noticeable to strangers."[16] Whether this desire to appear calm was a middle-class reaction against what they perceived as rabble, or an attempt to retain their dignity or their families' equilibrium in the face of persecution, or an assertion of Jewish pride to counter Aryan savagery, or a proclamation of female strength to rebut the stereotype of female frailty, it was noted more by (and in) women than men. Probably, men took this kind of behavior for granted whereas women, previously allowed and encouraged to be the more "emotional" sex, were particularly conscious of their efforts at self-control.

The Desire to Emigrate

A gender analysis of the *desire* to emigrate highlights women's particular expectations, priorities, and perceptions.[17] Women, whose identity was more family oriented than men's, struggled to preserve what was central to them by fleeing Germany. Men had businesses, clients, patients, political commitments, and, often, their World War I service, all of which tied them to Germany. Moreover, although women were less integrated than men into the work world, they were more integrated into their community. For women, the increasing hostility around them was unmitigated by a promising business prospect or a loyal employee or patient. Women's constant contacts with their own and others' children and with the community probably alerted them to the signals that come through interpersonal relations—and they took those signals seriously. Men's experiences were mediated through newspapers and broadcasts. Politics may have remained more abstract to them, whereas women's "narrower" picture—their neighbors, direct everyday contacts, the minutiae (and significance) of ordinary details—alerted them to danger at home. Summing up, Peter Wyden recalled the debates within his own family and those of other Berlin Jews: "It was not a bit unusual in these go-or-no-go family dilemmas for the women to display more energy and enterprise than the men. . . . They were less status-conscious, less money-oriented. . . . They seemed to be less rigid, less cautious, more confident of their ability to flourish on new turf."[18]

That men and women often *assessed* the dangers differently reflected their different contacts and frames of reference. But *decisions* to remain or to emigrate (in contrast to role reversals in other areas) seem to have been made by husbands—or, later, by circumstances. After the November Pogrom of 1938, some wives broke all family conventions by taking over the decision making when it became clear to them that their husbands' reluctance to leave Germany would result in even worse horrors.

The November Pogrom of 1938

The November Pogrom revealed the radicalization of Nazi persecution. Although the pogrom was called Kristallnacht (Crystal Night), which we understand to signify the broken glass of thousands of Jewish stores, homes, and synagogues, Jewish women's memoirs often focus not on broken glass but on flying feathers—feathers covering the internal space of the home, hallway, and front yard or courtyard. As in pogroms in Russia at the turn of the century, the mobs tore up feather blankets and pillows and shook them into the rooms, out the windows, and down the stairways. Jews were thus bereft of their bedding and the physical and psychological security that it represented. In addition, these items could not be readily replaced because of their expense and because the availability of domestic linens was severely limited in the looming war economy.[19] This image of feathers flying, of a domestic scene gravely disturbed, represents women's primary experience of the pogrom. The marauders beat and arrested Jewish men, sending more than thirty thousand to concentration camps. With brutal exceptions, which are worth noting because they may indicate more violence against women than historians have recognized to date,[20] most women were forced to stand by and watch their homes torn apart and their men abused.

As women cleaned up the wreckage of the pogrom, their most crucial task was to rescue their men. Wives of prisoners were told that their husbands would be released only if they could present emigration papers. Although no statistics are available to indicate their success, these women displayed extraordinary nerve and tenacity in saving a large number of men and in facilitating a mass exodus of married couples in 1939. Women summoned the courage to overcome gender stereotypes of passivity in order to find any means to have husbands and fathers released from camps. They had to organize the papers,

decide on the destination, sell property, and organize the departure. One example illuminates the ordeal facing many women. Mally Dienemann, whose
sixty-three-year-old husband was deteriorating rapidly in Buchenwald, raced
immediately to the Gestapo to prove that the couple were almost ready to emigrate. Next, she traveled to the passport office to obtain their passports, then
to the Emigration Office in Frankfurt, the Gestapo, the police, and the Finance
Office. She had to send requests to Buchenwald and to the Gestapo in Darmstadt: "Still it took until Tuesday of the third week, before my husband returned. . . . Next came running around for the many papers that one needed
for emigration. And while the Gestapo was in a rush, the Finance Office had
so much time and so many requests."[21]

Packing for Good

After the pogrom those Jews who remained in Germany tried desperately
to leave for anywhere—Latin America, Haiti, Cuba, Australia, Shanghai. As is
well known, profound obstacles to emigration existed. Even so, Jewish emigration was far from negligible. In September 1939 the number of (racially
defined) Jews who remained in Germany was 185,000, but this number diminished to 164,000 by October 1941.[22] Ultimately, about half of those Jews
who had lived in Germany in 1933 could save themselves through emigration
to safe countries.

When Jews packed, they believed that their departure would be permanent. Without exception, women took charge of the packing. It was so clearly
considered women's work that some women stayed behind to do it. Packing
was not only a necessity; it quickly became an art as Nazi rulings and red tape
made the process into a nightmare. In order to emigrate with one's belongings,
one had to obtain a permit from the Finance Department, which became available only after one provided lists of all the items one wished to take. One
woman spent an entire week writing "endless lists, in five copies each . . . every
item entered, every list neatly typed, and in the end I could only speak and
breathe and think in shoes, towels, scissors, soap and scarves." One could not
take just anything—only items purchased before 1933 were allowed. After
completing the lists, and often with ship or plane tickets in hand, Jews had to
await the authorization of the Finance Department. Again, connections and
bribes seemed to speed the process, and again, women without much previous

experience in the world of officialdom had to seek connections and master the art of bribery.[23]

With the arduous packing completed and papers in hand, many Jewish families sent their belongings in large containers to interim stations, often ports in Holland, to be stored until the owners knew their ultimate destination. The possessions of one family, who landed in Cuba, stayed in Rotterdam until the family arrived in the United States two years later. Some lost their possessions in the German invasion of Holland. Few people could pack all their belongings; the giant containers, and the surcharge that the Nazis demanded for every item, cost too much. Many had to sell most of their belongings. For many, "packing reduced a lifetime of possessions into three suitcases."[24]

Thus, many emigrants, the wealthy and the poor, tried to sell their homes and furnishings for a pittance, while mourning the loss of the haven they had created for themselves. The purchasers were Aryans, many of whom complained of *their* plight. A pastor's wife proclaimed, "We are suffering as much as you are," to which Alice Baerwald retorted, "With the difference that you're buying and I'm selling."[25]

Packing gave some women the opportunity to save valuables and a few mementos from the clutches of the Nazis. What they managed to smuggle out was paltry in comparison with what the Nazis stole from them. Still, it helped their families subsist for a short time when they arrived penniless at their destinations. Some women bribed the officials who came to their home to inspect everything that went into the containers, trunks, and suitcases. A few did this without consulting their husbands, as the women knew full well that their plans would have been vetoed. Other women engaged in even more dangerous schemes, such as smuggling jewelry or money abroad. Alice Baerwald concluded, "So, slowly we were taught how to become criminals, to attempt to circumvent every law."[26] And women were involved in "illegality" not only for personal subsistence or to help family but also to help the community at large. Beate Berger, for example, smuggled money from Berlin to Palestine in order to buy land for a children's home.[27]

Those Who Stayed Behind

Fewer women than men left Germany. Why was this so? There were still compelling reasons to stay, although life was becoming increasingly difficult in the 1930s. First, women, especially young women, could find jobs in Jewish businesses and homes or in Jewish social services.[28] And older, educated single women found a plethora of jobs in cultural and social service fields within the Jewish community. Martha Wertheimer, for example, worked as a journalist prior to 1933. Thereafter she plunged into Jewish welfare work while writing books and plays, contributing to the Jewish press, and tutoring English to earn extra money. She escorted many children's transports to England, advised Jews on emigration and welfare procedures, often worked twelve-hour days without pausing for meals, and took great joy in leading High Holiday services in Neu-Isenburg, at the League of Jewish Women's Home for Wayward Girls, and in organizing continuing education courses for Jewish youth who had been drafted into forced labor. Ultimately, she wrote to a friend in New York that, despite efforts to emigrate, she no longer waited to escape: "It is also worthwhile to be an officer on the sinking ship of Jewish life (*Judenheit*) in Germany, to hold out courageously and to fill the life boats, to the extent that we have some."[29]

Whereas the employment situation of Jewish women helped keep them in Germany, that of men helped them get out. Some men had business connections abroad that facilitated their flight, and others emigrated alone in order to establish themselves before sending for their families. Women's organizations agreed that wives should not "hinder" husbands from emigrating alone if there was no alternative.[30]

Another reason why more women than men remained behind was that before the war, men faced more immediate physical danger than women and were forced to flee promptly. As women feared for their men, they believed that they themselves would be spared serious harm by the Nazis. In retrospect, Ruth Klüger reflected on this kind of thinking and the resulting preponderance of women caught in the trap: "One seemed to ignore what was most obvious, namely how imperiled precisely the weaker and the socially disadvantaged are. That the Nazis would stop at women contradicted their racist identity. Had we, as the result of an absurd, patriarchal short circuit, perhaps counted on their chivalry?"[31]

Further, as more and more sons left, daughters remained as the sole caretakers for elderly parents. One commentator noted the existence of a whole slew of women "who can't think of emigration because they don't know who might care for their elderly mother in the interim, before they could start sending her money. In the same families, the sons went their way." For many, leaving aging parents—again, as statistics indicate, usually the mother—was the most painful act imaginable.[32]

As early as 1936, the League of Jewish Women saw cause for serious concern regarding the more general "problem of the emigration of women which is often partly overlooked and not correctly understood." The league reminded parents of their "responsibility to free their daughters too . . . [even if daughters] feel stronger psychological ties to their families than sons."[33] In 1936–1937, 54 percent of Jewish immigrants to the United States were men. Even as late as January 1938, the Hilfsverein, one of the main emigration organizations, announced, "Up to now, Jewish emigration . . . indicates a severe surplus of men."[34]

Fewer women than men seem to have received support from Jewish organizations in order to emigrate.[35] Moreover, young women and their families were often reluctant to consider Palestine, and the kibbutz, as an alternative for daughters. Total immigration statistics for Palestine compiled by the Jewish Agency indicate that between 1933 and 1942, 27,202 males and 24,977 females entered from Germany. Of these, the children and married people consisted of about equal numbers of males and females. The discrepancy can be seen among the 8,209 bachelors and 5,080 single females.[36]

The disproportion of Jewish women in the German-Jewish population came about partially because, to begin with, there were more Jewish women than men in Germany. In 1933, owing to male casualties during World War I, greater exogamy among Jewish men, and greater longevity among women, 52.3 percent of Jews were women. The slower rate of female emigration meant that the female proportion of the Jewish population rose to 57.5 percent by 1939. In other words, whereas in 1933 the average ratio was 109 Jewish women to 100 Jewish men, by 1939 the ratio had leaped to 136 to 100.[37] In 1939, one woman wrote, "Mostly we were women who had been left to ourselves. In part, our husbands had died from shock [or] . . . in a concentration camp and partly some wives who, aware of the greater danger to their husbands, had prevailed upon them to leave at once and alone. They were ready to . . . follow their husbands . . . but . . . it became impossible . . . and quite a few . . . became martyrs of Hitler."[38]

Elderly women, in particular, remained behind in disproportionate numbers. In 1933 the ratio of Jewish women over the age of sixty-five to Jewish men of the same age group was already 140 to 100. And, because many of the young had emigrated by 1935, the proportion of elderly Jews also increased. By 1937–1938, recipients of the Jewish Winter Relief included a large number of elderly women (as well as, in total, a larger number of women than men).[39] In 1939, there were 6,674 widowers and 28,347 widows in the expanded Reich. When Elisabeth Freund went to the Gestapo for her papers in 1941, she observed "all old people, old women," waiting in line. Freund's was the last train out of Germany. The women she described were trapped. In short, in slightly less than eight years, two-thirds of German Jews emigrated (many to European countries, where they were later caught up in the Nazi net), leaving a disproportionate number of the elderly and of women.[40]

Mary Felstiner has written, "Along the stations toward extinction . . . each gender lived its own journey." She is essentially correct. The Nazis attacked Jewish women and men primarily as Jews, and all Jews shared this agony. Yet, Jews were affected by, and reacted to, the Nazi onslaught in gendered ways. Women, focused on the home, saw their role as that of keeping the family together, maintaining a sense of normalcy amid desperation, and protecting their husbands and children. Their gender-based socialization helped them react to the Nazi threat earlier and to press their men to emigrate. And, as a result of gender differences, when the time came to escape, women, in larger numbers than men, were left behind. In referring to the male and female lines at Auschwitz, Felstiner concluded, "The two incommensurate lines on the ramp stretched back decades. Centuries."[41]

Notes

1. For a detailed account of Jewish women and families in Nazi Germany, see Marion Kaplan, *Jewish Life in Nazi Germany: Dignity and Despair* (Oxford: Oxford University Press, 1998).
2. Garlic today in Susan Neiman, *Slow Fire,* chapter entitled "Garlic" (New York: Schocken Books, 1992). "Like Jews" in Baerwald manuscript (by permission of the Houghton Library, Harvard University, bMS Ger 91, hereafter referred to as "Harvard ms.").
3. Robert Gellately, "The Gestapo and German Society: Political Denunciation in the Gestapo Case Files," *Journal of Modern History* 60, no. 4 (December 1988), pp. 673–674.

4. Erich Rosenthal, "Trends of the Jewish Population in Germany, 1910–1939," *Jewish Social Studies* 6 (1944), p. 262; *Blätter des Jüdischen Frauenbundes* (hereafter *BJFB*), 1/34, p. 7, and 3/35, p. 2; *Israelitisches Familienblatt* (hereafter *IF*), no. 8, 2/23/33, p. 9.

5. *IF*, 1/13/38, pp. 13–14, and 7/14/38, p. 12.

6. Corsetiere in Ruth Abraham, memoirs, Leo Baeck Institute, N.Y. (hereafter, LBI), p. 2; mother and daughter in Lisa Brauer, memoirs, LBI, p. 53.

7. *Jüdische Wohlfahrtspflege und Sozial Politik* (hereafter *JWS*) 7 (1937), p. 80.

8. Jobs for women in *JWS* (1933–1934), pp. 118–121.

9. Heroines in *BJFB*, 2/35, p. 12; husbands in *IF* 5/19/38, p. 19.

10. *IF* 2/17/38, p. 16.

11. Psychologists in G. W. Allport, J. S. Bruner, and E. M. Jandorf, "Personality under Social Catastrophe: Ninety Life-Histories of the Nazi Revolution," in *Character and Personality: An International Psychological Quarterly* 10, no. 1 (September 1941), p. 14.

12. Alice Baerwald, Harvard ms., p. 65.

13. Defending in Liselotte Kahn, memoirs, LBI, p. 21; small town in Jacob Ball-Kaduri, memoirs, LBI, p. 30; bribes in Brauer, memoirs, LBI, pp. 43, 57.

14. Palestine in Liselotte Kahn, memoirs, LBI, p. 23; England in Ann Lewis, memoirs, LBI, p. 264.

15. Abraham, memoirs, LBI, p. 2.

16. Depression in Hilde Honnet-Sichel, *Sie Durftennicht mehr Deutschesein*, ed. Margarete Limberg and Hubert Rübsaat (Frankfurt, 1990), p. 183; calm in Leo Gompertz memoirs, LBI, p. 10; "glad" in Hanna Bernheim, Harvard ms., p. 56.

17. For a full discussion of emigration, see Marion Kaplan, "Jewish Women in Nazi Germany before the Emigration," in *Between Sorrow and Strength: Women Refugees of the Nazi Period*, ed. Sibylle Quack (Cambridge: Cambridge University Press, 1995).

18. Peter Wyden, *Stella: One Woman's True Tale of Evil, Betrayal, and Survival in Hitler's Germany* (New York: Simon and Schuster, 1992), p. 47.

19. Erna Albersheim, Harvard ms., p. 28; Elsie Axelrath, Harvard ms., p. 43; Baerwald, Harvard ms., p. 72.

20. These exceptions seem to have occurred mostly in small towns (although for examples from Nuremberg and Düsseldorf, see Rita Thalmann and Emmanuel Feinermann, *Crystal Night* [New York: Coward, McCann and Geoghegan, 1972], pp. 70 and 81).

21. Mally Dienemann, Harvard ms., p. 35.

22. Herbert Strauss, "Jewish Emigration from Germany: Nazi Policies and Jewish Responses (I)," *Leo Baeck Year Book* (1980), pp. 317–318.

23. Lists in Brauer, memoirs, LBI, p. 56; before 1933 in Elisabeth Freund, memoirs, LBI, pp. 144–145; bribes in Brauer, memoirs, LBI, p. 57.

24. Rotterdam in Lilli Sussmann, memoirs, LBI, p. 5; "three suitcases" in Harold Basser in *We Shall Not Forget! Memories of the Holocaust*, ed. Carole Garbuny Vogel (Lexington, Mass.: Temple Isaiah, 1994), p. 202.

25. Baerwald, Harvard ms., p. 67.

26. Officials in Brauer, memoirs, LBI, p. 54; Freund, memoirs, LBI, p. 178; Ruth Glaser, memoirs, LBI, p. 71, and smuggling on p. 38; vetoed in Else Gerstel, memoirs, LBI, pp. 77–79; Baerwald, Harvard ms., p. 73.

27. Regina Scheer, *Ahawah: Das Vergessene Haus* (Berlin and Weimar: Aufbau-Verlag, 1992), p. 265.

28. *JWS* (1937), pp. 7–13, 27, 78–81; Avraham Barkai, "Der wirtschaftliche Existenzkampf der Juden im Dritten Reich, 1933–38," in *The Jews in Nazi Germany, 1933-1945,* ed. Arnold Paucker (Tübingen: J. C. B. Mohr, 1986), p. 163.

29. Hanno Loewy, ed., *In mich ist die grosse dunkle Ruhe gekommen, Martha Wertheimer Briefe an Siegfried Guggenheim* (1939-1941) (Frankfurt: Frankfurter Lern-und Dokumentationszentrum des Holocaust, 1993), pp. 6, 9, 13, 15, 22, 37.

30. *BJFB,* 12/36, p. 5. Among Eastern European Jews who returned east between 1934 and 1937, for example, the majority were male even though almost half of them were married. Maurer, "Ausländische Juden in Deutschland, 1933–39" in Paucker, ed., *The Jews in Nazi Germany,* p. 204.

31. Men beaten in Eisner, *Allein,* p. 8; Nauen (whose father was secretary of the Hilfsverein in Hamburg) interview, p. 15; Ruth Klüger, *weiter leben* (Göttingen, 1992), p. 83.

32. "Sons went" in *BJFB,* 4/37, p. 5. See also Glaser memoirs, LBI, p. 18; Erika Guetermann, "Das Photographien Album," memoirs, LBI. Men, too, felt grief at leaving their parents: see Stein-Pick, memoirs, LBI, p. 46. But more left, nonetheless.

33. "Overlooked" in *BJFB,* 12/36, p. 1; "responsibility" in *BJFB,* 4/37, p. 10; "psychological ties" in *BJFB,* 12/36, p. 1.

34. These statistics referred to 1936–1937, when 59.5 percent of the 11,352 Jewish immigrants to the United States came from Germany. *American Jewish Year Book 5699 (1938–39)* (Philadelphia: American Jewish Committee, 1938), pp. 552–554. Hilfsverein quotation in *Central Verein Zeitung,* January 20, 1938, p. 5.

35. For example, the number of emigrés supported by the emigration section of the Reichsvertretung der Juden in Deutschland broke down to approximately 4,161 men and 3,041 women in 1937. *Informationsblätter* (January–February 1938), pp. 6–7.

36. One survey of graduating classes from several Jewish schools in late 1935 showed that 47 percent of the boys and only 30 percent of the girls considered Palestine as a destination. *JWS* (Berlin, 1935), p. 188. Immigration statistics in "Jewish Immigration from Germany during 1933–1942 (includes Austria since 1938 and Czechoslovakia and Danzig since 1939)," reprint from "The Jewish Immigration and Population," issued by the Department of Statistics of the Jewish Agency.

37. *IF,* 2/27/36; Sybil Milton, "Women and the Holocaust," in *When Biology Became Destiny,* ed. Renate Bridenthal, Atina Grossmann, and Marion Kaplan (New York: Monthly Review Press, 1984), p. 301. See also Bruno Blau, "The Jewish Population of Germany, 1939-1946," *Jewish Social Studies* 12, no. 2, p. 165.

38. Andreas Lixl-Purcell, *Women of Exile* (Westport, Conn.: Greenwood Press, 1988), p. 92.

39. Data from 1933 in Rosenthal, "Trends," p. 248. In 1939, about 22 percent of Jewish women were widowed. Bruno Blau, "Die Juden in Deutschland von 1939 bis 1945,"

Judaica 7 (1951), p. 271. Of the total number of widows, 16,117 (57 percent) were sixty-five years old or older. Blau, "The Jewish Population of Germany," p. 165. Winter Relief in Vollnhals, "Jüdische Selbsthilfe bis 1938," in *Die Juden in Deutschland, 1933–1945,* ed. Wolfgang Benz (Munich: C. H. Beck, 1988), p. 405; *BJFB*, 10/38, p. 4.

40. Freund, memoirs, LBI, p. 146. See also Richarz, *Jüdisches Leben in Deutschland: Selbst-zeugnisse zur Sozialgeschichte, 1918-1945* (Stuttgart: Deutsche Verlags-Anstalt, 1982), p. 61; *JWS* (1937), pp. 96–97 (for statistics on the German Reich); *JWS* (1937), pp. 161–163 (for Hessen-Nassau); and *JWS* (1937), pp. 200–201 (for Koenigsberg).

41. Mary Felstiner, *To Paint Her Life: Charlotte Salomon in the Nazi Era* (New York: Harper-Collins, 1994), pp. 205–206.

CHAPTER THREE

The Missing 52 Percent
Research on Jewish Women in Interwar Poland and Its Implications for Holocaust Studies

Gershon Bacon

According to the Polish census, in 1931 women comprised some 52 percent of the Jewish community, which means that about 1.6 million of the 3.1 million Jews of Poland were female.[1] This rather pedestrian bit of statistical information would not be astounding were it not for the fact that the female majority of Polish Jewry finds little attention in the historical literature on the period. For example, Raphael Mahler's classic socioeconomic survey, *The Jews of Poland between the Two World Wars*,[2] contains not a single reference to women, and the most important narrative surveys of Jewish political and economic life in newly independent Poland[3] devote little or no space to women in Polish Jewish society. The exception that proves the rule is Celia Heller's book *On the Edge of Destruction*, which is the first effort to ponder the effect of sexual differences and roles on Jews' adjustment to Polish society.[4] The growing interest in Polish Jewry on the part of scholars in Israel, North America, and in Poland itself, manifested by a series of international conferences and two well-regarded journals, has done little to revise this lack of attention to women. My own survey of the field, completed in 1984, had no separate entries for women's studies and mentions only a few works that touch on the theme.[5] The state of research on Polish Jewry has changed little in the ensuing years. Shaul Stampfer's study on marriage age stands out as one of the few pathbreaking essays in the field.[6]

Why have topics related to Polish Jewish women attracted so little scholarly interest? Is this but another example of historians' "persistent tendency to assume that the male experience is the universal one"?[7] This explanation is certainly part of the answer, but another factor is that until recent years, the study of Polish Jewry was never far removed from the examination of internal Jewish politics and Polish-Jewish relations. In interwar Poland, the crucial categories that determined the direction of Polish-Jewish history were nationality (Jews versus non-Jews), class (the working class versus the middle class), and generation (youth versus their parents). Gender did not figure in the historical equation.

At a time of intense struggle for national rights, it is not surprising that the arena that attracted the most attention was national parliamentary politics, in which women's participation was negligible. In the six parliamentary elections in interwar Poland, only one Jewish woman, Ruzha Meltzer of the General Zionists, was elected out of the total of 107 Jewish deputies and senators.[8] Those arenas in which women's participation was more significant (such as voluntary organizations and sick fund councils) are the very ones generally neglected in historical literature.

The Promise of a Gender-Sensitive Approach

The few examples of the historical literature that take women's issues into account offer a hint of what we have been missing. Thus, in his history of Warsaw Jewry, Jacob Shatzky noted that Hasidic women offer an especially instructive example of adaptations to modernity within the traditional sector of Jewish society.[9] In Warsaw, the Hasidic woman could be quite worldly. If the Hasidic man rejected most of the attractions of secular culture and saw value only in Torah study, he could not and did not force his wife to keep her distance from Polish culture. A memoirist from that period observed that many young women from middle-class Hasidic homes studied in Catholic schools, read Polish books, attended the Polish theater, and wore the latest fashions.[10] Heller suggests that women played a significant role in their families' acculturation to Polish culture. In her view, for a substantial proportion of middle-class children, acculturation found encouragement at home, especially from mothers. Even before Poland became independent in 1918, the study of the Polish language, and of secular subjects, was much more acceptable for middle-class female children than for males. After independence, those girls became Jewish middle-class mothers who instilled in their children the love of the Polish language and culture.[11] Deborah Weissman's study of the Bais Yaakov (or Bet Yaakov) schools in Poland demonstrates the subtle transformation of women's role in the Orthodox community from that of a passive recipient of the values of the home to an educated, active defender of tradition.[12] A new Orthodox female elite emerged who served as teachers in their own towns and as role models for an entire generation of Orthodox women.

And yet there are hints that some religiously raised women were taking other paths. In one of the autobiographies of youth cited by Max Weinreich, we find the following observation: "A daughter of a well-known Hasid once announced that she ate ham. This is a characteristic trait among Hasidic daughters. Let them out of their cage and they become wilder than the most wild. . . . Their father can't take care of them. He must watch the kashrut of others."[13]

The insights and observations noted here are only a suggestion of what the historiography of Polish Jewry stands to gain from new perspectives that take an interest in women's experiences. In general, a Polish Jewish version of the processes analyzed so brilliantly by Marion Kaplan regarding Jewish women in Germany, and by Paula Hyman, Susan Glenn, and others regarding immigrant Jewish women in the United States, would be of immense value.[14] In Poland, the process of entering the middle class was highly charged with cultural and even national elements that made it worthy of historical and sociological analysis.[15]

Topics for Further Investigation

For purposes of illustration, I would like to suggest a few possible directions for further research.

Women's Voting Rights in the Kehilla

The nature of the *kehilla* (the Jewish community) was one of the most hotly contested topics on the political agenda of Polish Jewry in the interwar period. At the beginning of the twentieth century, the Zionists, Bundists, and Folkists all saw the kehilla as the building block of a new national Jewish identity, but only if it could be remade into a secular, democratic instrument, wherein religious support would be one of many services to the Jewish public or, in the view of more secularist nationalists, would be eliminated entirely. Orthodox parties, which developed at the same time, did their utmost to preserve the essentially religious nature of the kehilla, maintaining that even in a more democratic community their views should prevail because they represented the silent majority of the Jewish population. Changes did take place in the kehilla regime after World War I, with the adoption of almost universal suffrage, but voting rights were still limited to males.

Admittedly, women's suffrage was a new phenomenon in Polish politics, but various political movements within the Jewish community had allowed full female participation from the turn of the century (in the Zionist movement, for example, women had been allowed to vote since the Second Zionist Congress in 1898) and had championed that cause as part of the new secular kehilla they envisaged. Yet we hear nothing of a demand for equal participation of women in the elections of the kehilla.[16] The issue of women's suffrage, even for those parties which supported it vigorously, was evidently not a casus belli.

Women's organizations could, on occasion, put male political representatives in an uncomfortable position, as when members of the Jewish National Women's Organization approached Eliahu Kirshbraun, the deputy of the Orthodox Jewish party Agudat Yisrael (Union of Israel, or Aguda for short), to learn Aguda's views on women's rights. Regarding general political affairs, Kirshbraun maintained, Aguda supported full equality for women and would fight any discrimination against Jewish women. In Jewish life, however, Jewish women could not have equal rights because they had different religious duties from men. This was not Aguda's position but one dictated by authoritative codes of Jewish law.[17]

To what extent did women's lack of voting rights contribute to the neglect of women's issues in kehilla budgets? Some data suggest that Jewish women were not as politically conscious as Jewish men. In the 1919 parliamentary elections only 56 percent of eligible Jewish voters in Warsaw went to the polls (as opposed to 75 percent of non-Jewish voters), but the contrasts are even more stark by gender: 64 percent of eligible Jewish male voters in Warsaw cast ballots, but for Jewish women the figure was only 49 percent. (Among non-Jewish women, 75 percent voted.) The author of the study attributes these differences to systematic terror directed against Jewish voters.[18] A more recent analysis notes, however, that the voting in Warsaw on that day proceeded efficiently, without a single serious attempt to disturb it.[19] Whatever the case may be, the subject of Jewish political consciousness or the lack of such, among both men and women, deserves further exploration.

Women in Youth Movements and Political Parties

In his excellent study of the Zionist movement in Poland, Ezra Mendelsohn notes many complaints about the relative lack of female participation. He cites Puah Rakowski, one of the few female leaders of Polish Zionism, who blamed the Zionist leadership's adherence to traditional views that women should not take public office. She pointed to the success of revolutionary movements of the Left in Eastern Europe, which allowed real equality between the sexes, in attracting energetic and ambitious Jewish women.[20] Daniel Blatman, however, describes similar laments about the absence of women in Bund circles (see Chapter 4).

In his memoirs of the period, Yitzhak Schwarzbart, the Zionist leader, singles out for praise the few female Jewish student members of WIZO (the Women's International Zionist Organization), who represented a lonely minority. Jewish women were more likely to participate in the general Polish socialist movement or in the Bund than in Zionist organizations. Schwarzbart attributed this trend to a lack of Jewish education, which made women more likely to feel comfortable in organizations that had little or nothing to do with Jewish national pride. A second reason, in his view, was the moral stance of educated Jewish women regarding problems of the present and the future. They simply could not devote themselves to activity in the Zionist movement, which was more idealistic than practical. Although socialism also had a long-term mission, it was grounded in a struggle for direct and practical goals. By comparison, Zionism seemed a distant dream.[21]

These hypothetical explanations for the lack of women's participation do not obviate the need for a careful examination of the work of those women who did take part in political and organizational activities—in the Polish parliamentary campaigns, in the municipalities, on the elected boards of the sick funds and labor unions, and in the individual political parties, whether in women's auxiliaries or in the main body of the party.

Such an approach might, for example, reexamine the place of women in the Zionist pioneering movements and the *hakhshara* (training) farms and cooperatives, where a cult of historical national heroism sprang up.[22] Did this myth of armed heroism speak to the female members as well, or did they need an alternative vision? Beyond questions of ideology, practical questions about women in the movement deserve further exploration. For example, did the female members receive their proportionate share of the coveted certificates for immigration to Palestine? And were women on the kibbutzim in Poland relegated to "women's work"? As Levi Aryeh Sarid notes, "It is astonishing that the issue of relations between the sexes, does not find adequate expression in the literature and press of the movement."[23]

Polish Census Data

The many volumes of official statistical reports produced in interwar Poland have already served as the basis for a number of important studies on various aspects of Polish Jewry.[24] A gender-based analysis of the data, especially the wealth of information from the censuses from 1921 and 1931, would offer important insights. A few preliminary findings in this area show the potential uses of this material.

Jewish students, male and female. Mahler and others have called attention to the special and difficult situation of Jewish university students in newly independent Poland. In general, the position of Jewish students was constantly eroding, evidently because of ongoing discrimination in admissions policies, numerus clausus (Jewish quotas), and growing violence against Jews on the part of right-wing Polish students. In the 1930s not only did the percentage of Jews in the student body decline, but even the absolute number of Jewish students declined—from 24.6 percent of all students in institutions of higher education in 1921–1922 (8,426 of 34,266) to only 8.2 percent in 1938–1939 (4,113 of 49,987).[25]

When we divide the Jewish and general student body by gender, some significant differences emerge.[26] First, the ratio of Jewish women to female students is larger than the ratio of Jewish men to male students. Second, the relative proportion of women among Jewish students is quite high. It would seem that in Poland, as in other countries, Jewish women entered institutions of higher learning earlier and in greater proportion than their non-Jewish counterparts. Whereas female students made up only 23 percent of the general student body in 1923–1924 and 27 percent in 1928–1929, among Jewish students women comprised 33 percent in 1923–1924 and as much as 38 percent in 1928–1929.

Before we could draw any firm conclusions regarding these figures, we would have to obtain data on Polish Jewish students studying abroad. Most likely a large number of Jewish males, having been denied admission to various professional faculties in Poland, went to study elsewhere. On the face of things, though, it would seem that antisemitic practices either on the part of the universities themselves or on the part of the professions affected Jewish males more severely than Jewish females. This is not surprising, considering the departments in which Jewish men and Jewish women were enrolled: in the 1928–1929 academic year, for example, almost 45 percent of male Jewish students were in the department of law, as opposed to only 14 percent of female Jewish students. The largest enrollment of Jewish female students was in the department of philosophy (humanities and science): 70 percent of Jewish females but only 23 percent of Jewish males were enrolled in that department (and students of humanities did not enter competitive professions). The proportions of Jewish students (both male and female) in the law and medical departments shrank even further in the 1930s, as both the numerus clausus and "Aryan paragraphs" (resolutions passed by professional associations limiting membership to Aryans) steadily chipped away at Jewish representation in these fields.[27]

Even this preliminary analysis raises some important questions concerning the varied experience of the two genders in the academic world. Did Jewish women in Poland, as opposed to Jewish men, attend university as a kind of cultural finishing school, with little thought of entering professional life afterward? Were Jewish women physically safer than Jewish men in the face of right-wing student disturbances on the campuses?

Women's economic activity. Memoirs from the period contain a plethora of material about the varied economic activities of Jewish women. This abundance of data, however, does not mean that men and women participated equally in providing the family livelihood. Once again, the Polish census data and other economic survey materials from the period can provide us with the parameters for evaluating the largely anecdotal material found in the memoirs and biographies.

For the most part, the relatively plentiful scholarly literature about Jewish economic life in interwar Poland ignores the issue of gender. An important exception is Bina Garncarska-Kadari, whose studies on the Jewish working class take note of such issues as salary differentials. On the key issue of economic "activity" or "passivity" of Jewish women, Garncarska-Kadari offers some important correctives to the census data that underestimate the percentages of active Jewish women.[28] A few preliminary studies carried out in the 1930s also point to differences between the cities and the smaller market-towns with regard to economic activity by women and children.[29] We should take regional variations into account as well. The Polish statistical bureaus published a large number of local economic and demographic analyses of the census data, which would enable researchers to piece together the economic "pyramid" of Polish Jewish women and analyze how it differed from that of Jewish men.[30]

Yizkor Books

Although they are usually not the product of professional historians, the hundreds of memorials to destroyed communities have tremendous importance for many aspects of Holocaust research.[31] Even if the focus of this literature is the Holocaust period, considerable attention is also given to earlier eras, such as the interwar period. Approximately 90 percent of the material in the yizkor books is by or about men, but the remaining 10 percent offers precious testimony about the activities and views of women in traditional and modern roles and, not coincidentally, about the ways survivors of that world have constructed or reconstructed the memory of that period. A good example is the memoir that Yitzhak Nebenzahl presented of his grandmother Elke, who was "not just an *eshet hayyil* [a "woman of valor"—an ideally pious Jewish woman] who knew how to manage her business affairs and her household with understanding and diligence, but was blessed with a special feeling for matters of the kehilla and the community, with a sense of the spirit of the time." For instance, Elke did not object when her sons and grandsons decided to acquire a secular education; she even gave them her blessing. In addition to caring for her extended family, she chaired the local women's organization, which looked after the many social needs of the Jewish community. Her crowning achievement was the founding of the local *Bet Ya'akov* school, which she established over the objections of both the local Belzer Hasidim and "enlightened" families in the town, for whom Bet Yaakov was anathema.[32]

Alongside portrayals of traditional women like grandmother Elke, the yizkor books cite examples of women active in modern political parties and social movements. Thus in the book on Stryj, we find a short entry on Ita Becher, who worked during the day as a clerk but devoted all her free time to public service. A longtime member of Poalei Zion (a Zionist workers' party), she was single-handedly responsible for the financial upkeep of the local Labor Zionist kindergarten and often shared her meager salary with the needy. In addition to her volunteer work, Becher served in elective offices, as the Poalei Zion representative in the local sick fund and as secretary of the local federation of trade unions.[33]

Finally, the yizkor books enable us to trace the activities of women's organizations in cities and in towns large and small. They document, for example, groups for tending the sick and local Zionist women's groups.[34]

YIVO Autobiographies and Other Biographical Material

Paula Hyman makes extensive use of a number of published autobiographies of Jewish women (who spent at least the formative years of their lives in Eastern Europe) and of the YIVO collection of autobiographies of young people. These rich resources for the interwar period produced a stream of additional biographical and autobiographical material, most of which includes some discussion of families and women. A 1987 biography of Zionist leader Yitzhak Grunbaum, for example, contains the following passage:

> His mother taught him Polish and opened for him a window to Polish literature—and he was immediately captivated by the inherent charm of the new discovery. His mother was the daughter of a merchant who traded in Polish books, a branch that surprisingly was completely in Jewish hands. In the period which stood in the shadow of the cruel confrontation between tyranny and national aspirations, the mother was intoxicated by the atmosphere of intellectual rebellion, and breathed in the atmosphere of the new Polish literature. . . . Thus while the father shut himself up in his room and submerged himself in the latest issues of Ha'melitz . . . the mother would invite to her salon male and female friends to sit together and drink thirstily

from the fount of Polish literature. Every literary hero who fought against tsarist Russia or against the other enemies of Poland, became as a result of his deeds alone an admired figure in the reading salon of Mrs. Grunbaum.[35]

As Celia Heller has pointed out, the role of the mother as the engine of acculturation was a theme repeated in thousands of households. A careful culling of material from other biographies and autobiographies promises to enrich our understanding of Polish Jewish women.

Implications for the Study of Women during the Holocaust

The selected examples I have cited demonstrate the potential contribution of gender issues to our understanding of interwar Polish Jewry. In paying special attention to gender issues we risk drifting into an overly judgmental approach to the past; that is, we risk imposing our standards and our sensitivities on the past. But this is a problem of all historical research. The effort is well worth it.

In closing, I should like to offer a few thoughts on the implications of work on the interwar period for our understanding of women in the Holocaust. My firm conviction is that the two eras are connected. It would be a mistake to regard the Holocaust period, no matter how unique its horrors, as somehow detached from the rest of history. This point seems self-evident to me, but we often encounter the view that the Holocaust is sui generis, beyond standard historical explanations of background, causation, and precedent. How can we intelligently and fairly analyze the functioning and success or failure of Jewish communal bodies without the prewar background? Any analysis of Polish Jewry in the ghetto period must take into account the situation in the years immediately before the war, when we witnessed the progressive erosion of Jewish communal autonomy by Polish authorities, the decline of the rabbinate, and the marginalization of Jewish political leadership in the wake of the more general marginalization of parliamentary politics. In other words, at the onset of the German occupation, Polish Jews were at a distinct disadvantage in terms of their communal institutions. This disadvantage existed before the destruction and dislocations of the war and before the Germans began their campaign of systematic spoliation and ghettoization of the Jews.

Considerable evidence points toward a crisis in the Jewish family in interwar Poland, which made the harsh conditions under the Nazi occupation even more onerous. Did the differences in the ways women and men adjusted to Polish culture and language enhance women's likelihood of survival beyond the obvious advantage that they lacked bodily signs of Jewishness? In dealing with questions of relative status and survival potential, we must also take into account such factors as the enhanced role of the male breadwinner in the ghetto and the generally impossible conditions under which decisions had to be made given that German policies did not follow any normal canon of logic, utility, or sensibility. If the erosion of traditional values was stronger among certain sectors of educated women, how did this affect their attitudes and behavior during the war? If women felt a special closeness to Polish culture and, by extension, to Poland, was their disappointment with Polish persecution of the Jews proportionately greater? In sum, how were women's activities during the war conditioned by their prewar experiences?

These are just a few of the questions that emerge from a historical survey of women in interwar Poland. In dealing with the behavior of individuals and communities, we always have to ask ourselves how much of that behavior stems from long-term aspects of Jewish culture and how much from period-specific phenomena. For example, did the increasingly bourgeois nature of assimilated Jewish families make women more passive in family decision making, perhaps even more than in the traditional family? With only the available sources, I doubt that we can answer many of the questions I have posed. But surely any attempt to deal with them depends on our ability to determine the starting point for such analyses, which must begin with the status of women in Poland between the wars.

Notes

1. Szyja Bronsztejn, *Ludność Żydowska w Polsce w Okresie Międzywojennym* (Wrocław: Ossolineum, 1963): pp. 123, 148.

2. Raphael Mahler, *Yehudei Polin bein shtei milhamot olam: Historia kalkalit-sotsialit le'or ha'statistika* (Tel Aviv: Dvir, 1968).

3. See, e.g., Ezra Mendelsohn, *The Jews of East Central Europe between the World Wars* (Bloomington: Indiana University Press, 1983), pp. 11–83; Pawel Korzec, *Juifs en Pologne: La question juive pendant l'entre-deux-guerres* (Paris: Presses de la fondation

nationale des sciences politiques, 1980). See also the idiosyncratic but interesting work of Joseph Marcus, *Social and Political History of the Jews in Poland, 1919-1939* (Berlin: Mouton, 1983), pp. 163-182.

4. Celia Heller, *On the Edge of Destruction: Jews of Poland between the Two World Wars* (New York: Columbia University Press, 1977).

5. Gershon D. Hundert and Gershon C. Bacon, *The Jews in Poland and Russia: Bibliographical Essays* (Bloomington: Indiana University Press, 1984).

6. Shaul Stampfer, "Marital Patterns in Interwar Poland," in Yisrael Gutman et al., eds., *The Jews of Poland Between Two World Wars* (Hanover, N.H.: University Press of New England, 1989), pp. 173-197.

7. Barbara Alpern Engel, "Engendering Russia's History: Women in Post-Emancipation Russia and the Soviet Union," *Slavic Review* 51, no. 2 (Summer 1992), p. 311.

8. See the list in Yitzhak Schwarzbart, *Tsvishn Beide Velt-Milkhomes* (Buenos Aires: Tsentral-Farband fur Poilishe Yiden in Argentina, 1958), pp. 212-214.

9. Jacob Shatzky, *Geshikhte fun Yidn in Varshe*, vol. 3 (New York: YIVO, 1953), p. 371.

10. Y. Y. Frayd, *Yamim ve'Shanim*, 2 vols. (Tel Aviv: Dvir, 1938-1939), vol. 2, pp. 22-23.

11. Heller, *On the Edge of Destruction*, p. 227.

12. Deborah R. Weissman, "Bais Yaakov—A Women's Educational Movement in the Polish Jewish Community: A Case Study in Tradition and Modernity" (master's thesis, New York University, 1977).

13. Max Weinreich, *Der veg tsu undzer yugnt—Yesodes, metoden, problemen fun yiddisher yugnt-forshung* (Vilna: YIVO, 1935), p. 296.

14. Marion Kaplan, *The Making of the Jewish Middle Class: Women, Family, and Identity in Imperial Germany* (New York: Oxford University Press, 1991); Paula Hyman, *Gender and Assimilation in Modern Jewish History: The Roles and Representation of Women* (Seattle: University of Washington Press, 1995), pp. 93-133; Susan Glenn, *Daughters of the Shtetl: Life and Labor in the Immigrant Generation* (Ithaca: Cornell University Press, 1990).

15. For general views of the Polish middle class (including material on Jews and Jewish families), see Ireneusz Ihnatowicz, *Obyczaj wielkiej burżuazji warszawskiej w XIX Wieku* (Warsaw: PWN, 1971); Ryszard Kolodziejczyk, *Miasta, mieszczaństwo, burżuazja w Polsce w XIX Wieku* (Warsaw: PWN, 1979).

16. Ezra Mendelsohn, *Perakim nivharim be'toledot yehudei Polin bein shtei milhamot olam* (course reader, Hebrew University, 1971), part 2, pp. 164-165, citing *Arbeter Luakh* (1925).

17. *Haynt,* October 31, 1922, p. 4.

18. I. Mintzin, "Di Bateiligung fun di Yidn in di valn tsu di Poilishe Sejmn (1919, 1922)," *Bletter far Yiddishe Demografie, Statistik un Ekonomik* 1, no. 2 (April 1923), pp. 86-90.

19. Ludwik Hass, *Wybory Warszawskie, 1918-1926* (Warsaw: PWN, 1972), p. 66.

20. Ezra Mendelsohn, *Ha'Tenua Ha'Tsiyyonit be'Polin: Shenot hithavut, 1915-1926* (Jerusalem: Ha'sifriya ha'tsiyonnit, 1986), pp. 302-303.

21. Schwarzbart, *Tsvishn Beide Velt-Milkhomes*, pp. 127-128.

22. Levi Aryeh Sarid, *He'Halutz u'tenuot ha'noar be'Polin, 1917–1939* (Tel Aviv: Am Oved, 1979), p. 205.

23. Ibid., p. 499.

24. See, e.g., Jacob Lestchinsky, "The Jews in the Cities of the Republic of Poland," *YIVO Annual* 1 (1946), pp. 156–177.

25. Mahler, *Yehudei Polin bein shtei milhamot olam*, pp. 172–173.

26. Sources for statistics: *Rocznik Statystyki Rzeczypospolitej Polskiej* 3 (1924), p. 242; 4 (1925–1926), p. 421; 7 (1929), p. 428; 8 (1930), p. 415.

27. Mahler, *Yehudei Polin bein shtei milhamot olam*, p. 174, table 39.

28. Bina Garncarska-Kadari, "Ha'ovdim ha'yehudim be'Polin bein shtei milhamot olam (nituah statisti)," *Gal-Ed* 3 (1976), pp. 150–153; "Ha'matsav ha'homri shel shikhvot ha'ovdim ha'yehudim be'Polin (1930–1939)," *Gal-Ed* 9 (1986), pp. 146–147, 166–167.

29. N. S. Yedidowicz, "Di Yiddishe Bafelkerung fun Glubok in Tsifern," *YIVO Bleter* 2 (1931), pp. 414–420.

30. See, e.g., *Statystyka Polski, Seria C, zeszyt 58—Miasto Lwow* (Warsaw, 1937), pp. 96, 98, 116, for material about Jewish men and women who were active in light industry and in commerce in the city of Lvov.

31. For a guide to this literature, see Zachary M. Baker, "Bibliography of Eastern European Memorial Books," appendix 1 to Jack Kugelmass and Jonathan Boyarin (eds.), *From a Ruined Garden: The Memorial Books of Polish Jewry* (New York: Schocken Books, 1983), pp. 223–264.

32. Yitzhak Nebenzahl, "Elke Podrebaitel," in Michael Valtzer and Natan Kudish, eds., *Łancut—Hayyeha ve'Hurbana shel Kehilla Yehudit* (Israel, 1963), p. 173.

33. Natan Kudish et al., eds., *Sefer Stryj* (Israel, 1962), pp. 133–134.

34. Batya Hochberg, "Di Froyen-farayn 'Bikkur Holim,'" in *Sefer Lutzk* (Tel Aviv, 1961), pp. 239–241; Rahel Shperling-Shapira, "Agudat Nashim Tsiyyoniyot 'Devora,'" in David Shtokfish, ed., *Sefer Zgierz* (Israel, 1975), pp. 317–318.

35. Roman Frister, *Lelo Peshara* (Tel Aviv: Zmora, Bitan, 1987), pp. 14–15. The translation is my own.

CHAPTER FOUR

Women in the Jewish Labor Bund in Interwar Poland

Daniel Blatman

T he Jewish Labor Bund, a political movement established by Marxist intellectuals in Vilna in 1897, was an outgrowth of the condition of Eastern European Jews in the 1880s and 1890s. The large Jewish proletariat had become increasingly incorporated into the general urban working class, and the friction between the Jewish and non-Jewish proletariats was a principal factor in the emergence of a separate Jewish labor movement. The fact that Jewish workers were being dismissed from their jobs in the developing industries of urban Lithuania, Belorussia, and the Ukraine encouraged them to set up independent local organizations and also forced the Marxist Jewish leaders of the Bund to confront the issue of the national distinctiveness of the Jewish proletariat and the demand for Jewish cultural autonomy.[1] The question of women as a social group with distinct needs and, particularly, the issue of the Jewish working woman never came up at this time.

The revolutionary movement in Russia had a remarkably high proportion of women activists from the start. According to some estimates, 20 percent of revolutionary activists in Russia in the 1860s and 1870s were women.[2] Their representation in populist movements and groups was especially strong. Robert McNeal asserts that the principle of women's equality was already evident in the liberal Russian literature of the first half of the nineteenth century and that this literature influenced the way women, especially those from the aristocracy and the bourgeoisie, viewed themselves and their activity in society. An examination of the family background of prominent women Bundists of the early twentieth century suggests that they, like their Russian counterparts, may have derived their attitudes from the writings of Aleksander Pushkin or Aleksander Herzen. In fact, the Bund's membership included Jewish women veterans of the Russian populist movement of the 1860s and 1870s. Important women Bundists, such as Pati Kremer, Liuba Levinson-Aizenshtat, Anna Rozental, and Roza Levit, had had some higher education, and several had attended academic institutions in the West.[3] When they became activists in the labor movement, they were treated as the equals of their male counterparts.

The participation of women in the revolutionary movement had far-reaching repercussions for the participants. The Jewish family, ill disposed to see its sons join the revolutionary movement, was even less pleased to have its daughters join. Sometimes the parents ostracized these young women or even observed the bereavement ritual of shivah for them,[4] and this prospect strongly discouraged young Jewish women from activism in revolutionary parties. Nevertheless, several of the young Jewish women who joined the Bund before World War I came from traditional or Hasidic families, which were horrified by their daughters' actions. Esther Riskind, for example, whose Hasidic Chabad parents had intended to marry her off to a yeshiva student at age sixteen, was forced to leave home. She moved to Kharkow, where she became a leading activist in Jewish socialist student groups under Bund influence. Similar stories are told of other women Bundists who joined before or shortly after World War I, such as Esther Richter, Bella Shapiro, and Manya Rozen.[5]

Another deterrent to the participation of women was the nature of political work in the movement at the time: activism was quasi-underground and essentially illegal and thus presented considerable risk of official harassment, even imprisonment. Anna Rozental, an important Bundist, believed that work in the movement was intrinsically unsuitable for Jewish women. The Bundists' principal objectives in the early years were to contact as many Jewish workers as possible in industrial plants, workshops, and factories; to bring them the tidings of the movement; and to organize them for action. According to Rozental, few women had the organizational ability these goals required.[6]

Nonetheless, women's status within the movement was indistinguishable from men's, and this equality was carried over to the families of movement members. Most women activists who married chose their partners from among their ideological counterparts. (The phenomenon of families with two politically active spouses was typical of the vanguard of Jewish labor leaders in Eastern Europe.) Courtship and pairing patterns were totally subordinated to political goals. The ideology of the movement treated sexual attraction and love with suspicion, as threats to or distractions from the main goals of revolution. Moreover, the first (male) Bundists emphasized the purity of their relations with women. Nevertheless, young party activists tended to form romantic relationships with other members.[7]

Although the Bund had an explicitly revolutionary ideology in the years before World War I, its Jewishness meant that its attitudes concerning families and women were slightly different from those that characterized the general revolutionary movement in Russia. For example, women of the Bund were much more strongly inclined to have children than were women in the Russian revolutionary movement,[8] and the Bundist family retained rather traditional patterns of role division in the education of children.

It is no simple matter to determine the number of active women Bundists. The three biographical volumes published by Bundists in the United States after World War II provide details on 551 movement members and activists from the late nineteenth century to the Holocaust.[9] Ninety-four (17 percent) of these were women. This figure apparently overestimates the true number of women who were active in the movement because it includes twenty female members of Zukunft, the party's organization for young adults, who belonged to the various fighting groups in Poland and Lithuania during the Holocaust but were not important participants in party affairs before the war. Another twenty or so women whose biographies are included in the commemorative books were the wives of Bundists; it is doubtful whether all could be considered party activists. Thus the percentage of women in the Bund, both in Poland and Russia, was lower than the percentage of women in the Russian revolutionary movements.[10]

From Revolutionary Activity to Organization of Working Women

World War I, the Bolshevik Revolution in Russia, and the establishment of independent Poland at the end of the war inaugurated a new chapter in the history of the Bund. The party, which had based much of its work during the czarist period on illegal, clandestine activity, suddenly became a legal entity. Despite complex official constraints, after 1918 the Bund established organizations to serve Polish Jewry in the fields of education, culture, trade union-ism, and youth movements. Its new path in independent Poland led not only to changes in the party's structure and institutions but also to serious ideolog-ical turmoil, especially concerning the party's attitude toward the regime that had taken shape in the Soviet Union. After heated internal debate, the Bund aligned itself unequivocally with European social democracy by joining the Second Socialist International in the early 1930s.[11]

The repercussions of the Bund's decision to pursue legal political activity transcended ideology. The Bund had to build an extensive organizational and institutional infrastructure that could address the concerns of Polish Jewry, 3 million strong and divided among various political parties. For the first time in its history, the Bund had the opportunity to join with other Jewish parties in the attempt to construct Jewish cultural autonomy, a basic tenet of Bund ide-ology since the turn of the century. In the context of this reorientation, ques-tions about the status of Jewish working women in Poland and how to organize them were frequently discussed.

The modernization processes that swept Polish Jewry, coupled with the growing influence of Polish culture and language, were felt first among women, especially those of the urban middle classes, who were the main agents of acculturation within their families and society; men, in contrast, usu-ally opposed the infiltration of modern trends into the lives of their families.[12] The Bundists were aware of this "women's revolution," especially from the early 1930s on. True, these processes were studied in the general context of Polish society; however, their connection with the lives of Jewish women was clear. David Ajnhoren wrote in the daily newspaper of the Bund that the rev-olution was altering the foundations of society without warfare, victims, or violence. The modern woman, he pointed out, could be found in almost all occupations, from university teaching to athletic competition. Unlike her mother, she was dynamic, politically involved, and educated. She treated her children as friends and communicated with them by means of explanation and cooperation. She took account of new ideas in psychology and pedagogy in raising her children.[13]

To what extent did these trends concretely influence the real lives of the Jewish proletariat in Poland? With respect to the status of working Jewish women, as in other matters, the Bund evidently held several attitudes, some of which were mutually contradictory. The ideology of the Bund supported the idea of a complete integration of women in social and economic life. But the party put a brake on the creation of specific female organizations that could help in the implementation of that same integration. At the outset of Polish independence, Bundist and Zionist newspapers published articles on the Jewish woman. Thus the March 3, 1916, edition of *Lebensfragen,* the Bund journal in Poland, reported that the capitalist order prescribed a clear set of roles for women. In addition to the roles that had existed before—to bear children, to manage the home, and to be faithful wives—women were now to move into the factories. Thus women were to become cogs in the capitalist machine, obliged to continue to discharge their family duties while providing the sweat labor to maintain the very social and economic order that oppressed them. Only a socialist revolution that would alter the social order radically, the article concluded, could remedy the situation of women.[14] The Bund, then, continued to relate to women only from a class perspective, arguing that the capitalist system was the underlying cause of their oppression.

The party did, however, begin to give the special social roles of women more serious attention. It acknowledged that women exerted influence on social issues of importance to the working class, such as social entitlements, geriatric care, health concerns, and the problem of unemployment. It thus followed that women should enlist in trade unions and do their share in the struggle of the proletariat.[15]

Working women became important in the economic affairs of Jewish families. According to the population censuses, the proportion of Jewish women who were the primary family breadwinner rose from 25.8 percent in 1921 to 27.4 percent in 1931. This figure does not take into account women who ran family businesses; worked part time alongside the head of the household in workshops, small retail establishments, and the like; or engaged in such cottage industries as needlework and knitting, turning out goods that were sold in shops in the towns. Women accounted for 55.9 percent of Jewish wage earners in 1921 and 44.5 percent in 1931 (this drop reflected the effects of the economic crisis).[16] The percentage of wage-earning women was particularly high in "Jewish" industries—textile, apparel, haberdashery, and paper. In the early 1930s, women accounted for 35 percent of all Jewish workers in the textile industries of Lodz, for example, and 36 percent in Warsaw. The proportion of women was even higher in the lingerie industry: 44 percent in Lodz and 55 percent in Warsaw.[17]

Women's terms of employment and social insurance were far inferior to those of their male counterparts. In the industries with a high percentage of women, women's wages were only 50–60 percent of men's. The deterioration in the economic situation of Polish Jewry in the early 1930s and the increasingly negative attitude toward hiring Jews in various industries forced many middle-class families to join the ranks of the working class. Many young Jewish women who had completed primary school and expected to go on to further studies instead had to take supplementary vocational courses or accept unskilled jobs.[18]

The YAF: The Bund's Women's Auxiliary

In the early 1920s the Bund established a women's auxiliary, the Yidishe Arbeter-Froy Organizatsie (YAF). The formation of separate organizations for different groups of supporters was standard practice among parties of the Left; the Polish Socialist Party (PPS) also had a separate women's auxiliary. The main function of the Bund's women's organization, however, was not to deal with the needs of working women in particular but to serve as an extension of the party vis-à-vis the community of women.[19] Beynish Mikhalevich, a leading Bund ideologue of the 1920s, saw no difference between Jewish women and women workers in general and offered no support for the creation of a separate organization for this purpose. Rather, he emphasized the need for general social change that would transform the status and situation of women en passant. On the few occasions when he related to the issue of Jewish working women, Henryk Erlich, leader of the Bund in interwar Poland, said that their goal should be assimilation into the organizational structures of the Jewish working class and participation in the general proletarian struggle against fascism, against capitalism, and for social and cultural progress. He saw no point in a Jewish women's organization that concerned itself with the particular needs arising from women's living conditions, roles in the workplace, and status within the family.[20]

In the minds of the Bund leadership, the women's organizations, like its two youth movements, Zukunft and Sotsialistisher Kinder Farband (SKIF),[21] and other sectorial organizations established by the Bund, had to be separate because of the weakness of the revolutionary and class consciousness of these groups. The decision to establish the YAF evidently was adopted without any specific guidelines about its proper sphere of activities and tasks, except for the need to reach out to working women in an effort to enlist them in the party's activist cells.[22]

The party leadership's vision of YAF members as just like male members was probably incomplete.[23] One unique and critical need of working women was assistance in child care. In 1921, for example, there were more than 155,000 working women (Jewish and non-Jewish) in Warsaw alone.[24] The YAF, recognizing the growing importance of Jewish women's labor in supporting the family and appreciating the inadequacy of the solutions offered by the state, made intensive efforts to establish day care facilities for children of working mothers. In the early 1920s, such facilities were founded in Warsaw, Lodz, Lublin, Bialystok, Vilna, Piotrkow-Trybunalski, and other towns where the party was active. The center in Warsaw served 450 preschoolers in the early 1930s. During the summer vacation, the YAF sponsored half-day urban summer camps, but this activity placed an enormous burden on the limited resources of the YAF, and several day care centers and summer camps had to be closed because of budgetary problems.[25]

The need for both general and advanced education of Jewish working women eventually became central. The YAF activists were well aware that the affiliation of Jewish women with the Bund did not solve the problem of the living conditions of most Jewish women in the lower social classes, because their families continued to practice a style of life that limited women's responsibilities and authority to their traditional activities—cooking and taking care of the home. An informational system was therefore created, intended to modify the traditional ways of the Jewish family and to encourage Jewish women to change their attitudes toward their social lives and status. The YAF established women's clubs that sponsored lectures and classes on such issues as male-female relations in modern society, children's education and health, family planning, parent-child relations, and family budgeting. Many of the topics concerned the lives of the women themselves: their personal needs, their work schedules, their efforts to find time for housework, their annual vacation, fashion, home design, and the like. These activity groups made a special effort to augment the working women's basic education and literacy skills. Most important, the YAF entities provided working women with an after-work social framework that they had lacked.[26]

Thus the activity of the Bund's women's organization in interwar Poland manifested the pragmatism that typified the party in those years. Although the party leaders and organs attributed blatantly ideological goals to the YAF, the women's auxiliary developed a package of educational, informational, and social activities that attracted Jewish working women who did not necessarily subscribe to the party's ideological platform.

It is hard to estimate the number of women who participated in YAF activities. The party press obviously tends to overestimate the number of female activists as evidence of the success of the party's propaganda and organizational efforts. With this reservation in mind, the number of women participants in YAF activities in Warsaw in the late 1930s may be counted at about five or six hundred. In Lodz, an important interwar Bundist center, about eight or nine hundred Jewish working women participated in YAF activities during the same period, when Bund influence among the Jewish rank and file reached its peak. In Bialystok, Lublin, and Vilna, the corresponding figures at that time ranged only from one hundred to two hundred.[27]

Women and the Party: Mutual Expectations

In January 1928, shortly before the elections to the Polish Sejm, (parliament), the Bund issued an appeal to Jewish women, noting that their husbands worked hard, had limited social entitlements, and were worse off than their Polish counterparts simply because they were Jewish. After this description of the husbands' situation, the broadsheet addressed the women directly: "You're a mother. Your children play in the filthy streets without any supervision, without any care, without schooling. They are poor children, and the state is utterly unconcerned about their plight. They are poor Jewish children; they have no kindergartens, day care centers, or schools."[28] The broadsheet made no reference to the needs of the women themselves.

Throughout the interwar period, the Bund regarded the female population as a large body of potential supporters who, if persuaded to take part in party activity, would enhance its power immeasurably. The male leaders and spokesmen of the Bund tried ceaselessly to enroll Jewish women in activities that would serve the immediate political goals on the party agenda—not only the Sejm elections but also the Bund's struggle with the Jewish Communists for control of the Jewish labor unions in the late 1920s. In this struggle, which featured sporadic violence and subjected the Bund's ability to lead Jewish workers in Poland to a genuine test,[29] the party leadership urged women not to stand by passively: "The time has come for the working woman to do her share in preventing internecine strife. Few women, however, understand what is about to take place and know their role in this situation of a threat of a schism in Jewish society. . . . You must understand that these are the trade unions of your husbands, your brothers, and, when all is said and done, yourselves. . . . Any harm that befalls them means harm to the status and rights of the Jewish working class."[30]

In 1938, on the eve of the municipal council elections that gave the Bund its greatest electoral victory in independent Poland, a YAF leader in Warsaw, Dina Blond, urged working women to support the party's candidates because only a large party presence on the council could lead to improvements in day care centers, health and social insurance, geriatric care, and other matters of importance to them.[31]

The women who did become involved in some form of Bund activity concerned themselves with matters that *they* considered important, irrespective of the party's expectations. Moreover, they took an entirely different view of the reality in which they lived and the forces at work within the Jewish family and society. In a February 1935 edition of the Bund daily, *Naje Folkscajtung,* the author of an anonymous letter to the editor took vigorous exception to the assertion that Jewish working-class women had been released from the shackles of tradition and no longer heeded the rabbis and other religious leaders but had instead become active in trade unions and party branches. The writer argued that, in fact, most working-class Jewish women were typical Jewish housewives. The main reason they had not succeeded in stepping out of the traditional frameworks was that Jewish men, even those active in the Bund or the trade unions, had not done enough to enable women to attain the way of life advocated by the Bund ideologues and the YAF activists.[32]

What were the expectations of women who belonged to the women's auxiliary or the party itself? To what extent did the women, whom the Bund approached as potential party activists, believe that the movement met their needs? Did Jewish women who belonged in some way to the periphery of

Bund supporters, whether through their husbands' activities or through membership in a Bund-controlled trade union or through their children's participation in the Bund youth organizations, entertain expectations of becoming political or trade-union activists? Finally, how did women in the ranks regard the organization they had joined?

Rank-and-file women members evidently were skeptical about the possibility that membership in the Bund or the YAF might transform their lives. They perceived a large disparity between reality and the movement's promise of change and modernization. Not surprisingly, in many families of Bund supporters and activists, marital relations continued to follow the traditional patterns. The husband was the political activist, the worker who came home exhausted at the end of his day of toil and expected his wife to have prepared his supper on time. If a wife wished to take part in a women's-movement activity, her husband might pressure her to forgo the meeting so that she could greet him upon his return from work. Some women indeed avoided the activities organized for them by YAF in order to preserve domestic peace. Also, the burden of child rearing was mainly theirs, leaving most women little time to be active in party endeavors. Many women whose husbands belonged to trade unions continued to enroll their children in cheder and the traditional religious Jewish school system, attributing this to social pressure applied by relatives and neighbors.[33]

The Bund's efforts to organize Jewish women focused on their incorporation of women into the Jewish trade unions. The unions provided the party with its power base in Poland, and the Bund earned credit among members of the Jewish working class for its struggle throughout the interwar period for Jews' equal right to work, against discrimination in hiring, and for social benefits. In this respect, too, the party's goals and attitudes toward women's place in the trade unions were different from those of the women activists.

The issue of the unionization of Jewish women preoccupied the lower rank of YAF activists. They proposed establishing separate trade unions for women, but the Bund leadership rejected the idea. Women union members criticized the YAF and, indirectly, the Bund for not doing enough for women. They noted in particular that women members were not equal in status to their male counterparts in the existing entities, and many complaints of contemptuous and offensive treatment of women by men were recorded.[34]

YAF members also demanded a broader definition of trade unions in general. In the early 1930s, a fierce debate erupted on the issue of organizing Jewish domestics. Some YAF members called for the establishment of a separate union for these women, arguing that the working conditions of salaried domestics—long hours, paltry pay, and lack of formal social benefits—thrust them into a working milieu comparable to that of working women in England during the Industrial Revolution.[35] The significance of this debate transcended the ideological level; the debate also had obvious organizational implications.

The women's organization of the Bund had not succeeded in enrolling enough members to be regarded as important, a fact that bothered both ordinary activists and leaders of the YAF.[36] The organizers in the various towns stressed that in order to reach more women, the Bund had to adopt the measures that the YAF proposed—including the establishment of separate women's unions. But the Bund's political ideology as a socialist party frustrated the attempt to give women greater influence in its own institutions. Dina Blond, for example, attacked the idea of separate trade unions for women as contrary to the entire ideology and structure of the labor movement. A separate woman's organization, she said, would emphasize the isolation of women from the general proletariat rather than their equal status in it.[37]

True, the Bund had made some progress by establishing an entity for Jewish women that expanded their involvement in the Jewish labor movement and in political and trade-union affairs. However, the ideology continued to set an unbreachable limit in this respect. What mattered to the activists in the ranks was to organize as many women as possible under their banner, and they were prepared to go further than the Bund leaders in order to bring this about. They regarded the YAF as an organization devoted to the day-to-day needs of working women, not as one of many organizations in the party that aspired mainly to recruit supporters. For this reason, they insisted that the basic YAF framework be breached. They bombarded the editors of the party newspaper with complaints, accusing them of having published information on the problems of working women in Germany, France, or Spain without having devoted sufficient space to the problems of Jewish working women in Poland.[38]

Ultimately, the YAF continued to function as a bit player in the organizational system of the Bund in interwar Poland. At a general conference of the

Warsaw Bund in 1939, attended by 109 delegates in the Polish capital, the women's auxiliary was represented by only 2 members. In all, the Warsaw branch of the organization had only sixty-two women members that year (compared with a few thousand men). Furthermore, the YAF was undoubtedly one of the smallest party organizations in terms of membership. After more than a decade of arduous organizational work, the leaders of the party and of the YAF had not managed to create a large organization of Jewish working women.[39] Dina Blond admitted in 1935: "We have to tell the truth: we have not accomplished much. We have a small number of organizations, each with few women members in comparison with a vast numbers of women who can and should participate in it."[40]

About six months before the Nazi occupation of Poland, Haim Shlomo Kazdan, secretary-general of the Central Yiddish School Organization (CYSHO), the Yiddish school system in Poland, instigated a fierce internal debate concerning the status of women in the Bund. The party's influence in the Jewish community of Poland had just then reached its peak. Its successes in the municipal elections made it the strongest and most influential Jewish party. In view of such achievements, Kazdan asked, how could it be that no more than 10 percent of Bund members were women? All the social conditions seemed to lead toward greater participation of women. In certain occupational sectors, the number of women equaled or surpassed that of men. Furthermore, Jewish women outnumbered Jewish men in Poland, especially among the lower classes, because Jewish men emigrated in larger numbers. None of these circumstances translated into greater women's membership in the trade unions or party organizations. Kazdan blamed this on the modernization patterns of Jewish women in Poland. In his opinion, Jewish women were more susceptible to assimilation than Jewish men, more heavily involved in non-Jewish society, more likely to choose Polish as their vernacular, and, above all, more receptive to modern trends in social affairs and education. Even working-class Jewish women, Kazdan said, preferred to speak with their children in Polish and made efforts to integrate them into the general society and culture. Therefore, it was not surprising that the Bund and its political activities, which stressed the distinctiveness of Jewish culture, Yiddish education, and the political platform of the Jewish labor movement, reverberated so weakly in the hearts and minds of Jewish women.[41]

Kazdan's assertion was hotly countered by such party loyalists as Dina Blond. Rejecting his contention that assimilationist trends were the main reason for women's low rate of participation in the movement, Blond targeted the traditionalism of the Jewish family and the traditional roles it continued to impose on women. Child rearing, she argued, was the factor that dissuaded women from joining the Bund. Only the socialist program would ensure women's emancipation from these roles. Instead of blaming assimilation, she said, one should look to the opposite factor: the social conservativism of Jewish women.[42]

Other party members also tended to blame the traditional family milieu for the women's low participation rate in the Jewish labor movement. A member from Lodz noted that for many years Jewish women had been isolated from social involvement, distanced from positions of leadership, and unable to participate in political action. Most women had not yet shaken off this feeling of ghettoization, he continued; the only way to effect change would be to mobilize men to act vigorously in this matter as a major mission of family life. According to him, some men, despite their involvement in trade unions or local party activities, had never managed to integrate into routine family life the principles of gender equality and the need to involve women as full partners in labor-movement activity. This view was shared by many of the women members who expressed themselves on the issue.[43]

The changes that occurred in attitudes toward the status, roles, and organization of women in the Jewish Labor Bund from the late nineteenth century to the 1920s and 1930s in independent Poland chiefly reflect the fundamental transformation of life in Poland and in the Jewish working family. These changes affected the way Jewish women regarded their status in society and the way the Bund viewed the roles and problems of women and considered how to confront them.

One example of the change in women's perceptions of themselves is their conspicuously different attitude toward distinctively "feminine" matters, such as appearance and men's attitudes toward it. Zivia Horwicz, an important Bundist of the early twentieth century, would retort angrily to any allusion to her beauty by her male counterparts that such remarks were incompatible with the revolutionary and movement codes.[44] In the interwar period, in contrast,

YAF activists ascribed considerable importance to relations between the sexes and women's special needs. The YAF branches served as "advisory bureaus," so to speak, where women might obtain advice and guidance not only on the education and upbringing of children but also on such issues as feminine hygiene and fashion. A broad spectrum of women attended these sessions, some in their twenties and others in their forties and beyond.[45]

This type of activity totally transformed the role of the woman party activist. Not surprisingly, few of the women who had been important in organizing party activities in czarist Russia occupied important positions in the interwar Bund. One reason for this, of course, was their advancing age, but age did not prevent important male activists of the turn of the century from remaining politically active in interwar Poland. The place of the "revolutionary woman" was taken over by female activists of the women's auxiliary, such as Sara Schweber and Dina Blond, whose main efforts focused on organizational and informational work among women, or by such members as Bella Shapiro and Sonja Novogrodski, who concerned themselves mainly with education and cultural activity among women and youth. In the cities, branches, and YAF clubs, a cadre of local activists emerged that, even if identified with Bundist ideology, aspired chiefly to meet the needs of working women. Accordingly, these activists shaped the operational contours of the organization to which they belonged.

Not surprisingly, Bundist ideology found it hard to make the sudden transition from traditional to modern attitudes in matters of women's status and needs. This difficulty also beset the party in its ideological attitude toward other issues in the life of interwar Polish Jewry. The question of women's place in the Bund should be examined in view of this dialectic tension between political ideology and the changing realities of Jewish life—a tension that was not resolved until the onset of the German occupation in 1939. Nevertheless, there is no doubt that the Bund, unlike other Jewish political movements, made a real effort to integrate as many women as possible in party activity. Moreover, the issue of women's role in the party attracted more attention from the leadership in the Bund than, for example, in the Zionist parties, where the dominance of men among the leadership was absolute.[46]

Paula Hyman argues that Jewish society, despite the major changes that it underwent beginning in the last quarter of the nineteenth century, was still in the first stages of acculturation during the interwar period. Many political groups retained their traditional assumptions about Jewish society and the place of women in it.[47] The processes of change were only beginning in interwar Poland, and the change in ideology did not have enough time to produce far-reaching changes in the role of women in Jewish society or in Jewish political settings.

Notes

1. Ezra Mendelsohn, *Class Struggle in the Pale* (Cambridge: Cambridge University Press, 1970), p. 23; Henry J. Tobias, *The Jewish Bund in Russia from Its Origins to 1905* (Stanford: Stanford University Press, 1972), pp. 6–9; Jonathan Frankel, *Prophecy and Politics: Socialism, Nationalism and the Russian Jews, 1862–1917* (Cambridge: Cambridge University Press, 1981), p. 172.

2. Robert H. McNeal, "Women in the Russian Radical Movement," *Journal of Social History* 5, no. 2 (1971–1972), pp. 146–147.

3. Paula E. Hyman, *Gender and Assimilation in Modern Jewish History: The Roles and Representation of Women* (Seattle: University of Washington Press, 1995), pp. 76–77; Sydney S. Weinberg, *The World of Our Mothers* (Chapel Hill: University of North Carolina, 1988), pp. 46–55.

4. Miriam Raskin, *Tsen yor leben (di Rinfte Yorn)* (New York: Freiheit, 1927), pp. 19–23; Beynish Mikhalevich, *Zikhroynes fun a yidishn sotsialist,* vol. 1 (Warsaw: Lebens Fragen, 1929), p. 20.

5. Jacob Shalom Hertz (ed.), *Doyres bundistn,* vol. 2 (New York: Unser Tsait, 1956), pp. 131–133; Moshe Zalcman, *Bela Shapiro: Di popolere froyn geshtalt* (Paris, 1983), pp. 12–15.

6. Anna Rozental, "Froyn-geshtaltn in bund," *Naje Folkscajtung,* November 19, 1937.

7. Valadimir Medem, *Memoirs* (Tel Aviv: I. L. Perez, 1984), p. 142 (Hebrew).

8. McNeal, "Women in the Russian Radical Movement," p. 153.

9. Jacob Shalom Hertz, *Daynes Bundistn,* vols. 1–3 (New York: Unser Tsait, 1956–1968).

10. McNeal, "Women in the Russian Radical Movement," p. 144. The Jewish women members of the general revolutionary movement certainly warrant inclusion in this group of Jewish revolutionaries. According to McNeal (p. 159), roughly one-fourth of all women in the Russian radical movements in the second half of the nineteenth century were of Jewish origin.

11. Daniel Blatman, "The Bund in Poland, 1935–1939," *Polin: Studies in Polish Jewry* 9 (1996), pp. 59–60; Bernard K. Johnpoll, *The Politics of Futility: The General Jewish Workers Bund of Poland, 1917–1943* (Ithaca: Cornell University Press, 1967), pp. 82–142; Zvi Barzilai, *The Bund in Poland between the Two World Wars* (Jerusalem: Carmel, 1994), pp. 32–34 (Hebrew).

12. Celia S. Heller, *On the Edge of Destruction: Jews of Poland between the Two World Wars* (New York: Columbia University Press, 1977), pp. 241–244; Hyman, *Gender and Assimilation in Modern Jewish History*, pp. 83–92.

13. David Ajnhoren, "Gedankn iber der moderner froy," *Naje Folkscajtung*, February 18, 1930, and March 7, 1930.

14. "Arbeter froyn," *Lebensfragen* 5, March 3, 1916.

15. "Di froy un di gezelshaft," *Lebensfragen* 10 (no. 58), March 9, 1917.

16. Bina Garencarska-Kadari, "The Jewish Working Strata in Poland between the Two World Wars (Statistical Analysis)," *Gal-Ed: On the History of the Jews in Poland*, vol. 3 (1976), pp. 150–153 (Hebrew).

17. Bina Garencarska-Kadari, "Wages and Working Conditions of Jewish Workers in Poland, 1918–1929," *Gal-Ed: On the History of the Jews in Poland*, vols. 7–8 (1985), p. 127 (Hebrew).

18. Bina Garencarska-Kadary [*sic*], "Some Aspects of the Life of the Jewish Proletariat in Poland during the Interwar Period," *Polin: Studies in Polish Jewry* 8 (1994), pp. 244–245.

19. Relations between the Bund and the PPS are discussed in Abraham Brumberg, "The Bund and the Polish Socialist Party in the Late 1930s," in Chone Shmeruk, Yisrael Gutman, Ezra Mendelsohn, and Jehuda Reinhartz (eds.), *The Jews of Poland between Two World Wars* (Hanover, N.H.: University Press of New England for Brandeis University Press, 1989), p. 75–94; and Blatman, "The Bund in Poland," pp. 65–66. See also Puah Rakowski, *Zikhroynes fun a yiddisher revolutsionerin* (Buenos Aires: Tsentral-Forband fun Poylisher yidn in Argentina, 1954), p. 192; *Naje Folkscajtung*, June 6, 1934.

20. Beinush Michalowicz, "Arbeter froyn ziet bagrist," *Naje Folkscajtung*, March 19, 1926; "Di arbeter-froy vil oyfhern zu zien a mashin oyf zu kindln," *Naje Folkscajtung*, August 31, 1928; Henryk Erlich, "Unter der pan fun sotsialism," *Naje Folkscajtung*, April 4, 1930; "Der froyn-tog," *Naje Folkscajtung*, March 27, 1931.

21. The development of the Bund's youth organizations from the late nineteenth century to the years preceding World War II is discussed in Avraham Litvak, *The Way It Was* (Ein Harod: Ha kibbutz Hameuhad, 1945), pp. 172–182 (Hebrew); Jacob Shalom Hertz, *Di Geshikhte fun a yogent* (New York: Unser Tsait, 1946); Daniel Blatman, "Avraham (Abrasha) Blum and the Bundist Youngsters during the Holocaust," in Avihu Ronen and Yehoyakim Cochavi (eds.), *Third Person, Singular*, vol. 1 (Tel Aviv: Moreshet, 1994), pp. 305–313 (Hebrew).

22. Mordechai W. Berensztein, "Der 'bund' in poylen," in Shimon Federbush (ed.), *Yearbook*, vol. 1 (New York: American World Federation of Polish Jews, 1964), p. 206.

23. *Naje Folkscajtung*, June 22, 1935; Bernard Goldstein, *20 yor in varshaver "bund," 1919–1939* (New York: Unser Tsait, 1960), pp. 187–188.

24. "Di farhorevete muter un ire shlotslohze kinder," *Naje Folkscajtung*, February 14, 1928.

25. *Naje Folkscajtung*, July 13, 1926; July 30, 1928; March 29, 1929; July 3, 1929; May 25, 1930; August 3, 1931; April 1, 1932; and April 5, 1935.

26. "Faters, muters un kinder" (kleyne folkscajtung no. 12), *Naje Folkscajtung*, March 23, 1928; *Naje Folkscajtung*, December 25, 1928; Dina, "Ven di babe redt fun undz

aroys . . . ," *Naje Folkscajtung,* May 17, 1936; Dina, "A vort zu undzere lezerins," *Naje Folkscajtung,* October 17, 1937; Dina, "Urlob far der arbeter-froy," *Naje Folkscajtung,* June 9, 1939.

27. *Naje Folkscajtung,* September 12, 1936; February 13, 1938; and September 9, 1938.
28. "Yidishe arbetern, froy un muter!" *Naje Folkscajtung,* January 31, 1928.
29. Goldstein, *20 yor in varshaver "bund,"* pp. 244–248, 252–255; Joseph S. Hertz, "Der bund in umophengikn poylen, 1926–1932," *Di geshekhte fun bund* 5 (New York: Unser Tsait, 1981), pp. 35–37.
30. *Naje Folkscajtung,* April 4, 1930.
31. Dina, "Di arbeter-froyun di valen zum shtatrat," *Naje Folkscajtung,* November 13, 1938.
32. "Lomir zie ale helfn," *Naje Folkscajtung,* February 23, 1935.
33. *Naje Folkscajtung,* March 23, 1935; January 5, 1936.
34. "An alte ongeveitikte frage," *Naje Folkscajtung,* February 9, 1936; *Naje Folkscajtung,* January 9, 1938.
35. *Naje Folkscajtung,* December 12, 1937.
36. *Naje Folkscajtung,* March 30, 1935.
37. Dina, "Azoy vie di zakh iz," *Naje Folkscajtung,* January 16, 1938.
38. *Naje Folkscajtung,* December 25, 1928; March 11, 1935; and October 7, 1938.
39. "In yor fun groysen val-zig," *Algemayner yidisher arbeter-bund in poylen—varshaver komitet* (Warsaw, 1939), Bund Archives New York, MG-2/293. It is worth bearing in mind that the number of women who took part in or sent their children to YAF-sponsored social and cultural activities was much larger than the number of active women members of the YAF. Many working women saw the YAF chiefly as a place that could solve problems in their daily lives, not as an organization that entailed political activity.
40. Dina, "Tzwishen velche frojen," *Naje Folkscajtung,* May 10, 1935.
41. Haim S. Kazdan, "Froy un man in undzer bavegung," *Naje Folkscajtung,* February 10, 1939.
42. Dina, "Vo zenen di frajen?" *Naje Folkscajtung,* February 17, 1939.
43. *Naje Folkscajtung,* March 3, 1939; March 10, 1939; April 4, 1939.
44. Leon Berensztien, *Ershte shprotsungn, zikhroynes* (Buenos Aires: Farlang Yidbuch, 1956), pp. 148–149.
45. *Naje Folkscajtung,* September 12, 1932.
46. Ezra Mendelsohn, *Zionism in Poland: The Formative Years, 1915–1926* (New Haven: Yale University Press, 1981), pp. 339–340.
47. Hyman, *Gender and Assimilation in Modern Jewish History,* pp. 91–92.

CHAPTER FIVE

Ordinary Women in Nazi Germany
Perpetrators, Victims, Followers, and Bystanders

Gisela Bock

Among ordinary women in National Socialist Germany, where 35 million women lived by 1939, we find perpetrators, victims, followers, bystanders of racism and the Holocaust, and deplorably few resisters and rescuers.[1] The eight episodes that follow portray more or less ordinary German Gentile women engaged in different ways with other German Gentile women, German Jewish women and men, and German Gentile men. The sequence of these stories, which are characteristic of that time, follows the stages of the Nazi regime.

1. In the 1920s Margarete Adam, a deeply religious Catholic born in 1885, published several articles in the major feminist journal *Die Frau* and earned a Ph.D. in Hamburg under the supervision of Ernst A. Cassirer. (Cassirer was dismissed from his chair in 1933 because he was Jewish; he then left Germany.) In 1930, the *Centralverein deutscher Staatsbürger jüdischen Glaubens* published an essay on antisemitism by Adam with a response by Eva Reichmann, then editor of the Jewish journal *Der Morgen*. Adam, condemning the Nazis for their anti-Jewish racism, concluded: "Today no government, even the most antisemitic one, will find . . . the people's support for . . . the disfranchisement of the Jews as citizens of a polity. . . . Today, we philosemites know, . . . antisemitism is bound to decline and philosemitism will rise." Reichmann joined Adam in pleading not for "weary resignation, but hopeful optimism."[2]

The essays were followed by two epilogues with a striking turn of argument. Adam, who had written her essay in 1929, now pointed to the parliamentary elections of September 1930, when 6 million Germans (18.3 percent of the electorate) had voted for the "Hitler movement," making it the second largest parliamentary group after the Social Democrats. About 15 percent of the votes cast by women were for the Nazis; women comprised about 48 percent of the Nazi voters.[3] Adam confessed that she had become one of them, after months of inner struggle, not because of Nazi antisemitism but in spite of it. Her reasoning was that the Nazis seemed to be the only party in favor of the revision of the Versailles Treaty, against the widespread corruption, and against Bolshevism. Reichmann, in her epilogue, insisted that Adam was wrong in her political judgment. In 1933 Adam came to understand: she was fired from her teaching post and joined resistance efforts to persuade army officers and other public figures to revolt against the Nazi government. In 1937, at the time when most non-Jewish women and men had come to support or comply with Nazism, she was accused and convicted of high treason and sentenced to eight years of penal servitude. In 1946, she died of diseases contracted in prison.[4]

Adam was not quite an "ordinary" woman; she was an academic who engaged in a public exchange of views with a Jewish woman and who actively combated Nazism. But she was ordinary in that she was one of the growing number of women who, from 1930 on, voted for the Nazis, and her motives apparently resembled those of most Nazi voters: they voted for the party not because they agreed with everything the Nazis said but as a protest against the government in power.[5] Adam was ordinary in yet another sense: her vote was not based on women-specific motives. In fact, the female vote for the Nazis seems to have increased not because of Nazi pronouncements on women but for the same reasons that the male vote for the Nazis increased.

2. In April 1934, Emma Fischer, a twenty-nine-year-old unmarried and childless woman, learned that she was to be sterilized against her will. In 1931 Fischer had briefly stayed at a psychiatric clinic and had been diagnosed as schizophrenic. Faced with the involuntary procedure, she wrote a long letter of protest: "I am working regularly in the cigar factory since I left the clinic. I am able to earn the highest wage and my employer is satisfied with my work. . . . I have recovered and am now as normal as anyone else. . . . All human beings differ from one another. . . . I do not understand that I should be steril-

ized, I have not done any moral or sexual wrong. A nervous mental disease can happen to every human being and is just like any other illness . . . I do not have sexual intercourse with men and I do not intend to marry." Nevertheless, one of the newly created sterilization courts ordered that she be sterilized, and the operation was performed in 1935.[6]

National Socialism did not simply pursue a pronatalist policy to raise the number of births. It also had antinatalist goals, which were part of its complex and consistent racial policy directed against people who were considered "inferior" for ethnic or eugenic reasons. A law of July 1933 imposed sterilization on persons whose "inferior value" was seen to result from their actual or alleged hereditary disease, mostly mental or emotional. The law, aimed at "racial regeneration" by preventing such women and men from having children, was based on "the primacy of the state in the field of life, marriage and the family" and on the notion that the boundary between the political and the nonpolitical was itself a political issue.[7] About 1 million people were reported to the bureaucracy as "inferior"; four hundred thousand were actually sterilized. Several thousand died in the course of sterilization, most of them women. Reflecting their proportion in the German population, a minority of the victims were Jews, and half were women.[8]

3. Most of those who enforced the sterilization law were men. But many women reported presumable sterilization candidates to the "state doctors" who had the task of searching for the hereditarily diseased. From 1939, race hygiene was radicalized to include the killing of inmates of psychiatric asylums (perhaps two hundred thousand were put to death by 1945). Women were among the perpetrators as well as the victims of this "euthanasia." Nurses in the six killing centers assisted the "professional killers" and sometimes killed on their own.[9] They were not forced to perform this task and were not punished if they rejected it, as is evident from many cases when nurses resisted and sometimes were able to help their patients.[10] All Jewish inmates of such asylums were killed; this was the first instance of a systematic massacre of German Jewish women and men.

4. Some of the women who actively participated in both eugenic and ethnic racism were leaders of the Nazi women's elite groups and authors of the women's press. They urged women to accept the sterilization policy, identify possible candidates for sterilization, and reject marriage with Jews, Gypsies,

and other "racially inferior" persons. In doing so, they had to turn against traditional views of motherhood and of women as mothers. Female "maternalism" (*Mütterlichkeit*) became the object of racist polemic and was condemned as "sentimental humanitarianism," as were Christian charity and Marxism. "Women's maternalism" and "the female instinct to care for all those in need of help" were "acts against the race." Of "women's particular inclination toward all living beings," it was said that there was "scarcely any worse sin against nature."[11]

5. In 1933, the League of German Woman Doctors was among the first women's organizations to exclude Jewish members. In her memoirs, Hertha Nathorff, a Jewish doctor, described the Jews' expulsion. In April 1933, she attended a regular meeting of the league. A male Nazi participated and requested *Gleichschaltung* ("bringing-in-line"). A woman invited the "German colleagues" into another room. A Catholic woman protested: "What do you mean by German colleagues?" The answer: "Of course all those who are not Jewish."[12]

It was not only Jewish doctors who were ejected but also those non-Jewish doctors—very few—who refused to approve, in writing, of the expulsion of the Jews. Gentile women doctors adhered to race policies and belonged to Nazi organizations to a much higher degree than women at large, as did Gentile male doctors compared with men at large. Some of the women doctors also participated in the "medical" atrocities of the concentration camps.[13]

6. Christabel Bielenberg, who was born in Britain but became German by marriage, was involved in resistance activities. Through her efforts she met one kind of ordinary women who participated in Nazi persecution. Bielenberg was waiting in an office where four men, in heavy handcuffs, were dictating their accounts to four women typists. Suddenly one typist yelled at a prisoner because he insisted on reading what she had typed before he signed it. She slapped his face, and a moment later "she was powdering her nose and patting her hair, eyeing herself with some satisfaction in a small pocket mirror." Bielenberg's memoir continues: "I was shaking . . . this was cold, deadly hatred such as I never hope to have for any human being in my life again. I hated her, every living bit of her, and the fact that she was a woman made this hatred if possible more intense, for I think it was mixed with impotent rage and deepest humiliation that I belonged to her sex."[14]

The involvement of typists, stenographers, and telephone operators in Nazi activities was common. The telephone operators passed on innumerable messages and orders for the implementation of race policies, and the typists produced endless lists of expropriated Jewish property, documents in the sterilization courts, the minutes of the Wannsee conference, and countless other papers that are now evidence of persecution, racism, and the Holocaust.[15]

7. Miss K., a camp guard at the women's camp Ravensbrück, was a former unskilled pieceworker.[16] Like her, most of the camp guards came from a lower-class background and had been factory, office, or domestic workers. Upward mobility was the motive of many female guards in taking on the job. They either volunteered or were drafted in the female labor conscription of 1943. Usually only unmarried and childless women were hired, and if they became pregnant they were laid off. About 10 percent of the camp guards were women; women made up a smaller proportion of the staff of the *Einsatzgruppen* (extermination squads), and no women were among the personnel of the death camps Belzec, Chelmno, Sobibor, and Treblinka.[17] Among women at large, the camp guards and camp doctors were those who most closely correspond to the "ordinary men" Christopher Browning has portrayed. A survivor of Ravensbrück noted that these guards were "normal young girls," although she added, significantly, "in civil life"—not in the camp.[18]

In her youth, Miss K. had been a member of the Nazi girls' association (BDM), where she was socialized into the new values. These girls did not go through the traditional education for motherhood and family values. The BDM was not part of the Nazi women's organizations but of the Hitler Youth, and most girls' activities resembled those of the boys. Sports, not gymnastics, was the major pursuit and occasionally included shooting. When shooting was criticized as "unwomanly," the male leader of the Hitler Youth insisted that "we should not be confused by old men and old women who say that mothers should be the only educators of young girls." In fact, "all the energy of the girls was invested in assimilation to an external world which was imagined as male."[19] Many experienced the BDM as a liberating break with the family and traditional female norms. On the one hand, only a small minority of the BDM girls ended up as camp guards, like Miss K.; on the other hand, many more women than those in the BDM were taught similar womenly values. University students, for instance, were warned to avoid the Victorian "soft, over-feminine ideal of woman which is held by Western and oriental peoples, but does not correspond to the harsher German living conditions."[20]

Many female victims felt ashamed of belonging to a sex that included torturers. Lucia Schmidt-Fels, a German-French prisoner at Ravensbrück, described the women camp guards: "To the shame of our sex I must admit that women may be more malicious and mean, more hateful and petty than men as soon as they hold a position of power."[21] Other survivors, for instance Margarete Buber-Neumann and Ruth Klüger, underline stark differences among the female guards and argue that in general they were less brutal than male guards.[22] Still others noted the similarity of women's and men's acts. Claude Vaillant-Couturier, a former prisoner in Ravensbrück and Auschwitz, testified at the Nuremberg trial: "We may say that the men behaved in the same way as the women and that the women were just as wild as the men. There was no difference."[23]

8. Herr Paasch, a German merchant, was married to a Jewish woman. Their marriage protected her from persecution, but their relationship deteriorated in the 1930s and grew worse when his sister, Frau Kempfer, moved in with them in 1943. Quarrels took place between the two women and between husband and wife. In 1944, Paasch and his sister turned to the Secret Police's Department for the Jewish Question and submitted a denunciation against "the Jewess" Frau Paasch. Frau Kempfer accused her sister-in-law of having said that the Jews would be avenged, the German soldiers were murderers, the children killed in air raids were really killed by Hitler, and the war would result in Germany's defeat. In addition, Herr Paasch handed in his request for divorce; it was accepted. In July 1944, Frau Paasch was taken to Auschwitz and killed in the gas chamber.[24]

The Nazi dictatorship was based not just on terror and compulsion but also on consent and compliance. The denunciations were usually made in the name of the *Volksgemeinschaft* (people's community) but were often used to settle private conflicts and vendettas. Many denunciations were made by women, but they were clearly a minority. In the samples that have been studied to date, the proportion of women among the denouncers varies between 12 and 29 percent. The proportion of women among all victims varies from 9 to 20 percent.[25] What is important, beyond the numerical sex ratios, is that Gentile women, just like Gentile men, were likely to provide the Nazi bureaucracy with the information needed to render dictatorship and persecution effective.

The Larger Historical Perspective

It seems possible to draw some conclusions from the foregoing episodes. Most German Gentile women complied with Nazi rule, for all or most of its duration, as bystanders or, less passively, as followers. A minority were victims and a smaller minority were resisters or rescuers.[26] A larger and more powerful minority, including women of all walks of life and all social classes, actively participated in racist and genocidal policies; their beliefs, motives, and acts were similar to those of comparable ordinary men. The numerical ratio between those groups was different for women and for men. But belonging to one or the other sex did not determine the degree of involvement in racism and the Holocaust.

The fact that so many women, traditionally bound to the private sphere of home and family, came to be crucial for Nazi policies needs to be explained in a larger historical context. National Socialism tried, with some success, to do away with the traditional separation between the private and the public sphere, between the personal and the political. In principle, and often enough in practice, the personal and private was to exist and function exclusively for the benefit of the public and political, for the Volksgemeinschaft and the race, in the specific context of a dictatorship. The policy of antinatalism is one example. Another is the use of political denunciation by ordinary people in order to solve private and other conflicts and, conversely, the regime's use of such conflicts for its political ends. Yet another instance of the collapse of traditional boundaries is the Nazis' frenetic drive to organize the Germans. In a popular joke of the time a girl says, "My father is an SA member, my older brother is in the SS, my little brother is in the Hitler Youth, my mother is in the Nazi women's league, and I am a member of the BDM." "But when do you see each other?" "Oh, we meet every year at the Party Congress in Nuremberg." Family privacy could also be disrupted by *Blockwarte* (Nazi house guards), male and female, or by women leaders who intruded into the home to check, for example, that a Polish worker on a German farm was not allowed at the family dinner table. The collapse of private space was most dramatic when Gentiles hid Jews at home or elsewhere. Here the defense of private space could become a form of resistance.

To grasp the significance of this collapse of the traditional separate spheres, we need to revise the traditional view of Nazism as a regime that attributed to, imposed on, or left to women only the sphere of family and dutiful mother-hood. Not one of the reported cases of women adhering to Nazism or bearing responsibility for its crimes is the outcome of acts that women performed out of motherly concerns and as mothers. True, many of these women were mar-ried and had children, but this fact did not cause, and hardly shaped, their par-ticipation in Nazi rule.

Most types of women's participation were, in fact, a function of their extra domestic activity—their leadership in a Nazi organization, their employment in professional or white-collar jobs—and their desire to leave a low-paid job. Those women workers who remained on the job contributed in yet another way to the functioning of war and genocide. Employment and ambi-tion were just as decisive for the involvement of ordinary women in Nazi crimes as they were for most men, from the railway personnel who shipped the Jews to the death camps to the police who were sent east to kill Jews. And women, like men, were not forced to participate in immoral activities, even if they held jobs in which they were likely to become involved in genocidal policies.

Two gender-related differences may nonetheless be highlighted. What counts as ordinary in the case of men was often novel in the case of women. For instance, women had not traditionally striven for upward mobility except by marriage, and they would not traditionally turn to the police or to a political party to solve their problems. That many female perpetrators behaved brutally, however, should not be understood as necessarily indicating a break with tra-dition; idealized visions of the female sex were not descriptions of social real-ity. The novelty was rather that the regime purposefully used not only male but also female brutality for its ends. Second, fewer women than men were in-volved in direct and violent participation in the Holocaust. Yet I would suggest that, from the perspective of historical change and novelty, the lower numeri-cal share of female perpetrators is outweighed by their qualitative similarity to male perpetrators in their basic motives, attitudes, and acts.

Women's Contributions to the Nazi Regime

My attempt to place women's contribution to Nazi evil in a historical per-spective becomes clearer when it is set against three contrasting hypotheses that have been advanced.

Mothers and wives as victims. This is the view that ordinary German women, lacking power because of male domination, were not responsible for the dictatorship and crimes. For example, a number of American women who, after 1945, helped the Germans establish democracy, argued that women had been relegated to "Kinder, Küche, Kirche" and were therefore "not a part of policy-making in Nazi Germany."[27] In post-1945 Germany the same opinion prevailed. Later, American feminist writer Kate Millett saw Nazism as "probably the most deliberate attempt ever made to revive and solidify patriarchal conditions. . . . The part women were assigned to play in Hitler's Germany was to be one strictly confined to utter dedication to motherhood and family."[28] This view was seized upon by many German and non-German feminists who argued that "German women were the subjects of Nazi policy, not its agents."[29]

Mothers and wives as perpetrators. This hypothesis builds on a similar vision—that German women were reduced to the private sphere—but argues that this status made them accomplices and perpetrators of Nazi rule and the Holocaust. "In the Nazi world, man and woman operated in radically separate spheres," and women supported men's racist activities by focusing on motherhood and family.[30] Nazi rule in this view is a regime wherein German Gentile women, as holders of "the power of the mothers" and of the alleged "matriarchal" values of National Socialism, not only permitted but instigated German Gentile men to antisemitism and massacre.[31]

"Emancipated" women as perpetrators. A substantial number of Nazi women asserted women's equality with men while complying with racism and denouncing patriarchy as a Jewish invention. Scholars have identified them as "feminists."[32] The killing nurses have been identified as emancipated because they broke through female boundaries and did what men did.[33] Similarly, there is the argument that the female camp guards were not crueler than the men but only seemed to be because they too broke through gender boundaries and deviated from feminine behavior. "Emancipated" women are seen here as the most heavily involved in the Nazi evil of torture and killing.

What shall we make of these contrasts? German Gentile women, whether mothers and wives or not, were clearly not just victims. They were—just as German Gentile men were—also perpetrators, followers, bystanders, and a few resisters and rescuers. As to victimization, we should be careful to ask: victims of which part of Nazi rule? Of course Nazi rule meant, in a general sense, male domination and female subordination, no less under the Nazis than in German society before 1933 and after 1945 and in Western societies elsewhere. But the core of Nazi rule and its novelty (compared with other countries and other historical periods) was not patriarchy but racism. The female victims of Nazism were women who were considered "racially inferior" and those German Gentiles who resisted Nazism or sided with its victims.

Racial hierarchy prevailed over gender hierarchy, particularly in the case of female domination over "racially inferior" women and men. Female perpetrators acted in much the same way as male perpetrators and sometimes held key positions in racist and genocidal policy-making bodies. Usually these were ordinary women, just as ordinary as the women who did *not* participate, and just as ordinary as most male perpetrators. Female perpetrators were perpetrators not so much because they were female but because they believed themselves to be ordinary Germans, like the men. Hence, Christabel Bielenberg's feelings of shame about belonging to the female sex should be complemented by the statement of another ordinary woman: asked why she helped rescue Jews, she responded, "I was ashamed to be a German."[34]

It seems misdirected to identify ordinary women's contribution to Nazi evil as present in their activities as mothers and wives. True, wives (18 million in 1939) and mothers (9 million) helped stabilize the country and its rulers by their very existence; yet this is equally true for nonmothers (17 million) and nonwives (8 million). In 1939, 37 percent of the employed were women, and 53 percent of women were employed in factories, agriculture, and other jobs; in 1944, the respective figures were 53 percent and 57 percent.[35] In this wider sense, all Germans were responsible for the Holocaust, but not in their specific identities as women or men, and not because of their marital state, motherhood, or fatherhood. However, in order to explore the precise extent of women's participation in Nazi crimes, we should ask not who they were but what they did.

The assumption that German women's contribution to Nazi evil is located in their existence as mothers and wives seems misleading for another reason: it is grounded in the notion that Nazi rule essentially meant a radical cult of motherhood and separation of gender spheres. But as is shown in the cases I have discussed, the Nazi regime attributed greater importance to pursuing racist policies than to keeping women in their traditional sphere.

Women were not fired en masse from employment and driven back to home and hearth. Actually the number and proportion of women in the labor force increased, and so did the proportion of married women and mothers. Throughout the Nazi period the employment rate among women was higher in Germany than in most other Western countries.[36] The temporary decline of female university students, which almost paralleled that of male students, was due not to Nazi intervention but to economic depression. The one group of female academics that was excluded by Nazi intervention were the Jewish women, along with Jewish men. Altogether, the number and proportion of female university students and women in the professions (with the important exception of jurisprudence) did not decline but increased.[37]

Nazi propaganda and ideology did not include "Kinder, Küche, Kirche" or the biblical exhortation "Be fruitful and multiply." Actually, Nazi race hygienists often and deliberately polemicized against these slogans.[38] The number of convictions for abortion declined during most of the Nazi period in comparison with the years of the Weimar Republic (1923–1932: 47,500; 1933–1942: 40,000).[39] Under the Nazi regime, abortion was no longer simply prohibited but was practiced widely on "racially inferior"—Jewish, Polish, Russian, and hereditarily diseased—women. Abortion was now transformed from a gender issue into a race issue.

Racism and sexism were not of the same scale and importance for the Nazi rulers. In many areas the Nazis made concessions to Gentile women, sometimes revising their early pronouncements, but they were adamant in their views about race and especially about Jewish women and men.

The Relevance of Gender in Racism and Genocide

With regard to the female perpetrators, we need to explore not just their differences from males (and similarities with other women) but also their similarities with male perpetrators (and possible differences from other women). I have argued elsewhere that we do indeed need to explore differences between men and women victims; yet we also need to conceptualize the equal and nondistinctive treatment of male and female victims in the process of destruction, irrespective of sex and age.[40]

The indiscriminate killing of Jewish men and women and the priority of race relations over gender relations in Nazi eyes may, at first glance, appear to deny the relevance of gender in the study of the Holocaust. Rather, a gender-based perspective is legitimate and useful for several reasons. First, gender difference and gender hierarchy continued to play a prime role in German society at large. My argument is that gender difference played a smaller role in those activities of women that specifically contributed to Nazi race policy than in other women's activities. This argument can be explored only in terms of gender, not with a gender-neutral approach.[41] The fact that for the Nazis race as a *political* category was more crucial than sex should not blind us to the importance of gender as a *historical* category.

Second, gender should be conceptualized not just as differences but also as similarities between the sexes, as different degrees of difference, and even as the possibility of a historical erasure of gender difference and gender identity. We need to deal with the *relationship* between gender difference and gender similarity and with the relationships (including differences and similarities) *between* as well as *within* the sexes. This seems particularly relevant with respect to the Holocaust. Yet when male and female perpetrators perform similar acts and when male and female victims are killed alike, this does not mean that gender is unimportant. On a macro-historical level, the notion that in Nazism and the Holocaust, gender as a human relationship has receded and given precedence to race is the more striking against the background of centuries when the positions of men and women in society had been so different. On a micro-historical level, when Nazism elevated race to a crucial political concept, gender was not erased but relegated to a kind of underground. This is where historians need to discover the dynamics of gender—in terms of gender history as well as Holocaust history—and to distinguish between major and minor gender differences, obvious and subtle ones, and their changes over time (such as, in the case of the Einsatzgruppen, the transition from killing male Jews to killing women and children as well).[42] Not only did racism shape the historical expressions of gender, but gender also shaped the historical expressions of racism.

Gender refers not only to the relationship between sexual difference and similarity but also to sexual hierarchy and power—among other issues. In the Holocaust the crucial power relations were those between German Gentiles and Jews; searching for power relations between men and women among the perpetrators without considering their relationship to the victims (for example, in the argument that the female camp guards were not admitted to the higher ranks of the SS because they were disempowered as women) may easily border on cynicism. Among the victims, gender hierarchy was clearly subordinated to, even abolished by, more central power relations. This is where we may find the limits of a gender-based analysis of the Holocaust: male-female power relations cannot be conceptualized as a primary, independent historical agency; yet this limit, too, may be grasped only by studying the Holocaust through the perspective of gender.

Notes

1. These concepts are taken from Christopher Browning, *Ordinary Men: Reserve Battalion 101 and the Final Solution in Poland* (New York: HarperCollins, 1992), and Raul Hilberg, *Perpetrators, Victims, Bystanders: The Jewish Catastrophe, 1933–1945* (New York: HarperCollins, 1992). Another important account, which addresses both perpetrators and victims within an integrated framework, is Saul Friedländer, *Nazi Germany and the Jews*, vol. 1 (New York: HarperCollins, 1997).

2. Centralverein deutscher Staatsbürger jüdischen Glaubens e.V. (ed.), *Eine Aussprache über die Judenfrage zwischen Dr. Margarete Adam (mit einem Nachwort: Warum habe ich nationalsozialistisch gewählt?) und Dr. Eva Reichmann-Jungmann*, Berlin n.d. (Centralverein deutscher Staatsbürger jüdischen Glaubens, e. V.: December 1930).

3. Helen L. Boak, "'Our Last Hope': Women's Votes for Hitler," *German Studies Review* 12 (1989), pp. 289–310; Jürgen Falter, Thomas Lindenberger, and Siegfried Schumann, *Wahlen und Abstimmungen in der Weimarer Republik* (Munich: Beck, 1986), pp. 81–85.

4. Ursel Hochmuth and Gertrud Meyer, *Streiflichter aus dem Hamburger Widerstand, 1933–1945* (Frankfurt: Röderberg, 1969), pp. 266, 271–273; Eckart Krause, Ludwig Huber, and Holger Fischer (eds.), *Hochschulalltag im "Dritten Reich,"* vol. 3 (Berlin: Dietrich Reimer, 1991), pp. 1503f.; Hanna Elling, *Frauen im deutschen Widerstand, 1933–45* (Frankfurt: Röderberg, 1983), p. 173; Sybil Oldfield, "German Women in the Resistance to Hitler," in *Women, State and Revolution*, ed. Sian Reynolds (Amherst: University of Massachusetts Press, 1987), p. 88.

5. Jürgen Falter, *Hitlers Wähler* (Munich: Beck, 1991).

6. Undated letter in the court files: Staatsarchiv Freiburg, Gesundheitsamt Offenburg no. 12.

7. Arthur Gütt, Ernst Rüdin, and Falk Ruttke, *Das Gesetz zur Verhütung erbkranken Nachwuchses vom 14 Juli 1933* (Munich: Lehmann, 1934), pp. 5, 176.

8. Gisela Bock, *Zwangssterilisation im Nationalsozialismus* (Opladen: Westdeutscher, 1986), pp. 230–240, 351–360, 374–383. Of the 400,000 sterilized persons, 40,000 were in the territories that had been annexed as of 1938.

9. Gudrun Schwarz, "Verdrängte Täterinnen: Frauen im Apparat der SS (1939–1945)," in *Nach Osten: Verdeckte Spuren nationalsozialistischer Verbrechen,* ed. Theresa Wobbe (Frankfurt: Neue Kritik, 1992), pp. 197–227, esp. p. 214.

10. Bernhard Richarz, *Heilen, Pflegen, Töten: Zur Alltagsgeschichte einer Heil- und Pflegeanstalt bis zum Ende des Nationalsozialismus* (Göttingen: Vandenhoeck and Ruprecht, 1987), pp. 175f.; Henry Friedlander, *The Origins of Nazi Genocide: From Euthanasia to the Final Solution* (Chapel Hill: University of North Carolina Press, 1995), pp. 264–283.

11. Elisabeth von Barsewisch, *Die Aufgaben der Frau für die Aufartung* (Berlin: 7, 1933), pp. 13f.; Johanna Haarer, "Die rassenpolitischen Aufgaben des Deutschen Frauenwerks," *Neues Volk* 6, no. 4 (1938), pp. 17–19; Agnes Bluhm, "Das Gesetz zur Verhütung erbkranken Nachwuchses," *Die Frau* 41 (1934), pp. 529–538; Anna Ebert, "Das Sterilisationsgesetz und seine Auswirkung auf die Frau," *Völkischer Beobachter,* January 31, 1934.

12. Wolfgang Benz, ed., *Das Tagebuch der Hertha Nathorff* (Frankfurt: S. Fischer, 1988), p. 40.

13. Claudia Huerkamp, *Bildungsbürgerinnen: Frauen an den Universitäten und in akademischen Berufen* (Göttingen: Vandenhoeck and Ruprecht, 1996), ch. 8; Johanna Bleker, "Anerkennung durch Unterordnung?" in *Weibliche Ärzte,* ed. Eva Brinkschulte (Berlin: Edition Hentrich, 1994), pp. 126–136, esp. p. 132; Schwarz, "Verdrängte Täterinnen," pp. 211–215.

14. Christabel Bielenberg, *The Past Is Myself* (London, 1968), pp. 228–230. Cf. Elaine Martin, "Autobiography, Gender, and the Third Reich: Eva Zeller, Carola Stern, and Christabel Bielenberg," in *Gender, Patriarchy, and Fascism in the Third Reich,* ed. Elaine Martin (Detroit: Wayne State University Press, 1993), pp. 169–200.

15. Ursula Nienhaus, *Vater Staat und seine Gehilfinnen* (Frankfurt: Campus, 1995), ch. 5; Schwarz, "Verdrängte Täterinnen," pp. 203–210.

16. Dagmar Reese, "Homo homini lupus—Frauen als Täterinnen?" *Internationale Wissenschaftliche Korrespondenz zur Geschichte der deutschen Arbeiterbewegung* 27, no. 1 (1991), pp. 25–34.

17. Schwarz, "Verdrängte Täterinnen," pp. 206, 216, 221; Roger W. Smith, "Women and Genocide," *Holocaust and Genocide Studies* 8 (1994), pp. 315–334; Daniel J. Goldhagen, *Hitler's Willing Executioners* (New York: Knopf, 1996), ch. 13.

18. Dagmar Hajkova, *Ravensbrück* (Prague, 1960). The memoir is in Czech; the quotation is from a German translation in the Ravensbrück archives (p. 29).

19. Dagmar Reese, *Straff aber nicht stramm—herb aber nicht derb: Zur Vergesellschaftung von Mädchen durch den Bund Deutscher Mädel* (Weinheim: Beltz, 1989), p. 95. The previous quotation is from Baldur von Schirach, quoted in ibid., p. 57.

20. "Leitsätze für die körperliche Erziehung von Studentinnen an deutschen Hochschulen," in *Die Ärztin* 10 (1934), p. 118.

21. Lucia Schmidt-Fels, *Deportiert nach Ravensbrück* (Düsseldorf: Dehnen, 1981), p. 45.

22. Margarete Buber-Neumann, *Milena: Kafkas Freundin* (Munich: Albert Langen, 1977), pp. 192–194; Ruth Klüger, *weiter leben: Eine Jugend* (Göttingen: Wallstein, 1992), pp. 145–146.

23. *Der Prozess gegen die Hauptkriegsverbrecher vor dem Internationalen Militärgerichtshof* (Nuremberg: S. Fischer, 1947–1949), vol. 6, p. 238; cf. Ingrid Müller-Münch, *Die Frauen von Majdanek* (Reinbek, 1992), p. 40: "Es gab da tatsächlich keinen Unterschied."

24. Adelheid L. Rüter-Ehlermann and Christiaan F. Rüter (eds.), *Justiz und NS-Verbrechen*, Amsterdam 1968–1981, vol. 2, pp. 491–496. Cf. Robert Gellately, *The Gestapo and German Society* (Oxford: Clarendon Press), 1990, esp. ch. 5.

25. Gisela Diewald-Kerkmann, "Politische Denunziation—eine 'weibliche Domäne'?" *1999: Zeitschrift für Sozialgeschichte des 20. und 21. Jahrhunderts* 11, no. 2 (1996), pp. 11–35.

26. Sybil Milton, "Women and the Holocaust: The Case of German and German-Jewish Women," in Carol Rittner and John K. Roth (eds.) *Different Voices: Women and the Holocaust* (New York: Paragon House, 1993), pp. 213–249.

27. Quoted in Hermann-Josef Rupieper, "Bringing Democracy to the Frauleins: Frauen als Zielgruppe der amerikanischen Demokratisierungspolitik in Deutschland, 1945–1952," *Geschichte und Gesellschaft* 17 (1991), p. 65.

28. Kate Millett, *Sexual Politics* (Aylesbury, 1971), pp. 159, 161 (1st ed. 1969).

29. Bonnie S. Anderson and Judith P. Zinsser, *A History of Their Own* (New York: Harper and Row, 1988), vol. 2, p. 303.

30. Claudia Koonz, "Consequences: Women, Nazis and Moral Choice," in Rittner and Roth (eds.), p. 304.

31. Karin Windaus-Walser, "Gnade der weiblichen Geburt?" in *Feministische Studien* 1 (1988), p. 131; Karin Windaus-Walser, "Frauen im Nationalsozialismus," in *Töchter-Fragen: NS-Frauen-Geschichte*, ed. Lerke Gravenhorst and Carmen Tatschmurat (Freiburg: Kore, 1990), esp. pp. 69, 71.

32. Clifford Kirkpatrick, *Women in Nazi Germany* (London: Jarrolds, 1939), pp. 110–130.

33. Götz Aly and Susanne Heim, *Vordenker der Vernichtung* (Frankfurt: S. Fischer, 1993), pp. 198–203.

34. Frau Angermeier, quoted in Oldfield, "German Women in the Resistance to Hitler," p. 95.

35. Dörte Winkler, *Frauenarbeit im Dritten Reich* (Hamburg: Hoffman und Campe, 1977), pp. 195, 198, 201.

36. Clarence D. Long, *The Labor Force in War and Transition: Four Countries* (New York: National Bureau of Economic Research, 1952), p. 37.

37. Claudia Huerkamp, "Jüdische Akademikerinnen in Deutschland, 1900–1938," *Geschichte und Gesellschaft* 19 (1993), pp. 311–321; Huerkamp, *Bildungsbürgerinnen*, pp. 80–91, 281–295.

38. Bluhm, "Gesetz," p. 533; Ernst Rüdin (ed.), *Erbpflege und Rassenhygiene im völkischen Staat* (Munich: Lehmann, 1934), pp. 8–9.

39. Bock, *Zwangssterilisation*, pp. 160–163, 436–438.

40. Gisela Bock, "Gleichheit und Differenz in der nationalsozialistischen Rassenpolitik," *Geschichte und Gesellschaft* 19 (1993), pp. 277–310 (a slightly shorter version is in Bock and Susan James [eds.], *Beyond Equality and Difference* [London: Routledge, 1992]).

41. For male perpetrators, gender may have played a greater part than for female ones; social forms of masculinity, especially male bonding and heavy drinking, were mobilized for the process of destruction. See Browning, *Ordinary Men,* pp. 82, 103, 116; Robert J. Lifton, *The Nazi Doctors* (New York: Basic Books, 1986), pp. 159, 193–196, 210, 231, 312f., 443, 462; Goldhagen, *Hitler's Willing Executioners,* p. 533 n. 73.

42. Yitzhak Arad, *Ghetto in Flames* (New York: Holocaust Library, 1982); Yehoshua Büchler, "Kommandostab Reichsführer-SS: Himmler's Personal Murder Brigades in 1941," *Holocaust and Genocide Studies* 1 (1986), pp. 13, 16f.; Yaacov Lozowick, "Rollbahn Mord: The Early Activities of Einsatzgruppe C," *Holocaust and Genocide Studies* 2 (1987), pp. 221, 235.

PART II

Life in the Ghettos

The Nazis did not invent the ghetto. The term and the concept originated in Venice in 1516, when the authorities proclaimed that Jews were to be segregated into a secluded section of the city. Jewish ghettos existed throughout the Middle Ages in several Western European and Eastern European countries. They were, however, abolished with Emancipation in the late eighteenth and nineteenth centuries. The last ghetto (in Rome) existed until 1870.

The ghettos established by the Nazis represented a transitional phase in their policy to exclude Jews permanently from Europe—and from life. Hans Frank, the German governor of the General Government area of Poland (the part of Poland remaining after Germany and the Soviet Union had annexed regions in the west and east, respectively), admitted that the Germans sentenced 1.2 million Jews to death by starvation.

On September 21, 1939, when the occupation of Poland was barely accomplished, Reinhard Heydrich, head of the security service, announced that Jews were to be concentrated in big cities near major railroad lines. In these cities they were forced into designated areas that later became the Jewish ghettos. The goal of the German policy in 1939 was to facilitate the forced mass emigration and expulsion of Jews from all territories under German rule. This was a general directive; a specific law creating ghettos was never announced. Thus, the establishment of ghettos in Poland did not proceed in a uniform manner. The first ghetto was established in October 1939 in Piotrków Trybunalski in the General Government; the last ghettos were established in early 1943 in Silesia, an area annexed to the Reich.

Usually the ghettos were created after other punitive measures had stripped Jews of their jobs and businesses, confiscated their valuable possessions, barred their access to their savings in bank accounts, and deprived them of food. (Food-rationing regulations in Warsaw in 1941, for example, allotted each Jew a mere 184 calories per day.) As a result, by the time they were forced into ghettos, many Jews were already suffering from impoverishment and starvation.

Jews from the villages and towns were deported to the ghettos in the cities, which led to overcrowding. Sanitary facilities were overtaxed, and with few medicines available, disease was rampant. The Nazis cynically cited the unhealthy conditions (a direct consequence of their harsh policy) to justify the sealing of the ghettos as a preventive measure to save the population from the diseases said to be caused by the Jews. Of course, under the conditions of life in the ghettos, all the problems were exacerbated.

The two largest ghettos, in Lodz (160,000 people, in the Warthegau area, annexed to Germany) and in Warsaw (450,000 people, in the General Government), followed two different models. The Lodz ghetto, which was sealed on April 30, 1940, was completely isolated from its surroundings. Residents were issued script, a special currency that could not be exchanged outside the ghetto. There was no access to the Aryan side of the city, and all economic enterprises were controlled by the Judenrat (Jewish Council) under the surveillance of the Nazi authorities.

In the Warsaw ghetto, established in November 1940, connections with the Polish side of the city were possible until November 1941, when the walls of the ghetto were completely sealed and the death penalty was applied to Jews found outside the ghetto. Before then, however, many ghetto residents were able to move from one side to the other, despite the formal restrictions. Poles and Jews established an underground supply line between the ghetto and the Aryan side, and smuggling became a vital lifeline. Economic initiatives were introduced by individuals; Poles and Germans could establish small industries (known as shops), in which Jewish labor was greatly exploited. In addition to the Judenrat's social welfare efforts, a system of self-help organizations worked to assist the poor and destitute.

In both ghettos, however, the death rate was extremely high (112,463 people, about 20 percent of the combined population, died in Lodz and Warsaw during 1941–1942), mostly because of starvation and exhaustion. Even a minor injury or fever ended in death. Despite these draconian conditions, cultural life continued and even flourished. In the early years of the Warsaw ghetto, for example, there were concerts, plays, poetry readings, schools for children, adult education, and many underground publications.

Within the limitations imposed by Nazi policy, life in the ghetto was shaped by the administration of the ghetto, the population size, the relationship between the Jewish population and the Poles, and especially the level of isolation—whether the ghetto was closed or relatively open. Contacts with the city and surrounding villages were crucial for obtaining food supplies and for lessening the psychological impact of isolation and exclusion. In ghettos that were completely sealed, conditions quickly became extreme; by contrast, in ghettos like the one in Kraków, in which Jews could move in and out almost until its liquidation, food supplies were somewhat less scarce and morale was somewhat better.

Most ghettos in Poland were established before the mass killing started in the summer of 1941, and they were tightly sealed before deportation to the death camps began. In June 1941, when the Germans invaded the Soviet Union, they instituted a new policy: they began killing the Jews at hastily devised mass execution sites. As the German army swept through the Soviet areas with large Jewish populations—such as Vilna, Kovno, Minsk, Lvov, and Kiev—they murdered hundreds of thousands of people. (About 1.5 million Jews were massacred in these areas between June and December 1941.) These mass executions were carried out by German *Einsatzgruppen* (mobile killing and police units) with the assistance of local nationalistic groups.

It was during these mass executions that the "surviving" Jewish population was rounded up and put into ghettos. Thus the Jews in these newer ghettos had already experienced the loss of their family and friends and the destruction of their communities. They hoped that the worst was over and that the Nazis had an interest in keeping a small minority of Jews alive. The Jewish leadership tried to keep Jewish life intact and create work that would provide essential supplies for the Germans—a concept of "rescue through work." The belief that the remaining Jews could be saved if their work was essential to the Germans also prevailed in a number of other ghettos in Poland. The extreme examples of this strategy were the efforts of Mordechai Chaim Rumkowski in the Lodz ghetto.

In some ghettos this attitude was challenged by the youth movements, which urged noncompliance with the German orders and warned people not to report for deportation. It was only after the mass deportations from Warsaw (July–September 1942), however, that the youth movements and political parties prepared for resistance in earnest.

The mood of the ghetto dwellers who lived amid endless death, suffering, and fear was a combination of despair and perseverance, as they hoped to outlive the war and the Nazis. In the Warsaw ghetto, for example, many people believed that if they were able to survive the first year of ghetto life, they would be able to live through the war.

In spite of the alarming reports of mass killing in the East, and the news of the first deportations in the General Government, the actual mass deportations in each ghetto came as a surprise. They put a tragic end to all the efforts of the ghetto inhabitants to maintain hope and to enlist all their mental and social efforts to live to see the end of the war.

This part of the book begins with Liza Chapnik's moving account of the early days after the Germans captured her hometown of Grodno in July 1941. Through her words we feel the shock of her first encounter with German cruelty, the starvation of children in the ghetto, the Gestapo arrest of her father, and her growing understanding that every day in the ghetto would bring more Nazi sadism. We also see her developing resolve to do something to fight the Germans, and we follow her amazing activities as a member of the Jewish underground—and as a leader of the antifascist organization in Bialystok.

Chapnik's testimony is followed by a short story by Ida Fink, a prizewinning novelist. Fink captures the terror of a family's rehearsal for the inevitable knock on the door when the Nazis come to take them away. It is a chilling reminder of the fears that permeated ghetto life and of each family's attempts to outwit their tormentors.

Michal Unger's masterful analysis of "The Status and Plight of Women in the Lodz Ghetto" (Chapter 8) answers two questions that arise from the data on gender disparities in the ghetto: Why was the mortality rate higher for men than for women? And why were women, especially women in their twenties and thirties—in the prime of life—disproportionately put on the transports to be deported to the concentration camps? Drawing on memoirs, diaries, and stories written in the ghetto, Unger gives us a finely textured picture of ghetto life. She shows that women were somehow better able to cope with the harsh conditions—making soup out of potato peels, repairing torn clothing, working without rest, and adapting to the constantly changing situation—even though they were paid less than men. These same women, however—especially the single parents—were often overrepresented on the transport lists because they were the poorest segment of the ghetto. Because families headed by a single mother were more likely to be on welfare, they were the biggest drain on ghetto resources and the first to be targeted for deportation.

In Chapter 9, Dalia Ofer draws on a unique source: interviews of a cross section of women in the Warsaw ghetto. Through these interviews, conducted in 1942 by Cecilya Slepak for the underground archive established by Emmanuel Ringelblum, Ofer provides us with vivid portraits of the resourceful women in the Warsaw ghetto—portraits that parallel Unger's conclusions about Lodz. In the Warsaw ghetto, as in Lodz, there were more women than men. About half of the ghetto inhabitants were unemployed and were starving to death. Yet when we read about the women's efforts to obtain food and resources for their families, we have the impression of enormous strength, inventiveness, and resiliency. Some women turned to smuggling, taking great risks to provide for their families, yet seeing these risks as a natural part of their customary roles as caretakers. Others found more traditional work in soup kitchens and factories, formed liaisons with more powerful men, and did whatever they could to aid their family's survival.

Ofer captures the spirit of these women, who faced overwhelming forces with almost superhuman strength. But in the end, their destiny was not in their own hands.

CHAPTER SIX

The Grodno Ghetto and Its Underground
A Personal Narrative

Liza Chapnik

I was born in Grodno, Poland, in 1922. Everyone in my large family perished in the Holocaust: my parents, my grandmother, two sisters, my niece, my brother, and all my aunts, uncles, and cousins.

On June 21, 1941, I finished secondary school. That night, after our graduation celebration, my friends and I returned home to awful sounds, like a thunderstorm. We saw fire, but we couldn't even guess that a bomb had exploded. None of us realized that this was the beginning of the war for us (the Russians had occupied our part of Poland since 1939).

The next morning, the entire population of Grodno seemed to be running away to the East, to Russia, to escape from the Nazi plague. The way to the East was very arduous. German warplanes were flying overhead, and we could actually see the pilots throwing bombs at us. As we passed, the local peasants and villagers would come out of their houses with axes, shouting, "Jews and Communists, run away." They killed and injured many refugees.

On the sixth day of the war we reached the city of Stolbcy, where German tanks surrounded us. The Nazis arrested all the men and boys and put them into a camp. The women and girls were ordered to return home, although I, along with many others, did not leave the area. The men's camp in Stolbcy covered a large open area and held thousands of Soviet military prisoners. The

In this chapter and the other personal narratives, names have been given according to the author's recollection; first names were not always available and spellings could not always be verified.

prisoners had not been fed for five days and had nothing to drink, although the days were very hot.

I noticed a nice villa, not far from the camp. I went there and asked, in Polish, for some water and bread for the prisoners. They gave me a lot of food and water, and they blessed me in the name of Christ. Then I brought the food to the barbed wire and gave it to the soldiers. I repeated this procedure several times. At first the German gendarmes kept silent, but suddenly they began shouting and beating me, because I didn't want to go away. My sister Sara, and the women standing in the square nearby the camp, began to cry and shout, "They are murdering a little girl!" (Although I was nineteen, I was small and thin.) At that time, the people were not yet used to the Nazis' sadism.

After some time, the head of the camp, a young German officer, came over. The guard pointed at me and said, "The crazy girl does not want to go away without her brother." That evening my brother was released. We, and the remaining people from Grodno, began our journey home—through the fields, through the forests, and across the highways to Baranowicze—all the time trying to avoid the German army.

On the way back, my sister and brother left me with our relatives in Dereczyn, a little Jewish town near Slonim. One day, in the beginning of August, I decided to go to Slonim to visit some friends of my brother's, who were refugees from Warsaw. After walking in that direction for about an hour, I suddenly heard the sounds of women and children crying. I was frightened and hid in the hollow of a tall tree. The shouts and crying were awful, absolutely unbearable. I don't know how long I stayed, trembling, in the tree. Finally, a Belorussian woman walked by. She saw me and said, in Belorussian, "My little flower, what are you doing here?" She took me in her arms. I told her that I was going to Slonim. Her immediate reaction was, "Don't go there, the Germans have killed all the Jews." I couldn't speak; I was numb. On the way to her house, she told me to tell everyone that I was her niece, Danusia—her brother's daughter. She risked her life for me. (Notices had been posted everywhere warning that those who hid Jews would be immediately shot or hung.) When a neighbor came in, my benefactor said: "What a guest I have, didn't I tell you that my little niece would come? In a month we'll celebrate her fourteenth birthday." The neighbor looked at me and noticed that I resembled my "father," Peter: "Look, her nose, eyes, and mouth are like his."

After a few days I went to Slonim, where I learned that the Nazis had gathered about ten thousand Jews—children, women, and old people. They took them into the fields, forced them to dig large pits, placed the women and children on the edge of the pits, and shot them. The victims fell down into the pits, even though a great number of them were still alive. The earth continued to move with the struggles of people who were buried alive. So the local peasants were ordered to take their tractors and go over the place. The Slonim slaughter was one of the first war crimes committed by the German murderers. It took place just after the beginning of the war, in June 1941.

In Slonim, I went to the home of my brother's friends, Jankiel Goldfarb and his wife, Cylia. I knocked at the door, and Jankiel opened the door with an ax in his hand. I asked him what he meant to do. The answer was short enough: "The first Nazi who enters my room will be killed."

At that time there was no ghetto in Slonim, but Jews were forbidden to walk on the pavement. They were supposed to walk on the road amid horses and cars. All Jews were ordered to wear an identifying white armband with a blue Jewish star. The greatest shock for me was the sight of Lithuanians in Gestapo uniforms walking in the streets with children's heads on their swords. This was the atmosphere. Jankiel was the first who tried to convince me to work in the Jewish underground, and to fight against the Nazis for revenge. He had some contact with the Warsaw underground, and he told me about Wanda, a young woman who was a courier for the underground and who worked on the Aryan side—outside the Warsaw ghetto walls. (Jankiel Goldfarb and his wife later returned to Warsaw and took an active part in the Warsaw ghetto uprising.)

Although I didn't argue with Jankiel, I was not yet ready to leave my family and friends to work for the underground. This was only my first experience with the Nazis. In November I went back to my hometown of Grodno.

In Grodno two ghettos were established in November 1941. Ghetto 1, situated in the center of the city, was called productive because it contained workshops. In Ghetto 2, the nonproductive area along Skidelska Street, there were no workshops. (Ghetto 2 was eliminated before Ghetto 1.) The Nazis established a Judenrat (Jewish Council) to run the ghetto. The head of the Judenrat was David Brawer, the former director of the prestigious Jewish Tarbut gymnasium (high school). The fifteen members of the Judenrat included well-known and respected men: Lazar Gozanski (a lawyer), Zvi Bielko, Israel Lande, and Henryk Pudles, among others.

My family lived in Ghetto 1, at 6 Najdus Street. Soon after the ghetto was created, the watchman (guard) of my school had come to warn my parents that the Gestapo was looking for me. They had come to my school with a list of names of teachers and other intellectuals whom they were planning to arrest. The watchman saw the names of Grisha Chapnik (my brother) and Liza Chapnik on the list and wanted to reach us before the Gestapo came. Among the Grodno intelligentsia whom the Nazis wanted were our favorite historian, Aleksandr Wieliczkier, the mathematician Jerzy Kaminski, Rabbi Rozowski, Zilberfenig, the musician Josele Wigdorowicz, and others. All of them were shot in the first week after the Nazis occupied Grodno. Therefore my relatives and friends decided that Grisha and I should stay hidden.

During the day I was hidden in the apartment or in a large wardrobe, which our friends had put in the corridor that led to the attic. Through the back side of the wardrobe (which could be removed), I used to climb onto the roof. In the evening, when it began to get dark, some friends of mine would come to take me out to walk on the streets.

According to a German "order," three feet was enough space for a Jew in the ghetto, so all the apartments were terribly overcrowded. Our apartment, which consisted of two very small rooms, housed fourteen people: three families and a few single people. Despite the crowded conditions, we all were very friendly and shared each slice of bread.

After the Nazis occupied the cities, they issued an order directing Jews to turn over all their radios, and all gold and silver objects, to the Germans. We buried our radio, but a friend of mine, Lovka Lubich, hid his family's radio in the cellar. There we usually listened to the latest news from Moscow, sometimes from London, and we wrote down the news to distribute to others—mainly to the youth.

I told my friends, relatives, and neighbors in Grodno about the Slonim massacre and everything I had heard and seen. People didn't believe me. Each person hoped that the tragedy wouldn't touch him or her personally. But I wrote down what had happened in Slonim, and my brother prepared some leaflets in order to expose the truth about what the Nazis had done.

What I have remembered all my life about the atmosphere in the ghetto, through the half-century that has passed since then, are the ghetto children's eyes—their big, black, sad eyes, full of misery. The children in the ghetto were deprived of their childhood. Suddenly children—five, six, or ten years old— became grownups.

In the ghetto all Jews were potential victims of Nazi sadism. Members of the Gestapo would come to the ghetto—alone or with friends—for entertainment. This entertainment consisted of taking potshots at a child, raping a woman, cutting the beard off an old man, humiliating people in the street, and so on. This was everyday life in the ghetto. There were two Gestapo officers in charge of the ghettos: Kurt Viese was responsible for Ghetto 1 and Karl Streblow for Ghetto 2. They, along with Rinzler, who was in charge of the Kielbasin concentration camp near Grodno, would come to the ghetto to engage in sadistic "sports." Once Viese and Streblow, accompanied by some men from the Gestapo and the SS, entered Ghetto 1 and ordered members of the Judenrat to clean, with their bare hands, all the toilets in the neighborhood and then eat what they found there. After that, they were given an hour to clean the snow that covered the square near Perec Street, using only little spoons. This is how the Nazis entertained themselves. Another time, Viese, Streblow, Rinzler, and other Gestapo men came to Ghetto 1, and Viese announced that he was going to hang the prettiest girl of Grodno—Lena Prenska. The murderers were in need of an audience. They gathered people in Perec Street, near Tankus's bakery. Lena stepped on the little stool with her head raised, and when Viese took away the stool, she spat in his face and said, "You swines, your end is approaching."

Many people in the ghetto were starving. Some people preferred to kill themselves rather than suffer the constant assaults and humiliations. Some mothers gave their children poison (if they were fortunate enough to have some). I knew women dentists (who had access to arsenic) who poisoned their children, their husbands, and themselves. They were *not* trying to avoid the gas chambers; they had never heard of such things. Their sole aim was to avoid falling into the hands of the German murderers. (At that time, no one knew about the gas chambers, where millions of Jews perished. Then a Grodno Jew, Brojde, managed to escape from Treblinka in 1942. He told his story to Grisha

Chapnik and Helen Nirenberzanka, whose leaflets telling the truth about the death camp were distributed among the people in the ghetto and to those on the Aryan side.)

In October 1942, Gestapo men came to our apartment to search for Grisha and me. Grisha had already escaped to Bialystok, and I was in my shelter on the roof. When they didn't find us, they took my father. They warned him that if he didn't tell them where his son and daughter were, they would hang him. Our neighbors and relatives told me that my father was smiling as he left home. Maybe he went fearlessly, erect, and behaved with dignity because he was religious and for him it was "kiddush hashem"—sanctification in the name of God.

This was everyday life in the ghetto. In the atmosphere of this unbelievable terror, sadism, and slaughter, underground organizations emerged. At first all the youth groups—Hashomer Hatsa'ir, Dror, Komsomol, and Communists—had their own plans and met separately. Then Hashomer Hatsa'ir united with the Communists, and they worked together. Representatives of these groups—such as Zerah Silberberg (from Hashomer) and Mordechai Tenenbaum (from Dror)—came from Vilna and Warsaw to tell their members what was going on in those cities, and to make plans for local activities. Dodzki Rozowski from Hashomer Hatsa'ir founded a laboratory in which the group prepared false documents to enable their members to work on the Aryan side. These couriers established contacts with antifascist factions among the Russian, Polish, and Belorussian partisans, found weapons, and spread leaflets with the news about the massacre that had taken place in Slonim. Chasia Bielicka and Cyla Shahnes later transported the laboratory to the Bialystok ghetto.

There was a major division of opinion among the youth in the Grodno ghetto. One group urged us to prepare for armed resistance, that is, for an uprising in the Grodno ghetto. Everyone understood that any uprising in the ghetto was doomed to failure, but all the same, this group wanted to fight against the Nazis for the honor of the Jewish nation, and to avenge the deaths of their parents, other relatives, and friends. (Similarly, the fighters in the other ghettos—Warsaw, Vilna, and Bialystok—certainly realized that their uprisings would fail and that all the participants would perish.) The other group argued for leaving the ghetto at night and going to the neighboring forests where we could join the partisans and fight against the Nazis with them.

I am convinced that no uprising could have taken place in the Grodno ghetto. Eleven *Aktionen*—roundups of people for transport to the death camps—took place there, one after the other, within a very short period, leaving no time to prepare weapons or organize the resistance. In each Aktion, leaders and members of the underground were seized and many people were slaughtered.

In the end of 1942 and beginning of 1943, the youth movement made some attempts to send groups from the ghetto to the forest. The main obstacle was the lack of weapons. We had only a few pistols and one or two rifles. Many people who escaped were shot right near the ghetto fence, and others were recognized as Jews and shot in villages on the way to the forest. One man, Rejzner, who later returned to the ghetto, told us that he saw many corpses on the way to the forest.

In January 1943, the remaining people in Ghetto 2 were transported to the death camp. However, a group of eighteen young men and women, headed by Eliahu Tankus (from Hashomer Hatsa'ir), managed to escape into the forests. On the way, they were even able to buy several rifles in the village. One of the villagers, however, denounced the Jews to the Germans, and local policemen killed almost all of them. Among the victims were Miriam Pupks, Dalia Browarski, Haim Marash, Eliahu Tankus, and Shajke Mahes. After the failure of this group, Hersch Lifshitz tried to arrange some contacts with the Vilna ghetto underground. He managed to make an agreement with some railway workers, who transported a group of Grodno Jews to Vilna. Among them were Jezierski, Zamoszanski, Trachtenberg, and Liebicz. They also managed to buy some weapons and joined the partisans near Smorgon and Vilejka.

On the night of February 7, 1943, after the largest Aktion, a group of about thirty young people, headed by Leizer Lipski, Shai Hmielnik (from the Communists), and Shai Gorbulski, left the ghetto and went to the Nachski forest. They had a few pistols, which Rejzner had managed to obtain at the military hospital where he worked. The group joined partisan detachments and took part in such actions as the cutting of telephone lines. Gorbulski, Lipski, A. and G. Kapulski (son and father), Grach, and two brothers Peve were given awards by the Soviet government for their heroic actions. In June 1943, the Nachski forest was surrounded by German tanks and planes. The critical situation after the battle made the Nachski partisan brigade divide into smaller units and leave the Nachski forest. One group moved to the Lipchanski forest, and other groups moved to the forests near Slonim.

A very successful group of young women from Grodno worked as couriers on the Aryan side—outside the ghetto walls. These young women were given false documents and sent to the Bialystok underground. Among the five survivors of the Bialystok antifascist underground committee, four were Grodno girls: Chasia Bielicka, Bronia Vinicka, Ania Rud, and myself (Liza Chapnik). The fifth was Chajka Grossman, who played a leading part in the Bialystok uprising. Unfortunately, other Grodno girls, who were also sent to Bialystok to do underground work on the Aryan side, failed to get *Arbeitsamt* (work cards). These included Sara Shewachowicz, Fania Lipkies, and Andzia Jezierska, who was tortured severely but didn't betray anybody.

In November 1942 I obtained papers stolen from the magistrate of the city council. Leizer Lipski and Shai Hmielnik, the leaders of the Communist underground organization in Grodno, handed me this false document, with a Hitler stamp on it. Salomon Zukowski, whose handwriting was very good, filled in such false data as "Polish nationality" and "Catholic." He gave me a popular Polish name, Maria Mrozowska. Lipski gave me some names of contacts in the Bialystok underground. My task was made a little easier because Grisha, my brother, was already in Bialystok. He introduced me to Drejer, one of the leaders of the Communist underground.

Approximately one week after I left the ghetto, I went to the central police office to get a German passport. I gave them my false document and had my picture and fingerprints taken. In a month, I received a true *Personal Ausweis* (identity card) in the name of Maria Mrozowska. My first job was peeling potatoes at the railway station's canteen. After that, I found a job with Chasia Bielicka in the kitchen for SS men, where we peeled potatoes and other vegetables. We also cleaned their apartments.

Each night, I returned to the ghetto through one of our secret openings (for example, on Jurowiecka Street and Bielostoczanska Street). In the ghetto, I collected messages and assignments for missions on the Aryan side. My first task was to find safe houses and rooms (for the underground liaisons to meet with Polish, Russian, Belorussian, and German antifascists), and to locate and buy weapons. Usually, when we returned from the ghetto, Chasia and I exchanged information in our own code language.

When my safe room at 20 Grodnienski Street became spoiled (after a visit from the Gestapo), it took me a lot of time to find a suitable room with a separate entrance, a cellar, and so on. I finally found one at 12 Choroszczanska Street. There was a perfect underground cellar, and I could pull a few planks out of the floor to hide weapons, leaflets, documents, and intelligence service data. When liaisons came from the forests (two that I remember were Sergei Berkner and Natan Goldshtein), I hid them in this apartment.

During the war, Grodno had several connections to Bialystok. Not only were the Grodno couriers who had been provided with false documents sent there to go on working on the Aryan side, but also the last survivors of the Grodno ghetto—the "specialists" (skilled workers)—were transported to the Bialystok ghetto in February 1943. Those of us on the Aryan side managed to unite Polish, Russian, Belorussian, and even German antifascist groups into a large anti-Nazi organization. The committee that headed the underground organization coordinated the activities of all the groups. The members of the organization worked at the railway station, at the airport, in the Gestapo, at the Ritz restaurant for German high-level officers, at factories, and even in the National Belorussian Committee and other important places.

Until August 1943, when the Bialystok ghetto was liquidated, we were in close contact with the ghetto and carried the messages of its organizations. Between the destruction of the ghetto and April 1944, we supported the Jewish detachment Forojs ("forward" in Yiddish, referring to the Jewish partisan units), whose commander was Alexander Suhaczewski and whose commissar was Rivka Vojskowska. We provided them with medicines, compasses, maps, data, and some weapons. Forojs and the other Jewish partisan detachments took in all the people we managed to bring them—those who had escaped from the ghetto or transports.

In April 1944, the partisan brigade named after Kastus Kalinowski, headed by Colonel Nikolai Wojciechowski, came from Bialowieska Pushcha to the Bialystok forests. The brigade consisted of five detachments and was a part of the large Belorussian partisan unit headed by General Kapusta. The Soviet partisans had enough machine guns, rifles, pistols, radios, and other necessary equipment. But the Jewish platoon was badly equipped, and they couldn't get food in the villages as the Soviet detachments could. The Jewish partisans were often starving. When the Soviet partisan brigade came, they incorporated the

Jewish partisans into their brigade, but they distributed the Jewish partisans of Forojs among the other detachments of the brigade. We were disappointed because we wanted to preserve the Jewish platoon. However, our Jewish partisans were given weapons and took part in all the activities of the brigade.

The headquarters of the brigade appointed me chairman of the Bialystok antifascist organization. The members of the committee were Chasia Bielicka (who is now Chasia Borenshtein, living in Kibbutz Lehavot Habashan), the late Chajka Grossman (from Kibbutz Evron), Bronia Vinicka (now Bronka Klibanski, living in Jerusalem), Ania Rud (now living in Tel Aviv), the late Marylka Rozycka, and the late Burdzynski, whom we called Wujek (Uncle).

I shall give only a few examples of the activities of our Bialystok underground organization. First, we enrolled four Germans—Schade, Bohle, Kudlaschek, and Busse—in our underground work. They provided us with pistols, guns, intelligence service data, maps, compasses, and so on. (After the war, Schade wrote an article titled "Vom unpolitischen Director zum Widerstands Kampfer und Partisanen" [How a Nazi Party member became an antifascist fighter and partisan]).

Once, Colonel Wojciechowski asked me to bring our Germans to the forest to get messages directly from the headquarters. We were not sure the Germans would agree, because it was so dangerous. I can't say that Schade and Busse were enthusiastic, but finally they agreed. We invented a story that the Germans were going to the village to buy butter and honey and that I was their interpreter. We went in a carriage pulled by two horses, in which we hid some rifles, pistols, a map, and textiles for partisans' uniforms. The first meeting between the Germans and the partisans in the forest was extremely impressive and touching. On the way back, Busse and Schade told me that they couldn't say a word; they didn't believe their own eyes: "How could it be," they said, "that tanks, planes, Gestapo, the SS, and the famous German army, which conquered all Europe, are everywhere, and here, nearby in the forest, there are fearless partisans, fighters." After the war, Schade confessed that he was too ashamed to refuse to go to the forest: "How is it," he said, "that young Jewish girls go to the partisans every day, and he, a grown-up German, was afraid to go."

During the day we couriers carried rifles in pipes, parts of machine guns, and explosives. We passed members of the Gestapo, SS, and police. I should say that each step of the Jewish women on the Aryan side was extremely risky and dangerous. We seem to have lived on the verge of disaster—to have walked on the edge of a blade. We all assumed that none of us would survive, but it was our moral duty to fight the Nazis, to avenge our parents and our people.

Colonel Wojciechowski, head of the partisan brigade, and Chudinov, chief of the brigade headquarters, sent reports to the Central Committee and to the State Archivum, stating that the Bialystok underground, an antifascist organization, took an active part in the liberation of Bialystok and that we—the members of the committee of the antifascist organization—prepared everything for the liberation of the city. Chasia Bielicka and I had brought a detailed map of Bialystok and its surroundings to the headquarters. We marked where the airport was situated, how many airplanes there were, how many detachments, how many tanks, and so on. The Germans, before leaving the city, mined it in the hope of destroying the town. But we in the antifascist groups provided a map showing where the mines had been laid and where anti-aircraft batteries were situated. Thanks to the efforts of our underground antifascist organization, the Soviet military newspapers reported that Bialystok was liberated without victims.

CHAPTER SEVEN

The Key Game

Ida Fink

They had just finished supper and the woman had cleared the table, carried the plates to the kitchen, and placed them in the sink. The kitchen was mottled with patches of dampness and had a dull, yellowish light, even gloomier than in the main room. They had been living here for two weeks. It was their third apartment since the start of the war; they had abandoned the other two in a hurry. The woman came back into the room and sat down again at the table. The three of them sat there: the woman, her husband, and their chubby, blue-eyed, three-year-old child. Lately they had been talking a lot about the boy's blue eyes and chubby cheeks.

The boy sat erect, his back straight, his eyes fixed on his father, but it was obvious that he was so sleepy he could barely sit up.

The man was smoking a cigarette. His eyes were bloodshot and he kept blinking in a funny way. This blinking had begun soon after they fled the second apartment.

It was late, past ten o'clock. The day had long since ended, and they could have gone to sleep, but first they had to play the game that they had been playing every day for two weeks and still had not got right. Even though the man tried his best and his movements were agile and quick, the fault was his and not the child's. The boy was marvelous. Seeing his father put out his cigarette, he

Originally published in Polish in *Skrawek czasu* by Aneks Publishers, London, copyright © 1983 by Ida Fink. English translation first published in 1987 by Pantheon Books, a division of Random House. Reprinted here by permission.

shuddered and opened his blue eyes even wider. The woman, who didn't actually take part in the game, stroked the boy's hair.

"We'll play the key game just one more time, only today. Isn't that right?" she asked her husband.

He didn't answer because he was not sure if this really would be the last rehearsal. They were still two or three minutes off. He stood up and walked toward the bathroom door. Then the woman called out softly, "Ding-dong." She was imitating the door bell and she did it beautifully. Her "ding-dong" was quite a soft, lovely bell.

At the sound of chimes ringing so musically from his mother's lips, the boy jumped up from his chair and ran to the front door, which was separated from the main room by a narrow strip of corridor.

"Who's there?" he asked.

The woman, who alone had remained in her chair, clenched her eyes shut as if she were feeling a sudden, sharp pain.

"I'll open up in a minute, I'm looking for the keys," the child called out. Then he ran back to the main room, making a lot of noise with his feet. He ran in circles around the table, pulled out one of the sideboard drawers, and slammed it shut.

"Just a minute, I can't find them, I don't know where Mama put them," he yelled, then dragged the chair across the room, climbed onto it, and reached up to the top shelf of the etagere.

"I found them!" he shouted triumphantly. Then he got down from the chair, pushed it back to the table, and without looking at his mother, calmly walked to the door. A cold, musty draft blew in from the stairwell.

"Shut the door, darling," the woman said softly. "You were perfect. You really were."

The child didn't hear what she said. He stood in the middle of the room, staring at the closed bathroom door.

At last it creaked. The man was pale and his clothes were streaked with lime and dust. He stood on the threshold and blinked in that funny way.

"Well? How did it go?" asked the woman.

"I still need more time. He has to look for them longer. I slip in sideways all right, but then . . . it's so tight in there that when I turn . . . And he's got to make more noise—he should stamp his feet louder."

The child didn't take his eyes off him.

"Say something to him," the woman whispered.

"You did a good job, little one, a good job," he said mechanically.

"That's right," the woman said, "you're really doing a wonderful job, darling—and you're not little at all. You act just like a grown-up, don't you? And do you know that if someone should really ring the doorbell someday when Mama is at work, everything will depend on you? Isn't that right? And what will you say when they ask you about your parents?"

"Mama's at work."

"And Papa?"

He was silent.

"And Papa?" the man screamed in terror.

The child turned pale.

"And Papa?" the man repeated more calmly.

"He's dead," the child answered and threw himself at his father, who was standing right beside him, blinking his eyes in that funny way, but who was already long dead to the people who would really ring the bell.

CHAPTER EIGHT

The Status and Plight of Women in the Lodz Ghetto

Michal Unger

The second and last general population census in Poland before World War II was held on December 9, 1931. The data
from this census are used as indicators for comparison with data
from the Holocaust period. Such a comparison emphasizes the
anomaly and enormity of the Holocaust that descended on Polish Jewry in the war years. According to the census data, Lodz had a population of 604,829, of whom 202,497, or 33.5 percent, were Jews.[1] Among the
Jews, 96,658 (47.7 percent) were men and 105,839 (52.3 percent) were
women. It is estimated that from that time until the eruption of World War II
on September 1, 1939, the Jewish population of Lodz grew by about 30,000,
for a total of 233,000 Jews in the city on that date. One presumes that the ratio
between women and men did not change significantly in the interim. Thus
women held a certain numerical advantage from the beginning.

The first few months of the German occupation witnessed a mass exodus
from Lodz. It began on September 5, 1939, when the western part of Poland
was occupied by the German army and the Polish forces started to withdraw.
All men of draft age were called up to defend Warsaw. Many Jews joined the
outflux, which intensified after the city was occupied on September 8, 1939.
In December 1939 all Jews in Lodz were required to move into the ghetto—
which was sealed on May 1, 1940. On June 16, 1940, a census of the ghetto
population was taken by order of the Germans.[2] A total of 156,402 Jews were
recorded: 71,227 men (45.5 percent) and 85,175 women (54.4 percent), or
119.4 women for every 100 men. For Jews between ages twenty and forty-

five—those in their fertile years and their physical prime—the disparity was even greater: of the 64,430 members of this group, 27,281 were men and 37,149 were women.[3] Thus women comprised 57.7 percent of this age group.

According to these data, 76,598 Jews—about a third of the Jewish population—had left Lodz, and a majority of those departing were men. This exodus occurred in response to the mobilization of Jewish men for the Polish army at the beginning of the war. Some did not return, having been killed, captured, or transferred. Other men, particularly the younger ones, fled the city because of the regime under which Jews now lived: they faced numerous decrees, abuse, humiliation, abduction for forced labor, arrests, and the like. Men suffered from these more than women. Most of those leaving the city made their way to the General Government area or the Soviet Union. Thus, when the ghetto was formed, there were more women than men in Lodz, including many women with young children or elderly parents, who would surely have found the journey out of Lodz extremely difficult. Many testimonies reflect the frustration of women who were left alone and had to shoulder the burden by themselves under unspeakably harsh conditions. The author and poet Rivka Kwiatkowski-Pinchasik, an inhabitant of the ghetto, described the anguish of these women in a collection of stories. One of these stories, "The List," is about a young woman who, left alone in the ghetto with her young son and fearing that deportation will separate them, decides to volunteer for deportation.

> She vents all the bitterness of her soul on her husband, who had abandoned her and her son. He saved his skin by fleeing to Russia. Why did he have to flee on the very first day of the war? What frenzy gripped him when the Germans arrived? . . . "I have to get away, I have to flee. . . . The Germans won't dare harm the women." He's certainly gone on to big things there; he has a head on his shoulders. . . . He'll manage all right. He's probably found himself another woman. . . . Her love of and allegiance to her husband have turned into bitter hatred now that he has fled. . . . It's better to sign up together for life and for death! When he returns, if he returns, he'll return to an empty house.[4]

The realities of the ghetto exacerbated the numerical disparity between women and men. The Lodz ghetto *Chronicle* noted this fact on July 22, 1941:

Table 8.1   The Number of Deaths in the Lodz Ghetto

	1940 (May–December)	1941	1942 (January–July)
Men	3,448 (50.3%)	6,965 (60.8%)	6,773 (60%)
Women	3,403 (49.7%)	4,481 (39.2%)	4,500 (40%)
Total	6,852 (100%)	11,437 (100%)	11,273 (100%)

"There is a marked and steady increase in the number of women relative to the number of men. This is because the mortality rate of men is almost twice as high as that of women, and because of the labor transports."[5] The labor transports (deportations to labor camps outside the ghetto) began in December 1940 and continued as long as the ghetto existed. The vast majority of the 11,000 people swept up in these deportations were men.[6]

The main reason for the gender disparity in the ghetto, however, was the difference in mortality. Women have a longer life expectancy than men under normal circumstances, and even more so under ghetto conditions. One must take into account that the men's work was often harder than the women's, and this undoubtedly affected mortality. In addition, the impression one gets from testimonies and diaries written in the ghetto is that women adjusted better than men to ghetto conditions and coped better with the hunger and the harsh and changing circumstances.

Table 8.1 illustrates the difference between women's and men's mortality from May 1940 to July 1942.[7] The hardest year for the Jews in the ghetto was 1942, when starvation claimed more than 18,108 victims, approximately 40% women and 60% men. A clear trend is visible: virtual parity in men's and women's death rates in 1940 changed to a 20 percent disparity in 1941 and a similar disparity in 1942.

The numerical inequality of the sexes steadily grew. In 1941 there were 123 women for every 100 men. By 1944, the ratio widened to 137 per 100. The differences were more pronounced for those between twenty and thirty-four years of age: 151 women per 100 men in 1941, and 196 per 100 in 1944.[8]

Transport of Jews from other localities to the Lodz ghetto began in September 1941. The first to arrive were 3,082 Jews from Włocławek, 866 of whom were men (28 percent) and 2,216 women (72 percent).[9] In October–

November 1941, 19,953 Jews arrived from Central Europe: 8,263 men (42 percent) and 11,690 women (58 percent).[10]

The ghettos in the Wartheland district were liquidated in the course of 1942, and most of the Jews were sent to Chelmno, where they were murdered. Until September 1942, 14,350 refugees from these ghettos, mostly men and women of working age, were brought to Lodz. Even among these refugees, the women outnumbered the men.[11] In all, 37,385 people were taken to the ghetto between September 1941 and September 1942. This supplement, in which women formed a majority, also helped increase the ratio of women to men in the ghetto.

Deportations from the Lodz ghetto to the Chelmno extermination camp began on January 16, 1942, and took place in two main phases. The first phase, in which 54,978 people were deported, lasted until May 1942. The number of women deported in this period was 34,170 (62.1 percent of the total number of people deported).[12] The deported women comprised 44 percent of the women in the ghetto, while the deported men comprised 36 percent of the men in the ghetto. Women between the ages of twenty and forty were deported in numbers double and sometimes more than triple to those of men. For example, of the 727 people born in 1914 who were deported, 167 were men and 560 were women.[13]

The second phase began on September 1, 1942, with the brutal eviction of all hospital patients. From September 5 through September 12, in a cruel *Aktion* known as the *Sperre*, 15,685 people—mostly children, the ill, and the elderly—were deported. The number of women and girls in this deportation was 9,669 (61.6 percent of the total number of deportees).[14] In this case, too, nearly three times as many women over the age of twenty-five were deported compared with men of the same age group.[15] In all, 70,664 people were taken to Chelmno in 1942, of whom 43,839 (62 percent) were women.

The reason for the preponderance of women in the deportations was that women were, to some extent, the weak link in the ghetto. The persons selected for deportation in the first phase were welfare recipients, the unemployed, and families whose male breadwinners worked outside the ghetto. Women outnumbered men in these groups.

In spite of the large number of women who were deported, the numerical disparity between men and women persisted. Of the 88,036 people in the ghetto in December 1942, 38,262 (43.4 percent) were men and 49,774 (56.6 percent) were women.[16]

We have no data on the gender breakdown of the population for 1943. The total Jewish population of the ghetto in late 1943 was 83,132.[17] This was a relatively calm year, with lower mortality (4,581 deaths) than in previous years.[18] The main reasons were a slight improvement in nutrition and the fact that most of the remaining population was young and healthy, for most of the elderly and ill had been deported in 1942. Two deportations occurred in 1943; the first on March 30, when 945 people were deported to Chelmno, and the second on September 1, when 325 ill people were deported.[19] One presumes that the gender ratio did not change significantly that year. In March 1944, the ghetto population stood at 79,638, of which 33,607 were men (42.2 percent) and 46,031 women (57.8 percent). These numbers represent a slight increase in the proportion of women.[20]

Thus, the initial numerical advantage of women at the time the ghetto was sealed in 1940 grew as the years passed, because of the large percentage of men deported from the ghetto and the high proportion of women among Jews taken to the ghetto in late 1941 and 1942. The most important factor in the widening gender disparity was the higher mortality of men. By inference, women were better able than men to tolerate the ghetto conditions. For this reason, even though a larger number (and percentage) of women were deported from the ghetto in 1942, there was still a gender disparity in the ghetto.

Women at Work

The 1931 Polish census shows 31.5 working Jewish women for every 100 Jewish working men. Most of the women worked in the garment, textile, and paper industries.[21] These data apply to Poland as a whole. An industrial town such as Lodz may have had a slightly higher proportion of women workers, but it is reasonable to assume that one-third of the women in the city held jobs. Table 8.2 shows the occupational breakdown of women and men aged fourteen and over from the 1940 census. The census was conducted in the ghetto on June 16, 1940, less than two months after the ghetto was sealed, when most Jews presumably still reported their true occupations. In subsequent censuses, by contrast, most Jews described themselves as skilled in various occupations that the Germans needed.[22]

Table 8.2   Occupations by Gender in the Lodz Ghetto, 1940

Occupation[1]	Men	Women	Total
Unskilled laborers	6,512	4,779	11,291
White collar workers	5,532	2,536	8,068
Merchants	7,884	1,678	9,562
Teachers	727	543	1,270
Tailors/undergarment seamsters	6,280	8,649	14,922
Cobblers	2,450	4	2,454
Carpenters	1,119	—	1,119
Weavers	4,066	1,845	5,911
Knitters	2,666	2,070	4,736
Other	9,699	2,142	11,841
Not working	3,864	41,613	45,477
Total	50,799	65,859	116,651

[1]Occupations practiced by more than a thousand people are listed; those held by fewer than a thousand people are aggregated under "Other."

The most remarkable datum is that 41,613 women—63.1 percent of the total female population aged fourteen and above—did not hold jobs. Thus we see that 37 percent of women in Lodz held jobs on the eve of the war, a slightly higher proportion than in 1931. Most of the employed women did handicrafts, particularly sewing, weaving, and knitting.

Most of the ghetto population was unemployed in the second half of 1940. Initially, when the local German authorities under Friedrich Uebelhoer, governor of the district to which Lodz belonged, decided to set up the ghetto in December 1939, they envisaged the ghetto as a short-lived, provisional measure pending the deportation of all Jews from Lodz, for the city, as part of the Reich, had to be made *Judenrein* (cleansed of Jews).[23] The eviction was delayed for various reasons; in the meantime, the Jews remained in the ghetto while the Germans stripped them of all their property. At this point, the Germans did not accede to requests by M. C. Rumkowski, the *Judenaelteste* (Elder of the Jews) in the Lodz ghetto, to open workshops in the ghetto so that the population might earn a living. Consequently, few Jews worked during these months. From May to December 1940, about seventeen workshops were set up, mainly in needlework. They employed 4,982 people, or slightly more than three percent of the ghetto population, including 4,014 men and 968 women.[24]

Not until October 1940, when the Germans understood that the general deportation of Jews was not imminent, did the local German authorities decide to organize the ghetto in such a way that the Jews would pay their own way, sparing the Reich this expense. Because the Germans had stolen most of the Jews' money and property, the only way to achieve self-sufficiency in the ghetto was to organize a productive labor force. The Germans ordered the reopening of factories in the ghetto that had been shut down, purchased much machinery and had it brought into the ghetto, and made efforts to obtain orders for the ghetto enterprises, particularly from the Wehrmacht (the German army). It took Rumkowski and his associates until late 1940 to establish factories and recruit workers, but once they did so, they devoted all their energies to the project. Work was swiftly organized, and the number of workshops grew to approximately 120 by late 1943.

The organization of labor and the enormous profits the Germans derived from the Jews' toil provide the main explanation for the Germans' decision to refrain from liquidating the Lodz ghetto. While the other ghettos fell, Lodz operated until August 1944, when it was the last ghetto on Polish soil. The integration of women into the labor force progressed very slowly the first year. The many women without husbands bore the heavy dual burden of earning a livelihood and taking care of their families. Sara Selver-Urbach describes a courtyard around which several families dwelled, each with a different story of extreme hardship:

> In an apartment that was virtually a cellar . . . the Werzberger family lived with its many children. In a darkened room, on mattresses strewn across the moldy floor, lay the children—dirty, lice-infested, hungry, and ill. The beds and all other furnishings in the house had long since been destroyed for use as heating fuel. The father had been shot to death by the Germans at the time of the transfer from the city to the ghetto. Two children, still infants, one three years of age and the other only about one year old, had died during the first winter in the ghetto. Ever since the family had come to the ghetto, it had been living under severe deprivation at all times. Frantically the mother

wandered outdoors in search of sustenance for her remaining seven children, but her findings had been very miserable.[25]

The plight of these women was worse than that of two-parent families. The ghettoized Jews were quickly reduced to destitution and hunger. The hardships soon began to show their effects. People died of starvation and epidemics; many had no means of subsistence. In September 1940, after the Germans agreed to provide the ghetto with a loan of three million Reichsmarks, the situation improved somewhat. Rumkowski introduced a large-scale welfare system that provided a hundred thousand ghetto inhabitants with relief at a level that allowed them to survive, albeit with difficulty.[26] Because few women were working at this point, most of them presumably managed to make ends meet with the help of welfare support.[27] The abrupt upturn in male mortality, however, left many women widowed. Furthermore, the number of husbandless women increased when the deportations to the labor camps began. Many men, having been promised that their pay would be forwarded to their families, joined these deportations in the hope that they could provide for those they left behind in the ghetto. The promise was kept, but the wages hardly sufficed for the most rudimentary standard of living. Subsequently, when these payments became a burden on the community budget, the families of men working outside the ghetto were among the first to be deported, as were the welfare recipients (including a high percentage of women).

The watershed in women's employment in the Lodz ghetto was crossed in 1942, with the first deportations to the Chelmno extermination camp. At this point, the entire ghetto was transformed into a vast labor camp. Almost everyone, including women and children up to the age of ten, was quickly mobilized for labor; everyone else was deported. By April 1942, virtual parity existed in employment: 31,286 women and 32,985 men held jobs. The number of women working climbed steadily, and by late 1943, working women outnumbered working men by 43,346 to 30,436.[28] On March 1, 1944, there were 43,081 working women in the ghetto (54 percent) and 30,239 working men (38 percent; children composed the remaining 8 percent). At that time, the ghetto population stood at 79,638. Most of the women and men (53,412) were employed in factories and workshops.[29] On June 17, 1944, there were 42,486 working women and 28,945 working men out of a ghetto population of 76,476. Thus, 55.5 percent of the workers were women.[30]

The data show a radical change in the women's occupational profile. For decades, few women had accepted work outside the home because this behavior was socially unacceptable. The ghetto conditions, however, forced women to take part in the general struggle for survival. From 1942 on, they had no choice, because the Germans regarded anyone not working as unproductive and consequently superfluous. Therefore, labor became a prerequisite for survival. The result was that more than 90 percent of the women remaining in the ghetto after the 1942 deportations, took jobs and formed a substantial proportion of the ghetto labor force. This development modified the status and circumstances of women and affected other spheres of life.

The workshops, or *ressorts,* as they were known in the ghetto (an abbreviation of the German word *Arbeitsressorte*), were established at a rapid pace. The need to employ as many people as possible in order to spare them from deportation led to the formation of many ressorts in unsuitable quarters. Therefore, most of these facilities offered harsh physical conditions, including overcrowding and poor ventilation. These circumstances were aggravated in the winter by extreme cold, because of lack of fuel.

The ghetto Jews' main problem was hunger. It was German policy to starve the Jewish population. The provisions that reached the ghetto never neared the minimum needed for physical survival, and the food provided was of the poorest quality. The workers suffered in particular, because they had to toil as they starved; many collapsed on the job. Many workers reported to their jobs even when ill, otherwise they would have faced dismissal and the loss of the meager food ration that they were given at work. The work hours were long and exhausting, starting at eight hours per day and, beginning in February 1943, increasing to ten hours daily, from seven in the morning to five in the evening.[31] The workers were given a one-hour break for food, at which time they received the main component of their diet: a thin, watery soup that barely staved off starvation.

In late 1942, German involvement in ghetto affairs increased substantially, especially in the supervision of the workshops. Many German committees flocked to the ghetto, inspected the ressorts, monitored production, and placed orders. Jewish labor was meticulously supervised. The starving workers had to meet tight production deadlines, on which their fate and that of the ghetto depended. The labor itself was arduous and often done on a piecework basis. Most ghetto factories turned out apparel and textiles, chiefly for the German military authorities. The majority of the working women were employed in this industry.[32] For example, women were especially predominant in the millinery works, where 80 percent of the 1,400 workers in June 1942 were women;[33] in a rubber raincoat factory, where 410 of the 468 workers in May 1942 were women;[34] in a lingerie and dress workshop, where 800 women worked in May 1941;[35] and in carpet and straw workshops.

Author and journalist Yosef Zelkowicz, an employee at the ghetto archives and a contributor to the Lodz ghetto *Chronicle,* wrote a series of articles on the ressorts, their working conditions, and production. On May 15, 1942, Zelkowicz wrote about the upholstery workshop where women sewed mattress and pillow covers. Their remuneration was a paltry 86 pfennig per mattress cover. The conditions in this workshop were harsh. The employees, bloated with hunger, worked two shifts. In the first few months of 1942, the extreme hunger caused production to diminish by half. If in the past the seamstresses had sewn three to four mattress covers per day, they barely managed to complete one cover now, and their wages plummeted commensurately. Many women brought their young children to work, for lack of alternative care arrangements. These women shared their meager soup ration with their children, thus spreading their insufficient portions among several mouths.[36]

Rivka Kwiatkowski-Pinchasik describes the hardships of the toiling women in her short stories: "Their weary faces, their red, sleep-deprived eyes, and the endless peeling and peeling; women whose husbands have been sent off to hard labor, women whose children have been taken from them, alone, humiliated, despairing. Their clothes are torn and threadbare, their clogs damp and rotting. And with their scarred and stained fingers they peel frost-damaged potatoes, day after day, month after month."[37] Many women worked at home. *The Encyclopedia of the Lodz Ghetto,* written in the ghetto in 1943–1944, reports the following under the entry "Home Worker":

> Most home workers are women who accept work from the various ressorts. They receive their daily bowl of soup and their wages on a contract basis. Some of these women are the anonymous heroines of the ghetto. In addition to their paid labor, they keep up their housework, not only for the sake of their decimated families but also some-

times for non-relatives who have joined the family. Thus they safeguard the last vestiges of family life and, in many cases, the lives of the ill, the exhausted, and others whom the terrible conditions have placed at risk.[38]

The tradition of paying women less then men continued in the ghetto, and in the new social and demographic situation it had critical results. The disparity in women's and men's wages stood out on the early date of December 1939, when the community began to pay those mobilized for forced labor. Men were paid 1.75 marks a day and women only 1.25 marks. Sometimes the men's work was more strenuous, but women were paid less even when they worked on equal terms with the men, as often happened.[39] In a circular dated February 15, 1942, sent by Rumkowski to the offices and the ressorts, the Judenaelteste stipulated the remuneration of daily workers.[40] Women working outdoors earned 2.2 marks while men working outdoors earned 3 marks. Women working indoors received 1.7 marks while men received 2.5 marks.

The salary was computed on the basis of a sixty-hour week. Weekly remuneration for the unskilled ranged from 17.82 to 21.06 marks for men and from 15.12 to 17.82 marks for women; weekly remuneration of skilled workers was 22.68–24.30 marks for men and 21.06–22.68 marks for women.[41] The inequity in salary between men and women aggravated the situation of many one-parent families, where women were the only breadwinners.

Women at Home and in the Family

During the first two years of ghetto life, until the women became fully integrated into the labor force, most women were homemakers who attended to their families' needs—a formidable, strenuous task under ghetto conditions. The main concern was to feed the family. Starting in early June 1940, food distribution was handled in centralized fashion by the supply department of the Judenrat, and weekly parcels of commodities were doled out at a price. Various distribution centers were opened, where food rations were allotted.[42] Ghetto inhabitants, chiefly women and children, spent hours in line. Yosef Zelkowicz describes this aspect of ghetto life in one of his articles:

> She [the mother] has to join the bread queue at six a.m. The dairy cooperatives open at eight, and she must take her place in line there too

in order to obtain a quarter of a liter of milk for her little child. After that, she scurries from house to house to sell the milk to those with means for three pfennigs in order to redeem vouchers for soup at the public kitchen. . . . Later, she must run from neighbor to neighbor in order to prepare a pot of food. . . . When everything is ready, she stands at the gas burner for hours on end, blowing on the fire so that the soup in the pot will boil. In the meantime, night has fallen.[43]

The ghetto houses were dilapidated and poorly maintained. Most lacked such basic sanitary facilities as toilets and running water. Any cleaning or washing operation required tremendous effort.

The plight of the ghetto women worsened considerably after they joined the labor force. Women worked eight to ten hours in factories and offices and returned home after this exhausting day to begin their housework. An anonymous young woman describes in her diary the anguish that the gnawing hunger brought to her family:

> March 11, 1942 . . . I ate all the honey. I am selfish. What will the family say? I'm not worthy of my mother, who works so hard. Other than the hard work at the ressort, she also works for a woman who sells underwear in the street. My mother looks awful, like a shadow. She works very hard. When I wake up at twelve or one o'clock at night she's sewing, and at six a.m. she's back on her feet. I have no heart, I have no pity. I eat anything that lands near me. . . .
>
> March 14: . . . Father gave me his soup this morning. . . . Mother brought the bread ration from the ressort. I don't know what she lives on. She works the hardest and eats the least.[44]

To feed their families, women often improvised and invented "food" from the diverse commodities that they were given, some of them inedible. For example, the food rations included relatively large quantities of ersatz coffee, from which women would bake "cake."[45] There was much room for inventiveness with potato peels. To obtain this prized commodity at times of particular shortage, one had to present a doctor's prescription. In his diary entry of March 20, 1944, Oskar Rosenfeld describes a woman who was lucky enough to obtain two kilograms of potato peels after enormous effort:

The moment the mother stepped into the house, the children leaped upon her bag with the peels. Now it was time to work. They dumped the peels into a bucket, went down to the spigot in the freezing yard, and selected the peels that were suitable for use, and washed and cleaned them. At dusk, the tired children began to fall asleep in the middle of their work, but they had to continue. After the peels were washed, water was boiled in order to clean off the last bits of dirt. It was now midnight, and the housewife herself was spent. The two kilograms of peels have shriveled to half a kilo. Now she puts them in the grinder as if they were meat. . . . The mother has decided to prepare dumplings for the soup. . . . According to doctors, logical people and gastronomy experts in the ghetto, these things have nutritional value. Therefore, it would be a crime to forgo such a gift despite the monumental toil that it takes to achieve results.[46]

With the mammoth change in the lives of the ghetto women when they began to work full time, women became men's equals in bearing the burden of livelihood. When the women returned home, however, they resumed their traditional roles and carried the greater portion of the household burdens. The numerous textual sources that have survived from the ghetto period—diaries and literary works alike—show that women took for granted their continued obligation to do all the housework. They did not challenge this role, complain to their husbands, or ask them to take on some of the tasks. Few women imagined at this time that they even had the right to ask their husbands to share the burdens in the home.

With most family members at work, including children aged ten and older, the father's authority as the chief provider of the household was sometimes undermined, as was his status in the family. When a mother and children worked while the father did not—a situation that arose frequently—family tensions sometimes built up. Hunger and hardship were the main factors that affected interactions among family members. Some families nonetheless were united by hardship, maintained their integrity, and displayed great solidarity. Cases of self-sacrifice abounded, in which members of a family forfeited their food rations for an ill or weak relative or sold their food for medicine and the like. Oskar Singer describes a family in which the mother systematically gave up some of her food in order to strengthen her husband, whose physical condition was deteriorating. She sold all her possessions in order to buy medicine and nutritious food for him. Although she weakened herself gravely, she was unable to save her spouse.[47]

Many families went out of their way to eat at least one meal per day together, setting the table as they had in normal times and sharing their scanty rations. Some families symbolically marked the Sabbath and Jewish festivals by lighting candles, engaging in prayer, or cooking something more festive than usual. In many cases, the family structure and support did much to sustain the members' morale and struggle for survival. And in most cases, the living spirit in this struggle was the mother.

Elsewhere, however, family relations deteriorated, quarrels erupted, and family units dissolved. The Sperre of September 1942 left approximately fifteen hundred orphaned children in the ghetto. Rumkowski entreated senior officials' families to adopt them. The author of the September 22 ghetto *Chronicle* thought poorly of this idea, citing the breakdown of the family: "Here, in the ghetto, after three years of war, the concept of family has been erased from the lexicon, with a few exceptions. Any remaining illusions on the subject were completely dispelled after the deportation. . . . Instead of families, there are only 'family housing collectives' where all food commodities are weighed and doled out to family members, where strong family members deprive weaker ones of their food and set the stage for interminable family quarrels and conflicts."[48]

The quarrels had to do with the apportionment of food. Family members accused each other of unequal distribution and pilfering of rations. The various sources make it emphatically clear that women coped with hunger better than men. They exercised superior self-restraint, dividing their bread into daily portions, while many men frequently consumed several days' bread in one sitting. Women often showed greater responsibility than men toward family members, especially children. In his diary, young Dawid Sierakowiak describes clashes between his father and himself and between his parents concerning his father's behavior. On May 30, 1942, he wrote:

The internal situation at home is becoming extremely tense again. After two weeks of relative calm, during which Father divided his bread into equal daily portions, he became spoiled again. Last Thursday and again yesterday he devoured his whole loaf of bread, and today on top of it, half a kilo from Mom and Nadzia. . . . Today he bought our ration of sausage and ate over 5 dkg of it on the street (Nadzia was with him), so everyone's share of sausage was short. He has also managed to borrow 10 dkg of bread from Nadzia already. (Stupid girl. I take my portion of bread to the workshop with me now.) Father also bought his whole portion of meat today, and, having received a liter of whey at the dairy store for a whole family, he cooked it only for himself and lapped it all up. As a result, the rest of us have nothing to cook at home anymore, and are going to bed without supper.[49]

Sierakowiak's mother customarily shared her bread with his father, but the father did not appreciate this. His mother was deported to the extermination camp in the Sperre of September 5, 1942, as Dawid relates: "After the doctors announced the verdict, and when Mom, unfortunate Mom! was running like mad around the house, begging the doctors to spare her life, Father was eating soup that had been left on the stove by the relatives hiding in our apartment, and he was taking sugar out of their bag! True he was kind of confused, questioned the policemen and the doctor, but he didn't run out anywhere in the city; he did not go to any friends' connections to ask for protection. In a word, he was glad to be rid of a wife with whom life had become harder and harder, thus pushing Mom into her grave."[50]

The author and poet Yeshayahu Spiegel, in a short story entitled "Bread" that he wrote in the ghetto, describes a similar situation: a father who consumed his children's rations for lack of self-restraint. The father could not forgive himself for what he had done and spent many days mourning, praying, and smiting his breast in contrition. The mother also did not forgive him. From then on, she was beset with worry until she hit on the idea of sewing small cloth pouches where she might conceal the rations; thereafter she carried the pouches on her neck wherever she went.[51] In several cases, such quarrels led to divorce. The minutes of court hearings on conjugal affairs in 1944 evoke a bleak picture of serious crises in family relations. Women complained of the degradation, beatings, and abuse that had become their daily lot. Husbands refused to share their food rations and wages with their wives. Arguments often took place in front of the children, to their serious detriment. The men, in turn, complained that their wives had neglected the house, failed to tend to the cooking, and refused to take care of them.[52]

Overcrowding was another serious problem. Most families lived under grievously cramped conditions, sometimes with eight or ten people in a room. Population density was 40,105.7 people per square kilometer in May 1940 and 42,586.4 in January 1942, when the ghetto population reached its peak.[53] Normal conjugal life was difficult to maintain under such circumstances, and family tension often ensued.[54] Hunger and disease caused most of the women to stop menstruating and rendered many men impotent. This factor, coupled with unwillingness to bring children into a world so unstable and cruel, contributed to the low birth rate (only 2,306 children were born in the ghetto). These realities also contributed to the small number of marriages in the ghetto.

Nevertheless, many memoirs describe love affairs and relationships in the ghetto. Love flourished in the youth movements; however, the youngsters' situation was quite different from that of the older married adults, whose love lives suffered under the burdens of breadwinning, grueling labor, and starvation.

In sum, the realities of ghetto life created extreme situations. In this terrible ordeal, women seem to have outperformed men in the imperatives of endurance and adjustment, as manifested, inter alia, in their lower mortality. Ghettoization marked a significant departure from the prewar period in the lives of the Jewish women. The role of women in work and production in the ghetto was almost equal to that of men; ghetto inmates of both sexes shared the burden of supporting their families. Despite the equal duties, however, women were not given equal rights. The differences in women's status manifested themselves in lower wages and, above all, in their position in family life. Women assumed a large number of harsh obligations; while holding down arduous factory jobs, they had to shoulder all the other onerous burdens of housekeeping and care of family members. In this regard, men and women did not apportion the burden equally.

Women were unrepresented in the senior administration of the ghetto, which included factory managers and directors of Judenrat departments. In the lower echelons, women held important positions in several occupations. There were many women teachers and principals, some women physicians, and a few hospital department directors. Nevertheless, no woman attained any of the highest-ranking positions. Women were involved in cultural activities that were important in sustaining morale. But most culturally active women were young and at the beginning of their careers, so their impact in creative circles was slight.

Perhaps the plight of women in the Lodz ghetto, and the desperate situation of mothers, can best be summed up by the description from Dawid Sierakowiak's diary of his mother's deportation to the extermination camp:

> Dear mother, my tiny, emaciated mother who has gone through so many misfortunes in her life, whose entire life was one of sacrifice of others, relatives and strangers. . . . My poor mother who always accepted everything so willingly and who invariably continued to believe in God, showed them, in spite of extreme nervousness, complete presence of mind. With a fatalism and with heartbreaking, maddening logic, she spoke to us about her fate. She kind of admitted that I was right when I told her that she had given her life by lending and giving away provisions, but she admitted it with such a bitter smile that I could see she didn't regret her conduct at all, and although she loved her life so greatly, for her there are values even more important than life, like God, family etc. She kissed each one of us good-bye, took a bag with her bread and a few potatoes that I force on her, and left quickly to her horrible fate.[55]

Notes

1. Rafael Mahler, *Yehudey Polin beyn shtey milhemot ha-'olam* (Polish Jewry between the two World Wars: A socioeconomic-statistical history) (Tel Aviv: Dvir, 1968): p. 35.

2. Announcement No. 60 of June 12, 1940, posted in the ghetto by M. C. Rumkowski. Yad Vashem Archives, Zonabend Collection, 034/67.

3. The Jewish population was presumably slightly larger than this, because some Jews were not recorded in this census. The data, however, reflect reality rather faithfully and are indicative of the size of the population. The data are culled from the album of the ghetto statistics department, vol. 1, Photographic Archives, Yad Vashem, FA-74 (1): p. 8.

4. Rivka Kwiatkowski-Pinchasik, *Be-yadayim ne'emanot* (In reliable hands). (Haifa: Haifa Books, 1964): p. 87.

5. Lodz ghetto *Chronicle,* vol. 1 (Jerusalem: Yad Vashem, 1987): p. 194.

6. Yeshaya Trunk, *Lodzher geto: A historishe un sotsialogishe studie* (Ghetto Lodz: A historical and sociological study) (New York: Yad Vashem and YIVO, 1962): p. 181.

7. Lodz ghetto *Chronicle,* vol. 1, pp. 365–451; Lodz ghetto *Chronicle,* vol. 2, pp. 1, 91, 161, 215, 255–378. The table is based on data in Trunk, *Lodzher geto,* p. 238.

8. Abraham Melezin, *Przyczynek do znajomosci stosunkow demograficznych wsrod ludnosci zydowskiej w Lodzi, Krakowie i Lublinie podczas okupacji Niemieckiej* (Particulars about the demographic processes among the Jewish population of the towns of Lodz, Kraków, and Lublin during the German Occupation) (hereafter cited as "Demographic processes") (Lodz: Wydownictwa centralnej zydowskiej komisji historycznej przy ck zydow polskich, 1946): pp. 21–22.

9. Yad Vashem Archives, JM 1157.

10. Lodz ghetto *Chronicle,* vol. 1, p. 405.

11. Ibid., vol. 2, p. 215.

12. Ibid., vol. 1, pp. 365, 388, 405, 452; vol. 2, p. 1.

13. Yad Vashem Archives, JM 1157.

14. Lodz ghetto *Chronicle,* vol. 2, p. 307.

15. Icchak (Henryk) Ruhin, *Zydzi w Lodzi pod Niemiecka Okupacja, 1939–1945* (Jews in Lodz under the German Occupation) (London: Kontra, 1988): table on page 376.

16. Melezin, "Demographic processes," p. 17.

17. Lodz ghetto *Chronicle,* vol. 2, p. 378.

18. Ibid., vol. 3, p. 785.

19. Ibid., vol. 3, pp. 157–158, 502, 504.

20. Melezin, "Demographic processes," p. 25.

21. Bina Garnzareska-Kadri, "Temurot ba-matsav ha-homri shel shikhvot ha-'ovdim ha-yehudim be-Polin (1930–1939)" (Changes in the material circumstances of the Jewish working classes in Poland, 1930–1939), in *Gal-Ed* (historical collection on Polish Jewry), vol. 9 (1986): table on p. 169.

22. The census data, as produced on July 12, 1940, by the ghetto statistics department, are available in the statistics department album of the Photographic Archives, Yad Vashem, FA-74 (1): p. 8. See also JM-1157, Yad Vashem Archives, and Trunk, *Lodzher geto,* p. 93.

23. See Friedrich Uebelhoer's document of December 10, 1939, which makes the first explicit reference to the establishment of the ghetto, *Dokumenty i materialy do dziejow okupacji Niemieckiej w Polsce, Ghetto Lodzkie* (Documents and materials of the history of the German Occupation in Poland), A. Eisenbach (ed.) (Warsaw, 1946): pp. 26–31.

24. Statistics department album, vol. 2, Photographic Archives, Yad Vashem, FA-74 (2).

25. Sara Selver-Urbach, *Lu yehi boqer* (Would it were morning), "Monseset" (Tel Aviv, 1987), p. 170. The title of the chapter is a play on Genesis 10:26, the name of a nation which, in Hebrew, also means "courtyard of death." An English version is available in Sara Selver-

Urbach, *Through the Window of My Home: Memories from the Lodz Ghetto* (Jerusalem: Yad Vashem, 1986).

26. Announcement No. 123 of September 20, 1940, Yad Vashem Archives, Zonabend Collection, 034/129.

27. One of the Judenrat offices was a special secretariat for complaints and requests, headed by Renia Wolk. This office received thousands of letters from ghetto inhabitants. Hundreds of these letters, from 1940 and 1941, are kept in the Yad Vashem Archives (06/46/1-3). They illustrate with great clarity the social and economic distress and decline that were the regular portion of the Jewish inhabitants of the ghetto. A large number of these letters were written by women in distress.

28. Trunk, *Lodzher geto,* p. 340.

29. Melezin, "Demographic processes," p. 25.

30. Trunk, *Lodzher geto,* p. 340.

31. Leaflet no. 1 of February 1943, which stipulates the working hours at the ressorts and offices. Yad Vashem Archives, Zonabend Collection, 034-527.

32. In March 1944, 33,284 women worked in this industry, mostly in textiles and related occupations. See Melezin, "Demographic processes," p. 25.

33. Yozef Zelkowicz, "At the Millinery Ressort," June 8, 1942, Yad Vashem Archives, Zonabend Collection, 034/650.

34. Yosef Zelkowicz, "At the Rubber Raincoat Ressort," Yad Vashem Archives, Zonabend Collection, 034/647.

35. An article in *Gettozeitung,* the ghetto newspaper, nos. 11-12 of May 18, 1941, Yad Vashem Archives, Zonabend Collection, 034/595.

36. Yosef Zelkowicz, "At the Upholstery Ressort," Yad Vashem Archives, Zonabend Collection, 036/640.

37. Kwiatkowski-Pinchasik, *Be-yadayim ne'emanot,* p. 111.

38. *Encyclopedia of the Lodz Ghetto,* in the information bulletin of Beit Lochamei Haghetaot— Ghetto Fighters' House Archives, no. 8 (1955), p. 20.

39. Yad Vashem Archives, Zonabend Collection, 034/606.

40. Ibid., 034/510.

41. Trunk, *Lodzher geto,* p. 164.

42. Announcement no. 52, June 2, 1940, Yad Vashem Archives, Zonabend Collection, 034/59.

43. Yosef Zelkowicz, *Ba-yamim ha-nora'im ha-hem* (In those nightmarish days), notes from the Lodz ghetto (Jerusalem: Yad Vashem, 1995): p. 60.

44. Yad Vashem Archives, 06/52.

45. Lodz ghetto *Chronicle,* vol. 3, p. 174.

46. Diary of Oskar Rosenfeld, March 20, 1944, notebook 10, Yad Vashem Archives, 06/105.

47. Oskar Singer, "Der Tod von Litzmannstadt Getto" (Death of the Litzmannstadt [Lodz] ghetto), July 27, 1942, Yad Vashem Archives, Zonabend Collection, 034/613.

48. Lodz ghetto *Chronicle,* vol. 2, p. 236.

49. Dawid Sierakowiak, *The Diary of Dawid Sierakowiak: Five Notebooks from the Lodz Ghetto*, Alan Adelson (ed.) (New York: Oxford, 1996): p. 177.

50. Ibid., p. 219

51. Yeshayahu Spiegel, "*Malkhus Geto*" (Ghetto kingdom) (Lodz: Kleine Bibliotek Verlag, 1947): pp. 28–30.

52. Minutes of divorce court hearings in 1944, Beit Lochamei Haghetaot—Ghetto Fighters' House Archives, no. 862.

53. Melezin, "Demographic processes," p. 14.

54. Selver-Urbach, *Lu yehi boqer*, p. 179.

55. Sierakowiak, *The Diary of Dawid Sierakowiak*, pp. 219–220.

CHAPTER NINE

Gender Issues in Diaries and Testimonies of the Ghetto
The Case of Warsaw

Dalia Ofer

At the end of 1941, as part of his great effort to study and synthesize two and a half years of war life, Emmanuel Ringelblum, the initiator of the underground archive *Oneg Shabbat* in the Warsaw ghetto, asked Cecilya Slepak (perhaps best known for her translation of Dubnov's Jewish history series into Polish) to undertake a research project on Jewish women in Warsaw since the beginning of the war. Slepak deliberately selected her subjects from different social classes and occupations, including upper-, middle-, and lower-middle-class women, as well as some who barely made a living before the war and refugee women who had either been deported to Warsaw or escaped to the city. Among those interviewed were professional women with university educations, women who before the war had assisted their spouses in family-run stores, small business owners, and housewives.

The main goal of Slepak's study was to understand the metamorphosis of women from the eve of the war through the different stages of ghetto life until the spring of 1942. In the first part of each interview she asked about her subject's life before the war. She then moved on to the siege and bombardment of Warsaw and to everyday life after the occupation. The central part of the interview was dedicated to the move to the ghetto, its impact on everyday life, and the struggle for survival in the ghetto.[1]

This rich source presents women's voices in two senses: it consists of interviews with women, and the interviews are interpreted by a woman. Another important source of information are the ghetto diaries written by both men and women. In these diaries, gender issues are always presented in the general context of overall events, both before and during the ghetto period. At times the diaries touch on these issues directly, but more often they are raised indirectly in discussions of children, efforts to obtain food, the seizing of men and women for forced labor, and the escape of men to the East (which left women behind to care for their children). Such accounts reveal the vulnerability and vitality of women and their reactions to new and difficult realities. An analysis of the individual stories highlights both the commonality and particularities of women's social role, and their fate in the ghetto.

In this chapter, I shall discuss Slepak's conceptualization and conclusions. An understanding of gender issues as seen through her eyes and by the authors of the ghetto diaries also provides insight into their perceptions of other social issues connected to the ghetto.

Jews in Warsaw: Demographic Background

In 1939, the Jews comprised some 10 percent of the general population of Poland, which numbered approximately 32 million people. Warsaw, the largest city, was home to about 1 million people. In October 1939, the Jewish population of Warsaw numbered 359,000, or about 30 percent of the total.[2] In terms of employment, 47.6 percent of Warsaw Jews were self-employed, 37 percent were workers, and 12.7 percent had professional or white-collar occupations (teachers, doctors, lawyers, and so on). The remaining 2.7 percent of the workers were unidentified.[3] Of the first two groups, 46.8 percent were occupied in industry and 32.7 percent in commerce. The number of Jewish women who were employed outside their homes was small. For every 100 working men there were, on average, 31.5 working women, some 24 percent of the general Jewish workforce. In some fields, however, such as the textile and paper industries, Jewish women accounted for more than half the total workforce (55.2 and 63.5 percent, respectively). In the fashion industry, Jewish women comprised 43.6 percent of the female workforce. Women's salaries in most industries were half or less than half of men's.[4]

Many women of the lower middle class assisted in family-run businesses or worked in small stores. Although the number of professional women is not known, it was small; most educated women did not work after marriage. Those professions in which women were more visible were education (both Jewish and general), medicine (most women in this field were hospital nurses), and social work.

In April 1941, the number of Jews in the city reached a peak of 450,000, an increase of 57,000 since February 1940. The increase resulted from massive deportations in the neighboring smaller cities and towns,[5] and from the influx of Jews from the western borders and villages. Following the Nazi occupation, the number of women in Warsaw's Jewish population greatly exceeded that of men, as many men fled from the city, and others were deported to the forced-labor camps. (Many young people, most of them men, escaped to the East by crossing the borders to Vilna and to the Soviet-occupied zone.) On October 28, 1939, the Jewish population of Warsaw consisted of 164,307 males (46 percent) and 195,520 females (54 percent). Among those between the ages of sixteen and fifty-nine, the division was 104,273 men (44 percent) and 131,784 women (56 percent).[6] On January 31, 1942, there were 157,410 men and 211,492 women for a total Jewish population of 368,902. Whereas the numbers of boys and girls under age ten were almost equal (25,759 boys versus 25,699 girls), in the group aged ten to nineteen the number of girls slightly exceeded the numbers of boys (35,283 boys versus 39,790 girls). The great decrease in the number of men was seen in the group between the ages of twenty and twenty-nine, which included 19,747 men (35 percent) and 36,041 women (65 percent). This deficit in the number of men was less marked in the group between the ages of thirty and thirty-nine, which consisted of 29,155 men (41.5 percent) and 40,892 women (58.5 percent). This deficit of men persisted, although it decreased for the older segment of the population.[7]

The War and the First Year of Occupation

A number of women interviewed by Slepak described at length their reactions to the outbreak of war and the siege of Warsaw.[8] Women who were caught outside the city generally made a great effort to return home. All of them were aware of the basic political situation. During the siege, many of the women were occupied within the individual apartment buildings, which housed anywhere between a few hundred and a thousand people. The tenants of each building put together first-aid kits according to Civil Guard instructions, and some women mentioned that they had made use of the kits during the air raids. The women also described play groups and other activities that they, along with neighbors, initiated for the children in the houses. Some wondered how they had managed to overcome their fear and act efficiently during such difficult hours. The feeling of camaraderie expressed in their recollections is one explanation, although many noted that being active was itself a way to avoid hysteria.[9]

Several women (two of them professionals) reported that they had not been satisfied with the duties they performed in their own buildings. They had volunteered in the wider public sector, by offering help to refugees, mending uniforms for the soldiers, setting up public shelters, providing various kinds of aid in the hospitals, and even digging trenches.[10] For example, B.[1] (Slepak's subjects are known only by their initials), a nurse and a physical education teacher, reacted to the political tension in the spring of 1939 by joining the Civil Guard, whose task was to guide and assist the population in a national emergency. By the time the war broke out, she was second in command of her section of Warsaw. When her superior, a Polish officer, left the city, she took on his responsibilities. One of her first actions was to allocate a large public hall for the refugees so that basic care could be provided for them.[11]

The last days of heavy bombardments and shelling (September 25–27) were particularly traumatic. Many women described how their houses were directly hit and how they had to battle fire in order to escape, leaving their belongings—and sometimes wounded tenants—behind. A women whom Slepak called G. reported that after these bombardments, she was in shock for some weeks and did not even recall the Nazi entrance into the city. Other women, such as H., described their bewilderment when they saw the ruins of the city (25 percent of Warsaw's buildings had been hit by shells) and the looting that took place a day before the Germans entered. In contrast, the orderly march of German soldiers, they remarked ironically, was quite impressive.[12]

A recurring theme in many interviews was the discussion between husbands and wives on whether to leave Warsaw. The Polish government had issued a call to all young males to move eastward and form a new military line, and the men understandably wished to flee the advancing Germans. Women had to consider the prospect of being left alone, with all its attendant uncertainties. Some married women without children chose to flee with their husbands, while others decided to wait for the men to arrive at a safer destination before following.[13] Some young women offered to marry young men merely for the sake of crossing the border with them. To this end, they contributed all their savings.[14]

Testimonies and diaries describe the increased burden placed on women in the wake of occupation. Because men were at higher risk of being deported to forced-labor camps or being picked up for a day of hard physical labor (accompanied by abuse on the part of German or Polish supervisors), they tried to avoid being out of doors during daylight. As a result, the women became responsible for many chores, such as standing in line for bread or water, obtaining permission to retrieve personal belongings from confiscated homes, or repairing damaged businesses.[15]

Many families had lost their homes, and many men had lost their jobs. Thus, they needed to stay in public shelters, along with refugees arriving from other parts of Poland. The dislocation, lack of privacy, and shortages disrupted the prewar routines of couples and their children. Hence, the search for an available apartment, or for relatives or friends who could and would take them in, was a central activity for many in the first weeks after the occupation.[16]

Those who did not lose their homes often experienced systematic looting on the part of Germans and *Volksdeutsche* (ethnic Germans living in Eastern Europe). There was a prevailing sense of fear and uncertainty. Jews who lived in densely Jewish neighborhoods were more exposed to the looting and the risk of being seized in the streets. Rich people, however, were more likely to be "visited" by a high-ranking Nazi preparing a new home in Warsaw.[17]

Various portraits of energy, courage, and endurance emerge from Slepak's interviews. Her subjects were not timid about venturing outdoors without the armband marking them as Jews. They were ready to rely on Polish neighbors and friends to help them pass as Gentiles and also counted on their "good" (Aryan) looks. They did not hesitate to go to the authorities to demand or beg for help. If their husbands were taken for forced labor or arrested, for instance, they would attempt to get them released—by standing for hours or days in front of the office of Adam Czerniakow, the head of the Judenrat (Jewish Council), and sometimes even confronting the Gestapo. Needless to say, they were willing to work hard. Many testified that the new situation, in which the men were more often endangered and abused than the women, filled them with courage and a sense of mission. It was now their responsibility to take care of the family.

Thus the line between men's and women's roles became somewhat blurred. The numbers demonstrate the change in the role of women. In October 1939, of the 155,825 Jews employed in Warsaw, more than 33 percent were women, compared to some 24 percent before the war.[18] Nonetheless, most women still saw themselves primarily as helpmates. "I have to try hard, to use all means to make a living for my husband's sake and for my own" is a sentence often quoted by Slepak.[19]

Slepak also notes the sense of responsibility shown by daughters toward their parents. She describes C.[1,] a young woman of twenty-three, who had married a few days before the war broke out. After a traumatic failure to cross the Soviet border and join her husband, who had escaped to Vilna, she came back to her parents' home. She found that their house had been looted by the Germans and that all their food supplies—the family owned a restaurant—had been confiscated. She began to buy and sell all kinds of merchandise. She also started an affair with a Volksdeutsche who sublet a room in her parents' flat. This relationship enabled her to obtain the products she needed to reopen her parents' restaurant. In this way, she told Slepak, she and her parents had lived in relative comfort until their removal to the ghetto. This young woman's extramarital relationship (with a non-Jew, at that) was a clear flaunting of convention. Slepak, however, does not note any disapproval on the part of the woman's parents, who were able to stay in business because of their daughter's connections.[20]

Perez Opochinsky describes a similar departure from moral convention. He tells of the daughter of a Hasidic Jew, whose husband was killed in the Polish army in the first weeks of the war. This woman hosted in her apartment a number of men of less than respectable reputation. She fell in love with one of them—a thief—and married him. Her father, distressed, fell ill and died.[21]

Not all women changed their lifestyle after the occupation. Some had enough money and connections to reopen their businesses; others were even able to expand their enterprises and find new economic activities. G., an upper-middle-class housewife, had enjoyed extensive household help both before and after the outbreak of the war, and her social life had centered on meetings with friends in cafes and a weekly visit to the hairdresser and manicurist. In September 1939, she became active in all the Civil Guard tasks mentioned above, greatly aiding her neighbors. On September 21, her home received a direct hit from a shell, and the destruction left G. in a state of shock. But when things settled down, she concluded that life was too precious not to enjoy each moment. She did not want to change her style of life; she liked the way she spent her time, and her social relationships were important to her. Nevertheless, she felt that she should assume some responsibility for those poorer then herself who had suffered more from the war. Thus, she arranged for special space and services for refugees in her building, contributing money as well as time.[22]

Some regarded their efforts to continue customary activities as a means of boosting morale in the face of a frightening reality. Rachel Auerbach, a young journalist who lived in Warsaw before the war, describes in her memoirs the regular Sunday afternoon gatherings of friends and acquaintances in the home of Cecilya Slepak, which continued after war broke out. Auerbach attended one such meeting in November or December of 1939. The Slepaks at this time still had a nice apartment and their original furniture—even a piano—and Auerbach reported that the guests were served a noodle cake, which was unusual because of the food shortages. This social tradition lasted until the spring of 1940, when the Slepaks were forced to leave their home.[23]

Various other middle-class women, such as C., a corsetiere, managed to return to a more or less normal life following the occupation, until the move to the ghetto. Although C.'s store was hit by a bomb, she was able to salvage most of her merchandise and raw materials and reopen the store in a new location. Because she looked Aryan, she did not put on an armband. Her good relations with Polish customers and neighbors helped her carry off the impersonation; occasional customers did not suspect that she was Jewish.[24] Her situation was, to be sure, unlike that of G., who belonged to a different social class and had displayed a far different—basically hedonistic—attitude toward life. C.'s assertiveness grew out of the sheer necessity to make a living. She could not rely on her ailing husband (who had been severely beaten by the Germans) to provide for her family. Thus, her courage and risk taking seemed eminently reasonable in the context of the struggle for survival. G., in contrast, had the wherewithal to engage herself—perhaps uncharacteristically—in altruistic deeds.

Adam Czerniakow's diary speaks of women's courage and persistence,[25] but Haim Aharon Kaplan—a teacher in Warsaw who wrote a detailed diary from the beginning of the war until the mass deportation—strikes a more tra-ditional pose when he disparages women as weak, dependent on men, and in-clined to hysteria. Yet his own descriptions yield a different picture. His wife, for example, waited on line for hours, despite being ill, in an attempt to obtain permission to retrieve belongings from their confiscated home. When her efforts failed, she and two other women (one of them her Polish housekeeper) sneaked back to the house and took things out on their own. Moreover, Mrs. Kaplan, not her husband, was the one who carried the cash with her in days of danger.[26] Kaplan also describes men who took on such "women's chores" as buying food, but this activity did not signify a major change in their self-perception; they still expected to be served their evening meal.[27]

In reporting the responses of women to their new responsibilities, Slepak sometimes uses active verbs ("she succeeded," "she decided") and sometimes phrases indicative of a more passive attitude ("she understood," "she had to"). Two different types of self-understanding are implied. Some of the women took on responsibility and exercised initiative out of sheer necessity. Others found their situation challenging and used it to fulfill hidden potential. The first group clearly represented a traditional perception of women's responsi-bilities to care for men and family. Even when circumstances forced a change in their activities, these women remained essentially the same.[28] In contrast, women of the second group displayed a break with tradition. Even those who explained their motivation in traditional terms hinted at a new independence and willingness to depart from convention. An example of the second group is B., a dietitian who was in charge of the soup kitchens for the refugees. Only during the war and because of her particular situation, Slepak wrote, could this woman's potential be truly expressed. Her worldview did not allow her to be a passive participant during a difficult time. Thus, she initiated useful activities and reported being satisfied with her work, despite the long hours it re-quired.[29]

Many women became involved in house committees in their apartment buildings. These committees provided social services and support for poor families and refugees in the building. Opochinsky describes women who cooked and fed the children of poor families in their homes or who assumed the responsibility for keeping children occupied once the schools were closed. Men and women had the same voting rights on the house committees.[30] In the beginning it was rare for a woman to head such a committee or even be a member, but by the end of 1941, women's involvement and leadership had become more and more common, in part because men were weary of the extra commitment. One of Slepak's informants described power struggles within the house committees. Certain women, she reported, were interested in becoming head or secretary of the committee for reasons of power or status—whereas she just wanted to be of assistance.[31]

In the beginning of 1940, Emmanuel Ringelblum made the following terse notes:

> Women's perseverance—the main providers. Men don't go out. When [a man is seized for forced labor], the wife does not let go. She runs after [the kidnappers], she screams and cries "please, Mister"—she is not afraid of the soldiers. She stands on the long line—some are seized to work. Women of upper class sit in offices and answer questions. The beautiful hats have disappeared. In wartime [women] put on scarfs. When there is need to go to the Aleja Szucha [the Gestapo] the daughter or wife goes; in the worst scenario they stand and wait in the hallway. . . . Many have given up help at home and take care of their household, unlike in the pre-war days. The women are everywhere since the [men] have been taken to all sorts of work. . . . When a husband escapes and his wife has to be the sole provider. [Women] who never thought of working [out of their homes] are now performing the most difficult physical work.[32]

Ringelblum was aware of changes not only in the role of women but also in their sense of self. He refers with sensitivity to the issue of appearance, viewing the changes in dress as both a reflection of the transition in self-perception and an accommodation to the new reality. Women were careful not to be noticeable, not to catch the eye of a policeman, or a Nazi.[33]

The Move to the Ghetto

After the shock of the occupation of September 1939, the move to the ghetto was the greatest crisis for women and for the Jewish community in general. Beginning in March 1940, the Nazis started to mark off the Jewish quarter in the northern part of the city. They put up posters indicating that the quarter was an "infected area" (*Suechensperrgebiet*) and began to build a fence around it, funded by the Judenrat. In August 1940, the Nazis announced that Warsaw would be divided into three separate areas, for Germans, Poles, and Jews. The anxiety of the Jews who lived outside the Jewish quarter grew considerably, especially when families in the wealthier sections began to be driven out of their homes.[34]

In the weeks between October 28 and November 15, 1940, some 118,000 Poles were told to move out of the streets designated for the ghetto, and 138,000 Jews were ordered to move in. About 30 percent of the city's population was herded onto 2.4 percent of the land. Even after the ghetto was established, its borders kept changing: some of the streets with better apartment houses were taken out of its confines, and many families had to move more than once.

During the expulsion to the ghetto, Jews were allowed to take with them only what could be carried by hand. Furniture and other household goods had to be left behind or given to friends for safekeeping. This caused much pain, especially to those women whose activities and identity were centered in their home.[35]

All the women in Slepak's research describe the move to the ghetto as the greatest disaster for them. It was barely a year since some of them had recovered from the ruin inflicted on their homes during the bombings. Others had stayed in refugee centers for weeks and feared becoming homeless again.[36] Once the move to the ghetto became certain, the women were faced with the challenge of coping with an even harsher daily reality than they had anticipated.[37]

The ghetto was a closed confine whose gates were guarded by Polish, German, and Jewish police. This fact not only intensified the Jews' sense of isolation but worsened their economic condition. All economic enterprises on the Aryan side were unavailable to them, and food prices shot up. The shortage of basic food items and the lack of employment brought many who had somehow made a living in the previous year to the brink of disaster. To some extent, social differences became irrelevant. At the same time, however, the dichotomy between rich and poor became even sharper.[38] The ghetto population as a whole constantly moved toward impoverishment, and therefore most of the middle class disappeared. However, a small upper class emerged, consisting partially of people who had been rich before the war and partially of the new rich, who conducted business with the Germans or engaged in smuggling.

Because women significantly outnumbered men in the ghetto, single mothers represented a sizable portion of the population. But this group had few opportunities to find employment or otherwise earn money. Although the number of women in the labor force grew during the first year of the war, the ghetto offered fewer opportunities for employment at a time when personal needs grew even further.

In September 1941, there were 33,762 registered workers in the ghetto, of whom 18,979 were self-employed and 14,783 were salaried employees. Of the salaried employees, 61 percent (9,100) worked in institutions (including the Jewish police, the post office, and all social services including health). Most employees were men. An unknown number of women were engaged in trade. Yisrael Gutman estimates that some 30,000 people were either in forced-labor camps, working for the Germans in industries and other physical work in Warsaw, or employed in ghetto "shops" producing goods for the German army. (The shops, developed by German and Polish entrepreneurs, were run by Jewish managers and staffed by Jews laboring under harsh conditions.) Thus, some 65,000 people in the ghetto were employed. About half the inhabitants (200,000–250,000) had no regular income and were essentially starving to death. Most of the unemployed were women and children,[39] who were forced to sell their meager goods or beg for food or money.[40] Many of the unemployed, including most refugees, had hardly anything to sell.

Small Trade

Trade, as Ringelblum describes, generally involved women selling their household goods in exchange for food. This was a good market for Poles and other non-Jews who wanted to buy things at a low price. Trade was conducted in the area close to the cemetery and in a number of small alleys that had been run down even before the war.[41] Women would either sell their own belongings or would accumulate goods from neighbors and friends and sell them for a piece of the profit. Trading was not altogether safe. Anyone in uniform might approach the sellers and confiscate the goods or demand a bribe. The women also had to be wary of peddlers or hungry strangers who might grab their goods. Those women and men who served as intermediaries were in a somewhat better position. They did most of their trading door to door; in the hierarchy of small traders, they were a step up from the bottom.[42]

A number of women in Slepak's report speak of selling their household belongings, either immediately after moving to the ghetto or later, when other means of supporting themselves had been cut off. Selling personal goods was clearly a last resort. And for some, it served as a spur to more dramatic action to improve their condition.

C., the corsetiere who had lost her store, at first tried to sell whatever merchandise she had at home. Then she started to sell some of her belongings. Realizing that this was not a long-term solution, she looked for a way to get the merchandise from her ruined store, which had been sealed. She crossed over to the Aryan side disguised as the Polish maid of a Jewish family, bribed the gatekeeper of the house in which the store was located, and entered through the back door (which had been left unsealed by mistake). Back in the ghetto, however, there was little demand for her corsets. Therefore, C. began to cross over to the Aryan side on a regular basis, each time adopting a different disguise. She gradually renewed her business contacts with old customers, received orders, prepared them at home, and went back to deliver them, staying on the Aryan side for a few days each time before returning with food for her family, neighbors, and friends. In this way she made a living until the fall of 1941, when going over to the Aryan side became punishable by death.

C.[1], the young woman who worked in her parents' restaurant, helped her parents sell a good deal of furniture and other expensive belongings in order to set up a new restaurant in the ghetto. When her volksdeutscher lover left her, she and her parents were unable to keep the restaurant going. They sold off personal goods until the daughter decided to turn to smuggling.[43]

F., whose husband had been an artisan (possibly a shoemaker) both before the war and in the first year of the occupation, sold pairs of shoes in the market and to individuals. After her husband fell ill, she began to sell household items, although the market was flooded and the demand was low. Then, in early 1941, F. became pregnant. Reinvigorated, she realized that selling her possessions would never provide the bare minimum for her family, and she, too, turned to smuggling.[44]

Selling such small items as candies and cigarettes in the streets or in the shops was another way for women to make a living. Even women who worked in the shops, earning a few zlotys a day, tried to supplement their meager income through such sales.[45] For the most part, the women described here worked as individuals in the ghetto. If they crossed the ghetto walls to purchase goods to be sold in the ghetto, or for some other reason, they relied on past connections with Poles and on their Aryan looks. Their knowledge of Polish, together with intuition and ingenuity, were crucial for their success.

Smuggling

Under the official policy the Nazis allocated a meager supply of food to the ghetto of a few hundred calories per person per day. In December 1941, for example, the supply reached the low point of 184 calories per person. However, the actual allotment of food that reached the ghetto was a few times higher, owing to the smuggling of food into the ghetto. "Who knows," wrote Opochinsky, "if some day the smuggler will not be given a monument. He risked his life and saved a large number of the Jews of Warsaw from starving to death."[46] According to Gutman, smugglers were divided into two groups. The first was composed of organizers who operated in gangs and hired people to work for them. Because big money was involved in this traffic, these people became rich and quite powerful in the ghetto. The second group contained individuals who were willing to deliver goods to and from the ghetto out of sheer necessity.[47] Slepak's subjects seemed to form a third group of smaller traders and smugglers, mostly women who brought back more food than they needed for their own families. Such women renewed contact with Aryans they had known socially or through business relationships. Unlike the larger-scale smugglers, they operated either as individuals or as a team with their husbands.

Smuggling was a dangerous game, requiring patience, courage, and ingenuity. At times, being a woman had its advantages. Women did not hesitate, for example, to play on men's gallantry, or to appear poor and unhappy in order to receive sympathy. They were ready to risk their safety up to a certain point, counting on their intuition to warn them of danger and maintaining their composure and alertness. Often, however, they experienced chilling fear, especially when on the brink of getting caught.

F.[1] was an educated women—she had a Ph.D. in philology and had worked for an export firm in Lodz as a translator in four languages. In 1940, after the Lodz ghetto was formed, she and her sister escaped to Warsaw with the aid of a Polish friend. Unable to find a job that would use her language skills, she decided to learn to be a manicurist. She also engaged in trade on a small scale and managed in this way to make a living until the move to the ghetto. For a while she continued with small trade, first in the ghetto with her personal belongings. Then she brought bread, meat, and dairy products from the Aryan side into the ghetto. Each morning she waited long hours by the ghetto fence to find a chance to cross. She wore no armband and often changed her attire when crossing back and forth. Furthermore, she was inventive in hiding the products she smuggled into the ghetto. One day she was almost caught by two different agents. She saved herself with a combination of feminine charm and a bribe of three hundred zlotys (a considerable amount of money) but decided henceforth to give up smuggling.[48]

G., as previously described, was a woman of the Jewish upper middle class. During the first year in the ghetto, she lived on the "better" street. In December 1941, however, the ghetto was made smaller and she was compelled to leave her apartment and sublet space from another family. It was only at this point, she told Slepak, that the real war began for her. Her husband's business was ruined, he was unable to earn any income, and their savings were rapidly disappearing. Worried about suffering from shortages, G. started to use her social connections, both among the ghetto's upper middle class and with Poles on the Aryan side, to start trading in expensive furniture, pianos, art, Persian carpets, and the like. She would get up early in the morning and visit potential sellers in the ghetto and would then move to the Aryan side, where she met her Polish friends with an itemized list. This new enterprise went well; G. was able both to maintain her high standard of living and to support her sister (who had been forced to leave all her wealth on the Aryan side). She was also active in social aid, contributing money and time to refugee centers and inducing friends to join her.[49]

A number of common themes emerge from these stories. C., C.[1], and F. were all from a middle-class and law-abiding background and were driven by extreme circumstances into the illegal and dangerous world of trade. C. and F. were motivated by a sense of obligation as wives and mothers, F.[1] by the sheer need to survive. As C. put it, "The most important thing is life. I was ready to risk myself in order to live, but to get into danger in order to die did not make any sense." C. had a general rule and a clear goal, and she managed to escape the ultimate danger. Others did not. After December 1941, when being on the Aryan side became a capital offense for Jews, the number of Polish bounty hunters increased. This was a great blow to small-time smugglers. F., for example, was captured by a Pole, brought to the police, and put to death.

G. represents a somewhat different case. Her wealthy background provided her with a much wider web of social contacts and access to more valuable goods. Like the other women, she operated as a loner in the risky business of crossing over. Her stated motivation was the will to keep up her standard of living and to help her sister. As reported by Slepak, however, G. also took great pride in her ability to cope successfully with challenges and risks.

Opochinsky's survey on smugglers in the ghetto focuses on the large and well-organized operations, with special emphasis on the role of the intermediaries.[50] He also describes in detail the teamwork between husbands and wives. Women would stand with wagons in the ghetto marketplace, selling their wares and at the same time watching out for German police or other unwanted persons. From his account it is clear that women performed difficult physical work connected to smuggling. Young and old women would, for a few zloty, carry heavy loads on their backs. There were women pushing baby carriages loaded with sacks of flour, and girls on bicycles rushing by with heavy bundles.

Opochinsky also notes the social environment of the smugglers, their folklore, and the role of women in this context. He describes the underlying tension between the wives of smugglers who were the sellers and women buyers, as reflected in their small talk about the hardships of daily living, particularly the difficulties of providing food for children. Opochinsky also describes the relationship between husbands and wives involved in the smuggling, with the woman counting and holding the money while the husband kept a lookout. Despite competition, tension, and feuds, a certain level of cooperation among the smugglers was mandatory, and a sense of solidarity existed among them.[51]

Professional Women in the Ghetto

Of the sixteen women interviewed by Slepak, five were professionals—a higher proportion than was to be found in the general Jewish community. Two of them, B.[2] and Bir., were dietitians, B.[1] was a nurse and teacher of physical education, R. was an agronomist, Bt. a librarian, and F.[1] a philologist. B.[2], Bir., and R. used their professional skills during the first three years of the war, by working to organize public soup kitchens and establish a children's library. R., the agronomist, worked in a self-help organization in her hometown of Grochov. After arriving in Warsaw, she took part in TOPOROL, the organization for agricultural training. (TOPOROL initiated the cultivation of small plots of land in the ghetto, so that vegetables could be grown and distributed.) Diaries also refer to the important role of women in the health services, particularly as nurses (a special training program for nurses was established in the ghetto hospital) and as workers in the orphanages.[52]

Women participated in the planning and running of the soup kitchens and other aid institutions; however, they were not policy makers. They directed and worked in individual kitchens as cooks, waitresses, cleaning personnel, and the like. B.[2] and Bir. were on the supervising team, which operated from the central body that financed the soup kitchens, and Rachel Auerbach was the director of the kitchen at 40 Leszno Street.[53]

Most women and men had no experience in operating soup kitchens. An exception was Bir., who had worked in and supervised a workers' restaurant in Palestine and had worked in a kibbutz kitchen. Similarly, B.[2], a dietitian, was able to use her professional skills in the soup kitchen. Before the war, she had had trouble finding work in her field; now she served with great dedication, defining her job as a mission for the welfare of the Jewish community.[54]

Organizing the network of kitchens was a daunting task, given the scarcity of supplies, the number of people to be fed (about a hundred thousand in the beginning of 1942), the poor physical conditions, and the scarcity of professional staff. Good supervision was thus crucial. The first step was to offer basic courses to the workers on such subjects as nutrition, proper use of the equipment (of particular concern was the use of the minimum amount of coal or wood), and sanitation. Once the kitchens were in operation, supervision took the form of unannounced visits to the various kitchens and regular meetings with the directors, many of whom were women.

The directors' job was a difficult one. First, they had to use connections in order to acquire raw material and food. They were not always successful, and there were days when the kitchens could not operate for lack of supplies. In addition, the directors were also responsible for the proper running of the kitchen. The workers' personal cleanliness and tidy appearance were both deemed vital—cleanliness because of the prevalence of typhus and other diseases, and tidiness for reasons of morale. In some kitchens the workers even had uniforms and aprons that were washed regularly in a central laundry.

Not surprisingly, tension between the workers and the directors was common.[55] According to Auerbach, this tension came to the fore in the regular visits of the supervisors. They commented, for example, on the dirty cans and spoons used by those receiving food—something the workers could do nothing about. A far more serious cause of tension was the way food was distributed. People were assigned to a certain kitchen, where they handed in a coupon for each meal they received. Only those with coupons had the right to eat in a kitchen. But many others crowded in the entrance, among them young orphans who were not being provided for in any of the institutions and who waited for hours outside the kitchens in the hope of scrounging some leftovers or finding the opportunity to go through the garbage.

Auerbach describes these problems and the difficulties of enforcing rules aimed at allowing workers to enjoy some benefits from their work, while at the same time being honest and just in the distribution of the food. Clearly a great deal of power was connected with being even a worker in one of the kitchens, given the grave shortage of food.[56]

Soup was the food provided by the kitchens, and menu planning focused on putting together the most nutritious combination possible of whatever was available in the way of grains and vegetables (meat and milk products were almost nonexistent). Taste and texture were not overlooked. Memoirs by Auerbach and others speak of the efforts made to improve the taste and quality of the food. Nevertheless, the kitchens were of little help to the starving majority. They provided a crucial supplement for those who had some food of their own, but not enough to stave off starvation for those who did not.[57]

Were women more sensitive or more dedicated than men in managing the soup kitchens? We have no comparative analyses of kitchens run by men as opposed to women. Women's knowledge of home cooking was a limited advantage in running a large soup kitchen. According to Auerbach, Guzia, the cook at Leszno 40 (who had had a restaurant in Praga, a poor neighborhood of Warsaw), was proud of her skills, dedicated to her work, and labored to make a tasty soup. Yet her cooking habits did not accommodate the supervisors' demands for cleanliness. Many times she was insulted when she was told to change her apron or clean her nails, but she was unable to change her ways.

The sense of mission voiced by such kitchen supervisors as Bir., B.[2], and Auerbach was also expressed by other professionals, such as Bt. (the librarian) and R. (the agronomist). R. even noted, with some uneasiness, her feeling that she was deriving great satisfaction from her work even though the majority of the population was in deep distress.[58] Before the war, she told Slepak, she had been unhappy with her "narrow" work in a social service agency of the kehilla (the Jewish community). She recalled a colleague saying during the tense days of the summer of 1939, "I wish a war would start so that we could operate an extensive social aid program." When the war broke out she was in the early months of pregnancy, and she moved from Grochov to Warsaw to stay with her parents. Being pregnant did not deter her from devoting herself to aiding refugees; disregarding physical constraints, she walked in the bombarded streets carrying heavy loads for the refugee centers.

Following the occupation of Warsaw, she and her husband decided to return to Grochov. There she found her home damaged by the air raids. She spent long weeks making order out of the damage but then felt compelled to return to outside work. Soon she became a supervisor of the soup kitchen in Grochov. She had to walk seven and a half miles in each direction, but she was not discouraged. On the contrary, she reported, she was full of energy, "like a drunk person."

After being expelled from Grochov in December 1939, she, her husband, and their baby moved back to Warsaw. Unable to rent an apartment, they had to share a sublet with another family. "My situation," she told Slepak, "became more complicated. I had to find a way to function as a mother, a wife, and a professional worker." She did not give up but joined the communal kitchen organization in Warsaw, where she made a number of improvements.

The move to the ghetto opened even greater professional opportunities. When TOPOROL was established, R. was picked to head an agricultural school for teenagers who studied and worked in the small plots of the ghetto, seeking to improve the supply of vegetables. R. felt that they, too, had a mission that would help their fellows and would also change their own destinies.[59]

Women Workers in Shops and Industries

The industrial shops of Warsaw, where Jewish artisans and workers produced goods for German owners, turned out a variety of products: clothing for the army and high fashion for Germany's civilian market, leather goods, brushes, furniture and other wood products, tin cans, and many other items.[60] The shops, established during the spring and summer of 1941, employed 12,000–15,000 workers by July 1942.[61] Both the working conditions and the salaries—four to six zloty for a twelve-hour day—were deplorable. Opochinsky noted that the real draw of the shops was the 250 grams of bread distributed twice a day, along with three portions of soup and some ersatz coffee with saccharin and jam. The shops were also believed to offer a safe haven during the deportations of the summer of 1942—although in fact many shop workers were deported.

Of the women interviewed by Slepak, only F.[1], the philologist, worked in industry, having decided to quit smuggling after a close call with a Polish bounty hunter. In August 1941, she began working in a tin factory. She was paid six zlotys for twelve hours of work, of which one zloty went for a bowl of soup. The social environment of the place was difficult for her to deal with. Most of the workers were not Jewish, and there was a good deal of anti-semitism. Moreover, as the only educated woman, she was often harassed. In November she fell ill and lost her job.

In January 1942, on the brink of starvation, she was assigned to work in an ink factory in the ghetto. In this factory, too, most of the workers were women and many were not Jews. The Jewish workers were separated from the others, and everything they used (dishes, utensils, and so on) was marked in yellow. They were also paid less than the Polish women. F.[1] decided to supplement her income by doing manicures and other odd jobs for the nouveaux riches of the ghetto. A proud woman, she was determined not to rely on social aid in order to survive.

Opochinsky describes at length a shop that produced underwear. Some 80 percent of the workers were women.[62] The working hours were from seven in the morning until seven in the evening. Payment was by the piece, but the workers' efficiency was hampered by their being given more than one type of item to produce. The difficult working conditions, combined with fatigue and malnutrition, resulted in poor-quality merchandise. The worst days were those on which the shop did not have any orders. The women had to work the day in the shop because they were dependent on the bread and soup portions they received. But the hours dragged even more slowly than usual, and they were aware that when orders did arrive, their payment would be smaller than normal, as money would be deducted for the bread they had eaten.

In order to be in the shop by seven in the morning, working mothers had to get up at five to clean and care for their family. It was especially difficult to get up on freezing mornings, as warm clothes had long since been sold for food. While at work, the women worried about their children, who had been left alone. They feared random killing in the streets or by the walls of the ghetto. Despite their hunger, they saved part of their food for their children and thus they became ever weaker. Some 80 percent of workers in the shops died of hunger and typhus during 1941, but there were always others to replace the dead.

"It is easy to guess what happens to a mother when a child is under permanent danger of death," Ringelblum comments.[63] His notes speak of three- and four-year-old children passing through small holes in the ghetto walls to help smuggle goods. Not for nothing did the women in the shops worry about their children.

Some Concluding Remarks

I elected to work on diaries and personal documentation of the ghetto period, seeking to confront a direct and intimate viewpoint. I was also looking for the different voices of men and women as they described the reality of their lives. I soon discovered that references to certain issues, such as motherhood, male-female relationships, husbands and wives, and attention to beauty, were quite scattered. The diaries were dominated by the tremendous endeavor to carry on everyday life, although their authors also dealt with the wider public arena and the general meaning of events.

In my search for new materials, I came upon Cecilya Slepak's work. I realized immediately that I had not created a topic unthought of by the Jews under Nazi occupation. On the contrary, in their endless efforts to understand and document human conditions during the years preceding the final deportations, they realized that unless one understood the condition of women, one would not understand the general human condition. Slepak's report was so imposing and the personalities of the women so impressive that I found myself trying to walk in their footsteps, so as to understand their internal world and arrange what I was able to learn in a more general context. The diaries turned out to be a support or countertext to the individual interviews.

What emerges from these sources is a will to live so strong that at times it caused women to set aside convention. Women most often explained their coping strategies as natural reactions rooted in their duties to husbands, children, parents, or siblings. Some realized that the war had opened new opportunities for them and discovered capabilities they never thought they had. (This might be true generally of women on the civil front, under the stress of war.) Yet this discovery, too, was part of the basic framework of the fight for survival, both the women's own and that of their loved ones.

Some women were ready to manipulate sex for survival. The diaries and Slepak both refer to prostitution in the ghetto and to the establishment of sexual relationships in order to gain the protection of a powerful male. Some women were willing to play on the pride of men as protector of the "weaker sex." The mood of "eat, drink, and be merry" prevailed among the ghetto's upper middle class. In this context, ghetto diaries tell of men who established relationships with younger (sometimes married) women and neglected their own wives. Some women were ready to develop such a relationship for their own protection. Sometimes their husbands acceded to these extramarital affairs, hoping that they too would thereby gain safety. The other side of these stories was the suffering of the neglected wives and children, who were left with no protection.[64]

Most of the authors of the diaries and the women in Slepak's report were from the middle class that somehow managed to make it. They worked, they had some belongings to sell, and, until the date of interview or the last diary entry, they were still carrying on. When deportation started in July 1942, however, most of the distinctions between classes disappeared. The poorer population of the ghetto was the first to be deported, but most of the rest followed. Although the Germans were willing to delay the deportation of working men in the shops, most women were unable to obtain even this limited protection. The number of women who were connected to the shops decreased drastically. Some mothers who worked in shops were forced to hand over their children to save themselves.[65]

Nazi cruelty and brutality toward women were mentioned in many diaries as a symbol of the ultimate barbarity. Nazi behavior, as reported with dismay in the diaries, made a mockery of all cultural norms. When the deportations started, the abuse of mothers and children left speechless even the longtime witnesses of Nazi cruelty.

Notes

1. Emmanuel Ringelblum, *Last Writings,* vol. 2 (Jerusalem: Yad Vashem, 1992), p. 122 (henceforth Ringelblum 1992). An English translation of Ringelblum's notes was published in 1958 as *Notes from the Warsaw Ghetto: The Journal of Emmanuel Ringelblum,* ed. Jacob Sloan. This edition (henceforth Ringelblum 1958) is a selection from the Yiddish version that was published in 1948 as *Blater Far Geszichte.* Cecilya Slepak's research is to be found in the Ringelblum Archive (AR I/49), divided into a number of bands. Her subjects are identified only by an initial; where the same letter refers to more than one subject, I have added superscript numbers according to their order of appearance in the Yad Vashem Archive (YVA), and I use Yad Vashem signatures JM/217/4 and JM/215/3 (henceforth Slepak, followed by a band number).

2. Ruta Sakowska, *Ludzie z dzielnicy zmkniete* (Warsaw: PWN, 1993) p. 29, table 1.

3. Raphael Mahler, *The Jews of Poland between the Two World Wars: A Socio-Economic History on a Statistical Basis* (Tel Aviv: Dvir, 1968), p. 54.

4. Bina Garnazarska-Kedari, "Changes in the Material Situation of the Jewish Workers in Poland, 1930–1931" (Hebrew), *Gal'ed* 9 (1986), p. 169, table 8.

5. Yizhak Arad, Yisrael Gutman, and Avraham Margaliot (eds.), *Documents on the Holocaust* (Jerusalem: Yad Vashem, 1981), pp. 173–178 (henceforth DOH, 1981).

6. Anonymous, "Early Day—Course of Events, 1939–1940," in *To Live with Honor and Die with Honor: Selected Documents from the Ghetto Underground Archives "O.S." (Oneg Shabbat),* ed. Joseph Kermish (Jerusalem: Yad Vashem, 1986), p. 137 (henceforth Kermish 1986).

7. Sakowska 1993, p. 33, table 3.

8. G., aged thirty-eight, a housewife and mother of a thirteen-year-old girl, who is described as nouveau riche (Slepak, band 3); B.[1], aged forty-eight, a nurse and physical education teacher who studied in Berlin after World War I (Slepak, band 1); H., aged thirty, who was "very pretty—an Aryan look," from the lower middle class, and who worked in the stocking department of a large export enterprise but lost her job when the war broke out (Slepak, band 1).

9. G. (Slepak, band 3); Aharon Kaplan, *The Warsaw Diary of Chaim A. Kaplan,* ed. and trans. Abraham I. Katsh (New York: Collier Books, 1973), p. 45.

10. B.[1] (Slepak, band 1); B.[2], an unmarried dietitian (Slepak, band 3).

11. B.[1] (Slepak, band 1); H. (Slepak, band 1).

12. G. (Slepak, band 3); H. (Slepak, band 1).

13. For example, D., aged twenty-nine, was a cashier in an office where her husband was an accountant; C.[1], aged 23, was married a week before the war broke out. Her husband, a dental technician, left for Vilna and sent an emissary to cross the border with his wife, but they failed and she returned alone to Warsaw to her parents' home.

14. Perez Opochinsky (a member of the *Oneg Shabbat* archive), *Sketches from the Warsaw Ghetto* (Hebrew) (Tel Aviv: Hakibbutz Hameuchad, 1970), pp. 10, 18, 21; on the flight to the East, see also Kaplan 1973, pp. 70–71, 77. Kaplan did not discuss the issues men-

tioned earlier but cited the "great flight," which he (quoting others) estimated to have involved approximately 1 million Jews. The actual number was probably much smaller, not even reaching five hundred thousand.

15. Kaplan 1973, p. 43; See Slepak, band 1, on C., aged thirty, a lower-middle-class corsetiere, whose story is described in more detail later in this chapter.

16. Slepak, band 1; Kaplan 1973, pp. 44, 67; Ringelblum 1958, p. 40.

17. Kaplan 1973, pp. 46, 69; Ringelblum 1992, p. 96.

18. This estimate is based on the table of population and employment in Kermish 1986, p. 137 n. 7. I subtracted the number of men between the ages of sixteen and fifty-nine (104,273) from the number of those employed (155,825), which gave me the lowest possible number of employed women (51,555). Because not all the men were employed, the number of working women was actually higher.

19. See, for example, Slepak, band 1; F., age forty-two (Slepak, band 1). F. was from the lower middle class. Her husband was a shoemaker and she, a mother of three children, sold single shoes in the market. Her husband was caught one day in the street. When he refused to go for forced labor, he was beaten heavily and wounded severely. She obtained his release, after which he stayed home and could not work. See also *The Warsaw Diary of Adam Czerniakow: Prelude to Doom,* ed. Raul Hilberg, Stanislaw Staron, and Josef Kermish (New York: Stein and Day, 1979), pp. 88, 92–93, 102–103, 122, 162–163, 184–186, 202, 204–205, 214 (henceforth Czerniakow 1979).

20. Slepak, band 1.

21. Opochinsky 1970, pp. 11–12.

22. Slepak, band 3. See also Opochinsky 1970, pp. 47, 91–92.

23. Rachel Auerbach, *Warsaw's Testaments* (Hebrew) (Tel Aviv: Sifriyat Hapoalim, 1985), pp. 54–49.

24. Slepak, band 1.

25. Czerniakow 1979, pp. 92–93, 102–103, 108–113, 120–121, and passim. On the same issue, see Kermish 1986, p. 146 n. 7.

26. Kaplan 1973, pp. 16, 21, 42–45, 47.

27. Ibid., pp. 51, 55, 59.

28. In describing C., Slepak used active words; for F., she used a more passive language. I assume that this is the language the women themselves used in telling their stories to Slepak; if it is Slepak's choice of words, it is an indication of her perception of these two different women.

29. Slepak, band 3.

30. Opochinsky 1970, pp. 47–52; on equal voting rights, see p. 36. See also "A Description of Life in an Apartment House in Warsaw, Gesia St. 19" (anonymous) in Kermish 1986, p. 149.

31. Slepak, band 18.

32. Ringelblum 1992, pp. 51–52.

33. Ibid., p. 83.

34. For a detailed description of the stages in the planning and implementation of the ghetto, see Yisrael Gutman, *The Jews of Warsaw, 1939–1943: Ghetto, Underground, Revolt* (Bloomington: Indiana University Press, 1982), pp. 48–61.

35. On the move to the ghetto and the great panic among the Jews, see Ringelblum 1992, pp. 162–168; Kaplan 1973, pp. 209–218.

36. B.[1] described how painful it was to be in the shelter for refugees and how she and her husband missed their own place after a friend took them in. D. also described the difficult days in the refugee center after their house was destroyed in the bombing (see note 13). Ringelblum noted, "I heard that one person had to move seven times because of the changes in ghetto boundaries" (1992, p. 179).

37. K., a forty-two-year-old housewife, helped her husband in the family-owned stationery store (Slepak, band 1). She described how she lost her home and the store when the ghetto was established, and her difficulties in finding a home. She and her husband were arrested in April 1940; K. stayed in jail for a few months, was released and returned home. Her husband, however, was deported to Dachau and died there. An account of G.'s experiences (Slepak, band 3) is given in the text.

38. Ringelblum (1992, p. 208) wrote that Warsaw was divided into three sections. "The aristocracy in the following streets—Leszno, Elektoralna, Chlodna—the converted in Sienna and in all the rest, the poor souls."

39. Gutman 1982, p. 77.

40. Ringelblum 1992, p. 243. Rachel Auerbach wrote about a little boy who regularly visited her soup kitchen to beg for food. Asked "Where is your mother?" he replied, "In the street," in a tone of deep despair. See Rachel Auerbach, *In the Streets of Warsaw: 1939–1943* (Hebrew) (Tel Aviv: Am Oved, 1954), p. 24.

41. Opochinsky 1970, pp. 139–140.

42. A story is told by a thirteen-year-old boy about his mother, who received a food parcel from his brother in Russia in December 1940. They were very happy, he recounted, but then the mother had to sell most of the food in order to get the few zloty she needed for her trade. "From a Diary of a Boy" in Meilech Neustadt, *Destruction and Rising: The Epic of the Jews in Warsaw* (Hebrew) (Tel Aviv: Labor Union, 1946), p. 191.

43. Slepak, band 1; C.[1], in Slepak, band 1.

44. Slepak, band 1.

45. F.[1] (Slepak, band 1).

46. Opochinsky 1970, p. 142. See also the poem "Little Smuggler," by the Jewish Polish writer Henrika Lazobet, quoted in Gutman 1982, p. 436 n. 25; see also Auerbach 1954, pp. 36–39. Auerbach ended her piece on the smugglers, written on June 11, 1942, with the following sentence: "All honors to the unknown smuggler, the brave fighter on the walls of the besieged city" (p. 39).

47. Gutman 1982, pp. 67–68.

48. Slepak, band 1.

49. Slepak, band 3.

50. Opochinsky 1970, pp. 139–152.

51.   Ibid.; see also Auerbach 1954, pp. 36–39.

52.   On the medical services in the ghetto, see Charles G. Ronald, *Courage Under Siege: Starvation, Disease, and Death in the Warsaw Ghetto* (New York: Oxford University Press, 1992). On the school for nurses, see pp. 72–75; on the shortage of nurses, pp. 86–88; M. Lasky, *The Life of the Jews in the Warsaw Ghetto: Memoirs of a Doctor* (Hebrew) (Jerusalem: Shoah Library, n.d.).

53.   On the beginning of the soup kitchens, see Auerbach 1985, pp. 63–65; Ringelblum 1994, pp. 40–42, 70–71, 133–134.

54.   Slepak, band 1; Slepak, band 2.

55.   Auerbach 1985, pp. 92–94, 97.

56.   See Auerbach's description on the new management of her kitchen from the early days of the deportation (Auerbach 1985, pp. 109–112).

57.   Ibid., pp. 75–76; Auerbach 1954, pp. 22–23.

58.   Slepak, band 2.

59.   Slepak, band 2.

60.   Gutman 1982, pp. 72–77; Opochinsky 1970, pp. 177–191.

61.   Isaiah Trunk, *Judenrat: The Jewish Councils in Eastern Europe under Nazi Occupation* (New York: Macmillan, 1972), p. 81.

62.   Opochinsky 1970, pp. 184–191.

63.   Ringelblum 1992, p. 278; see also Mary Berg, *Warsaw Diary* (Hebrew) (Tel Aviv: Tversky, 1948), p. 64.

64.   Auerbach 1985, pp. 110–112. Avraham Levin, *Warsaw Ghetto Diary* (Hebrew) (Tel Aviv: Hakibbutz Hameuchad, 1969), p. 104.

65.   Levin 1969, p. 104.

PART III

Resistance and Rescue

For Jews, survival itself was a constant act of resistance, because the Nazis had targeted them for extinction.

The first stage of the Third Reich's anti-Jewish policies, which were applied in Germany in 1933 and subsequently in all the countries occupied by the Nazis, was the identification and labeling of Jews through registration, armbands, and yellow stars. Then Jews were deprived of their livelihood and savings: they were expelled from their occupations and professions; their shops, factories, farms, and trades were confiscated; and their capital, savings, and wealth were expropriated. As a result of these policies, Jews lost the resources to meet their basic needs for food and housing. They were also excluded from civic, cultural, and social life: Jews were forbidden to move about freely, to use public transportation, to sit on park benches, to eat in restaurants, and to attend concerts or the theater. Their children were barred from the public schools. Their contact with the world was further curtailed through curfews, restricted times for shopping, and the Nazis' confiscation of bicycles and radios.

From the outset, many Jews tried to resist these Nazi edicts—by setting up secret schools for their children, hiding family valuables or asking non-Jewish friends to hold them, transferring ownership of their businesses to non-Jews to avoid confiscation, holding clandestine cultural events, or simply violating some orders (for example, by hiding a radio in the basement). Each of these activities was illegal and punishable by death. These illegal activities endangered not only the individual who dared to break the rules but also his or her family or neighbors, because the Germans used the system of collective punishment in the occupied areas.

In the ghettos of Eastern Europe, as we have seen in Part II of this book, the list of illegal activities was detailed and endless. Almost any attempt to preserve the patterns of the Jews' former lives was illegal. Leaving the ghetto was also prohibited and very dangerous. Mothers who crossed the ghetto borders to find food for their children, and fathers who returned from a forced-labor detail with some bread hidden in their pockets, were considered smugglers and risked severe punishment and death. A rabbi who conducted a prayer service, a teacher who held classes in her home, and a leader of a youth group who taught Hebrew songs, were all knowingly engaging in illegal activities.

Nevertheless, both individuals and organized groups consciously chose to violate the Nazi laws. They were not only trying to survive; they were also defying the Nazis by retaining their dignity and humanity.

These were conscious acts of resistance. Although some scholars would consider this concept of resistance too broad—because it encompasses the instinctive behaviors of those who were simply struggling to live—we contend that these activities were also motivated by conscious attempts to defy the Nazis and to thwart their goal of depriving Jews of their humanity. In "Living on the Aryan Side in Poland" (Chapter 11), Lenore J. Weitzman argues that the crucial element in defining resistance is the motivation or intent of the actor. If an individual is trying to thwart, defy, subvert, outwit, or otherwise resist the aims of the oppressor, then he or she is engaging in resistance.

Bronka Klibanski (Chapter 10) begins this section of the book with a fascinating chronicle of her dangerous work as a courier for the underground youth movement in the Grodno and Bialystok ghettos. The ghetto revolts that took place in Eastern Europe in the last stages of the ghettos' existence, led mostly by the Zionist youth movements in cooperation with the Bund and the Communists, had the goal of maintaining Jewish honor. They had no hope of destroying the Nazis or sabotaging their war effort. But they wanted to resist the Nazis by fighting for the sake of human dignity and Jewish honor. These aims are illustrated in Klibanski's inspiring memoir.

The motivation of those who tried to escape from the ghettos and to pass as non-Jews on the Aryan side was different, but some of them were also engaged in resistance and rescue. Lenore Weitzman (Chapter 11) examines the overwhelming odds and dangers faced by Jews who were living on the Aryan side, most of whom were women. A minority were recruited by the Jewish underground to act as couriers for the resistance, but most were individuals who simply decided to defy the Nazis by passing. They risked tension-filled lives to save themselves and others and to survive as witnesses to the Nazi crimes.

Jews also became part of several different types of organized resistance movements. In addition to the underground movements in the ghettos, some Jews joined the armed partisans in the forests of Eastern Europe. Others worked with the many nationalistic anti-Nazi underground movements in both Western and Eastern Europe. The armed resistance and sabotage of the partisan movement in Eastern Europe did not become organized until 1942, when it was assisted by the Soviets; in 1943 it became a part of the Red Army's offensive. Although many partisan groups were openly antisemitic and would kill the Jews who escaped from the ghettos to join them, some were willing to enlist Jews to help them carry out food expeditions and sabotage.

Nechama Tec (Chapter 12) provides an illuminating account of an unusual Jewish partisan unit, the Bielski *otriad* (detachment). In addition to the typical partisan tasks of fighting and sabotage, it undertook the difficult role of trying to rescue other Jews. From the very start, Tuvia Bielski, its leader, insisted that the unit be open to all Jews, regardless of age, sex, state of health, or any other condition. Under his leadership, the Bielski otriad eventually included more than twelve hundred individuals. Tec contrasts the treatment of women in the Russian partisan units with their unconditional acceptance in the Bielski otriad. If a woman did not have special skills—as a nurse or a cook— she was not likely to be accepted by the Russian partisans unless she became involved with an officer. In the Bielski otriad, however, all women were accepted and no woman was coerced into a relationship. Many women remained unattached, although those who were living with a male fighter who defended the otriad enjoyed better living conditions and privileges.

In Chapter 13 Renée Poznanski appraises the role of women in the French-Jewish underground. On one hand, she points to their strategic importance and to the dangerous missions they undertook. On the other hand, she notes that their contributions were later ignored in both the historical literature and the collective memory in France: their heroic deeds were less likely than men's to be honored after the war, and they were less likely to be recognized in the official histories of the French resistance. Poznanski attributes these omissions to the multiplicity of collective memories in France and to the nature of the roles that women played in the resistance—which were either extensions of their traditional roles in society (such as supplying members with food or lodging or false papers) or were intentionally invisible (such as transporting arms to the fighters). It is a compelling account of how history was constructed.

The final chapter in Part III (Chapter 14) is Yehuda Bauer's thoughtful analysis of the life and activities of an unusual woman, Gisi Fleischmann, the political leader of the Slovakian Jewish community during the Nazi era. Although her position alone makes Fleischmann unique, what is even more unusual is her daring attempt to rescue Jews by bribing Nazi officials. Bauer reveals the complex and dramatic story of her heroic efforts to negotiate with the Nazis to save the Jews of other countries—the only endeavor of this scope undertaken by a Jewish community in all of Nazi-occupied Europe—as well as the Jews of her own community.

CHAPTER TEN

In the Ghetto and in the Resistance
A Personal Narrative

Bronka Klibanski

The war reached my hometown of Grodno and the entire Bialystok region on June 22, 1941, with a surprise attack by Germany on the Soviet Union. From the outbreak of World War II in 1939 until that point, we had lived under Soviet rule.

With the German invasion and the collapse of the Red Army, the world we had known was shattered. Overnight, our lives became public property. We suddenly found ourselves deprived of basic rights, unprotected by any law. We applied all our energy and ingenuity to the cause of finding food. Parents found it hard to adjust to the situation, leaving the burden of earning a livelihood almost exclusively to the children. To bring home something to ease the gnawing hunger, we sought any kind of work. Each day gave birth to new decrees and new humiliations. Jews were excluded from bread rations. First we were ordered to wear an armband with a blue Star of David and then, a week later, the yellow star. We were forbidden to walk on sidewalks but had to goose-step in the gutter. We saw no logic in these laws, only cruelty for its own sake and a bizarre wish to degrade us.

After the initial shock, we lifted our heads once again. We tried to make light of the situation, but we had hardly become used to it when a new blow fell and the Jews of Grodno were ordered to move into two ghettos, Grodno Ghetto 1 and Grodno Ghetto 2.

I shall omit from my testimony my personal recollections of the life in Grodno Ghetto 2 and shall move to my activities in the resistance movement in Bialystok. These activities grew out of my prewar involvement in Dror, a socialist-Zionist youth movement. Members of the prewar youth movements, Zionists and others, began meeting in the Grodno ghetto. In early January 1942 Mordechai Tenenbaum, a leader of the Dror movement, traveled to Grodno from Vilna on false documents. He told us what happened to the Jews of Vilna— they were taken to the Ponar forest, where fifty thousand out of about sixty thousand of them were massacred over a period of six months. He believed that the Germans intended to murder all the Jews under their control, and he exhorted us to be alert to everything around us, to put up resistance in any way possible, and to hide and try to escape when the Germans came to expel us from the ghetto. He told us not to cooperate with the Jewish police and not to believe their promises. He mentioned that a similar proclamation had been read at an assembly of Zionist youth organizations held in the Vilna ghetto on January 1, before he left. Now, at long last, we understood why we had been segregated from the rest of the population and enclosed in the ghetto. The Germans had contrived this situation in order to round us up and murder us with greater efficiency. Nevertheless, we found this truth hard to accept; somewhere in our hearts nestled the hope that we would be excluded from this fate.

Meanwhile, the Dror movement began to organize for the tasks that Mordechai Tenenbaum had assigned us, and in February 1942 the liaison officer, Bella Hazan, summoned me to the Bialystok ghetto for a members' meeting. I sneaked out of the ghetto, boarded a train to Bialystok without papers, and arrived safely. At the ghetto, I found a kibbutz, a group of about twenty young people living communally. They had come from the Vilna ghetto, with the help of the Austrian Feldwebel (staff sergeant), Anton Schmid. After the meeting, I returned to the Grodno ghetto and my family.

In April of that year, a member of the kibbutz, Hershel (Zvi) Rosenthal, came to tell me that we had to make our way to the Dabrowa, Suchowola, Knyszyn, and Jasinowka ghettos, situated between Grodno and Bialystok, to arrange for our comrades there to attend the movement's seminar in the Bialystok ghetto at Passover, despite the dangers of travel. After the harsh winter, spring erupted in full splendor, filling our hearts with strength and joie de vivre. For a short while, we forgot the ghetto and all our troubles. Traveling by foot and occasionally by wagon, we managed to visit each of the small, quarantined ghettos without mishap, demonstrating to our comrades that despite all the prohibitions and perils, one could circulate when necessary and feel free. To this day, I am still puzzled as to how we achieved this goal.

The seminar duly took place, under the leadership of Frumka Plotnicka, who came from the Warsaw ghetto especially for this task. We left the meeting strengthened in our resolve. Some of the participants did not return to their ghettos; a few, including me, were asked to stay behind in the Bialystok ghetto to work for the movement.

I did not imagine then that I would never see my family again; I had left them without a moment's hesitation because I had been brought up to believe that the movement took precedence over everything else. About six months later, in November 1942, the Germans surrounded Grodno Ghetto 2 in a surprise move. Everyone in my family, along with all the other Jews in the ghetto, was taken to the death camps. Thus I was not at their side in the last and worst moments of their lives. Since then, I have searched for them in every mound of earth that covers the soil of the former death camps in Polish territory.

I learned what had happened to my family from Mordechai Tenenbaum, who came as an emissary of the Jewish Fighters' Organization and the National Jewish Committee in Warsaw, to organize the resistance movement in the Bialystok ghetto. He found that the ghetto had been closed by the Germans in order to prevent the entry of Jewish fugitives from the ghettos in the Bialystok area, whose liquidation had begun on November 1, 1942. After overcoming many obstacles, Tenenbaum reached Grodno Ghetto 1, where he learned about the liquidation of Ghetto 2 and the deportations of my family. In fact the entire Bialystok area, including Grodno, was being steadily purged of Jews. Spared for the time being was only the Bialystok ghetto.

Day and night the deportation trains raced westward from the Bialystok region, delivering their human cargo to the death camps of Treblinka, Majdanek, and Auschwitz. How much time remained for the more than forty thousand Jews in the ghetto of Bialystok who were still alive? The extermination facilities could not murder all of us at once, so we waited and hoped. Most of the Jews in the Bialystok ghetto were assigned to work for the German army; they sabotaged their output and adopted a business-as-usual pose that camouflaged the fear of death. Perhaps, by some miracle, they might be spared after all.

In November 1942, the organizational activities of the movement were stepped up in order to prepare for self-defense and resistance against the Germans when they came to liquidate the ghetto. We were racing to finish our preparations: organizing the defense of the ghetto, stockpiling weapons, training people, and uniting all the underground movements in the ghetto. Tenenbaum, who had witnessed the large-scale deportation that began in July 1942 in the Warsaw ghetto, warned us again that all the ghettos were to be cruelly liquidated.

In the Bialystok ghetto, I took part in all the movement's operations: I worked in the vegetable garden, recruited new members, organized cultural activities, and helped the comrades who were digging the large bunker at 7 Chmielna Street. When work in the vegetable garden ceased, I took a job in a textile factory. I suffered from malnutrition and eventually fell ill, but I recovered when Mordechai Tenenbaum somehow arranged for me to receive calcium injections.

Tenenbaum threw himself into his work. At first, he labored to reinforce the Dror movement and instill it with a fighting doctrine. He organized target practice for members, set up an explosives laboratory, lured members of other movements, and tried to unite all the separate movements of the underground, particularly the most important of them: the Communists, the Zionist youth movement Hashomer Hatsa'ir, and Dror. Tenenbaum's charisma, vivid imagination, broad cultural and educational background, organizational skills, and integrity captured the hearts of everyone who came into contact with him, and he soon became the head of the ghetto underground and later the leader of the uprising. He brought two invaluable assets: the vast, terrible experience that he had gleaned from the ghettos he had lived in or visited, and his staunch belief in the role of the underground to defend Jewish honor and human pride. Thinking about the future, he initiated an underground archive, by collecting, with the assistance of Zwi Mersik, testimonies, diaries, historical works, and documents of the Judenrat, and even copies of German documents regarding the extermination of the Jews. His concern was to leave evidence of the Jews' experiences in the ghetto and their struggle against the Germans. The archives were taken out of the ghetto and hidden with a Polish friend called Filipowski.

In spite of all the hardships—congestion, uncertainty, deprivation—Jewish life continued in the ghettos as long as the Germans allowed it to continue.

Every day, however, someone's life was cut short for some trivial reason—mainly to remind the Jews who was master. But the Jews displayed an extraordinary ability to adjust, and we continued to survive and endure and hope, despite all the disturbing omens and reports about the death camps. We followed events on the eastern front and were encouraged by the first defeats inflicted on the Germans by the Russians. After Stalingrad, we became more confident that the Germans would not win the war. Our hearts were filled with the hope that perhaps they would not succeed in exterminating the remaining Jews.

The acting chairman of the Judenrat, Ephraim Barasz, met repeatedly with the heads of the German administration in Bialystok to try to convince them that the labor of all the ghetto inmates was useful to the war effort. German military and economic committees visited the ghetto frequently to see for themselves how vitally needed the Jews were, to pocket bribes, and to calm the suspicious ghetto inmates. The Judenrat carried out the Germans' instructions faithfully. They encouraged the Jews to obey German orders, to work hard, and not to endanger themselves by taking action or even thinking of resistance.

In this way the web of illusion was spun in the Bialystok ghetto—the myth that hard work and cooperation with the Germans would spare the inmates from the fate of the other ghettos. The Germans, aware of these beliefs, exploited them cynically to calm the Jews' fears and quell the spirit of revolt. This complacency persisted even after the first Aktion, the roundup for deportation in early February 1943, and lasted until August of that year, when the final liquidation of the ghetto began.

By late 1942, most of the ghettos in the region had been liquidated; only the youth movements—a predominant part of the underground, which had become a force to reckon with in the Bialystok ghetto—tried to devise methods of resistance. Concurrently, small groups from the underground were sent or made their way to the forest to establish a base where the survivors of the uprising and downfall of the ghetto would continue the battle as partisans.

Only the young people, such as our group of Dror, felt that we could do something. We knew that we could not stop the mass murder, but we understood that we had the power to sabotage the Germans' efforts if we could overcome the Jews' paralyzing illusions; fight the complacency and silence that the Germans were intent on evoking; preach vengeance; and find ways of taking action and, perhaps, effecting rescue. We had to defend ourselves for the sake of human dignity. We were not concerned for our own lives; nor did we regard the lives of the few as holier than those of the masses. Under these circumstances, faced with genocide, the supreme value was not life, but the manner in which death was met. This attitude of resistance and revolt, espoused by Tenenbaum, became widely accepted.

It was my privilege to belong to one of the movements whose members acted in this cause. I was not one of the leaders, but a rank-and-file member of a team of Dror activists. One day Mordechai Tenenbaum suggested that I cross to the Aryan side to serve as a liaison officer for the movement. In late 1942 only one liaison officer, Tema Shneiderman, remained alive. Other experienced officers had been caught by the Germans, and I was to replace them. At that time, the Polish population of Bialystok was ordered to apply for German identity cards. I did so, too, using a forged birth certificate as proof that I was a Christian. I had to leave the ghetto frequently to carry out each stage of these arrangements: reporting to the police station, registering, depositing my birth certificate, being photographed with a shield bearing my identity number, being fingerprinted, and finally receiving the valid document.

It was dangerous to cross to the Aryan side. I was to leave the ghetto early in the morning with a group of Jewish laborers. Then I would swiftly take off my yellow stars and would leave the group at a suitable moment, when the German guards were distracted. Each step had risks: I could be caught leaving the ghetto; the Germans might discover that I was Jewish or that my birth certificate was forged. But luck was with me, and I left for my new posting on the last day of 1942. On the Aryan side, Tema Shneiderman helped me find a room and a job as a maid in the apartment of three German railroad operators. I later used their help when I rode the trains to purchase arms and deliver them to Bialystok and to the ghetto. This, my main task, was the most dangerous of all.

In my job outside the ghetto as a liaison for Dror, I also carried out many other missions: gathering intelligence, concealing Mordechai Tenenbaum's underground archives on the Aryan side, maintaining communications with other ghettos, and so on. It was a lonely life—a life in which I could rely only on myself and my ingenuity. Later I learned that several other women from other movements also went over to the Aryan side, but for reasons of secrecy none of us were told about the others. I gained enormous strength and self-confidence from the exchange of letters, from frequent visits to the ghetto, and especially from the friendship and love that developed between myself and Mordechai Tenenbaum, in the shadow of the inevitable end. I knew that Mordechai would perish after leading his comrades to battles that would claim most of the participants' lives. I did not try to persuade him to act in any other way. My life, too, could end at any moment. Despite everything, I remain grateful for the assignment I was given, a mission that taught me to overcome my selfishness and transcend these dark and bitter times.

On my very first day on the Aryan side, the fact that I was living alone, which was not customary for a young woman of my age at that time, naturally provoked my neighbors' suspicions that I was Jewish. The last Jews in the Grodno ghetto were murdered at this time, and the surviving members of the underground, particularly young women, attempted to flee to the Bialystok ghetto—not knowing that there, too, the first Aktion had begun. Some of them came to me, and I had to hide them in my room until the Aktion was over. This subterfuge made the neighbors even more suspicious of me, and to this day I am puzzled about how I managed to protect those who came to me, and to avoid arrest myself. I took on various patterns of behavior that were evidently part of my nature—composure in the face of danger, steadfastness in times of stress, and outbursts of anger and fury at the sight of injustice or degradation. Because of my reserved, polite, and detached demeanor, the Poles perceived me as a girl of fine upbringing who did not fear to speak her mind. This image, my non-Jewish appearance, and my knowledge of Polish permitted me to survive and act as I did.

Each of my underground comrades on the Aryan side chose an identity that was not far removed from her own, and this stratagem helped us succeed and survive. Some camouflaged themselves as pious Christians, others as villagers, others as laborers. Some found it hard to disguise themselves and returned to the ghetto; others were captured by the Germans because they lost their nerve or the falsity of their papers was discovered. Despite the tortures they underwent, they never betrayed anyone.

We lost several brave women; one tragedy occurred when several veteran couriers and liaisons were stopped at the checkpoint between Bialystok and Warsaw and were caught with money that had been given them for delivery to the underground. Two of them, Lonka Koziebrodzka and Bella Hazan, were caught while passing as Poles and taken to the Pawiak Prison in Warsaw and then to Auschwitz, where Koziebrodzka died of typhus. Others, such as Tema Shneiderman, were killed in resistance operations in the ghettos.

It was not by chance that women were chosen as liaisons or couriers. It was easier for us to disguise ourselves. Until the Bialystok ghetto uprising began in August 1943, we worked on the Aryan side, hardly communicating with one another and never collaborating. This situation changed when the uprising commenced. The heavy siege that the Germans imposed on the ghetto rendered us useless to the rebels. Even so, I moved around the outside of the ghetto in the hope that I might find some way to communicate with comrades inside in order to help them. When the uprising broke out, two women from Hashomer Hatsa'ir slipped out of the ghetto. Together we tried to make contact with their comrades who had joined the partisans. We knew that a small group of Jewish partisans—mostly Communists but some from Hashomer Hatsa'ir—had assembled in the forests surrounding Bialystok after having fled the ghetto between January and April 1943. The members of this group had frequently visited the ghetto to maintain communications and receive food and weapons. Few in number and poorly equipped, they often changed hiding places to avoid detection by the Germans and the villagers. I had not had any contact with them before the uprising.

August 16, 1943, was the first day of the uprising in the Bialystok ghetto. Chaika Grossman (head of Hashomer Hatsa'ir in the Bialystok ghetto and later a member of the Israeli Parliament) and I met in the street with the forest group's liaison, Marylka Rozycka, and through her we established contact with the partisans there. I wandered daily, as if dazed, around the ghetto walls and the surrounding streets, looking for Jews that I could help. At this point, we pledged all our energy to saving fugitives from the deportation trains and helping the group of partisans who sheltered them.

The uprising lasted more than three weeks. Mordechai Tenenbaum was killed, or committed suicide, and with him died the great majority of his fighters. I was unable to assist the fighters and my loved ones, and I suffered for my inability to be with them. Although I came in contact with some survivors of the uprising, I managed to save only one and later to procure him a rifle. Another time I met on the street a man who had escaped from Treblinka and was hiding in the St. Rocha church. I brought him to the partisans, but he was later killed in a battle against the Germans. All these events were frustrating, and I thought bitterly that in the end none of us would survive.

Members of the resistance who had escaped from the trains or gone into hiding joined the forest group—some on their own initiative and others with our assistance. Thus the size of the group soon doubled, from fifty to one hundred members. The newcomers were in abysmal physical and psychological condition. Because they did not have weapons, they could not go on "food missions" or participate in operations against the Germans. Their morale suffered. Some had lost the will to live; perhaps this is why many of them were killed shortly afterward. We tried to encourage them and give them food, weapons, and medications that we had brought from the town to the forest, but their needs exceeded our abilities.

Our group of young women initially numbered six and then five: two Communists, two women from Hashomer Hatsa'ir, and one from Dror. Our sixth member, Rivkele Medajska, lost her life helping Jews who had gone into hiding outside the ghetto and who were in great danger before she was able to lead them to the partisans. We also had ties with several women who lived independently on the Aryan side, such as Janka Malewska, Lodka Bodak, and others. We met with them and sometimes sheltered people with them until they could move to the forest. These women never let us down; one even paid with her life and that of her daughter for aiding two men who had escaped from a camp by giving them shelter until their transfer to the partisans.

It was not until the spring of 1944 that the first squad of Soviet paratroopers reached the forest surrounding Bialystok and begin to unify the groups operating there, including Jews and Soviet prisoners of war who had escaped their captors. Our partisan group, known as Forojs (Forward), joined them and thus crossed an important watershed. The Jewish partisans' situation improved greatly once they joined the larger partisan camp, although they were not spared humiliations as Jews. We became liaisons at the Soviet headquarters of the large partisan formation. The unit was well organized and worked in coordination with the Red Army; it had all the equipment it needed and communicated directly with partisan centers in Minsk (the capital of Belorussia) and Moscow.

According to instructions, an antifascist committee was set up in Bialystok in May 1944 under one of our Communist comrades, Liza Chapnik. In addition to ourselves, the committee was composed of some prewar Communist Party members, Poles, and Belorussians who lived in the city and had managed to survive the mass arrests in the fall of 1941. Four members of the committee, amazingly enough, were Germans; two of them were Nazi Party members who had been powerful executives with large textile companies. Contacts with them had been established by several Jewish women who had been employed in their business—and who were sheltered by them when the ghetto was liquidated. These Germans—Schade, Bohle, Kudlaschek, and Busse—even visited the partisan headquarters in the forest shortly before the Soviet forces liberated Bialystok in late July 1944.

We five women liaisons effectively constituted the executive core of the antifascist committee. We stayed in touch with non-Jewish comrades who worked in such places as the Bialystok airport and German military installations. They fed us information on the movements of army units, the positioning of anti-aircraft batteries, and the number of warplanes and other craft. One member of our group used this information to prepare detailed sketches of German military and aircraft formations, which were forwarded by partisan headquarters to the Soviet military command.

I also had a Polish contact, an officer from the AK (the Polish national underground army), Dr. Filipowski, who worked in a German pharmaceutical warehouse and provided me with medicines and equipment for the partisans. He also safeguarded Mordechai Tenenbaum's underground archives, which had been smuggled out of the ghetto and are kept today in the Yad Vashem Archives in Jerusalem. Another Polish comrade, an elderly man named Burdzynski, would come and visit one of us whenever it was necessary to allay a landlady's suspicions; these visits were interpreted as proof that we were Christians.

In the last few weeks of the German occupation, fleeing soldiers—including Belorussians, Ukrainians, and others from the German auxiliary units—passed through our area. We were ordered to convince them that the Soviet authorities would give them amnesty if they defected from the enemy army and turned over their weapons to us. In many cases we were successful, and by liberation day we had a bunker full of weapons.

One of the operations we planned was to blow up German vehicles by using magnetic bombs that had been parachuted to the partisans several weeks before liberation. To take possession of these explosives, I had to travel toward the front in a train compartment full of German soldiers in order to meet with a group of partisan saboteurs. The Polish engine driver saved me from trouble by inviting me to travel in the engine. I caught up with the partisans en route to their mission and thus participated, by chance, in blowing up a train that was rushing German reinforcements to the crumbling front. However, we did not have an opportunity to use the few bombs I had obtained.

Liberation came on July 27, 1944, a beautiful, clear summer day. Earlier, the SS men who had lived in the area had fled Bialystok in panic, and one of their special commando units had set the entire downtown area ablaze. Three of us—Ania Rud, Liza Chapnik, and I—had taken shelter in a German bunker; the others had gone to the forest. But now, the flames that had danced over downtown Bialystok had finally subsided. A strange silence hovered in the air, as if the whole city were holding its breath.

The first to come were the Soviet sappers, searching for mines. When we heard Russian being spoken, we cautiously stepped forward to meet them, but only after satisfying ourselves beyond doubt that they were indeed Soviet soldiers. Then came the tanks. We ran to kiss their grimy crew members and thank them for having liberated us from the Germans at long last. Our joy was boundless, our smiles unlimited. We organized a small parade the next day, clutching red flags and marching to the outskirts of the city, where we welcomed the general who led the troops into the town. He was moved to receive this kind of welcome on Polish soil. We were drunk with happiness that day, having witnessed our people's murderers in flight.

But what then? How were we to go on? What followed were days of mourning and bereavement. There were no homes left, no families. I wandered through the streets looking for familiar faces. Once a Russian soldier whispered to me: "Nye platch, dyevushka; lubimiy tvoy vernyetsa"—"Don't cry, my girl; your lover will come back." I did not even feel the tears streaming down my face.

After the liberation of Bialystok, we helped arrest collaborators who were known to have revealed the hiding places of Jews and handed them over to the Germans. Our partisan commander, Colonel Nikolai Wojciechowski, went to Leningrad and subsequently to Siberia to practice his profession, engineering. He later became an alcoholic and finally, I heard, committed suicide. Of the

Jewish partisan group, which had attained the size of more than one hundred members after the uprising in and liquidation of the ghetto, only fifty or so survived. Most of them went to Israel. Two members of our women's group, Liza Chapnik and Ania Rud, chose to move to the Soviet Union; the other three—Chaika Grossman, Chasia Bielicka, and I—went to Israel after a short stay in Poland working with child and teenage survivors. In the past few years, my two comrades who had elected to live in the Soviet Union joined us, together with their families, in the mass immigration to Israel of Soviet Jews.

What typified the group of liaisons to which I belonged? Each of us had belonged to a youth movement, either leftist, Zionist, or Communist; the main feature we shared was probably the ideological education our respective movements had provided. The values that informed our education were Jewish and universal. We had learned at an early age to be frugal; to improve ourselves; to transcend trivialities, egotistic inclinations, and cheap temptations; and to work on behalf of the collective. These values, which we internalized along with our hatred of the Germans and our wish to exact revenge, may explain, at least partially, our actions in the underground and after the war. Complementary to these ideals were the education we received at home and our own personality traits, such as courage and audacity.

It is important to note the respectful and admiring attitude the Soviet command and partisans evinced toward our group of liaisons. We were awarded citations and our names and activities were mentioned in newspapers, books, and periodicals (without mention of our Jewishness).

We saw no need to wage a feminist struggle to ensure our human dignity; we earned respect by behaving and acting in ways that spoke for themselves. In comparison to the men, it seems to me that we women were more loyal to the cause, more sensitive to our surroundings, wiser—or perhaps more generously endowed with intuition—and more resolute in our commitment to change reality while accepting that some things are unattainable. We did so without despairing, without giving up, and without ceasing to try.

CHAPTER ELEVEN

Living on the Aryan Side in Poland
Gender, Passing, and the Nature of Resistance

Lenore J. Weitzman

I t was both illegal and dangerous for Polish Jews to defy Nazi orders that required them to live in ghettos. Jews who escaped from the ghettos and tried to pass as non-Jews were referred to (at that time) as living on the Aryan side—the side of the city that lay beyond the ghetto walls. Those who lived on the Aryan side risked the constant threat of death. In Warsaw, for example, once the ghetto walls were sealed in November 1941, Jews who were caught outside the ghetto were shot. Those who tried to live on the Aryan side also faced formidable obstacles in securing the basic necessities of life: food (when food was rationed), work (when the Germans controlled work permits), and a place to live (when the penalty for harboring Jews was death). Even normal activities like walking down the street or riding on a streetcar could be dangerous because police patrols routinely closed off streets and checked everyone's documents. Because Jews who were trying to pass had to use false or forged documents, they were always vulnerable to exposure.

In Poland, most of those Jews who survived on the Aryan side were women. Some of them were recruited by the Jewish underground as couriers for the resistance. They smuggled information, passports, people, and weapons into and out of the ghettos, and they established safe places to hide people and documents. However, most Jews on the Aryan side were not part of an organization: they were individuals who were simply trying to survive by outwitting the Nazis.

It was a dangerous strategy that required nerves of steel. Even those Jews who had contacts outside the ghetto and who managed to obtain good documents and a place to live still risked being recognized or having someone merely suspect that they looked Jewish. The Gestapo offered rewards (a kilo of sugar or a bottle of whisky—valuable commodities in war-torn Poland) to Poles who found Jews outside the ghetto, and there were bounty hunters who searched for Jews to turn over to the Gestapo or to blackmail. Trying to pass with a young child or an elderly parent—or any second person—increased the chances of some mishap that could lead to death.

In spite of the danger, as ghetto conditions worsened and as more people began to suspect the Nazis' ultimate aim, passing seemed like the only way to survive the Nazis. There was also talk about "survival as resistance," and some young people were urged to try to escape to the Aryan side to survive for their people.[1] For most Jews, however, life on the Aryan side seemed much more perilous than coping with the hardships of daily life in the ghetto.

There were also many practical reasons why most Jews felt that they could not make it on the Aryan side. Many had been worn down by the starvation and disease in the ghetto and knew that their weakened appearance would immediately betray them. Others were worried about their lack of financial resources: how could they bribe the guards at the gate or pay for food or rent when the Nazis had already confiscated their assets? Still others were sure that their "Jewish looks" would give them away. Finally, there was the problem of language. Many Polish Jews could be identified by their "Jewish Polish"—their distinctive accent, inflection, or style of speaking Polish—or by their limited knowledge of the language.[2]

Another critical reason why many young men and women who might have been able to pass on the Aryan side chose, nevertheless, to remain in the ghetto was because they were bound to their families: they wanted to be with them and they felt responsible for them—for an aging mother or father, or a younger sister or brother, or for their own children. Those who were young and strong and employed in the ghetto were often the critical lifelines for their families. Although the rules were constantly changing, the families of workers were often exempt from deportations, and the food that workers received might help keep their families from starvation. In addition, those who thought of escape were afraid that their loved ones might be punished, because the

Germans applied principles of collective responsibility and collective punishment. Thus many of those who might have been able to survive on the Aryan side were also those who had the most compelling reason for remaining in the ghetto—their concern for their families. This combination of positive and negative forces—the desire to be with and help one's family in the ghetto, and the threats and dangers of the Aryan side—limited the number of Jews who tried to pass.

Nevertheless, my research suggests that at least 10 percent of the Jews who survived the Holocaust were those who passed on the Aryan side. Obviously, my "sample" is limited to those who succeeded.[3] The number of Jews who tried to pass but did not succeed is likely to be even greater, because many of those who tried were caught and did not live to tell their stories.[4]

It is important to distinguish between passing, which is the subject of this chapter, and hiding, which is not. Jews who were passing had to rely on their own wits and initiative to take care of all the practical details of life. In addition, they were always "out in the open" and had to engage in continual social interaction with their Polish neighbors, co-workers, and landlords. In contrast, Jews who were hidden typically avoided all contact with Germans and Poles. They relied on someone else for their food, shelter, and protection. Although some people who were hidden may have passed from time to time, the subjects of my research were always passing for at least one full year (the average in Poland was three full years).

My first quest, as a sociologist, was to find out what types of people tried to pass and what skills, characteristics, and circumstances enabled them to succeed. I shall address these issues below, but after years of interviewing and analyzing the experiences of hundreds of survivors, it seems clear to me that the single most important factor in their success was sheer luck. Without luck, no amount of good looks, initiative, linguistic fluency, money, or contacts was enough.

My research draws on four primary sources: my own in-depth interviews with more than fifty survivors who passed (and who are now living in the United States, France, and Israel); written testimonies drawn from the main testimonies archive at Yad Vashem in Jerusalem; videotaped testimonies from the Fortunoff Video Archive at Yale University; and published books, including autobiographies.

Two brief methodological notes are necessary. First, the interview sample was generated by a "snowball" procedure involving personal referrals, survivor organizations, and written testimonies.[5] Because there is no systematic list of people who tried to pass, a random sample was not possible.

Second, the statistical analysis presented here is based solely on the sample from Yad Vashem, which was drawn as follows. I (and my research assistants) read through the approximately 6,500 testimonies contained in the main testimonies archive of Yad Vashem in 1992–93. We identified more than 800 testimonies that mentioned false papers, forged documents, passing, living illegally, or living on the Aryan side.[6] Approximately half of those 800 testimonies were given by people who passed in Poland. After eliminating cases in which there was not enough information for our analysis or in which the person was not really passing, we drew a random subsample of 248 Polish testimonies to code.[7] The statistics reported below are based on this subsample.

The Decision to Pass

On Their Own: Alicia and David Lose Their Mothers

Alicia[8] was reared in a cultured, upper-middle-class professional family in Warsaw. Her parents were well educated and spoke Russian, German, and Polish at home. When the Germans invaded Poland in September 1939, Alicia was away visiting relatives. In the early winter she and her aunt took a train back to Warsaw. By then all Jews over the age of twelve were required to wear a Jewish star and to obtain a special permit to travel. But Alicia was not yet twelve, and her aunt decided that neither she nor Alicia would wear the star. It was Alicia's first experience with passing:

> My aunt was from Danzig and so German was her mother tongue. When we arrived at the railway station in Otwock the place was full of Germans. . . . They heard us talking in German and came over to us in a very kindly manner and invited my aunt, who was then sixty years old, to sit with them in the car that was reserved especially for the Germans. They talked to us the whole trip and kept saying what a nice woman and lovely granddaughter. . . . I think there was something about this experience that later gave me power . . . because I knew I could be accepted as a Pole and a German.[9]

Alicia's interpretation proved to be correct. Many of those who passed had a prior (though often inadvertent) experience with passing, which gave them the confidence to do it. It also provided them with anticipatory socialization into the role.

Months later, Alicia and her family were forced to move into the Warsaw ghetto, where their standard of living deteriorated rapidly. But they felt safe and secure. She remembers that her mother, a cultured middle-class woman, actually felt "lucky" to have a job as a cleaning lady in the post office. Then, one day, when Alicia and her mother were at the post office, the Germans suddenly came in screaming and shooting. The workers were forced into the courtyard, while the Germans stood above, firing shots into the crowd in the courtyard. Alicia's mother was shot and killed right in front of her. For Alicia, who was not yet fourteen, the shooting changed everything: she decided that she had to do something to save herself: "I don't remember mourning, I don't remember pain, I don't remember sorrow. I do remember one thing: a feeling that now I'm saving myself—a very clear feeling. I knew it and I felt as if I was on a train and I'm going to jump off."[10] She called a non-Jewish friend of her mother's, who agreed to help Alicia escape from the ghetto.

Although one might assume that the decision to pass was usually the result of months of preparation and planning, the data suggest that many people, like Alicia, made a spontaneous decision, when they suddenly found themselves alone.

Losing his mother had the same effect on David.[11] His story begins in the early days of the Warsaw ghetto, before being caught on the Aryan side was a capital offense for Jews. David's mother suggested that he try to sneak out to buy some food. The family had nothing to eat, and she thought that David would not be identified as a Jew because he spoke Polish without an accent and had the manners of a street-smart kid.

It was unusual for an Orthodox Jewish boy to speak perfect Polish, but David had an unusual education. One day at cheder (the traditional Jewish school for religious boys), David's teacher had hit his hand with a stick to chastise him, and David refused to return to the school. Although his parents were upset by his refusal, they eventually sent him to a regular Polish school. There he learned flawless Polish—his family spoke only Yiddish at home—and David became "accustomed to Polish ways, to their mentality, their songs and games, and to Christian prayers." By the time the war broke out in 1939, David had spent five years in the Polish school and was thoroughly accepted by his peers. So, David explains, he began to be a smuggler:

> I got some clothes that I could hide food in and it just looked like I was fat. I did not always succeed and sometimes the police caught me: they would take all my food and throw it away and beat me until I was bloody and throw me into the ghetto. . . . But for me it was an adventure, and I began to be very successful.

By the time he was sixteen David had established a network of suppliers and smugglers and supported his family in an almost opulent style. While "there were children on the street who were starving to death," his family could afford to eat chocolate and give food to other people.[12]

David's life changed dramatically on the day of the first big *Aktion*—the round-up of Jews for deportation from the ghetto (in July 1942):

> One morning at seven A.M. we began to hear shouting: Out! Everyone get out of the house and come down. . . . They were shooting. . . . One second, just before we go out of the door, my mother took me by the neck and with my little sister she pushed us both into the cabinet and locked it and took the key with her. . . . The two of us stayed there. . . . We heard them come into the room . . . they shot around . . . and then they left.
>
> And after all this there was . . . this terrible silence . . . as if there are no more people in the world. . . . Then we heard the whistle of the train. . . . I never saw my mother again. That was the last time I saw her. She was taken to Treblinka.[13]

Like Alicia, David did not decide to try passing on the Aryan side until he faced the loss of his mother and the inevitability of his own death if he stayed in the ghetto. (His father was taken two weeks later.) Thus losing one's parents—and more specifically, losing one's mother—was often the impetus for the decision to try to save oneself. As Natalie, one of the women I interviewed, said, you do not think of it "until you are all alone and 'free.' But what a horrible 'freedom' it is: you are without any family. Yet it is not until you have this 'freedom' that you can even think of saving yourself."[14]

Although the decision to pass may have been spontaneous for some, the groundwork had been laid by the progressive victimization of the Jewish population. By the time they decided to pass, most of the survivors in the Yad Vashem sample had witnessed the physical harassment, killing, or deportation of members of their family (49 percent had endured the killing of at least one member of their immediate family), and almost two-thirds had themselves experienced harassment and physical violence.

Both Alicia and David made the decision to escape from the ghetto without consulting anyone else. This was the most common pattern among the 248 people in the Yad Vashem sample: 52 percent made the decision alone.

Family Help and Support

In the second most common pattern (found in 20 percent of those sampled), a family member, typically a parent, took the initiative in suggesting and arranging for a child, especially a daughter, to pass. Typically a father would buy the false documents or arrange for someone he knew (a former business associate, patient, client, or neighbor), to help his children pass. In Ida Fink's semi-autobiographical novel *The Journey,* for example, her father, a doctor, bought birth certificates for his two daughters from one of his patients.[15] In other cases mothers asked old friends, neighbors, former nursemaids, trusted customers, or priests to help their daughters find a job, false papers, or a place to live.

In some cases the parent did not help with specific plans but took the initiative by urging a daughter or son to escape. In fact, several parents begged a child to escape and put all the family's resources into saving that one child. These children were sent off with the mission to live for their family.[16] It is interesting to note that having your parents urge you to leave has the same sociological function as having parents deported—because both sever the bond that tied so many others to their families in the ghetto and prevented them from leaving.

In still other cases the parents planned a later escape for themselves but were caught in an Aktion before they got out. Many Jews were unprepared for the swiftness with which the Nazis liquidated the ghettos and seized everyone, irrespective of their "protected" documents and work passes and exemptions.

Other parents made it through the first stage of the escape but were caught or betrayed soon after they arrived at their "haven" on the Aryan side. For example, Ella's father was a well-to-do businessman who entrusted his former business partner with the jewels he brought from the ghetto.[17] One day Ella arrived at her father's apartment and discovered that he had been taken to the Gestapo. His partner had betrayed him so that he could steal the jewelry. His only act of contrition was to allow Ella to run away before the Gestapo returned to catch her.

Help from Non-Jews and Other Jews

Other Gentiles, however, were faithful friends to Jews who passed.[18] Of those in my sample, 16 percent benefited from the help of non-Jews who suggested or arranged their passing. For example, Suzie's father, a successful businessman, was friendly with a German industrialist whose wife offered to save Suzie and her sister:

> At that time they had already started to kill old people and cripples and his wife said that if they would begin taking young people she would take me and my sister to Germany and get us jobs as maids.
>
> [When the time came] my father managed to buy "real" identity papers for us. There were lots of false papers on the market but he found a Ukrainian woman who sold him her real papers in her maiden name. . . . So if they ever checked, it was real. . . . I remember I learned the Ukrainian pater nostra so I would know something.[19]

Another 6 percent of the Yad Vashem survivors learned about the possibilities of living on the Aryan side from Jewish friends and acquaintances. It was easier to get in and out of the ghettos when they were first established, and many people managed to get past the gates to sell or trade on the Aryan side. At that time some people tried to establish new identities on the other side, but many came back to the ghetto—to see their families or to escape the constant tension. Thus talk and gossip about the Aryan side was "in the air" in the ghettos (where gossip was generally abundant): someone knew someone who had thought about it, or was planning it, or had already left, or had been betrayed to the Gestapo. This lore was accompanied by a thriving black market in false documents, although not all were aimed at creating a new identity.

Defiance: Bronka and the Jewish Underground

For another group of people the decision to live on the Aryan side was not really a decision to pass: it was a response to a call from the Zionist youth movement and a way of performing vital work for the Jewish resistance. Although only 4 percent of the sample from the Yad Vashem archives made the decision to pass because a Jewish organization suggested it or helped them, the theoretical significance of this minority is much greater than their numbers would suggest because of the roles they played in the resistance and the pattern of their lives on the Aryan side.

In Poland, Lithuania, and other parts of the former Soviet Union, it was primarily women who lived on the Aryan side to work as couriers for the resistance. These women were the lifeline of the Jewish underground. Consider the strong motivation and confident tone in this quotation from my interview with Bronka Klibanski about her decision to pass—which parallels the gripping events she reports in Chapter 10.

> Mordechai Tanenbaum spoke at a meeting of my Zionist youth group
> . . . [and told us how the Vilna Jews were forced to dig a mass grave
> and were shot in the forest of Ponary]. He was the first to make us un-
> derstand . . . that this is the German policy—the physical extermina-
> tion of the Jews. And at that time, there were not many people who
> understood this. The older Jewish leaders didn't believe him. They
> didn't believe such a policy could exist . . . because it was so inhu-
> man. . . . They could not face it. But we, I, believed what he said
> to us.
>
> He told us also of his plans, what we have to do. . . . and *I was
> ready to do it. . . .*
>
> I was ready to do anything to fight the Germans . . . and to take
> revenge for what the Germans were doing to our people.[20]

A Last-Minute Opportunity

Finally, some Jews (only 3 percent of the sample) never made a conscious decision to escape or pass but, at the last minute, found themselves
in a situation where they could do so. Samuel Oliner, for example, tells of

the chaos of an Aktion in the middle of the night, when his stepmother told him to run away:

> "Run, run my child; run away so that you will save yourself."
> "But mother, where shall I go?"
> "Go. Go anywhere. Hide. Hide. Hide. They are killing us all. I am sure of it now. . . . Shmulek I love you. I know God will protect you."
> Bursting into tears I ran toward her, but she pushed me away. "Go. There is no time. Go quickly and hide. Run into the country-side. Save yourself."

Still in his pajamas, Samuel ran outside and climbed onto the roof to hide: he was the only Jew in Bobowa to survive the Aktion.[21]

The data that I have presented on how Polish Jews made the decision to pass are summarized in Table 11.1 on page 197. It also shows some interesting gender differences in the Yad Vashem sample. Men were more likely than women to make the decision to pass on their own (71 percent versus 44 percent). For women, a family member was more likely to have suggested passing or to have offered to help (this was true for 24 percent of the women versus 10 percent of the men). Women were also more likely to have been aided by non-Jewish contacts (19 percent versus 7 percent) and were slightly more likely to be recruited by a Jewish organization (to be couriers for the underground). Overall, men were more likely to have acted independently, while women were more likely to have received help from others.

One possible explanation for these findings is that men and women are accustomed to using different vocabularies to explain their behavior; that is, men are more likely to say that they acted independently, while women are more likely to admit that they received help. However, there is more reason to believe that these reports are real. In fact, they parallel later differences between the men and women when they were living on the Aryan side. There, too, the men were more likely to be loners, were less likely to confide in others, and were less likely to receive help from others. In contrast, the women were more likely to be affiliated: they were more likely to have contacts with others while passing, and they were more likely to receive help from others.

Table 11.1 How Polish Jews Decided to Escape and Pass

	Percentage of All Men and Women	Percentage of Women	Percentage of Men
Made the decision alone	52	44	71
Family member suggested it, helped them	20	24	10
Non-Jewish friend or contact suggested it, helped them	16	19	7
Jewish friend or acquaintance did it, suggested it, or helped them	6	6	7
Jewish organization suggested it, helped them	4	4	1
Spontaneous, in the situation	3	3	3

Note: Total N=248. Because these figures are rounded to the nearest percent, columns may not add up to 100%.

Double Lives versus Secret Selves

The way one decided to pass (or was recruited into passing) was related to one's psychological experiences while passing. Compare, for example, the experiences of David, the young smuggler who decided to pass after his mother was taken in an Aktion, with those of Bronka Klibanski, who became a courier for the underground.

When David escaped from the ghetto, he went to the home of Stashik, a young friend from his smuggling operation. Stashik and his family were overjoyed to see him alive and invited David to stay with them. After a short time, however, it became evident that David was endangering the family: he had nightmares every night and would scream and call out in his dreams—in Yiddish. Because Stashik was a member of the Polish underground, he could not risk making his neighbors suspicious. He offered to take David to the home of his father, who was already hiding six other Jews in his cellar. David agreed but soon found that he "could not stand being locked up in the cellar with the other Jews." He decided to leave and take his chances on the streets. That decision was one of the many examples of David's good luck: four days later the Germans found the hiding place and shot all the Jews, along with Stashik's father.

With no place to live, David's life on the Aryan side was filled with terror and constant tension: "Every minute you are in danger for your life. You are not a human being." A critical event for David was witnessing the shooting of two Jewish girls in a Warsaw park:

> Once I went into a park and I saw two girls, and by some instinct I knew they were Jewish. . . . they were dressed in normal clothes, and they had a "good look" but I knew. . . . Naturally, I said nothing to them. I was just sitting there. . . .
>
> There were all kind of people at that park, Germans and others. One man came toward those girls. I could see what was happening, he started talking to them. Then he pulled out a gun and shot them on the spot, both of them. . . . I was about three or four hundred meters away, sitting on a bench.
>
> The minute he finished with them he started walking toward me, and I, I had the cap of a Polish youth movement . . . and I decided that I'm not running away, so I stood up, took one apple, ate it and walked toward this man. It was very hard for me, I didn't think much, I acted by intuition . . . I walked straight to him, he looked me in the eyes, I passed him and he didn't stop me.[22]

As soon as he left the park David decided that he could not live with the tension on the Aryan side: "And then I went out of the park. . . . and then I decided: I'm going back to the Jews. . . . back to the ghetto, to the Aktionen . . . to die with the rest of the Jews. In the ghetto it was a relief, I felt like I belong to the same people, and whatever is going to happen with everyone else will happen to me. . . . On the Aryan side you are fighting for your life all the time. . . . Even with all the dangers in the ghetto it is better than the Aryan side."[23]

The day after David returned to the Warsaw ghetto, his luck ran out: he was caught in an Aktion and herded into a cattle car bound for Treblinka. "By this time there were rumors and songs in the ghetto about Treblinka as a cemetery for Jews. . . . some Warsaw Jews had escaped from Treblinka and had come back to the ghetto to tell others that it was a death camp. But we did not believe it because you cannot live with the feeling that you are going to die . . . so you know but you don't know."[24]

Nevertheless, David knew enough to know that he did not want to stay on a train to Treblinka. Along with two others, he managed to lift up some of the boards from the floor of the train and drop down on the tracks:

DAVID: The moment my head hit the tracks I lost consciousness.

After I woke up I got up and ran to the forest . . . I sat [there] a little and then I went back to the ghetto. . . .

LW: I don't understand that. Why?

DAVID: Because I was too afraid to stay on the other side. I cannot live on that side. It was too dangerous. It is too hard to fight.

If you have one week to live with Jews, O.K. you want to live. And after the week you can start to worry. But if you are out of the ghetto you worry for every minute. Even if it is one week—it was easier in the ghetto.[25]

After David returned to the ghetto, he was put on a work crew whose task was to go through the apartments of those who had been deported. In 1943, when the Warsaw uprising began, he decided to escape again. After another series of miraculous experiences, he ended up in the area of Tarnopol, where he worked on several farms and managed to survive until the Russians came.

Before hearing about David's experiences, one might assume that it would be easier to pass if one was alone. Indeed, the conventional wisdom among Jews at the time was that it was always unwise for someone who was trying to pass to have any contact with other Jews. Yet, when we compare David's testimony with Bronka Klibanski's, we see that Bronka's underground contacts actually made it psychologically easier for her to pass because, in Erving Goffman's terms, they provided her with a "backstage" to sustain her "frontstage performance."[26]

Although both David and Bronka had to maintain their secret selves—the self of their Jewish identity—only Bronka was living a double life. She had one life as an Aryan and another as a member of the resistance, where she could express her true self. Even though Bronka had to keep switching between her "real self" and her "Aryan self"—while David stayed in his Aryan role twenty-four hours a day—it was David who, alone in the Aryan world, was more likely to feel lost and without purpose. Bronka, in contrast, sustained both her secret self and her presented self, with help from her network of co-conspirators.

Both theoretical and practical reasons suggest why life on the Aryan side was easier for Bronka. Not only did she have a political ideology and a purpose, but she was also in contact with other people who supported who she really was—what Cooley called her "looking glass self."[27] Cooley showed that we come to see ourselves as others see us, and we therefore rely on others to reflect the image we have of ourselves. When others see us as strong and competent, it sustains and reinforces our self-image. On a more practical level, the possibility of a backstage allows one to relax and to rebuild one's energy for the next performance. Without that backstage—and someone to share who one "really" is—the constant tension can be unbearable (as it was for David).

Contrast David's attitude with the following quotation from Bronka:

> I wasn't afraid . . . I was determined, determined to do something to take revenge for what the Germans were doing to our people. And this gave me strength . . . I thought it was necessary to defend ourselves. When the Germans would come to take us to death, we have to fight, we have to do everything not to make it easy for the Germans. We realized that we will not be able to fight against the Germans because they are stronger this time. But what we wanted was to take some revenge. To do something to make them, this terrible work, more difficult.
>
> It was not important to me if I will remain alive or not. It was not important at all. And I never thought I will survive.[28]

Who Passed? Age, Class, and Gender

The demographic characteristics that most clearly distinguished those who passed from the overall Jewish population were age (they were more likely to be young), marital status (they were more likely to be single), and gender (they were more likely to be female). They were also more likely to come from middle- or upper-middle-class homes.

When the Nazis first entered Poland, the median age of those who eventually passed was twenty (the mean was twenty-two). About 50 percent of

those who later passed were under twenty, and another 25 percent were between twenty and thirty, and another 20 percent were between thirty and forty.
Only 3 percent were over forty. Because the median age of the sample is so
young, it is not surprising that most of them (64 percent) were not married
when the war began and that a significant minority (47 percent) were still
students.

Among the half (53 percent) who were employed before the war, the most
frequently listed occupations were in the small trades (a pattern that was typical for the Jewish population at that time) or the professions (which included
those who were lawyers, doctors, teachers, professors and other professionals).
The figure for the professions is much higher than we would expect in a normal distribution of the Polish Jewish population.[29] Similarly, the fathers of
those who were students were much more likely to be economically well off: 45
percent of them were well-to-do businessmen or professionals. (The other half
were either artisans or in the small trades.)

In our own independent assessment of the prewar social class of those
who later passed, we ranked 48 percent as middle class, 30 percent as upper
middle class, and 7 percent as upper class. Only 15 percent were either poor
or "just getting by." (Of course, all these indicators of status are for the period
before the war began. The Nazi onslaught brought turmoil and economic devastation for most previously middle- and upper-middle-class Jewish families.)
Together these data suggest that those who passed were more likely to be from
relatively well educated families of considerably higher-than-average socioeconomic status.

Why Women?

The last demographic characteristic that distinguishes those who passed
is gender: 69 percent were women. There are several reasons for the predominance of women. First, Jewish men could easily be identified as Jews: in
Poland, it was highly unusual for anyone who was not Jewish to be circumcised, so physical evidence of circumcision was considered proof that a man
was Jewish. Whenever Nazis or Poles suspected a man of being Jewish, they
told him to drop his pants.

A second factor was the differential psychological effect that circumcision—or the lack of it—had on men and women. Because men knew that they
could be identified, they were probably more fearful of passing to begin with,

and less likely to try it. In addition, when they did try it, they were always aware that they could be exposed, and that, in turn, may have made them more self-conscious and vulnerable. In contrast, women could be confident that they could not be unmasked by a physical examination.

The great importance of these psychological effects is illustrated by the men who did not display them—that is, those who were so confident in their Aryan roles that even physical evidence of their circumcision did not undermine their credibility. Stephan, for example, was a blond, blue-eyed young man who had false documents and worked at a German air force base with other Poles.[30] He had grown up in a small village with a one-room school and spoke Polish like a native. He also spoke German, because his village was near the German border, but was reluctant to speak it "because I was afraid that my German would sound as if its roots were Yiddish, not pure German." When the Germans in charge of the base found out that Stephan spoke German, they put him in charge of his group and transmitted instructions through him. As a result the other Poles treated him as a leader. One day the commander of the base told Stephan to take ten men to the doctor for a checkup:

> I told the doctor I stand here under orders for you to give everyone a checkup. . . . After he finished he said, "What about you?" He told me to take off my shirt. He checked me with a stethoscope, he checked my heart. I am used to this exam, it is like the ones we had in school, and I never imagined he will command me to take off my pants. He could never imagine that I, who am speaking German, am really a Jew.
>
> But when I had to take off my trousers I could not hide what they had done to me when I was 8 days old—it was cut.
>
> The doctor said, it looks like a Jew's. I told him that my mother told me that when I was a small boy I had an operation. And the doctor asked me if I had pimosa—that is, when dirt gets in between the folds of the outer skin and then you must take it off. And it is a surgery that is like a circumcision. That is what he told me. I knew this illness is a possibility but I did not know the name was pimosa . . .
>
> And then he told me it is very dangerous—if you fall into the hands of the Gestapo they will say you are a Jew. So I suggest to you

that you write home . . . and tell your parents to go to the hospital and get the records of your operation. Then bring them to me. Of course, that day I started thinking of how to escape from that place.[31]

Most of the other men who successfully passed in Poland were similar in their absolute self-confidence. Oswald Rufeisen, for example, was so successful in convincing the German police that he was a trustworthy Pole that he had access to their secret plans to liquidate the Mir ghetto. He managed to use his position to warn the Jews (and helped hundreds to escape in time). When he was unmasked as an informer, the Germans assumed that "I did it because I was a Polish patriot. Even then they did not suspect that I was a Jew."[32]

Nevertheless, each of these men was very conscious of his physical vulnerability and was careful to avoid undressing and washing in the presence of other men. Similarly, David, the young smuggler, who eventually found work helping a Ukranian farmer, told the farmer that he was a "simple" person who preferred to sleep in the barn with the animals. That way he did not have to wash and undress in the farmer's small house (and, equally important for David, only the cows would hear his Yiddish nightmares).

These examples suggest that if one is confident and convincing in one's assumed identity, others will often explain away discrepant information. In fact, what is most surprising about the experiences of both men and women who passed is the extent to which others (who accepted them) unconsciously helped them by assuming that there were reasonable explanations for behaviors or traits that might have given them away.

Thus, the predominance of women among those who passed may be explained, at least in part, by the fact that women were more likely to believe that they could pass initially, and were more self-confident when they embarked on their new lives. Men, by contrast, were more reluctant to try, just as Jews with other distinguishing physical or social characteristics, such as dark hair, or a prominent nose, or a distinctive accent, were afraid that they would be identified. But there were some Jews with each of these characteristics who were successful nevertheless.

A third factor that contributed to the larger number of women who passed was the greater cultural assimilation of Jewish women in Poland before the war. Celia Heller's pioneering study suggests that Jewish women were typically allowed more freedom to explore and absorb Polish language, literature, and culture. They became the "engines of acculturation," bringing Polish culture into their homes.[33] Similarly, Gershon Bacon (Chapter 3) notes that Jewish girls, even those from Hasidic homes, were more likely than Jewish boys to attend regular Polish schools and to become familiar with Polish literature, customs, and fashions.

The sex-segregated educational system also provided Jewish boys and girls with different sets of skills and opportunities. Most Jewish families gave priority to their sons' Jewish education and sent them to special schools, the cheder and the yeshiva. Jewish girls were not permitted to study in these male schools, and because Jewish education was not as critical for them, they were often sent to Polish public schools. This pattern of divergent educational tracks for Jewish girls and boys persisted through the institution of compulsory (but still sex-segregated) "public" education in Poland.[34]

Ironically, the "inferior" non-Jewish education that Jewish girls were more likely to receive provided them with knowledge and contacts that helped them to pass—such as the ability to speak colloquial Polish, familiarity with Polish customs (and Catholic prayers and rituals), a sense of the patterns and nuances of social interaction, personal networks and contacts in the non-Jewish world of their Polish classmates, and sometimes a few friends to whom they might be able to turn for help.[35]

The final factor that explains the predominance of women among those who passed was their different socialization, and the different social roles they had traditionally assumed. Women were socialized to pay attention to the social sphere, to be sensitive to the feelings and reactions of others, to adapt and fit in, and to read finely tuned nuances that were critical for passing. These "feminine" skills were less likely to be nurtured in men.[36]

The foregoing discussion leads us to two possible hypotheses to explain the predominance of women among survivors who passed. The first is that more women tried to pass to begin with (because of men's physical vulnerability and the psychological insecurity it fostered). The second is that both men and women tried to pass, but a larger percentage of women were successful (because of the physical, psychological, educational, and social differences discussed above). I am inclined to believe that both hypotheses are correct, even though we will never have the appropriate data to test them.

One further caveat is in order. It is important to note, once again, that one's traits or efforts were not the only factors that determined one's success with passing. The responses of others and the larger political climate were absolutely critical. Thus in explaining the success (or failure) of those who passed, we must always be wary of explanations that focus solely on the person trying to pass. So many forces beyond their control worked against Jews living on the Aryan side—not the least of which were the Nazi policies that offered incentives for Poles to catch Jews (and death for those who sheltered them.)

In recognizing the importance of these external factors and the actions of others, it is useful to note that the outside world was accustomed to treating men and women differently. Even though the Germans and Poles who controlled access to everything, from a train ticket to an identity card, did not know when they were helping a Jew, they were aware of the person's gender and they knew whether they were helping a man or a woman. And they were more likely to be helpful to a woman. (Women were also more likely to ask for help.)[37] Thus women who were passing may have found the external world more hospitable.

Life on the Aryan Side

Most people who escaped from the ghetto did not have a clear plan for how they would establish their new lives. Typically their first concern was to get far away from the place where they had been living, so that no one would recognize them. They often headed for the nearest big city, where they assumed that they would be more anonymous. Overall, almost half of those who were passing in Poland (46 percent) lived in large cities; another 15 percent lived in small cities. Few lived in small villages (12 percent) or rural areas (10 percent). The remaining 11 percent lived in both urban and rural areas. (A few others were passing as Poles in POW camps or forced-labor camps or concentration camps.) Only a quarter of those who were passing remained stable: only 9 percent stayed in one place and only 16 percent moved only once. Most moved a few times (54 percent), some moved very often (16 percent), and others were constantly on the run (6 percent).

The first step for most people was a train ride. Helene and Sarah, two sisters who managed to escape from the last roundup in their ghetto with both money and false papers, began their journey on the train. Because they had no place to live, they lived on trains, traveling from town to town. One day the

Germans stopped their train and told everyone on it that they were being taken for forced labor in Germany. Helene was terrified. Although she knew her papers were good, she was sure that she would be exposed if she had to live in close quarters with real Polish girls. She was sent to work in a brick factory in Heidelberg, where the other Polish girls began to suspect that she was Jewish: "I looked Polish but maybe my German was too good or I didn't use the right Polish expressions. . . . They opened my mail and saw I had only one sister. They wanted to know why? Poles had large families . . . where was my mother, my father, my sisters, my brothers? If you were alone you were immediately suspicious."[38] Helene was "lucky" to become ill with appendicitis. Before the other women had a chance to report her to the Gestapo, she had to be transferred to a hospital (where she was in a multinational group of POWs, removed from Polish scrutiny).

Although it may seem counterintuitive, Helene's instinct that she might be safer in Germany, where there would be fewer Poles who could recognize her as a Jew, was correct. She was also correct in feeling unsafe in a group of Polish women. The "ideal" situation for many Polish Jewish women turned out to be a domestic job in Germany, where they had no contact with Poles.

The most common "occupation" among the women who passed was domestic work: 35 percent of the women found domestic jobs and another 6 percent worked as nannies. These jobs had the advantage of limiting the women's exposure to, and scrutiny by, a large number of people. (They had the disadvantage, however, of making exploitation easy, because all domestics were totally dependent on their employers.)

The functional equivalent for men was farm work: the largest single group of men who passed, 22 percent, found work on farms. Working for a single farmer afforded them some privacy and a similar shield from the outside world. These two occupations—domestic work for women and farm work for men—were the ones that Alicia and David found.

Alicia, the young girl whose mother was killed in the ghetto post office, was advised to go to a church where young people were being registered for forced labor in Germany. She assumed that they needed workers and would accept everyone who registered. However, the recruiting station turned out to be a terrifying place for a Jew: the first step in the process was an inspection of the recruits to see if any Jews were hiding among them: "They lined us up to look us over. . . . There were two blond girls with us who were dressed in a Polish national costume with huge crosses. They looked very theatrical. . . . The inspectors [spotted them immediately as Jews] and took them out and shot them in front of our eyes. They kicked them. It was horrible. The Poles were very upset too. . . . They took out between 16 and 18 people and shot them on the spot."[39] Alicia was lucky to find herself "adopted" by another young woman, who protected her during the inspection. When the officers came to examine Alicia, her friend began flirting and implied that the two girls were "a package deal" who could make the officers very happy.

After a second inspection at the German border, where officials were again looking for Jews, the recruits were taken to a camp where they signed up for various types of work. Alicia opted for farmwork (instead of a factory) so that she could avoid close contact with other Poles. However, she did not look like a hearty farm girl:

> I was taken to a place called Nowgat, to an employment office and they waited for the farmers to come take who they wanted to work. It was like a slave market. The Polish boys were heavy and fat and I weighed only 52 kilos [about 114 pounds]. . . . they took everyone but me and I was really scared. I was afraid they would dump me in some kind of factory and I would be with other Poles and they could recognize me. It was a very scary moment.
>
> And then a short fat woman came: she said she was very sorry she was late, probably there was nothing left. She wants a girl but has demands: she wants a girl who knows German, who can read or write German, and who knows arithmetic because her husband is the head of the village and there are things to do and there is also translation. She also needs to know how to milk cows. . . . She was standing in front of me and I said I could read and write German.[40]

Alicia took a big chance: being able to read and write German was totally inappropriate for someone with papers identifying her as the daughter of a farmer and a laundress. She knew that she should appear to be as plain as possible, but she was so afraid of being rejected that she tried to impress the woman. Once again, Alicia was lucky. She was accepted and given "a nice room with a good bed and a closet." Her next ordeal came when she was taken to the cow shed and told to milk the cows: "I had never even seen a live cow in my life." Alicia had no choice: she had to admit that she did not know how to milk the cow. Her employer taught her, and she was pleased with Alicia's work, but the gaps between Alicia's papers and her skills were too great to go unnoticed. Her employer decided that Alicia was clearly of a higher social status than her papers indicated, and therefore she must be hiding her true identity. The woman then figured out "who Alicia really was." Fortunately, the explanation did not harm Alicia: "My boss decided I was the daughter of a Polish general. She told all her friends that she has a maid who was the daughter of a Polish general. In her eyes someone who know languages at my age must be the daughter of a general."[41]

Alicia's experiences were typical in that luck played a critical role in her life, in that she found employment as a maid, and in her intuitive realization that she was better off with a single family. However, her living conditions were better than most, and most of the Polish women in the Yad Vashem sample remained in Poland.

Because most of those who were passing were from urban backgrounds, they felt more comfortable and safer—whatever the reality—in a city in Poland. The ideal abode was a room of one's own with a separate entrance, but choices were limited in war-torn Poland, and Jews who were passing more often lived in rooming houses or shared a room with someone who needed the money from a lodger. The lack of privacy added to the feeling that one was always being watched and evaluated. Every move, every conversation, and every possession opened the door to a revelation that could trigger detection.

Sandra Brand, for example, had her husband's picture in her wallet. When her documents were inspected, his Jewish appearance aroused suspicion.[42] For others it was the lack of pictures that was problematic: How could a young girl not have pictures of her family? Where were they, and why didn't they send her presents for Christmas? For still others the giveaway was a trait or a habit or an expression. Sonya brushed her teeth every day; Pessia didn't eat pork; Celia was so serious; Helena rejected the Polish boys. The possibilities were endless. Niusia, for example, decided that her eyeglasses made her "look Jewish":

> You know the Christians, the Polish, they didn't wear eyeglasses. So
> I had to take them off when I was in the street. I had to go without

them and I couldn't see. I was afraid . . . I was always afraid I had said something that could have made somebody understand that I am a Jew. That somebody will tell and that I will have to go to the Gestapo. . . . Every step and every word, everything, was under control. What to say and how to look and how to speak and how to move. . . .

Every night I tried to remember what I have done and what I have said—from the morning, the beginning of the day. It was like seeing a movie picture. I saw the whole day and I heard everything, every word I said, who I met and what they said . . . and maybe I said something wrong or did something wrong and maybe I have to change my dwelling. Maybe it is impossible for me to live anymore in this place. It was terrible to think it all over at night. It was just terrible to live like that. And of course, I was always afraid.[43]

In spite of the incredible dangers they faced, more than 60 percent of those who were passing tried to provide help for someone else (56 percent of the women and 40 percent of the men helped someone in their family while passing, and 35 percent of the women and 41 percent of the men helped a Jewish friend).

Crises

Everyone who passed encountered situations where they were sure that they had reached the end. Recall Alicia's terror at the recruiting station and David's fear when he was put on the train to Treblinka. For Bronka, the crisis came on a day when she had been buying guns from the peasants in the countryside and was smuggling them back to the ghetto:

The Germans were at the railway station looking for smugglers—not smugglers of arms—because they didn't realize that there could be girls smuggling arms. But food was scarce in Bialystok so there were many, many Polish women who were smuggling food from the countryside.

So I had some guns in my valise and I saw the German at the train station. I noticed him from a distance because you had to notice everything. . . . [He had] a dog, a very big dog.

The first thing when I noticed him was that I thought I had to go back because he could arrest me. But I noticed that he noticed me. So I had no choice. . . .

So I went to him and I talked to him. . . . he looked at my valise, and then at me, and he asked me what I had inside. I told him, I have lard and eggs and butter. All these things were illegal—it was not permitted to bring them to the city. It was smuggling.

And I asked him with a nice smile if he wants me to open it. And he said, no, no, no, thank you very much, because there was no need to open it because I told him I have all of these things that I was not permitted to have. So if I told him the truth, there was no need to open. It was finished.

He told me to go with him to the station. We waited for the train together. I didn't know if I was under arrest or not. When the train arrived, he took me to the conductor of the train, and he asked him to give me a good place to sit where no one would bother me. And he told the conductor not to let anyone look at my valise, that nobody should bother me. And so I got back safely to Bialystok with the arms.[44]

Not everyone was as lucky. Both Bronka Klibanski and Bella Yari-Hazan (another courier) were strikingly beautiful and seemed invulnerable. But eventually Bella's luck ran out when she, too, faced a crisis while traveling. Bella was using a ghetto-manufactured travel permit and was carrying materials for the underground, which she had tied up in small bits in her long blond braids.[45] The police had been alerted and were looking for the false travel permits. Although Bella managed to get rid of the incriminating evidence, the Germans were certain that she was working for the Polish underground, and they brutally interrogated, beat, and tortured her. She managed to withstand the torture and never confessed. Eventually she was sent to Auschwitz, where she continued to pass as a Pole.

Traits That Helped or Enabled One to Pass

Data from the Yad Vashem testimonies affirm the importance of many of the traits we have already noted. The statistics and discussions here serve as a summary and a distillation of the factors that are embedded in the individual cases discussed above. The following factors were mentioned in more than half the testimonies as critical to the survivors' success on the Aryan side: a self-confident personality (75 percent of the testimonies), the ability to speak the local language without an accent (66 percent), having non-Jewish friends and contacts (62 percent), personal appearance (61 percent), and "proper" or good documents (56 percent).

Self-Confidence and Defiance

We have already seen examples of the importance of self-confidence and a willingness to stand up to Germans, such as Bronka's amazing courage in dealing with the police when she was smuggling arms. Similarly, even though David talked about his constant fear, his actions—especially those in the public park—showed his confidence and defiance.

Many of those who passed had, even before they moved to the Aryan side, some prior experience with passing that added to their self-confidence. Recall, for example, Alicia's train trip with her aunt: she knew that she could be accepted as a Pole and a German. Although I do not have systematic data, many other testimonies mention a prior experience with passing. Nechama Tec, for example, realized, "I had *fooled* the enemy. I was smarter than they because they did not recognize the Jew in me. They were not so powerful after all!"[46] Even though some of these experiences were inadvertent, they were nevertheless emboldening. They also provided anticipatory socialization into playing the role of a non-Jew.

Language and the Lack of an Accent

Data from the Yad Vashem testimonies emphasize the importance of both the technical and the social aspects of language. It was not language alone, but also access to the social settings in which the Polish language was learned and spoken, that facilitated passing. In the United States in 1998, it is hard for many of us to envision the extent to which Poles and Jews in prewar Poland "lived in different worlds, linguistically and socially, . . . and each felt like a stranger in the world of the other."[47] According to Celia Heller, the rigidity of the social lines between Poles and Jews in the period between the two world wars came very close to that of the color line in the United States.[48] Language was one of the clearest indexes of this segregation. In the 1931 Polish census 79 percent of the Jews of Poland listed Yiddish as their mother tongue.[49] Although there is still some question about the meaning of this statistic, it is clear that many Jews in Poland did not speak Polish, or did not speak it well, or spoke it with a distinctive Jewish accent.[50]

Many of those who were able to pass were unusual because they had attended Polish schools and spoke Polish without an accent. As David said, if he had not left the cheder, he would have spoken only Yiddish, the language of his home. In fact, it was language alone that doomed his younger sister: although she "looked O.K., she only spoke Yiddish."[51]

In addition to Polish, knowledge of German was often useful. Although some Jews who were passing were afraid to let others know that they understood German (because it was similar to Yiddish and might betray their Jewish background), many others took advantage of being able to understand German. For example, Bella Yari-Hazan, the courier for the resistance, managed to get a job in Gestapo headquarters because she understood German:[52]

> I decided that it would be useful [to the underground] if I could work for the Gestapo. So I went and asked for work as a cleaning lady because I understood German—from Yiddish [even though my Polish was not so good]. The Germans did not know the difference between good and bad Polish because they could not speak Polish. But if they said I should bring them tea I understood them. When I cleaned their rooms I could go over things and find papers for the underground.
>
> My real job was to find things for the underground. As a young attractive girl with blond hair and two braids I could get away with it.

Non-Jewish Friends and Contacts

Although most of those in the Yad Vashem sample describe themselves as having a strong Jewish identity, they nevertheless had extensive contact with non-Jews, either through school or through work. The importance of these contacts is clear: 87 percent of those who passed received some help from non-Jewish individuals, 8 percent received help from the non-Jewish underground, and 4 percent received help from a Christian organization dedicated to helping Jews, such as Zegota.

Women were more likely than men to receive help from non-Jewish individuals (91% of the women versus 80% of the men), and they were given more of different kinds of help. The forms of assistance that Jews received while passing included being given a place to sleep for a night or two (76 percent of the women versus 59 percent of the men), being given a place to live for a week or more (86 percent versus 63 percent), being provided with food (76 percent versus 68 percent), being given help in getting documents (77 percent versus 71 percent), being introduced as a relative (25 percent versus 9 percent), and being given a job or help in finding employment (53 percent versus 48 percent). Although many of these differences are not large, the pattern is consistent: when we look at both the amount and the diversity of help, we find that others were more willing to help women than men.

Appearance

Although the perceived importance of blond-haired, blue-eyed Aryan looks has been mentioned throughout this chapter, many testimonies suggest that manner and bearing were just as important as physical appearance. Most of those who were passing went to great lengths to try to conform to what they saw as the appropriate bearing and manner. Sandra Brand, for example, despite her blond hair and blue eyes, constantly had to remind herself to "shed her timidity and to walk with confidence."[53] She also worried about her "Jewish" habit of using her hands when she spoke, so she bought a fur muff and tried to keep her hands tightly clenched while speaking. Similarly, Nechama Tec writes, "We knew that Jews could be recognized by the sadness in their eyes . . . my parents kept telling me, 'pretend you're happy. Think about happy things. You must have happy eyes.' "[54]

Identity Cards and Documents

During the German occupation of Poland the police would routinely close off a section of streets and check the documents of every single pedestrian. Perfect Polish and Aryan looks were no protection from an immediate arrest if one did not have a valid *Kennkarte* (a Polish identity card). A bad forgery might be even more dangerous than no card at all, because it might make the police suspect that a Jew was trying to pass. For example, when sixteen-year-old Hannah found herself in one of these dragnets, she tore up her false identity card, because she was afraid it was not good enough.[55] She was arrested for not having a Kennkarte and ended up being sent to Auschwitz as a Pole. She continued to pass in Auschwitz until the camp was liberated.

In the Yad Vashem sample, 86 percent of those who passed had documents that helped them. Most common were identity cards (84 percent had them), birth certificates (50 percent), work cards (34 percent), travel permits (27 percent), residence or food cards (21 percent), and baptismal certificates (19 percent).

If one was using false papers, the best papers to have were real documents with someone else's real name, because the Gestapo would often call to verify that a person was properly recorded in the records of a town or village.[56] About 38 percent of the Yad Vashem sample managed to obtain real documents and to substitute their own picture for the one on the card. Bella Yari-Hazan, for example, asked a Polish nurse, with whom she worked in the ghetto hospital, if she could have the nurse's identity card. The underground substituted Bella's picture on the card and then matched the stamp that covered part of the photo.

Although Bella knew the real person whose papers she carried, most Jews acquired documents bearing strangers' names and thus risked a chance encounter with that person or someone who knew her or him. That is exactly what happened to Rachel.[57] At the police station for what she thought was a routine re-registration, the policeman looked at her application with disbelief. He asked her to follow him into his office, where he told her that he knew that she was "not Anna because I know her. She was a maid in my parents' house and she and I were lovers." Rachel was shaking, sure that she would be handed over to the Gestapo. But the policeman smiled and said, "But I see that you're a beautiful woman and I like you. So maybe we can work something out . . . I'll give you your new papers and I'll keep you safe if you and I could be friends, if you'll stay with me."[58] Rachel was trembling but managed to smile as she promised to come live with him. Then he led her back to the desk and gave her a new identity card. That afternoon, Rachel and her son packed up their few possessions and left on the first train.

If one could not get real documents with the name of a real person, it was best to have real papers with false names (which about a third of the Yad Vashem sample possessed). Blank forms and stamps might be stolen (or supplied by friendly clerks), and the bearer could fill in a false name and biographical data. Finally, the most common and the least valuable documents were total fabrications—which about 51 percent of the sample had. (Because some people had more than one set of documents, these percentages add up to more than 100 percent.)

The most common way of getting documents (a way used by 39 percent of the sample) was through non-Jewish friends. This method was more common among women (44 percent of the women versus 29 percent of the men). Only one-third of those who obtained papers paid for them, even though there was a thriving black market in identity documents during the war. The problem with purchased documents was that one was never sure of the quality of the documents.

Nathan's family, for example, paid a friend of a friend to buy documents for them on the black market.[59] The documents were very expensive and had to be paid for in advance. A clerk at the City Hall stayed in his office late at night and surreptitiously copied the names and personal data of real people onto new identity cards. Because the clerk was working in dim light and under great pressure, he had no time to match the age and occupation of the purchaser with the document. After spending a fortune to obtain his false documents, Nathan found himself with a name he detested, an occupation he knew nothing about, and an ID card that made him ten years older than he actually was. An educated middle-class man, he was always embarrassed when someone examined his card and saw that he was an apprentice shoemaker: "I did not look like a shoemaker, and my hands, everybody who saw them, knew that they were not the hands of a cobbler. . . . I cried when I saw those papers. . . . I can't tell you how horrible I felt because I had to show it to everybody who wanted to see it. . . . but we had no money to get them changed."[60]

A second risk of purchasing identity documents on the black market was the possibility of blackmail. After the war, Nathan found out that the clerk who had supplied his family's documents later tracked down some of his customers and forced them to keep paying him off throughout the war.

The Issue of Resistance

Was living on the Aryan side a form of resistance? If the essential element in resistance is the motivation to outwit, defy, subvert, thwart, or otherwise resist the aims of the oppressor—as I would assert—then many of those who were passing on the Aryan side were resisting by defying the Nazis and trying to thwart their goal of destroying the entire Jewish people. Although there is some controversy about this definition of resistance, most analysts agree that the intention or motivation of the actor is the critical element in defining resistance.[61]

There is also some controversy about whether we can accept retrospective definitions of motivation (such as those given in testimonies years later). Many historians assert that we can only rely on what people wrote at the time. Although this position seems especially inappropriate for those who were passing (because no sensible person would keep a diary while passing), the rationale for this stance is that people who write about long-ago experiences reinterpret their motivation in light of subsequent events and new definitions of desirable behavior. However, it seems evident that similar considerations structured what one said or wrote during the Holocaust as well. What one thinks (and writes about) is always influenced by personal concerns and by the universal human need to create self-sustaining explanations for one's behavior.

Thus it was natural to define the decision to pass as a way of resisting the Nazis, or as a way of obeying one's parents who urged one to live for the family, or as a way of surviving to bear witness to the Nazi crimes. Similarly, those who described the decision to pass as something that others arranged for them, did not have to feel guilty or responsible for those who did not make it, because the survivor had not "chosen" to abandon them.

Thus any report of one's motivation is influenced by social definitions of what is or was desirable, and that is no less true of those who wrote about their intentions during or right after the Holocaust. In addition, because we can learn about motivation only from self-reports, and because the issue of motivation lies at the heart of most definitions of resistance, we have to rely on the explanations that people offer for their own behavior. And if we do so, then we must acknowledge that resistance was often a critical component of the motivation to try to survive on the Aryan side. Thus, if we follow the widely accepted view of resistance—as behavior that is motivated by the intention to thwart or defy the aims of the oppressor and thereby has a larger political agenda than "merely" living[62]—then we should conclude that many of those who lived on the Aryan side saw themselves as resisting the Nazis: they were consciously defying Nazi orders and deliberately trying to subvert the murderous intentions of the Nazis.

Some of them were also trying to save themselves and others so that some few might live to bear witness to the Nazis' crimes. This later rationale was similarly employed by the Jewish underground which, at various times, sent valued members to the Aryan side for safety. Their goals were also to rescue Jews, save lives, and ensure the survival of witnesses to the Nazi crimes.

When one looks at the full spectrum of the literature on Jewish resistance, which includes many activities that were defined as passive and spiritual resistance,[63] it is surely valid to consider the efforts of those on the Aryan side to bear witness, save Jewish lives, and thwart Nazi goals, as the very essence of Jewish resistance during the Holocaust.

Women and Resistance

Although most scholars endorse this broad concept of resistance, we may nevertheless ask why most accounts of resistance during the Holocaust have focused on armed resistance. Is it just a coincidence that this is the form of resistance that more men were engaged in—in contrast to those in which women were more prevalent, such as rescue activities? Although a full discussion of this issue is beyond the scope of this chapter, there are several factors that help us understand the focus on male-based armed resistance—and the parallel neglect of women's resistance activities.

First, armed resistance was more likely to be noticeable and public—involving acts such as blowing up railroad lines or a German canteen. In contrast, rescue activities, such as saving a child, involved a multitude of steps that had to be performed quietly and unobtrusively. Many of the tasks involved in saving oneself and others were invisible and needed to be invisible. They were either totally secret or known to only one or two others. This emphasis on secrecy and invisibility was in stark contrast to the publicity-generating acts or the "glory actions" that captured the public's attention and were remembered as triumphs of the resistance.

Second, many of the women involved in rescue activities were not part of a formal organization. Women were more likely to be involved in private acts of rescue organized through friends and social networks. Many of their activities were extensions of their prewar roles in the home and in charitable organizations. The activities of individuals were not less numerous than those of groups: for example, Susan Zuccotti concludes that one-half of the Jews who were saved in France were saved by individuals who were not part of any organization.[64] However, as Renée Poznanski shows (Chapter 13), women were not part of the institutional structure of recognition and remembrance that emerged after the war. Both women and men later defined the women's resistance activities as private acts, rather than as national heroism.

Third, even when women did take part in organized resistance activities, their roles were more often defined as auxiliary than as central. As Poznanski illustrates, even though women were often given the most dangerous missions of transporting weapons and guns (because women were "naturally disguised"), what they were doing was defined as helping those who blew up the trains. The roles they were assigned, their lack of leadership positions, and the humble labeling of their tasks all contributed to women's lower level of recognition and honor after the war.

Fourth, in both Western and Eastern Europe, what were defined as women's activities, especially if they involved women and children, were, simply put, typically devalued. As Deborah Dwork has shown, because this type of resistance involved saving children, and because it was mainly done by women, it did not count as much.[65] In addition, the women rescuers generally did not seek publicity, left few records of their activities, and disappeared from public life after the war.

Finally, and most simply, the official version of resistance embodies a male perspective, and in that perspective guns and arms typify resistance. Even though the most authoritative Holocaust scholars—such as Yisrael Gutman and Leni Yahil[66]—have explicitly embraced a much more inclusive concept of resistance during the Holocaust, the focus on armed resistance has nevertheless prevailed. The irony of this perspective is that scholars generally agree that these exploits, however spectacular and brave, had little or no larger military value (and in many cases they were actually counterproductive).[67]

If we place the activities of those who were living on the Aryan side in this larger context, it is not surprising that they have received relatively little attention. They were, for the most part, ordinary people, acting independently, trying to remain invisible, and they were primarily women. Even when they helped or rescued others, their activities had to remain unobtrusive and unrecognized. But in the end, passing was a means of saving lives, and I am grateful that so many of them lived to tell their story.

Notes

1. Rose Zar, *In the Mouth of the Wolf* (Philadelphia: Jewish Publication Society, 1983), p. 6.
2. Celia S. Heller, *On the Edge of Destruction: Jews of Poland between the Two World Wars* (Detroit: Wayne State University Press, 1977), p. 68.
3. In both the Yad Vashem and Yale samples discussed later in this chapter, about 10 percent of the Holocaust survivors who voluntarily gave testimonies reported living on the Aryan side. I assume that this estimate of the percentage of Jews who passed is conservative, because those who survived by passing may have been less likely to give testimonies than those who survived the concentration camps.
4. All of the survivors I interviewed talked about other Jews who were caught. In addition, Poles would not have created the "sport" of catching Jews who escaped from the ghetto if there had not been so many Jews to catch.
5. I am especially grateful to Professor Yisrael Gutman and Dr. Mordecai Paldiel of Yad Vashem for helping to arrange the interviews in Israel, and to Vardit Hortman, my assistant, and Professor Anita Weiner, my colleague, for accompanying me and being my second eyes and ears during the interviews.
6. This was a very time-consuming process because the Yad Vashem Archives were not computerized in the fall of 1992, when I began my work, and there was no master list of testimonies. I am especially grateful for Neta Frishman's dedicated assistance and support in every phase of the archival research.
7. To be able to organize this vast array of information, I developed a seventeen-page questionnaire that I used to record and code the basic information and events in each testimony. I (and my assistants) also recorded many stories, quotations, and excerpts from the narratives. I am indebted to Gali Avrahami, Na'ama Begin, Gabriel Bar-Shaked, Emmanuel Darmon, Karen Dengler, Neat Frishman, Vardit Hortman, Aryeh Julius, Bluma Lederhandler, Karen Margolet, Iris Mazel, Eugenia Melchoir, Julia Vercholantsev, Ella Walner, Olaf Walner, Eva Weitzman, and Maria Westerman for their assistance.
8. Each of the cases drawn from the Yad Vashem archives is identified by its file number in the main testimonies archive. I have used the full names of those who have publicly spoken about, written about, or allowed others to write about their experiences. Others are identified only by first names, which, in some cases, have been changed because of restrictions on the files or because of my own concern about identifying people who are no longer alive. Alicia is Yad Vashem testimony #03–4297, translated from Hebrew by Iris Mazel, January 6, 1993.

9. Ibid., pp. 2–3.

10. Ibid., p. 10.

11. Personal interview with David, Jerusalem, June 6, 1994. This is also a Yad Vashem testimony, which had not been given a file number when it was translated from Hebrew by Neta Frishman in June 1993.

12. Ibid.

13. Ibid.

14. Personal interview with Natalie, Los Angeles, August 1994. The reaction was not always immediate, as it was for Alicia. Yitzhak Sternberg, for example, was depressed and indifferent after he lost both his mother and his brother in the Aktion in Chodorov: "At first, I did not care about anything. I did not care about what might happen to me. I did not hide. . . . What else could they do to me?" Personal interview, Kibbutz Lochameh HaGetaot, Israel, May 3, 1993. See also Yitzhak Sternberg, *Under Assumed Identity* (Haifa: Chidekel Press, 1986).

15. Personal interview with Ida Fink, Holon, Israel, July 11, 1993. See also Ida Fink, *The Journey* (New York: Farrar, Straus and Giroux, 1990), pp. 2–3.

16. Solomon Pearl, the author of *Europa, Europa,* said that his mother's parting words, telling him that he had to live, were what kept him going. Personal interview, Givataim, Israel, June 19, 1994.

17. Personal interview with Ella, Miami Beach, March 11, 1994.

18. For a more extended discussion of help from non-Jews see Nechama Tec, *When Light Pierced the Darkness* (New York: Oxford University Press, 1987); Eva Fogelman, *Conscience and Courage: Rescuers of Jews during the Holocaust* (New York: Anchor Books, 1994); Samuel and Pearl Oliner, *The Altruistic Personality* (New York: Free Press, 1988); and Mordecai Paldiel, *Sheltering the Jews: Stories of Holocaust Rescuers* (Minneapolis: Fortress Press, 1996).

19. Personal interview with Suzie, Ramat Gan, Israel, June 22, 1994.

20. Personal interview with Bronka Klibanski, Jerusalem, June 12, 1993, and June 21, 1994.

21. Samuel P. Oliner, *Restless Memories* (Berkeley: Judiah Magnes, 1986), p. 11.

22. Personal interview with David, Jerusalem, June 7, 1994.

23. Ibid.

24. Ibid.

25. Ibid.

26. Erving Goffman, *The Presentation of Self in Everyday Life* (Garden City, New York: Doubleday, 1959).

27. Charles Horton Cooley, *Human Nature and the Social Order* (New York: Charles Scribner's Sons, 1922).

28. Personal interview with Bronka Klibanski, Jerusalem, June 12, 1993.

29. Although there is no category that is comparable to the classification we used, Raphael Mahler lists only 5 percent of the Jewish population in "services, liberal professions" in his economic profile of the Jewish population of Poland in 1921. Mahler, *Yehude polin en shte milhamot ha-olam* (Tel Aviv: Dvir, 1968), p. 61, as cited in Ezra Mendelsohn, *The*

Jews of East Central Europe between the World Wars (Bloomington: Indiana University Press, 1987), p. 36.

30. Yad Vashem testimony of Stephan, p. 35, translated by Karen Margalit, July 15, 1993.

31. Yad Vashem testimony of Stephan, p. 20. On his next day off, Stephan escaped to Hungary, where he joined the underground.

32. Personal interview with Oswald Rufeisen, Haifa, June 15, 1994. See also Nechama Tec's fascinating account of his life in *The Lion's Den* (New York: Oxford University Press, 1990).

33. Heller, *On the Edge of Destruction.*

34. In 1918 the new sovereign state of Poland instituted a system of compulsory public education, but the required courses could be taken in schools that were run by the Jewish community. As Ezra Mendelsohn notes, in practice this meant that parents had the option of sending their children to schools that were run by the Jewish authorities, which included curricula with Jewish subject matter. In some of these schools, courses were taught in Jewish languages (either Yiddish or Hebrew). (Mendelsohn, *The Jews of East Central Europe between the World Wars.*) Because all Polish schools were sex segregated, and because it was considered more important for boys to receive a Jewish education, boys were more likely to remain in schools on a Jewish track, while their sisters were more likely to attend ordinary Polish schools. Although I have been unable to locate any hard data on the different educational tracks of Jewish boys and girls, it is clear that the Jewish community at that time believed that these differences existed and was concerned about losing their young women. This concern led to the establishment of the *Beys ya'akov* schools for girls. (Personal conversations with Paula Hyman and Gershon Bacon, September 1997.)

35. Among the less religious and more assimilated segments of the Polish Jewish population, both girls and boys were more likely to receive secular educations. Most, but not all, of those who passed benefited from these secular educations.

36. However, those men who passed successfully either had or were able to acquire a similar sensitivity. Here we are suggesting differences between most men and most women, not between the men and women who passed.

37. It is possible that women are simply more willing to report that they asked for help and that they received help. But I am inclined to believe that differences between women and men are real, because of the consistent pattern of women's greater involvement with people in every sphere of this research.

38. Testimony of Helene R., #15, Fortunoff Video Archive, Yale University.

39. Yad Vashem testimony of Alicia, #03–4297, translated by Iris Mazel, January 6, 1993, p. 15.

40. Ibid., p. 17.

41. Ibid.

42. Personal interview with Sandra Brand, New York, March 6, 1989.

43. Testimony of Niusia, #87, Fortunoff Video Archive, Yale University.

44. Personal interview with Bronka Klibanski, Jerusalem, June 12, 1993.

45. Personal interview with Bella Yari-Hazan, June 20, 1994.

46. Nechama Tec, *Dry Tears* (New York: Oxford University Press, 1982).

47. Tec, *When Light Pierced the Darkness,* p. 36.

48. Heller, *On the Edge of Destruction.*

49. Ibid.

50. Ibid.

51. Personal interview with David, Jerusalem, June 6, 1994.

52. Personal interview with Bella Yari-Hazan, June 20, 1994.

53. Personal interview with Sandra Brand, New York, March 6, 1989; see also Sandra Brand, *I Dared to Live* (New York: Shengold, 1978).

54. Tec, *Dry Tears,* p. 68.

55. Personal interview with Hannah, Miami Beach, March 10, 1994.

56. Mordecai Paldiel was especially helpful in discussing different types of forged documents with me.

57. This story is paraphrased from the testimony of Paul D., #48, Fortunoff Video Archive, Yale University. Paul D. was passing with his mother, and he was waiting outside the office when these events transpired.

58. Ibid.

59. Personal interview with Nathan Gross, Tiberias, Israel, December 1988.

60. Ibid., p. 5.

61. For example, see Roger S. Gottlieb, "The Concept of Resistance: Jewish Resistance during the Holocaust," *Social Theory and Practice* 9 (1983), pp. 31–49; Leni Yahil, "Jewish Resistance—An Examination of Active and Passive Forms of Jewish Survival in the Holocaust Period," in *Jewish Resistance during the Holocaust,* proceedings of the conference on manifestations of Jewish resistance, Yad Vashem, Jerusalem, April 7–11, 1968 (Jerusalem: Yad Vashem, 1971); Michael R. Marrus, "Jewish Resistance during the Holocaust," *Journal of Contemporary History* 30 (1995), pp. 83–110.

62. Ibid.

63. Yahil, "Jewish Resistance." Yisrael Gutman, for example, mentions the "stubborn daily struggle for survival by defying Nazi regulations and terror, or the culturally oriented underground . . . in the spheres of education, religion, and the arts." Yisrael Gutman, "Jewish Resistance: Some Questions and Answers," in *The Historiography of the Holocaust Period,* ed. Yisrael Gutman and Gideon Greif (Jerusalem: Yad Vashem, 1988).

64. For example, Susan Zuccotti concludes that one-half of all the Jews who were saved in France were saved by individuals who were not part of organizations (*The Holocaust, the French and the Jews* [New York: Basic Books, 1993]).

65. Deborah Dwork, *Children with a Star* (New Haven: Yale University Press, 1991), p. xliv.

66. Yahil, "Jewish Resistance"; Gutman, "Jewish Resistance."

67. For example, see Marrus, "Jewish Resistance during the Holocaust."

CHAPTER TWELVE

Women among the Forest Partisans

Nechama Tec

M uch of western Belorussia, now known as Belarus, is covered by thick, swampy, partly inaccessible forests. Under the German occupation, from the summer of 1941 until the summer of 1944, this area became a haven for a variety of prospective Nazi victims and an important center for the Soviet partisan movement.

The forest population was changeable and diverse. The first arrivals were former Red Army soldiers who had eluded capture by the enemy during the initial stages of the German-Russian war. They were followed by escaped Soviet prisoners of war and by guerrilla organizers sent specially from Moscow.[1] By 1942, young Belorussian men were fleeing to the forest to avoid conscription for forced labor in Germany. They were joined by a stream of Jewish fugitives who had survived the overcrowding, disease, starvation, and other abuses in the nearby ghettos.

For the Jewish ghetto runaways in particular, life in the woods posed serious challenges and threats. Most Jews in prewar Poland (77 percent) had lived in urban centers; they had little experience with the requirements for survival in a forest environment. Also, many of the ghetto runaways were women, children, or elderly men—easy targets for unruly partisan groups. Some of these fugitives were robbed and murdered; others were stripped of their meager belongings and chased away. Usually only young Jewish men with guns stood a chance of being accepted in a non-Jewish partisan group.

The Jews, faced with the threatening and unpredictable environment of the forest, devised unusual strategies of survival. Some of them successfully cooperated with non-Jewish partisans; others formed their own units, which varied in composition, size, and ability to withstand the overpowering dangers. At times these newly created detachments were transformed into family camps. One of these Jewish groups, known as the Bielski otriad (the brothers who formed it were the Bielskis, and *otriad* is a Russian word for partisan detachment), took on the dual role of rescuers and fighters. Eventually it became the largest armed rescue organization of Jews by Jews, numbering more than 1,200 individuals—men, women, and children.[2]

The three Bielski brothers, Asael, Tuvia, and Zus, belonged to the small minority of Jews who were peasants before the war. The only Jews in their isolated village, they were poor, with limited schooling. But they were familiar with the countryside and very independent. The brothers refused to submit to Nazi persecution and, in the summer of 1941, escaped into the countryside. With the help of Belorussian friends, they acquired some arms. In the summer of 1942, with more than thirty followers, they formed a partisan unit with Tuvia Bielski as commander.

Tuvia Bielski, a strong leader, insisted from the start that all Jews, regardless of age, sex, state of health, and any other condition, would be accepted into the unit. Some saw this open-door policy as a threat to the group's existence, but Tuvia argued that large size meant greater safety, and eventually his forceful personality prevailed.

The Bielski otriad managed to neutralize some of the surrounding dangers by cooperating with the Soviet partisans in food collection and in military ventures. Different partisan groups were assigned to different villages from which to acquire provisions. Faced with armed men, the peasants had no choice but to part with their limited supplies. At first the joint military moves were aimed at the acquisition of arms and goods. Later, they included such sabotage activities as cutting telephone wires, blowing up bridges, and derailing trains.

From 1942 until 1943, the Bielski partisans led a nomadic existence. Toward the end of 1943, they established a more permanent home in the Nolibocka forest. At this stage the camp came to resemble a shtetl (a small town). The establishment of factories and workshops in the camp transformed part of the Bielski detachment into a supplier of services to the Soviet partisans. The usefulness of the otriad helped to counter some of the non-Jewish partisans' complaints that the Jews ate too much, depriving the "real" fighters of food.[3]

In addition, the exchanges that grew out of the workshops and factories improved the economic situation in the Bielski unit, so that it was not necessary for the young men to go on so many dangerous food-finding expeditions. Finally, the work itself must have contributed to the workers' psychological well-being.

Life in the forest revolved around safety concerns and the acquisition of food. Inevitably, characteristics such as physical strength, perseverance, fearlessness, independence, mobility, and courage were highly valued. Conversely, those defined as lacking in these attributes were devalued and sometimes mistreated. These included the Jewish fugitives, women, children, the old, and the sick.

Women, and Jewish women in particular, faced different prospects in Russian partisan units and in the Bielski group. Officially, the Soviet government praised women's contributions to guerrilla warfare, claiming that women partisans symbolized supreme dedication to the patriotic struggle for the country. In reality women who joined Soviet partisan detachments were relegated to unimportant duties. The closest they came to combat was as scouts or intelligence agents, and even these jobs were assigned to them only rarely. Eagerness to participate or special fitness did not tip the scale in their favor. Estimates of the percentage of women in the entire Russian partisan movement range from 2 to 5 percent. And despite the official attitudes, the Russian partisan leadership in the forest was convinced that this small proportion of women was all that the movement could effectively absorb.[4]

Some experts claim that the principal reason for admitting women into Russian partisan detachments was their usefulness as sex partners. A woman, the argument continues, was defined as a necessary part of an officer's equipment, and "officers from a brigade commander down to the battalion commanders 'married' the women enlisted in the unit. Usually, women became the property of the officers, which by implication gave them officer status, with such attendant privileges as quarters with the brigade staffs, relief from combat assignments. . . . The women, in turn, were often willing to content themselves with their contribution as officers' 'wives.'"[5] Most high-ranking Russian partisans had a mistress. In recognition of this arrangement, such a woman was called a "transit wife."[6] Because women were aware that powerful male partisans could shield them from danger, it is not surprising that "every woman in the forest dreamt of becoming a wife of a commandant. Indeed, young girls would sleep with Russian commandants, political heads or whoever was in a position of power." Conversely, "unless a young woman was ready to become the mistress of a Russian officer she would not be admitted into an otriad." And if a partisan, any male partisan, helped a woman in any way, he expected to be paid with sexual favors.[7]

Although most male partisans were eager to have sex with women, they also accused them of promiscuity. The very women they desired as sex partners they viewed with contempt. In conversations between men, for example, the word *whore* was often substituted for the word *woman*.[8] All women in the forest, defined as sex objects and excluded from participation in valued activities, were in a dependent position. Jewish women—and most of the women in the Belorussian forests were Jewish—were in even more dependent and vulnerable positions than Christian women. Whereas many non-Jewish women came to the woods because of a special attachment to a man, Jewish women came to avoid death. Even before they came to the forest they knew that the possibility of rape and murder was real.

Among the Soviet partisans, the overall hostility directed toward all women was even more vigorously applied to Jewish women. Over time, these negative attitudes became stronger and more common, largely because of changes in the composition of the partisan group. Toward the end of the war, in order to prevent future punishment, some Nazi collaborators switched sides and joined the partisan ranks. Invariably they brought their antisemitism with them, creating a more pervasive anti-Jewish atmosphere.[9] Some officers who had Jewish mistresses were under pressure to terminate their relationships. A few refused to give in; others broke off their connections to these women.[10]

Few of the Jewish women who reached the forest gained entry into Russian partisan detachments. Most of those who did became sexually involved with partisan officers. But not all who sought entry were ready to trade sex for protection. And only a fraction had the requisite youth and good looks to qualify for such transactions. Special skills could overcome these barriers. A physician, a nurse, or a good cook would be accepted into a detachment even though she refused to become someone's mistress or did not qualify as one. Doctors were in especially short supply, as were nurses, and they would be welcomed into any otriad.

In the Bielski otriad, the elite were the Bielski brothers, their wives, some relatives, close friends, and those who worked at the headquarters. Next in importance were the young men with guns, who were the otriad's defenders. Indirectly they defended their community through participation in joint anti-German moves, but they devoted most of their energies to gathering provisions. Food expeditions were exhausting and dangerous, sometimes ending in the death of the participants.

Below the armed men in the hierarchy were artisans. They enjoyed more privileged positions after the fall of 1943, when the otriad built workshops and factories. Most members of the otriad—anyone who arrived without a gun and without highly valued skills—occupied the bottom of the social structure. These people performed only unskilled labor, such as working in the kitchen, chopping wood, or taking care of the cows or horses. Contemptuously called *malbush* or *malbushim* (Hebrew for "clothes," but no one seems to know how the term acquired its negative meaning),[11] this group included older people, women and children, and many intellectuals and professionals, whose skills were useless in the anti-intellectual climate of the forest, where good manners and a cultural background were irrelevant and even inappropriate. The use of coarse language became a commonplace. Cursing and heavy drinking were widely accepted. Most partisans agreed that drinking made life easier and helped one forget the dangerous situation. Tuvia Bielski's wife, Lilka, claimed that drinking "a cup, a glass . . . kept away illnesses."[12] Some people even felt that Tuvia's success in his dealings with Russian partisans was enhanced by his ability to "outdrink them and . . . curse like they did."[13]

The malbushim, who ate only what was officially allotted to them by the otriad, reacted to their lot in a variety of ways. Some tried to make the best of the situation, saying: "We were not starving, we also did not have an abundance, some had more than others. We had enough. We would collect berries in the forest, mushrooms. This helped, too."[14] Others maintained that there was enough bread and that it was of excellent quality. Still others were less satisfied and insisted that they were hungry but justified the practice of giving more food to the higher-ups: "The Bielski family ate better. It was their right, it was coming to them."[15] Another malbush, resigned to his fate, said: "Those in power had to eat better. There is no equality in any place and there was no equality in the forest either." Finally, one respondent said: "I was not a

Communist, never thought that people should have the same. Those who did not go for expeditions would get soup, sometimes bread and potatoes in peels. There was no salt. If the cook liked you, you would get a piece of lung or some such object that was swimming in the soup. If he did not like you, you would get watery soup."[16]

People in the Bielski otriad, as in most groups, could occasionally improve their situations or their social rank. The road for social mobility, however, was significantly different for men and women. Both men and women could earn more food by taking on extra work: spending extra hours on kitchen jobs or in guarding the camp would entitle a person to more food but would not affect his or her ranking. To improve their status, some men would acquire a gun and go on food-finding expeditions. This would remove them from the position of a malbush. Some of these men, after obtaining a gun, distinguished themselves as scouts and fighters and became a part of the elite.

No such opportunities were available to women, who were barred from food missions because the men believed that the presence of women on an expedition would endanger an already perilous situation. (Chaja Bielski was an exception: her prominent husband, Asael, would occasionally take her with him.) In the rare instances when a woman alone reached the Bielski otriad with a weapon it was confiscated. Guns belonged to men and not to women; this was the law of the forest. Raja Kaplinski, the official secretary of the otriad, justified this custom: "What did she think, she will come to our camp and shoot at birds? Tuvia needed to give the gun to a man who went with an expedition to bring food."[17]

Unless a woman had special skills, upon entering the Bielski otriad she became a malbush. She stopped being a malbush when she became attached to an "appropriate" man—usually an uneducated lower-class youth, a partisan fighter with a gun, who belonged to a higher class in the forest. The privileges of such a fighting man included the possibility of choosing a sexual partner, often a woman from a formerly socially superior background, someone a simple, uneducated young man would not even have dreamed about before the war. In fact, most "forest marriages" involved prewar higher-class women and prewar lower-class men.

There were no official weddings. When a man and a woman shared a tent or a bunker and acted like a couple, others began to treat them as married. It has been estimated that about 60 percent of the adults lived as couples. Most former partisans say that these "marriages" were stable and lasted a lifetime.[18]

Most people in the Bielski camp agreed that a woman needed someone to take care of her and that this someone had to be a "proper" man.[19] One young woman explained, "Even though we women did not go out to fight and did not go for food missions, we were exposed to military actions. The Germans would attack us. A woman who had a man with a gun felt more secure."[20] Some believe that the man-woman relationships in the woods were based on more than an exchange of services and goods. One woman, attached to a man who would have been socially beneath her before the war, said, "I do not agree that women were selling themselves, but it was not love either. To be sure, men rather than women would select a partner. But if a woman did not like a man no one forced her. She was free to reject a man, any man. . . . A friend of mine, an educated girl from a good home, . . . became involved with a carpenter, very common. Still, he saved her life, she really loved him later on. These were two different worlds. They had a wonderful marriage. Now too many women marry without love."[21]

Life was hard for an unattached woman, even in the Bielski otriad. Usually such a woman was dressed in rags, with shoes that were falling apart. If she had no shoes, she had to wait for her turn to see the shoemaker. But if she had nothing with which to bribe him, her turn would never come.

Nonetheless, while many young women were sexually active, in the Bielski otriad no one coerced any of them into a relationship. Unlike women in the Soviet detachments, women in the Bielski otriad had the freedom to refuse a suitor. In fact, some of the women who could have had lovers opted for celibacy. They rarely blamed the Bielski otriad for their difficulties. Instead, they would emphasize again and again that if it were not for this group they would have never made it.[22]

Many Jewish women in the Bielski otriad were critical of the men they married or refused to marry. Sulia Rubin, for example, was part of the elite of her town. When she reached the Bielski otriad in November 1942, her privileged background gained her entry into the bunker of another privileged family, who were apparently impressed by her prewar social class. But her background did not prevent her from becoming a malbush. "Every ziemlanka [bunker] had a 'nebbish,' 'a hanger-on,' a malbush—I was it. Not fit for anything. They took me in only reluctantly." She had a hard time adjusting in the forest and eventually married a crude, uneducated young man, a fighter. As the wife of this common but "important" man, her situation improved drastically and she was able to help her friends. Yet the fact that her marriage endured did not keep her from voicing disdain for men's behavior:

> I did not see one man sacrifice himself and go to the grave with his children. My cousin went. She could have survived. A German wanted to protect her. She was gorgeous, with blue eyes and dark curly hair. She won the beauty contest of the town Druzgieniki. Her name was Mina Bencjanowski. During a deportation a German wanted to take her to the side that was spared. She said: "Aber meine Kinder" (But my children). "Die Kinder kan ich nicht" (The children I cannot), was his answer. "Da gehe ich mit die Kinder zum Todt" (Then I will go to death with my children). Not only did the men not sacrifice themselves for their children and wives, but when a man's wife was barely dead he would already look for a woman with whom to have sex. This happened to me. We were hidden during an Aktion. This man's wife was taken away not long before that and he was trying to make out, first with my sister, then with me. . . . I wanted a prince on a white horse to come and take me, but there was no one like this. I was attractive, young. Sure, men wanted me, but only for sex, not for my soul. I was cured of all men. I tell my husband when he is jealous: "Don't be afraid. I don't need any men. I don't want them." Many of my girlfriends feel the same way. We had them up to here [she places a hand above her mouth].[23]

Is Sulia Rubin right when she says that many of her women friends resent men and have no use for them? Perhaps. What led to this hostility? Was it the inequality of the relationship? Was it the women's dependence?

The Bielski otriad automatically admitted, fed, and sheltered every Jewish woman who reached the forest. Its former members agree that no woman there was ever forced or raped or sent away.[24] In sharp contrast, acceptance of a woman into a Soviet detachment was rare and contingent on special skills or on the willingness to become the mistress of a powerful man. Some women were raped by Soviet partisans, and some were sent away.

With few exceptions, all women, in all partisan groups, were excluded from combat duty and from leadership positions. Whatever influence a woman had was usually channeled through a man to whom she was sexually attached. Do these male-female distinctions mean that despite the devastation, some patriarchal traditions continued to flourish? Is it possible that the forest, with its demands of physical strength, perseverance, fearlessness, and resourcefulness, perpetuated or reestablished these patriarchal patterns? Clearly, whether these patterns were a continuation of old traditions or newly emergent arrangements, they in some way shaped the lives and destinies of men and women differently.

Notes

1. Some of these Soviet soldiers may have been willful deserters, but others were probably left behind during the rapid and chaotic retreat. See Yitzhak Arad, *Ghetto in Flames: The Struggle and Destruction of the Jews in Vilna in the Holocaust* (New York: Holocaust Library, 1982), p. 30; Hersh Smolar, *The Minsk Ghetto, Soviet Jewish Partisans against the Nazis* (New York: Holocaust Library, 1989), pp. 4–8. It has been estimated that in the first six months of the war the Germans took more than 3 million Soviet soldiers as prisoners. See Earl Ziemke, "Composition and Morale of the Partisan Movement," in John A. Armstrong (ed.), *Soviet Partisans in World War II* (Madison: University of Wisconsin Press, 1964), p. 143. Nazi policies toward Russian POWs consisted of economic exploitation and murder. The economic exploitation was an intermediary step that led to eventual death. See Rueben Ainsztein, *Jewish Resistance in Occupied Eastern Europe* (New York: Barnes and Noble, 1974), p. 243; Martin Gilbert, *The Second World War: A Complete History* (New York: Henry Holt, 1989), p. 373.

2. For more information on the Bielski otriad see Nechama Tec, *Defiance: The Bielski Partisans* (New York: Oxford University Press, 1993).

3. It appears that the combat activities of the partisans have been highly exaggerated. Whatever military encounters took place reflected the avoidance of direct enemy confrontations that is characteristic of guerrilla warfare. Henri Michel, *The Shadow War: European Resistance, 1939–1945* (New York: Harper and Row, 1972), pp. 278–279; Jack N. Porter, ed., *Jewish Partisans: A Documentary of Jewish Resistance in the Soviet Union during World War II* (New York: University Press of America, 1982), p. 9; J. K. Zawodny, "Guerrilla and Sabotage: Organization, Operations, Motivations, Escalations," *Annals of the Academy of Political Science* 341, (May 1962), pp. 8–18. Even after the tide of the Russian-German war turned in favor of the Soviet Union, it took quite a while before the Soviet partisans became an effective force. Some are convinced that the partisan fighting was much less extensive than officially claimed. See Nechama Tec, *In The Lion's Den: The Life of Oswald Rufeisen* (New York: Oxford University Press, 1990), pp. 201–202.

4. Porter says that the literature of the partisan movement does not acknowledge that women were treated in a sexist fashion. See Jack N. Porter, "Jewish Women in the Resistance," in *Anthology of Armed Resistance to the Nazis, 1939–1945,* ed. Isaac Kowalski (New York: Jewish Combatants Publishing House, 1986), vol. 1, p. 292.

5. Earl Ziemke, "Composition and Morale of the Partisan Movement," in Armstrong, *Soviet Partisans in World War II,* p. 147–148.

6. Hersh Smolar, personal interview, Tel Aviv, Israel, 1988–1990.

7. Chaja Bielski, personal interview, Haifa, Israel, 1987–1991; Pinchas Boldo, personal interview, Haifa, Israel, 1990; Abraham Viner, personal interview, Haifa, Israel, 1990; Lili Krawitz, personal interview, Tel Aviv, Israel, 1989.

8. Hersh Smolar notes that some women also used these expressions.

9. In the last year of the war, an estimated 10 to 20 percent of the Soviet partisans were former Nazi collaborators. See Ziemke, "Composition and Morale of the Partisan Movement," p. 147. Jewish partisans reported stepped-up antisemitism in the Soviet otriads. Among these partisans are Zorach Arluk (personal interview, Tel Aviv, Israel, 1988), Jashke Mazowi (personal interview, Tel Aviv, Israel, 1989), and Itzyk Mendelson (Yad Vashem Testimony, no. 3355/186).

10. Ester Marchwinski, Yad Vashem Testimony, no. 03/33567; Josef Marchwinski, Yad Vashem Testimony, no. 03/3568.

11. Shmuel Amarant, "The Tuvia Bielski Partisan Company," in *Nivo shel adam* (Expressions of a man) (Jerusalem: Published privately with the help of Misrad Hahinuch ve Hatarbut, 1973). This chapter was translated from Hebrew into English by R. Goodman.

12. Lilka Bielski, personal interview, Brooklyn, New York, 1989.

13. Sulia Wolozhinski-Rubin, personal interview, Saddle River, New Jersey, 1988.

14. Tamara Rabinowicz, personal interview, Haifa, Israel, 1990.

15. Cila Sawicki, personal interview, Tel Aviv, Israel, 1989.

16. Luba Garfunk, personal interview, Tel Aviv, Israel, 1989.

17. Raja Kaplinski, personal interview, Tel Aviv, Israel, 1988–1989.

18. Personal interviews with Chaja Bielski and Raja Kaplinski.

19. This view was expressed by almost everyone—for example, Chaja Bielski, Eljezer Engelstern, and Shmuel Geler.

20. Pesia Bairach, personal interview, Tel Aviv, Israel, 1990.

21. Lili Krawitz, personal interview.

22. Two examples of the many women who share these attitudes are Ester Krynicki Gorodejski Berkowitz and Cila Kapelowicz. See Ester Krynicki Gorodejski Berkowitz, "Sichrojnes fun der Deitscher Okupacje" (Memoirs from the German Occupation), in *Mir,* ed. N. Blumenthal (Jerusalem: Memorial Books, Encyclopedia of the Diaspora, 1962), pp. 587–602. Cila Kapelowicz reached the Bielski otriad after she escaped from the Mir ghetto and after the few relatives and friends with her were murdered by Russian partisans. She now lives in South Africa. I interviewed her when she was visiting Israel in 1987.

23. Personal interview with Sulia Rubin, who was told this story secondhand. Whether Sulia's secondhand observation applies to many more cases is not so important. What matters here are her perceptions of reality, not reality itself.

24. When Arkie Lubczanski, one of the Bielski partisans, was banned from the otriad, his "wife" was not included in this order. In fact, she voluntarily left with him but then returned alone because no Russian otriad would take her. She was readmitted without any problem.

CHAPTER THIRTEEN

Women in the French-Jewish Underground
Shield-Bearers of the Resistance?

Renée Poznanski

Bertie Albrecht, Marie-Madeleine Fourcade, Danièle Casanova, Marianne Cohn, Mila Racine, and Ariane Knout—these are some of the women in the pantheon of Resistance heroes glorified after the liberation of France. These few lauded women are the exceptions: they were venerated primarily because they were killed for the cause. Moreover, our memory of resistance in France is segmented: each interest group—Jewish, Communist, Gaullist—has its own specific and particularistic memory. Thus the commemoration of each of these women has been confined to the political press of her own movement.[1] This applies particularly to the heroines of the Jewish Resistance: the martyrdom of Marianne Cohn and Mila Racine, for example, is mentioned only in the Jewish press.

If the subject of women in the French Resistance has been ignored in historical literature and collective memory, this is doubly the case for Jewish women. Since the 1970s, however, specific memories have begun to emerge, and a few works have appeared that examine the role of women in the French Resistance or investigate the definition, forms, and importance of the Jewish Resistance.[2] All these studies begin by deploring the silence of the previous years. All cite figures intended to show how large the number of women Resistance activists—or Jewish Resistance activists—really was. They retell the activists' stories, which are sometimes humorous or moving but always heroic and often tragic. They describe missions performed mainly or exclusively by women—or by Jews—behind the scenes and reveal the brilliant feats they accomplished. Finally, they assess the price paid by those women or Jews who did not return from their missions.

It seems as if the authors of these works are seeking to legitimate the role of women or that of Jews in the collective memory of the Resistance by demanding that France acknowledge the importance of their contribution to the liberation of the country.[3] In fact we are faced with a historical problem. Undoubtedly the recent attention to the role of women is largely the result of the development of feminist consciousness, as the outpouring of studies on the Jewish Resistance is a direct result of the revival of Jewish consciousness in France.[4] In both cases, however, it is the broader conception of the Resistance as a whole that is involved in ongoing revision.

The findings of studies specifically devoted to French women in World War II bear witness to the attention now paid by historians to that topic. Of the 1,059 awarded, only 6 women received a *Compagnon de la libération,* the highest honor awarded to a French citizen for Resistance activities. This disparity clearly expresses the small place accorded to women in the epic of the Resistance.[5] Women themselves seem to have undervalued and even concealed their participation in the Resistance in the immediate postwar years.[6] One possible reason is that once "normality" was in sight, women naturally returned to their former place in society. Furthermore, as the Resistance movement developed and became institutionalized, it was integrated into traditional structures of public participation, such as political parties and the army, which had previously been male monopolies. A third reason is the nature of women's participation in the Resistance. Because women's activities were based on everyday life, they were more difficult to pinpoint than such male activities as political developments or military action.[7]

Women were indeed active in the Resistance, but primarily in its infrastructure. Frequently they directed the social services of the various movements, supplying members with food, lodging, means of communication, and false papers; this practice was clearly an extension of women's traditional role in society.[8] Battalions of female liaison agents were particularly effective in the information services and the escape networks; they transported arms and supported the fighters.[9] Women rarely took part in the fighting, however, and even when they worked on the movement's tracts and clandestine journals, they were more often the typists than the editors. But without their support, the dazzling exploits of the fighters would not have been possible.

Jewish resistance in France—that is, resistance mounted by Jews—followed the traditional patterns of Jewish political and social activism in France. It reflected the composition of French Jewry, a mosaic of national and political identities that included the community of Jews who had lived in France for many generations and also successive waves of immigrants from Eastern or Central Europe. Some Jewish Resistance activists, women and men, were part of the general Resistance movements in France. Most of them were of French nationality. In fact, it would be difficult and unproductive to study the role of Jewish women in the Resistance apart from the role of women, or that of Jews, who engaged individually in the various movements. In both cases, we are faced with the same fundamental issues: the influence of anti-Jewish persecution in France (which did not spare women); the stages of this persecution, which paved the way for the enlistment of Jews in the Resistance; the time-honored forms of political participation of French Jews; their integration into the movements without the emergence of any specific Jewish characteristic but with a different fate in the case of capture; and the methods of action characteristic of women, Jewish or otherwise, in the Resistance.[10]

Thus the meeting of the two dimensions, Jewish and female, sheds no new light here. The example of Madeleine Dreyfus, granddaughter of Captain Alfred Dreyfus, is symbolic in this respect. Dreyfus, an exemplary French Jew, had been trained by the *Eclaireurs* (the Scouts) and served as a social worker in the *Secours national* (National Social Service). In response to the roundups of Jews for deportation in the summer of 1942, she joined the Resistance group Combat, where she operated in the social service that had assumed responsibility for prisoners and internees and prepared the logistical infrastructure for escape across the Pyrenean border. The contacts she developed in her work enabled her to equip members of her family with false papers. Arrested as a member of the Resistance and jailed by the Gestapo as a Jew, she was sent to Drancy and then deported to Auschwitz, where she died of typhoid fever.[11]

Although one individual Jewish woman's experience may not be generalizable, an examination of the different collective and Jewish settings in which Jewish women Resistance activists operated illuminates several characteristics specific to them.

In the Bosom of the Communist Resistance

Even before the war, Communist militancy had begun to play an important role among Jewish immigrants in France. It was sustained by a large influx of political immigrants and encouraged by the creation of a special agency within the French Communist Party, the *Main d'oeuvre immigrée* (MOI, or Immigrant Labor Force), which was divided into language groups so as to offer militants who were still strangers to French society a convenient vehicle for political integration. The formation of specialized groups was a traditional part of the Communist Party's institutional strategy. Just as there were groups of immigrants, there were women's committees and thus Jewish women's committees. The Party's intention was neither to assure better representation for the groups concerned nor to decentralize power but rather to ensure the assimilation of Party themes and slogans, which were adapted to the characteristics of each respective social setting. There was no time for lengthy didactic indoctrination; for rapid mobilization it was better to co-opt existing stereotypes than to attempt to modify them. The Party's clandestine press and subsequent policies reflected these intentions, whether directed at women in general or at Jewish women in particular.[12] Thus the clandestine texts for women stressed the harsh conditions of daily life, the food shortages, the exorbitant prices of goods on the black market, and the workers' wages, which had been slashed nearly to zero.[13]

These emphases were chosen because women suffered the effects of poverty most directly. They also provided a convenient backdrop for efforts to coach the population in the spirit of resistance. The Communists, aware that women were less at risk than men of being arrested for subversive activity, organized public demonstrations for women on these ostensibly apolitical themes. As the Prefect of Police reported, the clandestine Communist Party worked to deploy "non-Communist female elements in a campaign of unrest on behalf of prisoners and children."[14] Indeed, for many months, delegations of women regularly marched on city halls to demand coal, better delivery of supplies, information about relatives who were prisoners of war, and the liberation of those who had been interned. In occupied France—in Vitry-sur-Seine, Montreuil, Bagnolet, and elsewhere—dozens turned out to demonstrate in front of public buildings.[15]

These same slogans were carried into the Jewish immigrant settings, with modifications suited to the special situation of the Jews. Thus demands for the return of POWs were replaced by demands for the liberation of Jews interned after the roundup of May 14, 1941. On June 16, 1941, Anna Repkovski, a militant in the women's section of *Solidarité* (the Jewish Communist organization in Paris), organized a delegation of women that marched to the Loiret camps where Jews were interned. More than one hundred women insisted on seeing their husbands at Pithiviers. The French administrators of the camps refused the request, but they did allow the women to distribute the bread they had brought.[16] In this campaign of unrest, led by Jewish women, the municipality or the Office of the Prefect—that is, the Vichy administrative services—was sometimes replaced by the *Comité de coordination des oeuvres juives* (Jewish Charity Coordination Committee), an organization that the Germans had imposed on the Jews to coordinate the Jewish welfare agencies.[17] From July 20 to July 31, 1941, almost five hundred Jewish women participated in daily demonstrations against the Coordination Committee, seeking the liberation of their husbands, who were interned in the camps at Pithiviers and Beaune-la-Rolande.[18] By implication, the women demonstrators held this Jewish organization—in which the Communists (and particularly Solidarité) did not participate—responsible for the internments. Although goals associated with internal Jewish politics thus intervened in this case, the Communists used the same technique of mobilizing women in order to create unrest.

Women were also instructed to inundate members of the Vichy government and its representatives in the occupied area with letters of protest and liberation demands and to try to arouse public opinion.[19] During the winter of 1941, Solidarité distributed the following exhortation: "Tell all the children to write letters to their teachers, doctors, and dentists. Tell all the families to write to the Office of the Prefect, the Red Cross, the German officer Dannecker [Theodor Dannecker was then the head of the Judenreferat of the Gestapo in Paris], various French personalities, and, in general, to all Frenchmen. The scandal of Drancy must be known to all."[20]

Jewish women obeyed these directives, and the letters poured in. All handwritten, and some copied out by a child in round, careful script, these letters expressed "the continual fear of receiving the short but oh so terrible message" telling of the execution of a son or a husband and implored Xavier Vallat, the *Commissaire général aux questions juives,* to intercede. "Each night is a night of anguish . . . ; we shake when we hear a knock on the door, our hearts pound as we open each letter," wrote "Wretched Jewish mothers and wives" in May 16, 1942. The letters demanded explanations of the insistent persecution of Jews. All the letters were written on behalf of a group: by an anonymous woman on behalf of all the internees' wives, or by a child on behalf of the internees' children. They differed from individual petitions in that, although their contents were not political, they were the products of a letter campaign orchestrated by the Communist Party.[21]

Apart from this policy of encouraging women to give voice to their unrest, the Jewish Communist leadership urged them to support their men, whose decision to join the Resistance altered their family's daily routine or placed them in danger. When the Communist Resistance proclaimed a moratorium on production for the Germans, women were urged to join a widespread solidarity campaign "to support the laborers who choose to suffer hunger rather than work for the Nazi gangs."[22]

After the irrevocable decision to embark on armed struggle, however, the priorities changed. The Party sought to strengthen the ranks of the fighters.[23] Moreover, after the summer of 1942, the threat of destitution was no longer the Jews' main concern. They now lived under constant fear of deportation, and it was imperative to hide in order to escape the roundups. The Central Committee of the PCF (the French Communist Party) defined the role of the Jewish women's committees in a circular dated January 1943: "The women's committees should be linked to the defense movement [in order to provide] protection and assistance for the Jewish mother and her child, to meet the needs of Jewish families and conceal them with their children, to participate in the general struggle of French women for better supplies, to instill in Jewish women the will to fight, to resist deportation, and to resist the separation of wives from their husbands and children."[24]

Practically speaking, the activities connected with the struggle against deportation—that is, with the specific plight of French Jewry—were entrusted to the women. The men were sent to fight; it was the responsibility of the Jewish women in Solidarité and later in the National Movement Against Racism (MNCR) to rescue Jewish children in the Paris region.[25] In addition to tasks directly associated with deportation and the development of solidarity with those directly affected by persecution or repression, Jewish women were asked to support the combat by accepting the sacrifice of their husbands and children. During the fighting for liberation, when all resistance activity was devoted to armed combat, the roles of men and women remained clearly differentiated: armed struggle for the men, logistical and social support for the women. The appeal in issue 20 (June–July 1944) of *Jeune combat,* the journal of the young Jewish Communists, is typical: "Girls! Form intelligence services, health groups, and groups of solidarity with the fighters. Young Jewish men! Come and swell the ranks of the fighting units of the patriotic militia."[26]

The overall resistance strategy of the Communists in France thus gave women an important role. The characterization of mothers, wives, and daughters as martyrs was widely exploited in the press as a forceful mobilizing theme. In its efforts to exhort the mothers and fathers of France to aid the persecuted Jewish children, the clandestine monthly journal *Fraternité* gave mothers precedence over fathers.[27] On the assumption that the repression would not affect them to the same extent, the mothers were called on to demonstrate their indignation publicly and to support actions taken by the men, despite the repercussions that this behavior might have on their daily life. Their mission was to urge close relatives to join the combat and to facilitate the fighters' efforts. They were also responsible for all activities connected with the fight against deportation.

The Jewish women's committees were used to convey instructions in Jewish immigrant settings in the same way that non-Jewish Communist women's groups were used elsewhere, but the mission of the Jewish women was adapted to the specific conditions of antisemitic persecution. Their role in this Communist political strategy related principally to rescue activity. The price paid for following these directives also differed for Jewish women. By this time, Jews were forbidden to practice most trades that might provide them with a livelihood. They had been dismissed from all administrative positions, dispossessed of their shops, and barred from any job in the occupied zone that brought them into contact with the public. Only those who made apparel and gloves for the German army could still work. The Party offered no alternative employment.

Moreover, the Jews suffered more than "mere" joblessness and poverty. Immigrant groups, especially Jews and including women, were especially vulnerable to police repression. The archives of the *Préfecture de police* contain statistics on the number of "undesirable" women—those deemed guilty of subversion—interned in the Tourelles prison of Paris between September 22, 1941, and April 5, 1943. The figure grew steadily until late August 1942, when it plunged from 340 to 56, reflecting the mass deportation of Jews—men, women, and children. Three transports left Paris each week, with a thousand Jews per transport. These convoys were filled by massive roundups that swept up every Jew in sight. The data suggest that most of the undesirable women at Tourelles were Jewish; the fate that awaited them was Auschwitz.[28]

The Jewish Communist women also played a major role in the logistical support of armed Communist groups. The MOI commandos were formed in the spring of 1942.[29] Jewish immigrants from Romania and Hungary accounted for 90 percent of the first of the four detachments created. The second detachment was made up entirely of Jews. Women, most of them Jewish, played an essential and well-defined role in the actions carried out by these armed units. Believed to have a "natural disguise" because no one would suspect a woman of being a dangerous terrorist, the women took on the most perilous assignments. As liaison agents, they were sent on rescue missions when an underground chief feared that his cover had been blown.[30] According to Louis Gronowski-Brunot, the political head in the MOI leadership troika, "They came into contact with many people and, unlike us, carried compromising documents. At the same time, they demonstrated an almost maternal devotion to their work. Despite the difficulties of supply, they never forgot to bring a few sweets; sometimes they ordered a steak in a restaurant, wrapped it in a sheet of paper, and slipped it into their handbag."[31] Olga Bancic, who directed the liaison service of the FTP-MOI groups (the fighting units of the MOI), was arrested by the *Sections speciales* (repressive police units) together with the twenty-two other foreign Communist members of the Manouchian Resistance group listed on the *Affiche rouge*.[32] She was guillotined in the courtyard of Stuttgart Prison on May 10, 1944.[33]

The technical team of the armed action was made up exclusively of women, because their traditional role in society made it easier for them to perform the necessary tasks. With arms for the fighting units concealed in their shopping baskets, they made long and dangerous trips through the streets of Paris. The "Jewish women in action" supplied the fighters with propaganda

and ration cards; later on, they provided them with bombs.[34] In the planning
of armed operations, the women helped to locate the targets—for example, by
studying the itinerary of a German army unit and verifying exactly where and
when it would pass. A woman could more easily carry out these reconnaissance
operations without attracting attention.[35] Once the target was chosen and the
attack plan drawn up, it was a woman who delivered the explosives or guns to
the partisans. After the operation, it was also a woman who recovered the arms
at a predetermined rendezvous in order to allow the partisan to escape without
this compromising package.

Another sector of Communist resistance activity entrusted almost exclusively to women—chiefly Jewish women of Austrian origin—was the TA, or
Travail allemand (German labor). Established in the summer of 1941, this organization devoted itself to infiltrating places frequented by Germans, where it
distributed propaganda (particularly the service journal *Soldat im Westen*) and
recruited militants. The TA was directed by Arthur London, but most of the
work, especially the dangerous task of recruitment, was carried out by women,
who used their charm to strike up conversations with German soldiers and
sound out their intentions. Irma Mico was responsible for all the Paris groups
working for the TA from September 1943 on.[36]

Although armed combat and raids remained basically the domain of the
men, there were exceptions: one of the women's groups specialized in placing
grenades under German trucks, and such individual women as Dina Krisher,
Simone Motta, and Jacqueline Szynckmann were members of *Carmagnole,* an
armed group in Lyon that "did the railways, the garages, the factories, the
transformers, the Germans, the municipalities, the militiamen." Dina Krisher
explained in her testimony, "I didn't perform the traditional work of women in
the Resistance"—thereby acknowledging that women had traditional work.
After an action in the liberation of Villeurbanne, during which she killed two
Germans, she was arrested but, by acting the part of a simple and innocuous
woman, managed to secure her release the next day.[37] Thus she used and
abused the female stereotype in the performance of her missions.

It is worth adding that even the leaders of these all-women groups were
under the authority of the leadership troika or the sector commander, and all
such officials were men. Cristina Boïco, for example, directed the intelligence
service that suggested military targets, but it was Boris Holban who decided on

them. Catherine Varlin, who joined the leadership troika of the 35th FTP-MOI brigade in Toulouse in 1943 and led the FTP of the Meuse region in 1944, remains an exception. Furthermore, she was almost reassigned to liaison work and was able to reassume regional responsibilities only by volunteering for the command of a region that nobody else wanted.[38]

Ultimately, the non-French Jewish women in the Communist Resistance organizations performed the same functions as all Jewish immigrants, men and women alike, and the same functions as women in all the Resistance organizations. A team of female liaison agents in Castres, for example, was instructed to meet recruited volunteers who wished to join the Scout maquis; in this role, the women frequently exploited their "natural disguise." Liliane Marx, head of this team, pushed her baby carriage through the public park opposite the station, carrying a collaborationist journal under her arm as a sign identifying her to potential recruits.[39] Anne-Marie Lambert (Bonnard) smuggled documents and money from Switzerland for the *Organisation juive de combat* (OJC). Convoys to Spain always included young women who rode in separate compartments in order to report to headquarters that all had gone well.[40] And Annette Zyman, an activist in the OJC Commando of Nice, applied her feminine charms to entrap a White Russian (an opponent of the Communist regime) who had been responsible for denouncing Jews.[41] Consequently, women generally provided liaison or logistical support services for actions carried out essentially by men, or they invoked hallowed social and cultural perceptions in organizing actions themselves.

The size of the group of Jewish women activists in the Communist Resistance is an important characteristic, as are the exceptional number and audacity of the male Jewish immigrants who made an important contribution to the Resistance.[42] Several factors explain the large numbers of Jewish Resistance fighters. The pattern of the persecution of Jews—discrimination followed by dragnets—had banished the entire Jewish population from society, thus facilitating their move toward clandestine action. Young Jewish men and women, eager for vengeance after the Aktionen of the summer of 1942 in which their close relatives had been deported, set the pace of the Communist-led armed struggle in Paris. In fact, they were the sole remaining Communist armed group after the arrest of all members of FTP headquarters in January 1943.[43] Resistance activity was the natural outgrowth of the underground life that had become the inevitable fate of many young Jewish families. And the Communist Party strategy of apportioning resistance duties among specific social groups—immigrants, women, Jews—exploited these particular situations to the utmost. As a consequence, although the Jewish Communists' methods of action mirrored the methods of non-Jews, it was among the Communist women militants, Jews and non-Jews, that a group emerged with a single-minded focus on rescuing the Jews from deportation—that is, an activity devoted to the specific situation of the Jews.

From Assistance to Humanitarian Resistance

In addition to the Jewish men and women who engaged in political or armed combat, others attempted to alleviate the hardships caused by the increasingly severe discriminatory legislation. These social endeavors, made even more imperative by the war, which created deprivation and poverty, were an "autonomous and almost exclusive element of the integration of women in public life."[44] Antisemitic legislation made this observation most applicable in Jewish settings. As impoverishment made inroads among French Jews and as thousands of foreign Jews were interned in camps in France, most Jewish organizations, in both the occupied zone and the so-called free zone, opted for social work. Despite the antisemitic legislation by the Vichy government, social assistance in the south of France developed to an unprecedented degree. Not only was it legal, but it frequently received the support of the administrative authorities and even the good will of certain social services of the Vichy regime. When the anti-Jewish dragnets spread and the pace of deportations increased, social assistance gradually gave way to rescue work. The hitherto legal activities went underground, and the assistance evolved into humanitarian resistance. At the heart of this action was the rescue of Jewish children and youth, and in this respect the women, some affiliated with the Jewish Scouts movement and others with the Jewish organization *Oeuvre de secours aux enfants* (OSE, or Children's Charity), played a central role.

The OSE focused on the rescue of children and the provision of medical assistance to the persecuted Jewish population.[45] After the armistice of 1940, OSE social workers went into the internment camps, where more than forty thousand alien Jews had been incarcerated, some of them settling there permanently.[46] In the first six months of 1942, more than 3,400 families availed themselves of the services of OSE social workers and doctors. Finally, the OSE created numerous homes for refugee children from Central Europe and Poland, for Jewish orphans, and for children whose destitute parents could no longer care for them.[47] Most members of the OSE staff were women.

In the summer of 1942, the pace of roundups and deportations increased. Whereas it had been possible earlier to use various legal maneuvers to free all the children and many of the Jewish inmates in the camps and to improve the internment conditions of the others, it now became imperative to protect as many Jews as possible from deportation. Illegal action, arising "spontaneously" from the social workers' activity in the camps, became the norm. The women social workers immersed themselves in clandestine rescue activity that grew in intensity and extent in the subsequent months.[48]

When the Nazis defeated France, in June 1940, the French Jewish Scouts (*Eclaireurs israélites de France,* or EIF) established rural labor camps, which employed teachers who had lost their jobs as a result of the Vichy laws, housed young men and women who had been forcibly banished from society by anti-semitic legislation, and accommodated teenagers and young adults released from the internment camps that the French government had set up for aliens. In Lautrec, Charry, and Taluyers, these "pioneers" divided their time among agricultural work, carpentry, electricity and masonry workshops, theoretical courses, sports, and study circles devoted to intellectual and spiritual de-velopment, with strong emphasis on Jewish subjects.[49] The young women took turns working in the linen room, the kitchen, and the farmyard. Isaac Pougatch, who ran the Charry camp, wrote, however, that the women were "jealous of the boys who work in the fields, and [they] go there whenever they have time. They particularly enjoy gardening."[50] Thus, the traditional gender-based division of tasks persisted. Furthermore, the back-to-the-land ideology of the movement automatically boosted the prestige of the tasks that had been assigned to the young men.

During the summer of 1942, the many young Jews who were classified as aliens because their parents—who had typically come to France from Eastern Europe in the interwar years, or who were part of the influx from other coun-tries overtaken by the Nazis (Austria or Germany) in the early years of the war—were not French citizens, and who had found a haven in the EIF camps, faced the threat of deportation. This situation led to the creation of the *Sixième,* the

Youth Social Service. Composed of eighty-eight young Scouts (boys and girls) who worked throughout the southern zone, it concealed Jewish youngsters who were threatened with deportation. The organization disguised itself within the social affairs department of the official *Union générale des israélites de France* (UGIF), the agency created by the Vichy government to replace and control all previous Jewish organizations. When the Commissaire général aux questions juives ordered the dissolution of all youth organizations, especially the EIF, the Sixième came under the administrative authority of other UGIF directorates, thus promoting indirectly the development of collaboration between the EIF and the OSE.[51]

The clandestine OSE network for hiding children, organized by Georges Garel in the autumn of 1942, used a dual circuit of social workers: some were responsible for contacts with parents, and others were in regular contact with the hidden children. Twenty-nine social workers maintained fictitious jobs with charities affiliated with the religious or secular institutions that housed the children—the Amitié Chrétienne, Cimade, the Sainte Germaine charity in Toulouse, Pastor Monod's charity in Lyons, the National Aid in Limoges and Périgueux, the Fund for Compensation and Family Allocations in Grenoble, and many other private charities. This non-Jewish support infrastructure was motivated by social and philanthropic goals and was run mainly by women. Hence it is no coincidence that of all the Righteous Gentiles honored by Yad Vashem for their work in rescuing Jews in wartime France, 69.6 percent were women.[52]

In 1943, the OSE leadership, assisted by members of the Zionist youth movement *Mouvement de la jeunesse zioniste* (MJS), began to organize clandestine emigration of children to Switzerland. Because children were involved, women again played a major role, this time as victims as well as rescuers. Mila Racine and Marianne Cohn were arrested while escorting a group of children to the Swiss border and paid for their efforts with their lives. In all, 7,500–9,000 Jewish children were saved in France by the joint action of the OSE, the EIF, the MJS, and their French contacts.[53] Women—Jewish and non-Jewish—were essential in this rescue activity. This explains why all studies on the contribution of women to the French Resistance, unlike studies on the Resistance in general, devote much attention to the rescue of Jews.[54]

A Problem of Historiography

If historical works on the Resistance have long overlooked the role of women, the reason is the return of political society and scholarship to their traditional emphases, in which the Resistance is understood exclusively as a political and military phenomenon, and women are reduced to the role of shield-bearers in a combat waged by men.

Jewish women who were active in the Resistance did not make their presence felt in postwar Jewish political society. They were not represented on the board of the *Conseil représentatif des institutions juives de France* (CRIF), the outgrowth of the Jewish resistance organizations and an agency to which the Communists belonged. As an essentially political organization, CRIF had no room for social organizations. What had been humanitarian resistance reverted to its former condition as social work or educational activity. The Jewish Communist organizations were no more interested in revolutionizing women's status than they were in revolutionizing the status of Jews in French society.[55]

The memory of the Resistance, also largely shaped by the Communists, undervalued the contribution of aliens in general and hence of alien Jewish women. Should the contribution of foreigners to the liberation of France be emphasized? With the antisemitic laws revoked, why should Jews be differentiated from the rest of French society, even for purposes of analysis? These women had organized the logistical infrastructure of the Resistance but rarely participated in armed combat or in policymaking in the various movements. They had played an essential role in the rescue of the Jews, but was this truly a major segment of the Resistance? As Paula Schwartz suggests, "a revised notion of the Resistance is [clearly] needed."[56] Yet, it is not so much the consideration of the new forms of political participation created by the social and political setting of occupied France that is required. Rather, all components of civil society should be integrated into a history of the Resistance that would no longer focus only on the tip of the iceberg.[57] By reassuming their place in the history of the Resistance, Jewish women reintegrate civilian society into the heart of history and superimpose a pluralist vision of French society.

Because the social infrastructure of the Resistance is not discussed in most of the documents and archives that historians use in their work, this particular "history from below" relies more heavily than most on oral sources.[58] Few women provided testimonies on their Resistance experiences in the immediate aftermath of the war; thus, oral testimonies made more than thirty years after the fact have become vital in any attempt to reconstruct this social dimension of the history of the Resistance.[59] Moreover, because the Communist and Zionist memories of the Jewish Resistance in France compete so keenly for the limelight, it is difficult to analyze rescue or combat strategies irrespective of contemporary ideological polemics. These methodological problems and the contemporary sense of "winners" and "losers" in the shaping of collective memory make it particularly problematic to historicize the role of Jewish women in the French Jewish underground—at the very time when the historicization of the Resistance as a whole requires consideration of all its constituent parts and social substrata.[60]

Notes

1. Henry Rousso, *The Vichy Syndrome: History and Memory in France since 1944* (Cambridge: Harvard University Press, 1991) (*Le syndrôme de Vichy, 1944-198 . . .* , Paris, Seuil, 1987, p. 106).

2. On the historiography of the French Resistance, see Jean-Marie Guillon, "La Résistance, 50 ans et 2,000 titres après," in *Mémoire et histoire: La Résistance,* ed. Jean-Marie Guillon and Pierre Laborie (Toulouse: Privat, 1995), pp. 27–44.

3. See, for example, Rita Thalmann, "Femmes juives dans la Résistance et la libération du territoire," *Le monde juif* 152 (1994), p. 181.

4. Renée Poznanski, "Reflections on Jewish Resistance and Jewish Resistants in France," *Jewish Social Studies* 2, no. 1 (1995), pp. 124–158.

5. Paula Schwartz, "Redefining Resistance: Women's Activism in Wartime France," in *Behind the Lines: Gender and the Two World Wars,* ed. Margaret Randolph Higonnet, Jane Jenson, Sonya Michel, and Margaret Collins Weitz (New Haven: Yale University Press, 1987), p. 144. And see Catherine Varlin, "Une ville engloutie: La résistance des femmes juives," in RHICOJ, *Les juifs dans la Résistance et la Libération: Histoire, témoignages, débats* (Paris: Le Scribe, 1985), pp. 101–103.

6. Dominique Veillon, "Elles étaient dans la Résistance," *Repères* 59 (1983), pp. 9–12; Laurent Douzou, "La Résistance: Une affaire d'hommes?" *Cahiers de l'Institut d'histoire du temps présent (IHTP)* 31 (1995), pp. 11–24.

7. Paula Schwartz, "Partisans and Gender Politics in Vichy France," *French Historical Studies* 16, no. 1 (1989), pp. 126–151.

8. Bertie Albrecht headed the social services of Combat and, later, of the *Mouvements unis de résistance (MUR).* See Yvette Bernard-Farnoux, "A la suite de Bertie Albrecht au service

social des Mouvements unis de Résistance," in RHICOJ, *Les juifs dans la Résistance et la Libération,* pp. 104–108. Schwartz, "Redefining Resistance," p. 147.

9. Women accounted for 99 of the 708 agents of the Jade-Fitzroy intelligence network and more than half of the 211 members of the Françoise network; Marie-Madeleine Fourcade directed the Alliance network. Dominique Veillon, "Les réseaux de résistance," in *La France des années noires,* ed. Jean-Pierre Azéma and François Bédarida (Paris: Seuil, 1993), p. 410. On the role of women in the escape networks, see Margaret L. Rossiter, *Women in the Resistance* (New York: Praeger, 1986).

10. On Jews in the Resistance and the contribution made by the restoration of a collective dimension to their individual actions, see Poznanski, "Reflections on Jewish Resistance."

11. Michael Burns, *Dreyfus, a Family Affair, from the French Revolution to the Holocaust* (New York: HarperCollins, 1991).

12. Some women had reservations about this focus on specific women's themes; see, for instance, Edith Thomas, *Le témoin compromis* (Paris: Viviane Hamy, 1995), pp. 118, 173.

13. A Yiddish-language tract issued by the *Mouvement des femmes* in March 1942: "March 8, Day of Struggle for Women's Demands. To the Jewish Women," translated into French by Annette and Aby Wieviorka, *Le monde juif* 125 (1987), p. 31.

14. *Archives nationales* (AN), F60, 502, Prefect of Police to Darlan, July 3, 1941. All translations from French are my own.

15. These demonstrations are mentioned in the fortnightly reports on "La situation à Paris," issued by General Intelligence and kept in the archives of the Office of the Prefect (Préfecture de Police, or PP) in Paris.

16. David Diamant, *Le billet vert* (Paris: Renouveau, 1977), p. 42.

17. On the establishment of the Coordination Committee, see Renée Poznanski, "Avant les premières grandes rafles: Les juifs de Paris sous l'Occupation (juin 1940–avril 1941)," in *Cahiers de l'IHTP* 22, ed. Léo Hamon and Renée Poznanski (1992), p. 39ff.

18. "Note sur les manifestations des femmes des internés civils," YIVO Archives (New York), UGIF, I-13.

19. PP Archives, "Situation à Paris," May 18, 1942.

20. *La presse anti-raciste sous l'occupation hitlérienne,* Paris, Union des juifs pour la Résistance et l'Entraide (1950), pp. 39–40; see other examples in *Unzer Vort* 36 (December 6, 1941), translated into French by Annette and Aby Wieviorka, *Le monde juif* 125 (1987), p. 28.

21. AN, AJ 38, 5. See other examples in Renée Poznanski, *Etre juif en France pendant la Seconde Guerre mondiale* (Paris: Hachette, 1994), p. 347ff. Because the Germans had adopted the policy of executing hostages in retaliation for attacks carried out in Paris against German soldiers, Drancy served as a hostage reserve.

22. *Unzer Vort* 36 (December 6, 1941).

23. The strategic choices of the Communist Party in France during the war are discussed in Stéphane Courtois, *Le PCF dans la guerre* (Paris: Ramsay, 1980).

24. Translated into French by Annette and Aby Wieviorka, *Le monde juif* 128 (1987), pp. 176–178.

25. David Diamant, *Les juifs dans la Résistance française, 1940–1944* (Paris: Roger Maria, 1971), pp. 134–136. In this way 607 children were dispersed in the Paris area between July 1942 and April 1943 by the militants of these two organizations. See David Diamant, "Les juifs de Paris dans la Résistance," manuscript, Musée de la Résistance, Ivry.

26. Archives of the Centre de documentation juive contemporaine (CDJC) XXII-7.

27. CDJC, XXII–5; *Fraternité* 9 (August 28, 1943). In February 1944, lengthy articles were devoted to the roundups of POWs' wives in Paris: CDJC, XX–5; *Fraternité* (17 February 1944) (southern zone).

28. PP Archives. These figures appear in reports on the "Situation à Paris." The convoy of June 22, 1942, took sixty-six women incarcerated in the Tourelles prison—slightly more than one-third of the internees at that time—to Auschwitz. See Serge Klarsfeld, *Calendrier de la persécution des Juifs en France, 1940–1944* (Paris: FFDJF, 1993), p. 242.

29. Stéphane Coutois, Denis Peschanski, and Adam Rayski, *Le sang de l'étranger* (Paris: Fayard, 1989), p. 122ff.

30. Boris Holban, *Testament* (Paris: Calmann-Lévy, 1989), p. 122.

31. Louis Gronowski-Brunot, *Le dernier grand soir: Un juif de Pologne* (Paris: Seuil, 1980), p. 173.

32. The Manouchian Resistance group was the last of the armed Communist groups—composed of foreigners—remaining in the capital. The Affiche rouge had been displayed throughout the country as part of a vast campaign of propaganda against the Résistance, called the Army of Crime.

33. Holban, *Testament*, p. 122. The trial of the twenty-three resistance fighters is discussed in Courtois et al., *Le sang de l'étranger*, p. 335ff. On the execution of Olga Bancic, see Jacques Ravine, *La résistance organisée des juifs en France* (Paris: Julliard, 1973), p. 219.

34. Abraham Lissner, *Un franc-tireur juif raconte...* (Paris, 1969), p. 21ff., 45.

35. Holban, *Testament*, p. 118.

36. See Courtois et al., *Le sang de l'étranger*, p. 130, and Irma Mico's testimony in Gronowski-Brunot, *Le dernier grand soir*, p. 156.

37. Dina Krisher, "Combattante à Carmagnole," in RHICOJ, *Les juifs dans la Résistance et la Libération*, pp. 98, 100.

38. Varlin, "Une ville engloutie," pp. 101–103.

39. Alain Michel, *Les Eclaireurs israélites de France pendant la Seconde Guerre mondiale* (Paris: EIF, 1984), p. 187.

40. CDJC, DLXXII-40, testimony of Jacques Roitman.

41. CDJC, DLXI-38, testimony of Annette Zyman.

42. Philippe Joutard and François Marcot (eds.), *Les étrangers dans la Résistance en France* (Besançon: Museum of Resistance and Deportation, 1992).

43. Courtois et al., *Le sang de l'étranger*, pp. 164–165.

44. Hélène Eck, "Les Françaises sous Vichy: Femmes du désastre?" in *Histoire des femmes en Occident*, ed. Georges Duby and Michelle Perrot (Paris: Plon), p. 194.

45. On the OSE, see Martine Lemalet (ed.), *Au secours des enfants du siècle: Regards croisés sur l'OSE* (Paris: Nil Editions, 1993).

46. OSE report, "Six Months of Work: January–June 1942," reprinted in ibid., pp. 187–206. The internment camps are discussed in Anne Grynberg, *Les camps de la honte* (Paris: La découverte, 1991). On the number of Jews interned, see Poznanski, *Etre juif en France,* pp. 266–267.

47. On November 1, 1941, the OSE had 1,200 children in its care. Archives of the Central Consistory during World War II, Rue Saint Georges, Paris, CC-22/23, OSE, Montpellier, December 15, 1941.

48. CDJC, CCXVII-12a, report on the Garel network, undated, unnumbered. On the transition from legal social activity to clandestine operations, see Renée Poznanski, "De l'action philanthropique à la résistance humanitaire," in Lemalet, *Au secours des enfants du siècle,* pp. 57–82.

49. Various reports issued in 1941 and kept at Yad Vashem, 09/11-3. See also CDJC, DLXI-30, Anny Latour's interview with Isaac Pougatch.

50. Isaac Pougatch, *Charry* (Paris: Oreste Zeluck, 1945), p. 34. Robert Gamzon's diary describes how "girls" were assigned to these tasks. See Gamzon, *Les eaux claires* (Paris, EIF, 1981).

51. CDJC, CCXVII-11, Lyons, October 1, 1944, "Report on the Activity of the Youth Social Service (the *Sixième*), 1942–1944." See the testimony of Liliane Klein-Liber, "Témoignage sur les opérations de sauvetage," *Annales, ESC* 48, no. 3 (1993), pp. 673–678.

52. On the performance of the Garel network, see CDJC, CCXVIII-104, testimony of Georges Garel on the clandestine work of the OSE; CDJC, CCXVII-12a, report on the Garel network, undated, unnumbered; and Lucien Lazare, *La résistance juive en France* (Paris: Stock, 1987), p. 211ff. For a list of Righteous Gentiles up to 1992 see Lucien Lazare, *Le livre des justes* (Paris: J.-C. Lattes, 1993), pp. 237–245.

53. Estimate by Hillel J. Kieval, "Legality and Resistance in Vichy France: The Rescue of Jewish Children," *Proceedings of the American and Philosophical Society* 124–125 (1980), p. 366.

54. See, for instance, Margarete L. Rossiter, "Le rôle des femmes dans la Résistance en France," *Guerre mondiale et conflits contemporains* 155 (1989), pp. 53–62.

55. On the CRIF, see Poznanski, *Etre juif en France,* pp. 625–633, 651–654. A return to normalcy, achieved by armed warfare, is what awaited the youth, according to the September 10, 1944, issue of *Jeune combat,* entitled "Luttons pour notre avenir heureux" (Let us fight for a happy future), Bund Archives, New York.

56. Schwartz, "Redefining Resistance," p. 147.

57. "The history of the Maquis is not just a history of the men in the woods, it is just as much the history of the women who stayed behind. This has vital implications for research into women and the Resistance." Roderick Kedward, "The Maquis and the Culture of the Outlaw," in R. Kedward and Roger Austin, eds., *Vichy France and the Resistance: Culture and Ideology* (London: Croom Helm, 1985), p. 247. The development of the maquis would not have been possible without the general support infrastructure of the population. The resistance in the maquis is therefore no longer only the account of surprise attacks; it is also an aspect of social history.

58. On the contribution that oral sources can make and the pitfalls of using them, see Danièle Voldman, ed., "La bouche de la vérité: La recherche historique et les sources orales," *Cahiers de l'IHTP* 21 (November 1992).

59. See Lisbeth Trallori, "La résistance passée sous silence," in *Femmes et fascismes,* ed. Rita Thalmann (Paris: Tierce, 1986), pp. 171–187; Schwartz, "Redefining Resistance," p. 149; and Rossiter, *Women in the Resistance.* For an analysis of that silence immediately after the war, see Douzou, "La Résistance," p. 15.

60. Efforts should be made to quantify the participation of Jewish women Resistance activists, both those who operated within the Communist organizations and those who belonged to special rescue organizations. In particular, the extent of their participation should be compared with that of men in the Resistance, of non-Jewish women, and of the Jewish population as a whole.

CHAPTER FOURTEEN

Gisi Fleischmann

Yehuda Bauer

Modern Jewish society, especially the tradition-bound parts of it, was inhospitable to female leadership or even significant female participation in the public sphere. Women had circumscribed roles as daughters, wives, and mothers, and participation in decision making of a social and political kind was not among these roles.

In the Zionist movement in Europe, women were becoming prominent in activities relating to social welfare through the Women's International Zionist Organization (WIZO) and similar groups, which paralleled the growing Hadassah Organization in the United States. By the 1930s, Hadassah had become a powerful political organization, but its leaders, while influential up to a point, were still part of a male-led political structure, which the women accepted, sometimes reluctantly. In Palestine, the outstanding female leader of the American Hadassah, Henrietta Szold, became the director of Youth Aliyah, the organization that aided German-Jewish youth; however, she was not a member of the Jewish Agency Executive (the governing body of the Yishuv, the organized Jewish community in Palestine).[1] In Europe, too, WIZO had no political power. In the early 1930s, women who were part of WIZO, or WIZO-like groups, came to prominence as the problem of refugees became urgent and their experience in social welfare work became useful. In Holland, Gertrude van Tijn (Cohen) became the secretary of the committee that dealt with refugees, most of whom were from Germany.[2] In Berlin, Recha Freier founded Youth Aliyah, which in Palestine was taken over by Szold; Cora Berliner became a prominent member of the German Jewish leadership, and other women also emerged as powerful figures.[3] In Czechoslovakia, there arose a group of women who knew each other fairly well, and who became responsible for matters concerning refugees. In Prague, Marie Schmolka, Irma Polak, and Hannah Steiner were all connected with WIZO and Jewish refugee work.[4] In Bratislava, there was Gisi (Gisela) Fleischmann.

Female participation among the leadership of Jewish society in Poland prior to the Holocaust was practically nil. Not only in Orthodox and ultra-Orthodox circles was such participation unthinkable, but liberal and even socialist groups and parties, whether they were assimilationist, Bundist, or Zionist, also lacked any practical application of gender equality. Women could be teachers in schools, or activists for local social welfare, but their public role was limited to influencing their husbands, when they had the urge to do so and the husbands were willing. It was the males who filled the leadership positions. The force of Jewish traditions and their impact on even nonreligious Jewish circles were considerable; in the area of traditional gender roles they were even more powerful.

The Nazis decreed that only Jewish males should constitute the forced leadership groups known as Judenraete or Aeltestenraete. As a result, with just one minor exception, Jewish women did not participate in these bodies. Their functions in Polish, Belorussian, and Baltic ghettos were the traditional ones of social work wherever possible, and artistic life whenever *that* was possible. A certain degree of contradiction was evident in that while more and more families were led by women after the death of their husbands, these women's input into group leadership was practically nonexistent.

It was in the unofficial and rebellious circles that feminine leadership became possible. The underground political parties, especially the left-wing ones, accepted female leaders as a matter of course—or so it seemed at first blush. In Vilna, after the tragic death of the Communist leader Itzik Wittenberg (July 1943), the Communist underground was led by women.[5] Because women could move about in Nazi-occupied Poland more easily than men, women were able to take on the important role of emissaries between the ghettos.[6] But only under exceptional circumstances and under the pressure of totally new conditions were the old taboos set aside. It is against this background that Gisi Fleischmann emerged.

Gisi Fleischmann, born in 1892, was the daughter of Julius and Jetty Fischer, owners of a hotel and a restaurant in the old Jewish quarter of Bratislava.[7] Jetty Fischer was the aunt of Rabbi Shmuel David Halevi Ungar of Nitra, who was to become the acknowledged leader of Slovak Jewish ultra-Orthodoxy. Gisi's kinship with the famous rabbi was to play a part in her activities during the Holocaust.

Gisi and her younger brothers, Desider and Gustav, grew up in an Orthodox environment and became Zionists while in their teens. The family restaurant became a meeting place of Zionists, probably at a fairly early date. The meetings must have been conducted in German or Hungarian, the languages of the Jewish intelligentsia, for most of the participants knew little or no Slovak, the language spoken by the poor. This language barrier created difficulties between the Jews and the Slovaks, who had been developing a national consciousness since about the middle of the nineteenth century, with a trend toward exclusivity. As was often the case in Eastern Europe, most of the Jews belonged to the urban culture of the reigning power, in this case the Austro-Hungarian monarchy, and they were perceived by the Slovaks as a Germanizing and Magyarizing factor. In the late 1930s, 136,000 Jews lived among some 2.5 million Slovaks, and the Jews constituted a large part of the bourgeois, merchant, and artisan classes. Slowly, a Slovak intellectual class began to emerge, in competition with Germans, Hungarians, and Jews; the radical nationalist elements among this group grew as the crises of the interwar period revealed the weak structure of Slovak society.

Zionism started slowly in Slovakia. Most Slovak Jews were at least nominally Orthodox. However, away from the ultra-Orthodox strongholds of Nitra, Topolcany, and some other places, which boasted yeshivas, Orthodoxy was easygoing and co-existed with a pro-Zionist tendency. Zionist youth movements began to flourish in the 1930s under the influence of neighboring Polish movements. The Communists were a strong presence in Slovakia, with indigenous leaders, and in the 1930s many Jewish youths joined them. On the fringes were extreme assimilationist groups and a small but important number of converts to Christianity. No Jews were included among the Communist leaders.

By the mid-1920s Gisi Fleischmann, a young wife and mother of two daughters, was no longer Orthodox or observant. She co-founded the Bratislava branch of WIZO and became its second president. Her political involvement in Zionism became more and more intense, and in 1938 she became head of the Bratislava branch of HICEM, the agency that dealt with emigration to all countries other than Palestine.

In 1938–1939, Fleischmann moved into formal leadership roles. She became a member of the Slovak Central Refugee Committee and as such a member of the group that advised the local representative of the Joint Distribution Committee (JDC), Joseph Blum. No love was lost between Blum and Fleischmann. But in 1939 or 1940 he moved to Budapest, although he remained responsible for JDC operations in Slovakia and Hungary (together with his American colleague, S. Bertrand Jacobson). As a result, Gisi became for all intents and purposes the JDC person in Bratislava. In the spring of 1939 she went to London, with Oskar Neumann of the Zionist organization of Bratislava and Robert Fueredi of the Central Refugee Committee, to solicit the help of the British in getting Jewish refugees out of Slovakia. The mission was a failure, as was a JDC conference in Paris that summer. No real help was forthcoming from the JDC at that point, and no places were found for Jews to enter. On the day the conference ended, the Germans invaded Poland. Fleischmann was invited to remain in London, but she refused to abandon her family (both her husband and her mother were ill) and her community, and she returned to Bratislava.[8]

In her private life, too, radical changes were occurring. She had sent her two daughters, Judith and Alice, to Palestine—first Judith just before the war, and then Alice just after the war broke out—with immigration certificates of children and pioneers. Her husband was a sickly person, and with the death of her father, she had to look after her frail mother. Her refusal to leave Bratislava was, I think, more a question of responsibility to her husband and mother than one of communal responsibility. I do not believe that she would have refused to follow her two daughters had it not been for her family in Bratislava.

In late 1939 and 1940, she became involved with illegal immigration transports to Palestine that were organized partly by the Mossad and Revisionist representatives in Austria but later mainly by Berthold Storfer, a Jew who had been recruited by Adolf Eichmann to organize Jewish emigration. In an abandoned munitions factory on the outskirts of Bratislava and at another location nearby, hundreds of refugees waited for ships to take them down the Danube to the Black Sea. But it was not until early September 1940 that the river boats finally came. Until then, the Central Refugee Committee, under Gisi Fleischmann, had to take care of them, with little help from the JDC or anyone else. That meant raising large funds from an increasingly impoverished Jewish community and then distributing the money to the refugees.[9] According to testimonies collected by Joan Campion, Gisi was involved personally in delivering and distributing food, caring for children, and organizing cultural activities for the refugees.[10] It was that rare combination of organizational talent, intellectual ability, and emotional involvement, together with a great deal of political savvy, that made Gisi Fleischmann's personality so unique—some might say, so feminine.

Slovakia had become autonomous in October 1938 and then declared its independence, at the bidding of Nazi Germany, in March 1939. The government was led by the fascist Hlinka party, under a virtual German protectorate, and headed by the Catholic priest Jozef Tiso. Anti-Jewish pogroms followed; in the course of one of them, Fleischmann's brother Gustav was fatally injured. A process of so-called Aryanization was initiated, in which Jews were deprived of their property. An attempt by the Zionists, whose leadership now included Gisi Fleischmann, to establish a Jewish umbrella organization in Slovakia was aborted by the opposition of the ultra-Orthodox.

A Slovak Judenrat (called Ú.Ž—Ústredna Židov) was established as early as September 1940, at the instigation of Dieter Wisliceny, who had been sent by Eichmann to be the Slovak government's Advisor on Jewish Affairs. To head this body, the first Judenrat outside Poland, the Slovaks nominated a respected Orthodox official, Heinrich Schwartz. The Zionists, after some hesitation, joined the Judenrat but opposed Schwartz, recognizing only later that he had done his best to resist the demands of the venal Slovak officials. Against this background, Blum in Budapest complained to the JDC parent body in the United States about the unreliability of the Zionist leadership in Bratislava, naming Fleischmann, among others. The New York JDC, however, had no way of intervening in local disputes even if they had wanted to. Help from the United States, which had never been significant, came to a virtual stop by the end of 1941, when the Japanese attack brought America into the war.

The "final solution" was decided upon some time in 1941, probably in the late spring. In July 1941, the mass murder of Jews at the hands of the SS and the German regular army began in newly conquered Soviet territories. The

Wannsee conference (of some of the German ministries and the SS leadership on the implementation of the "final solution") of January 20, 1942, dealt with some of the administrative aspects, and its protocol reflects some of the internal discussions among the Nazi leaders. In Slovakia no obstacles were expected to the murder of the Jews. In fact, Slovakia was the only country in Europe where the local puppet government actually asked the Nazis to deport the Jews. This was a result of a Slovak commitment to supply a large number of laborers for Germany; unable to fulfill their quota, the Slovaks suggested that twenty thousand Jews be deported instead. To avoid being burdened with the families of the productive workers, they asked the Germans to accept the wives and children as well. Eichmann at first did not want the families; in early 1942 Chelmno was the only extermination camp in operation, and that facility was kept busy murdering the Jews of the annexed territories of western Poland. But he finally decided to deport the families as well, at first to the Lublin region in Poland. The young people and some of the others were sent to build the camp at Auschwitz. Among them were the women who built the women's camp at Birkenau.[11]

Slovak Jews heard rumors about the impending deportations and pleaded with the government heads, including Tiso, not to deport the community. They also turned to the Vatican, which lodged a protest on March 14, 1942, to no avail. The deportations started on March 26, with a transport of young girls and women. From then until October, some fifty-eight thousand Jews, out of a community of ninety thousand, were shipped to Poland.[12]

From the early days of the Ú.Ž, Gisi Fleischmann was a member of the organization. She headed the department of emigration, which was natural because of her prior involvement with HICEM and the JDC. She tried desperately to get as many Jews as possible out of Slovakia. She must have belonged to the Zionist leadership group that worked within the Ú.Ž, which at first opposed Schwartz.

The threat of the deportations led Neumann, who was in charge of the youth department of the Ú.Ž, to send members of the Zionist youth movements to Slovak townships and communities to warn them about the danger. But most leaders and individuals in the communities refused to listen; they decided that it was best to report to what they thought would be forced labor, in order to avoid reprisals against their families.[13] As the deportations proceeded, a sizable minority, consisting of an Orthodox group led by Rabbi Ungar, along with members of the Zionist youth groups, and a number of unorganized people—some seven thousand people at least, or about 8 percent of the total number of Jews—fled to Hungary.[14]

During the spring of 1942, an underground leadership consisting of Gisi Fleischmann, Oskar Neumann, Wilhelm Fuerst, Tibor Kovač, Andrej Steiner, and some others, crystallized at the Ú.Ž. They used to meet in Gisi's office. They were all opposed to Arpad Sebestyen, the frightened and ineffective Orthodox schoolteacher who then headed the Ú.Ž. They were soon joined by Rabbi Michael Dov-Ber Weissmandel, Rabbi Ungar's son-in-law and Gisi's second cousin by marriage. The members of this Working Group (*pracovná skupina*) at first attempted legal rescue, trying to obtain certificates for individuals, showing them to be economically important for Slovakia. Then, apparently in late June, Weissmandel suggested that they try to bribe Wisliceny, who was supervising the deportations. The only Jew who was in contact with Wisliceny was a traitor named Karel Hochberg, who headed a department for special tasks at the Ú.Ž and supplied Wisliceny and the Slovak fascists with technical help and information regarding the Jews to be deported. After some hesitation, the Working Group decided to approach Wisliceny through Hochberg. A sum of money—Weissmandel claims it was twenty-five thousand dollars—was given to Hochberg on August 17, and a second sum was exchanged toward the end of September. After that, only two transports left for Poland, which convinced the group that the bribe had been effective.

It seems clear that the Working Group was headed by Gisi. For an ultra-Orthodox man like Weissmandel this was no doubt a radical departure: a woman, and a Zionist to boot, heading a group of which he was a member! He explained his participation by referring to her strong personality, her commitment, and her wisdom; it was precisely because she was a woman, he says, that individuals who otherwise would have quarreled accepted her leadership. He does not mention what must have been a decisive fact for an ultra-Orthodox Jew: Gisi was a relative, and this must have neutralized the traditional fear of and superciliousness toward women. As for the other members of the group, their testimonies indicate great admiration for her steadfastness, courage, and altruism, and especially for her sharp intelligence and general qualities of leadership.

Determined attempts were made to bribe the corrupt Slovak officials and the Germans. Kovač, Steiner, and Gisi herself were active in this endeavor, using funds obtained in part from the JDC in Switzerland.[15] Fleischmann was the one who phoned and sent letters through emissaries, and she also went to Hungary to try to convince the local Jewish leadership to help their Slovak counterparts. She failed miserably—the Hungarian Jewish leaders were concerned about their own legal status and refused to engage in what they feared would be illegal operations.

Only gradually did it dawn on the Working Group that the deportations not only meant great suffering but were aimed at the murder of every Jew. They tried to send non-Jewish emissaries to the Lublin area, where they could receive occasional messages from and send parcels to deportees. Then, in the summer, they learned that the deportees had been sent "beyond the Bug" river; a letter from Fleischmann to Switzerland says, "I almost despair of believing that we shall ever see anyone of our friends again."[16]

As we now know, it was not Hochberg's bribing of Wisliceny that stopped the deportations, but the bribing of the Slovak officials. In addition, the relatively large number of Jews who were protected by various documents left only a few available for additional transports, and a directive from Berlin agreed that there was no point in pressing for the deportations of the remaining Jews. Also, the Vatican intervened a second time, in June 1942. When the deportations ended, fewer than twenty-five thousand Jews were left in Slovakia.

The belief that they had succeeded in stopping the deportations by bribing Wisliceny made the Working Group undertake a much larger program: trying to reach Himmler through Wisliceny in an attempt to stop the trains to the extermination camps from all over Europe. Apparently only Fleischmann and Weissmandel pressed hard within the group for what became known as the Europa Plan; the others did not think that it had much chance of succeeding. It is amazing that the underground leadership of a remnant of a Jewish community in a satellite state tried to rescue the Jews of all Nazi-occupied Europe in a daring plan of ransom negotiations with the murderers—and this effort was led by a woman.

Continuous talks were held with Wisliceny after the first contact, in November 1942, and money for the bribe was solicited both from the JDC and from emissaries from the Yishuv emissaries who had established themselves in

Istanbul. Most of the initial two-hundred-thousand-dollar down payment was transferred to Bratislava, illegally of course, during the spring and early summer of 1943. But as we now know, the negotiations lacked a concrete basis. Wisliceny had received the approval of Himmler to conduct negotiations in November but then received no further instructions. Himmler's initial agreement appears to be related to his desire to open options for negotiating with the Americans. He saw the Jews as a logical conduit for such contacts. In the summer of 1943, he ordered Wisliceny to stop the talks, perhaps because he had found alternative routes that might lead him to the Americans.[17]

While the negotiations around the Europa Plan continued, the danger of renewed deportations arose again, especially after March 1943, when Slovak antisemitism was combined with German reminders that there were still Jews in Slovakia. The Working Group mobilized all its resources in order to avert the danger by massive bribery—and again, it succeeded. At the end of 1943, Neumann became the head of Ú.Ž, and the Working Group thus became the official leadership of Slovak Jewry.

Gisi Fleischmann was arrested in early 1944, when an attempt to bribe an important official misfired and the Germans traced the bribe to her. She spent four months in prison before her friends succeeded in obtaining her release. Offered a certificate of entry to Palestine, she again refused the opportunity to escape, apparently because of her feeling of responsibility for the community and for her ailing mother.

It seems clear, from her letters and the memoirs of the surviving members of the group, that they all feared a deterioration of the situation in Slovakia prior to liberation, whether because of the ravages of a German retreat or because of a rebellion in Slovakia that would bring with it a German invasion. In the end, elements in the army, along with that part of the underground that was loyal to the Czechoslovak government in exile in London, and the Communist underground, already active in partisan detachments in the mountains, all pressed for a rebellion. The pro-Czechs and the army officers wanted to rehabilitate Slovakia in the eyes of the Allies, whereas the Communists wanted to help their Soviet mentors. The preparations went awry, however, and the rebellion broke out prematurely, on August 29, 1944. It was followed immediately by the entry of German troops. In their wake came an Einsatzkommando of the SS, which turned against the Jews. Shortly afterward, Alois Brunner, one of Eichmann's most evil henchmen, came to oversee the "final solution" of the Jewish question in Slovakia.[18]

Because the Working Group, under Fleischmann's leadership, believed that their tactic had worked during the previous regime, they tried to apply the same tactic to the new circumstances. They went to the Nazis and offered them goods in return for a cessation of the deportations of Jews, despite warnings even from some friendly SS contacts not to offer negotiations with Brunner. When they were told to ask the Jews of Bratislava to report for deportation to Sered, they obeyed. When their community list was taken by the police, they complained to the SS but did not spread the word to the community to hide. As a result, toward the end of September 1944, most of the Jews were arrested and taken to Sered. Gisi, brutally interrogated at Sered by Brunner himself, pleaded for her life, but to no avail. On October 17, she was shipped to Auschwitz, along with an order from Brunner that she be liquidated. On October 18, she was separated from the rest, but no one knows how she was killed.

The month of September, the last period of the Working Group's activity, casts a dark shadow over all of them, and on Gisi as their leader. They could have had no illusions by then, but they acted just like many of the Jewish Councils in Poland. They could have warned the Jews, but they didn't; they could have refused the demands of the Nazis—even though this would have made no difference—but they didn't. But then, we were not in their place, and we don't know how we would have acted.[19]

What is there to say in conclusion? Do gender studies provide us with an additional perspective on a case like this? I think that the answer is yes. This is, surely, a secondary perspective, the chief one being the story of a political underground group and its attempts to rescue Jews, within the context of the Slovak fascist state and the German policies toward the Jews—policies that did not differentiate between the fate of women and that of men. But from the aspect of social history of the Jews, the story of a woman and a leader who climbed the ladder of traditional female involvement in Jewish welfare and migration matters and became the only political leader of a Jewish underground— the only underground anywhere in Europe that united all the political factions of a country (with the exception of the Communists), and the only group anywhere in Europe that tried to rescue not just its own Jews but Jews of other countries as well—is significant. The case of Gisi Fleischmann can and should be addressed as an important manifestation of the development of Jewish society and of the female role in it. She was a courageous woman, a brave leader, a person who wanted to enjoy life, who had a happy family around her, but who chose to stand at the head of a group that tried to save a community. I don't know of any other woman who did something similar during the Holocaust, or indeed even before that. All I can say is that I think she did her best, and that she should be recognized as a role model, despite all her mistakes. She was the stuff heroines are made of.

Notes

1. Sandra B. Kadosh, *Ideology versus Reality: Youth Aliyah and the Rescue of Jewish Children during the Holocaust Era, 1933–1945* (New York: Ann Arbor University Microfilms International) (Ph.D. thesis), 1995.

2. Yehuda Bauer, *American Jewry and the Holocaust* (Detroit: Wayne State University Press, 1981), especially pp. 356–379.

3. See, for instance, Wolfgang Benz, ed., *Die Juden in Deutschland, 1933–1945* (Munich: C. H. Beck, 1988).

4. Livia Rothkirchen, "The Jews of Bohemia and Moravia: 1938–1945," in Avigdor Dagan, ed., *The Jews of Czechoslovakia,* vol. 3 (Philadelphia: Jewish Publication Society, 1984); Bauer, *American Jewry and the Holocaust,* p. 34.

5. Yitzhak Arad, *Ghetto in Flames* (Jerusalem: Yad Vashem, 1980).

6. Vladka Meed (Miedzyrzecki Feigele), *On Both Sides of the Wall* (New York: Holcaust Library and Schocken Books, 1979).

7. The personal history of Gisi Fleischmann has been described a number of times, especially in Joan Campion's book, *In The Lion's Mouth* (Lanham, Md.: University Press of America, 1987); and in Hannah Yablonka, "Gisi Fleischmann" (Hebrew), in Akiva Nir, ed., *Prakim bekorot shoat Yehudei Slovakia* (The history of the Holocaust in Slovakia) (Givat Haviva: Moreshet, 1984), pp. 103–108.

8. Bauer, *American Jewry and the Holocaust,* especially pp. 356–379.

9. Dalia Ofer and Hannah Weiner, *Dead-End Journey* (Lanham, Md.: University Press of America, 1996); Dalia Ofer, "The Rescue of European Jewry and Illegal Immigration to Palestine," in Michael R. Marrus, *The Nazi Holocaust,* vol. 9 (Meckler: Westport, 1989), pp. 199–222.

10. Campion, *In the Lion's Mouth.*

11. Yehuda Bauer, *Jews For Sale?* (New Haven: Yale University Press, 1994).

12. Livia Rothkirchen, *Hurban Yahadut Slovakia* (The destruction of Slovak Jewry) (Jerusalem: Yad Vashem, 1961).

13. Oskar Neumann, *Im Schatten des Todes* (Tel-Aviv: Olamenu, 1956); Ya'akov Ronen, "Tnuot hanoar bemachteret beSlovakia" (Youth movements in the underground in Slovakia), in Nir, *Prakim bekorot shoat Yehudei Slovakia*. Also in Bauer, *American Jewry and the Holocaust*, pp. 356–270, and *Jews For Sale?* p. 73.

14. All this is described in great detail by Gila Fatran, *Haim ma'avak al hisardut?* (Was it a struggle for survival?) (Tel-Aviv: Moreshet, 1992). Much of the material on Gisi Fleischmann herself also comes from Fatran's book.

15. Bauer, *Jews for Sale?* pp. 62–101.

16. A respected Canadian colleague of mine, Professor John S. Conway, has accused the Working Group of being collaborationists who betrayed their community by negotiating with Wisliceny; he even says that they knew about the mass murder in 1942 and failed to inform their community in order to save themselves. Nothing could be further from the truth. They warned the community not to report for the deportations months before they knew what the German plan was. They encouraged the flight to Hungary, and they engaged in negotiations to try to stop the deportations. John S. Conway, "Fruehe Augenzeugenberichte aus Auschwitz: Glaubwuerdigkeit und Wirkungsgeschichte," in *Vierteljahreshafte fuer Zeitgeschichte (VHZG)*, 1979, vol. 2; and "Der Holocaust in Ungarn," *VHZG*, 1984, vol. 2. Critiqued in Bauer, *Jews for Sale?* pp. 70–73, and in Fatran, *Haim ma'avak al hisardut?* pp. 159–160, 206–208, 235–238.

17. Bauer, *Jews For Sale?* pp. 62–101.

18. Fatran, *Haim ma'avak al hisardut?* passim.

19. Ibid., pp. 247–261.

PART IV

Labor Camps and Concentration Camps

The Nazi camps—a central means of exerting terror and exploiting people in the interest of the regime—were of several types: concentration camps, forced-labor camps, and extermination camps, as well as assembly and transit camps where people were collected before deportation. Although the name of each kind of camp reflects its major function, extensive killing of prisoners occurred in all camps, and the number of deaths escalated as the war proceeded to Germany's final defeat. The high death rates in all camps were the result of the inhuman conditions—violence, starvation, and the spiritual and physical degradation of the prisoners—which were intended to break the human spirit and the will to live.

Concentration camps were first established in Germany, at the outset of the Nazi regime. In the beginning, their purpose was to "re-educate" Germans who opposed the Nazis. To this group of inmates were added "professional and habitual criminals" and "antisocials," such as homosexuals, Roma and Sinti (Gypsies), prostitutes, and the "work-shy"—men who had, without adequate reasons, refused employment offered to them on two or more occasions. After the pogrom of November 9–11, 1938, the concentration camps were packed with German Jews; those who survived were released only after they were able to prove that they would leave the country. The families of the Jews who perished at this time were expected to pay for their cremation and to collect the container of their remains.

Forced-labor camps were constructed in Eastern Europe after the beginning of the war and later in Germany itself. At first the occupied populations and Soviet prisoners of war were used as free labor to aid the Nazi war economy. On September 26, 1939, after completing the occupation of Poland, the German authorities introduced forced labor for the Jewish population in the General Government (the area of Poland that was not annexed either to Germany or to the Soviet Union). At least 437 labor camps were established for Jews in occupied Poland. At first it was primarily men who were seized in the streets and deported to dig trenches along the new border with the Soviet Union. Later, when the system was more developed, the Jewish Councils were ordered to provide the needed laborers, and they prepared lists of potential deportees from the community according to age and physical ability.

By the end of 1942 there were two types of labor camps: SS camps, established near large ghettos and administered by the SS authorities, and factory camps established by private German companies and enterprises and administered by the "factory guard" (*Werkschutz*), which reported directly to the company management. In the SS camps, as in the concentration camps, men and women were housed in separate quarters. In factory camps, however, men's and women's quarters were built in the same area without fences or partitions. Women were often assigned to the most arduous "male" tasks because the private companies had to pay the SS for the laborers they "leased," and they were charged less for women.

Extermination camps were established in Poland in the fall of 1941 as part of the "final solution." The first death camp began operations at Chelmno in December 1941; Jews from Lodz were gassed there in vans. From then until the summer of 1944, when the area was conquered by the Red Army, some 320,000 people were murdered in Chelmno. The death camps in Belzec, Sobibor, and Treblinka were established in spring 1942 to accomplish *Aktion Reinhard,* the planned murder of all Jews in the General Government. All Jews deported to these camps—more than 1.7 million—were murdered, using carbon monoxide gas generated by a gasoline or diesel engine.

Auschwitz-Birkenau, the largest extermination camp, was first established as both a labor camp and a concentration camp. Systematic gassing of prisoners began in March 1942. At its height, Auschwitz operated four gas chambers, using Zyklon B and crematoria: 1.25 million people were murdered there, most of them Jews, along with tens of thousands of Gypsies, Poles, and Soviet prisoners of war.

Upon their arrival at Auschwitz, both men and women were stripped of their belongings and went through a selection process in which most of them were sent directly to the gas chambers. Those chosen for work—mostly young males but also some women—went through regular follow-up selections in which the weak and sick were identified and sent to be gassed. After the initial selection, workers were stripped of their identities. Numbers were tattooed on their arms, their hair was shaved, and they were issued one garment at random—typically a stripped pajama uniform—and perhaps a pair of wooden clogs. Hard labor, freezing winter temperatures, starvation rations, malnutrition, and unsanitary living conditions left little hope for survival. Chance and luck, more than any other factors, explain why some survived. However, the few who were able to work indoors, "organize" extra food, or link up with a family member or a good friend, had a slightly better chance of remaining alive.

The "final solution" and the gassings were top-secret operations, and the Nazis went to great lengths to conceal the truth. Despite scattered rumors, most victims were unaware of where their deportation would lead them, believing that they were going to be resettled. The Nazis continued their deception even in the death camps. The gas chambers were made to look like showers, and the victims were told that they were going through a process of disinfection.

The first three chapters in Part IV present rich descriptions of the lives of women prisoners in the Auschwitz-Birkenau concentration camp, the Skarżysko-Kamienna labor camp, and the "model ghetto" and concentration camp of Theresienstadt. Part IV begins with Lidia Vago's moving memoir of her "life" in the camps (Chapter 15). Vago starts with the sudden degradation of her highly respected professional family after the German army occupied their small town. We follow her journey in the cattle cars to the selection ramp at Auschwitz (where her forty-six-year-old mother is sent to her death), through the humiliating shaving, to the women's work camp, where she and her sister are assigned to work in a factory. Her simple acts of resistance—such as writing down a poem to share with others (an offense punishable by death)—are not detected, and the sisters somehow manage to survive. We are struck by the illogical and arbitrary pattern of their treatment, the constant precariousness of their lives, and how much their survival was a matter of chance.

Felicja Karay's fascinating analysis (Chapter 16) makes extensive use of testimonies and diaries to provide a vivid portrait of daily life in the labor camp of Skarżysko-Kamienna, the largest camp in the Radom district of Poland. Karay illuminates the social structure of the camp, the living conditions, life in the barracks, the organization of commerce and trade, intimate relationships, the underground, mutual assistance networks, and cultural expression in the form of songs, poems, and concerts. She points to many little things that enabled some women to avoid personal deterioration and carve out a less brutal existence.

In Chapter 17, Ruth Bondy provides a beautifully written portrait of the experiences of women in Theresienstadt and the family camp in Birkenau. At

first we note the similarities in the reactions of the men and women: for example, when offered a chance to join a husband or wife on a transport, both men
and women were likely to volunteer to go with their partners, believing that
they would be resettled together. But Bondy's finely nuanced observations of
daily life also reveals many differences. In Theresienstadt, for example, the
women organized their living space to become the family's after-hours home,
where women cooked scraps of food, darned the men's torn socks, repaired
worn clothing, and searched for fleas and lice. All the women's memoirs about
Theresienstadt describe the unceasing and unsuccessful war against dirt and
insects. Bondy observes that the women suffered more from filth, bedbugs, and
fleas, while the men suffered more from hunger. The women seemed to bear
the hunger, and they deteriorated more slowly than the men.

The last four chapters in Part IV address the question of gender differences more directly, focusing on a number of issues embedded in the descrip-
tive writings of Vago, Karay, and Bondy.

In Chapter 18 Myra Goldenberg analyzes the memoirs of three survivors
of Auschwitz-Birkenau and follows the threads of three common themes. The
first is the translation of homemaking skills (such as sewing a pocket to save
bread) into life-saving adaptations in the camps. The second is the prevalence
of nurturance and social bonding as coping strategies. In all three memoirs, the
narrator tells us that a sister or surrogate sister or mother pulled her from hope-
lessness and helped her survive. The final theme is the women's heightened
physical vulnerability and fear of the possibility of sexual assault. Goldenberg
recounts the women's shame and humiliation while standing naked, being
shaved, having to endure body searches, and being terrorized by the rumors of
rape. She concludes that men and women's experiences of the Holocaust were
not the same: gender permeated and defined "different horrors" within the
"same hell."

Joan Ringelheim (Chapter 19) echoes the theme of women's physical vulnerability but asserts that we do not know much about it because of the silence
that has surrounded the topic. Does the silence reflect the reluctance of women
survivors who do not want to discuss sexual abuse, or the reluctance of the
researchers who do not want to hear about it? She urges us to stop shielding
ourselves in our interviews with survivors lest we lose the opportunity to hear
their full stories in all their complexity.

A very different conclusion is asserted by Lawrence Langer (Chapter 20). He argues that gendered behavior played a severely diminished role during the Holocaust. Even if, he writes, small communities of women survived through mutual support, it is wrong to valorize them because a darker subtext of the "tainted memories" haunts both male and female survivors. Although he notes that the origins of humiliation were often dissimilar for men and women, he claims that the ultimate sense of loss unites former victims in a violated world beyond gender. Langer contends that the reality of life for both men and women was dominated by painful circumstances in which they had no choice. For example, he points to the inversion of birth into death: childbirth, normally a life-affirming event, became a death warrant for the mother. Both male and female survivors suffer from these tainted memories when they cannot fully celebrate the birth of their own children because they remember the fate of pregnant women and their unborn children in the camps. He concludes by urging us to face the chaos of the survivors' lives with unshielded eyes and not to create a "mythology of comparative endurance."

In the final chapter, Sara R. Horowitz (Chapter 21) echoes Langer's assertion that "the trauma of the Nazi genocide did not end with liberation of the camps but continues to color what happens later." Both authors note that survivors' experiences after the war—even their happiest moments, such as the birth of a child—are inevitably colored by their memories of other children and mothers who could not be saved, and of their own parents, who did not live to share the joy of having grandchildren. Whereas Langer asserts that these traumas are not gender specific, Horowitz disagrees, arguing that this "gender wounding"—a shattering of something important to one's womanhood or manhood—is very different for men and women. She concludes that both men's and women's experiences were gendered: the Nazis assaulted gendered identities, and the trauma of victimization was often experienced as a gender wounding. Even though gender was not the totality of their lives, we cannot fully understand what happened to men and women in the Holocaust without understanding the gender dimension of their experiences.

CHAPTER FIFTEEN

One Year in the Black Hole of Our Planet Earth
A Personal Narrative

Lidia Rosenfeld Vago

I was born on November 4, 1924, in Gheorgheni, a small town in the Carpathian Mountains of Transylvania, which belonged to Romania at that time. My father, Dr. Endre Rosenfeld, was a general practitioner, and my mother, Dr. Jolan Harnik, was a dentist. My sister, Anikó, is two and a half years younger than I am. My parents were assimilated Hungarian Jews, who had started learning Romanian only when they transferred to the university of Cluj from Budapest after World War I. We spoke two languages at home: Hungarian, and German because we had German (or rather Sächsische or Schwäbische) governesses. My parents did not know Yiddish, nor did I ever hear my grandparents or my divorced grandmother from Debrecen speak this language.

In September 1940, northern Transylvania, including our area, the Szekelyfold (Seklerland), was annexed to Hungary. Tragically, the lot of the northern Transylvanian Jews was thrown in with that of Hungarian Jewry. From October 1940 until June 1943, I attended the newly founded Jewish Gymnasium in Kolozsvar (Cluj), because a numerus clausus quota system suddenly deprived thousands of Jewish youngsters of a public education. This was the happiest and most fulfilling period of my youth, maybe of my life. We students were preparing feverishly for the *matura* examination in the spring of 1943, but we also had fun at dancing parties.

In December 1943, after graduating from the Jewish Gymnasium with an excellent-graded matriculation certificate, I went to the Notre Dame de Sion Institute in Budapest, where I studied French and English. Quite a few students there were Jewish, and the nuns were equally kind to all of us.

On Sunday morning, March 19, 1944, the German army marched into Hungary and occupied the whole country. It was the beginning of the end for Hungarian Jewry. It was almost three months later, on Friday morning, June 2, that two gendarmes came to our home to escort my family to the local police station. I started to sob when my mother was ordered to hand over her wedding ring. She had a strong character, and while she rubbed her finger with soap, she sternly chided me: "Aren't you ashamed of humiliating yourself in front of them?"

We spent that sleepless Friday night on the bare floor of an office at the police precinct. The sudden degradation and predicament of our highly respected family seemed so absurd, so unbelievable, as if it were happening to other people. None of us cried. Most Jews from our town had already been deported to an unknown destination.

On June 6 we were herded into cattle cars, with more than eighty people to a car. No one had enough space to lie down or to sit on the floor with legs outstretched. Our rucksacks and shoulder bags served as seating cushions, and from time to time we stood up and sat down, to alleviate muscle pain. We were so cramped for space that it was quite a task to reach the toilet bucket in the middle of the car. The stench was unbearable. Those sitting close to the bucket held up sheets for some privacy, because, after all, we were civilized people.

When we crossed the Slovak border at Kassa and the SS had collected us from the Hungarian gendarmerie, my self-controlled father, a veteran of World War I, broke down and wanted to commit suicide. He was anguished that he had not concealed his morphine, which the gendarmes had taken away from him in the ghetto. My mother gently chided him: "How can you talk like this? You have two children."

We reached our final destination in darkness, in the early morning hours of Saturday, June 10. A deadly silence prevailed for several hours. Not for a moment did my sister and I fear extermination. It was beyond our wildest pessimistic fantasies. Of the eighty-odd tormented souls of our cattle car, only three were ultimately to be condemned to life in hell in Auschwitz-Birkenau.

Prisoners in striped uniforms yelled instructions in German and Hungarian: "Get out quickly, leave everything behind, and stand up in separate rows, women and men. Those who are ill, or cannot walk, will travel in trucks. The physicians among the men should stand over there with their first-aid kits." As we waited for the fulfillment of our destiny, we saw the doctors' group at our left, and our father with his kit, for the last time.

Our turn came in front of the SS "doctor," who turned to my mother and asked, "Kannst du gut laufen?" This simple German verb had only one meaning for us, namely, to run. But it turned out later that for them it meant "to walk," or "to go on foot." She said hesitatingly, "Not so well." The officer made a sign for her to go to the right, and for us to go in the opposite direction. Our forty-six-year-old mother was murdered because of a semantic misunderstanding.

We were led through a small forest toward a red brick building, the Sauna (bathhouse). There were low benches along the wall of a long corridor-like anteroom, the undressing room. We were instructed to leave our clothes behind, neatly tied, and to remember where we had put them. We were allowed to take our shoes along, however, which saved many lives during the Death March and throughout the harsh winter.

We entered a large hall in which several women barbers (not hairdressers) were set up. Working as if in a race against time, they rudely cut our hair, leaving us bald and clean shaven everywhere on our entire bodies. The culture shock proceeded as our female bodies were stripped of their fig leaves and exposed to the lascivious gaze of the German soldiers. Oh, no! It was a fleeting, terrifying, agonizing thought. But the soldiers couldn't care less. I decided not to feel ashamed, humiliated, degraded, defeminized, or dehumanized. I simply looked through them. It was an act of defiance, although no one else realized it.

I was given a long black evening gown to put on. Who could have been so foolish as to bring it there? Empty-handed, we were marched to our lodgings, a huge barren compound surrounded by electric barbed wire, with rows upon rows of rudimentary wooden huts, most of them unfinished, and no blade of grass as far as the eye could see. It was the quarantine B III Lager, dubbed Mexico for its poor condition, as we were to learn later. The huts had no bunks, just the wooden floor and an unfinished, leaking roof. At the entrance was the small room of Hella, our *blockowa* (a veteran Jewish inmate who was head of the block), and her cousin Annie. The block was divided into two wings, and at the other end was a small latrine that could be used only at specific times. A makeshift open-air latrine was at a distance from our block. No scrap of paper of whatever sort could be found anywhere, and there was no water. A nearby ditch ran with brownish dirty water, whose origin could not be determined. Signs reading "Seuchengefahr" were posted to warn of epidemics.

As soon as we had occupied our living space on the floor, I tried to approach our omnipotent, probably omniscient blockowa. "Where are our mothers, children, and grandparents?" Hella pointed toward dark clouds of smoke with flames shooting up here and there in the distance. "There are your mothers and children going up in smoke just now. Cholera yassna vengerki"—this phrase sounded like swearing, the last word clearly meaning us, Hungarian women. "Why have you come here now? You had good times, while we were dying. Don't say you didn't know." Hella realized that I was reasonable, and she told me to pick up a few "pebbles" from the walkway. At closer inspection one could see that they were crushed coke with discernible fragments of bones! The pervasive stench was almost unbearable. Most of the women lived, or rather vegetated, under a haze of self-deception. "They are burning garbage" was the common illusion.

One day, also in the early days, I had an embarrassing encounter in the latrine. My respected and beloved literature and history teacher from our Jewish Gymnasium, Dr. Magda Gönczi, was sitting next to me. It was humiliating to meet her there in the filth and stench, one year after my graduation. Coincidentally, another literature teacher from our school, Lenke Steiner, was in the same block, as were other former pupils, though not my friends. Maybe my presence there, the former star of our school, induced these two teachers to deliver impromptu lectures on literature and to suggest that I recite poems. We had a captive audience. After the war, nobody could tell me where, when, and how these two dear teachers had met their end.

Soon we were all so weak and ill that nothing mattered, except being able to get up from the hard floor in the morning (after about a week we each received one thin blanket). Sanitary conditions kept deteriorating because of the lack of water. Nearly everybody suffered from dysentery, and we couldn't help relieving ourselves, standing at attention in rows of five, during the tormenting *Zählappells* (roll calls), which lasted for several hours on end. For me dysentery came as a lifesaver, as I had been constipated, because of inhibitions, since the ghetto and throughout the journey in the cattle cars—a period of at least ten days (which I remember as two full weeks, if that is possible).

At night we were not allowed to go to the latrine, and we used the brown bowls from which we sipped our meager soup—five women from the same bowl, counting each *schluck*. Anikó "washed" the bowl and my underpants in the sewage ditch, because I had no strength left.

The overall filth was aggravated by the last menstrual period that all the women had. We knew that it was to be the last, and we were "grateful" for the bromide added to our so-called coffee, which allegedly was intended not only to tranquilize our nerves but also to stop our biological function.*

On July 8 (I found the date in the *Kalendarium,* the chronicles of Auschwitz), exactly four weeks after our arrival, we were ordered to file past an SS officer, and lift our dresses above the knees. No real selection took place, just a knee examination. Anikó and I, and most of the girls from our group of about one thousand, were found fit for "extermination through work." Then we were taken to the Sauna again, where we were branded like cattle. The tattooing on our arms was performed in a large hall, by a desk, where our personal data were registered and our numbers were given to us on a small slip of white linen with a yellow triangle. I was A-9618, and Anikó was A-9617.

The symbolism of our new identity as a mere number, a nonentity, a non-person, is the uttermost memento of Auschwitz and of all the other death and concentration camps. After our registration and the tattooing, we took our first shower since the day of our arrival. We received disinfected underpants and dresses, and we set out in the direction of the *Rampe* (the unloading point at Birkenau) where we had arrived. Our destination was the women's work camp known as A Lager (or B I a), across the railway line. Sometimes we happened to see truckloads of different "commodities" being transported somewhere. The most painful sight was a multitude of baby carriages. Where had all the babies gone?

A delegation of civilian engineers or managers of the Weichsel-Metall-Union munitions factory had come to the camp to hire workers. Because we

*There is no evidence that bromide was added to any food or liquid in the camps.

were the slaves of the SS, the company paid them minimal wages for our work. The managers walked past the rows of their prospective forced laborers and picked out the women they considered suitable for factory work. One of the Union men reached our row of five, looked at us, and to our amazement he thought aloud, "Hm, da hab ich was" (Hm, I have something here). And he picked out only Anikó and me.

There were heart-rending scenes as some mothers were separated from their daughters and sisters from each other. Some were picked for the Union, while the others remained there, to be employed in different *Aussenkommandos* (outdoor work squads) or to go on transports to other camps. In some cases, but not all, for reasons unknown to me, the Union men relented and agreed to take the desperate mothers or sisters as well.

We were marched over to the two Union blocks in the more established work camp, the B Lager (B I b), just next to this A Lager and adjacent to Crematorium II. Living conditions were slightly better. Only four women slept in a *Koya* (bunk), and we, the Hungarian newcomers, were mixed with the others, mostly Poles, Greeks from Saloniki and some Greek islands, and a few Belgians.

The factory was situated in Auschwitz, some three or four kilometers from our camp. We worked in the day shift, from six in the morning to six at night, with half an hour's lunch break. This routine lasted until the beginning of October, when we were moved over to the new women's camp in Auschwitz. Then Anikó and I, along with many other women, were transferred to the night shift. Our sheltered existence in the Union *Kommando* (work squads) and in the new women's camp in Auschwitz was, undoubtedly, our life preserver—at least until the Death March.

Anikó was lucky to work at a *kontrolle* (checking) table, but I worked in the *Fräserei* (milling section), standing at various types of milling machines for eleven and a half hours a day. My ankles were swollen even when I was lying down. My usual task was to cut down to a given size the round edge of a thumbtack-shaped tiny metal component of something, or I had to sharpen the tack. The work was so monotonous, and I was so weak and weary, that I was in constant danger of dozing off and cutting my fingers, which happened once or twice. I was "grateful" to the SS *Aufseherin* (the supervisor), who awakened me with a forceful slap on my face. Each day I had to finish about two thousand such pieces, which I took to the scales of Hertha Ligeti for weighing in the nearby *Kontrolle* section. Then my pieces were individually measured with a gauge. If the number of rejects (*Ausschuss*) happened to be above a certain minimal amount, suspicion of sabotage arose, and I would receive twenty-five whippings.

The SS woman kept a close eye on us, and the kindest warning for the slightest infringement of discipline was a box on the ear. Once she probably counted the minutes I was spending at the toilet (sometimes I went there to sleep for a few minutes) and waited for me by my machine to hand out this really humane remonstration, plus her usual threat: "I will send you out of here through the chimney."

I was lucky that my German civilian technical supervisor was Meister Jupp from Westfalen, and pitied the Kontrolle girls, who had pug-faced Meister Klein, who was forever sniffing out and denouncing saboteurs. Meister Jupp's benevolence to me started with an angry chiding: "Why're you so awkward?" "Because I have never done anything like this in my life." "What did you do in your life?" "I passed my *Abitur* [high school graduation exam], and I wanted to become a physician, like my parents." Could he have thought that we were criminals? From that day on, he brought me garlic nearly every day, and seeing how happy and grateful I was, he jokingly called me Fräulein Knoblauch (Miss Garlic). Of course, I shared my precious source of vitamins with Anikó, who shared it with her boyfriend, Victor Beja from Saloniki, who toasted their bread on a furnace and smeared it with the garlic. Victor successfully repaired the sole of Anikó's shoes, probably risking severe punishment, but he didn't get away with another gallant gesture to his darling Anikó. He was a silversmith, and he made her a necklace with a medallion from some nice-looking, but not exactly precious, metal. After giving Anikó the necklace, he didn't come to work for several days, because somehow he had been found out and received twenty-five lashes. He did not betray Anikó, so she was not caught and punished.

Several mechanics were in charge of the maintenance of my machine. One of them, who became a good friend, was Simi Fuchs from Marosvásárhely, owner of a library and a former "illegal" Communist in Romania and then in Hungary. He had arrived at Auschwitz with his wife and two children, but he knew that he had no family any more. After two or three months in the Union,

Simi and Hertha Ligeti started a romance, and I sometimes mediated messages between them. They pledged marriage, just in case they happened to survive. They did, and Hertha came to Romania, and they settled in Cluj.

Once while Simi was repairing my machine, he mentioned his library and his love for literature, and I told him that I used to recite poems. Simi asked me if I would be willing to write down as many poems as I remembered, for him to take to the men's camp. I agreed, and he brought me paper and pencil, possession of which was punishable by death. I jotted down verses by my favorite poets.

About three years later, in Cluj, he told me that he had been active in the underground in Auschwitz, and added, smiling: "I also 'recruited' you when you mentioned your knowledge of many poems by heart. You had no idea that you acted for the underground movement, and made an important contribution in keeping up the morale among the Hungarian men."

In addition to Simi, two other men sometimes repaired my machine. Giorgio Montecorboli was Italian, and we couldn't really talk, but we understood each other thanks to my knowledge of Romanian and French, and my twelve years of Latin. He suddenly disappeared in October, and I was shocked to learn that he had been "selected."

I remember less fondly the other Italian, Leon Urbach, because he was sly and took advantage of my trust. Paul Kunya, a pharmacist from a village in our area, promised to help us in some way. I don't remember how he managed to find Leon as a messenger, and not a Hungarian man from the factory. Leon brought me a portion of margarine from Paul, which we resisted the temptation to eat but used as a cosmetic cream on our cracked lips and dry skin. Only after the liberation did we hear from Paul that he had sent us more margarine several times. Leon had apparently taken the risk of keeping it himself. Once, during one of the air raid alarms, he tried to make a pass at me, which I rejected in disgust. I was committed to my boyfriend, Bela.

On one of the first days of October we were transferred to a new small women's camp in Auschwitz I. Our transfer to our new lodgings was preceded by a selection for *Krätze* (scabies). The selected women were supposed to be isolated in special Kratze-blocks until they could return to work, but they probably were sent to the crematorium.

Stark naked on the cold October day, we had to file past an SS doctor and an SS Aufseherin from the factory. We were naked so that no blemish could be hidden, nor any unpermitted "luxury" items that we may have "bought" or "organized."

I went first, was found fit, and turned toward the already examined women. When I got to them, I looked back and nearly fainted. Anikó was standing in front of the selector, who examined her carefully, like a real human doctor (without touching her, though, or maybe he touched her only with his gloved hand), and made a gesture for her to join the Krätze group. At that moment, however, she suddenly ran toward me. The Aufseherin, who knew her from the factory, had intervened, explaining that the rash on her midriff and her arms and hands looked like scabies but were "only oil Krätze, because she works with grease."

Once every several weeks we received clean underpants. To my utter revulsion and pain, I once received a pair of underpants sewn from a *talles* (a prayer shawl). It was unmistakable, with the dark stripes on the border, and the characteristic fine weave of cloth. I was not the only one who received such underwear, and I felt sorry for the religious girls. Nevertheless, we had to tolerate this degradation.

After the middle of December I suddenly ran a high fever (probably around 40 degrees Celsius, or 104 Farenheit) and was unable to stand by the machine. For the first time during my camp life I had to go to the infirmary. A kind woman doctor was there, who spoke Hungarian. She was from Udvarhely, a town not far from ours. I had acute bronchitis, and Dr. Boehm had me admitted to the *Revier*.

The Revier was a simple infirmary; it would be a gross exaggeration to call it a hospital. I was to remain there until the afternoon of Thursday, January 18, 1945—the evacuation of Auschwitz. A Belgian woman was brought to my bed, to share my straw mattress. I was surprised to see that her breasts were tightly bandaged, and I asked what had happened to her. She had been pregnant when she arrived at Auschwitz, and in due course the pregnancy began to show. Although she knew that she could not be allowed to live, she desperately hoped for a miracle and put all her energy into her work in the Union. She gave birth to a girl in December or the beginning of January, and the baby was taken from her to be killed with an injection, probably of phenol. She said to me excitedly: "I did not want to see my daughter. I did not love her for a moment. I will find my husband, and we will have more children."

On January 6 Anikó came sobbing to the Revier and told me about the hanging of the four heroines for their part in the *Sonderkommando* revolt—a desperate attempt of these inmates to destroy the crematoria and carry out a mass escape. Of course, we already knew about the tragedy. The night shift had to watch the execution of two girls, then the returning day shift was forced to attend the hanging of the other two girls. Anikó was hit by the Aufseherin because she closed her eyes. She told me, "Just think of it, one of them has a younger sister here." I couldn't have imagined that Estusia Wajcblum's sister, Hanka, would be my friend more than four decades later, and that we would work together to perpetuate the memories of our four martyred heroines with a memorial sculpture at Yad Vashem, in Jerusalem.

On Thursday afternoon, January 18, somebody made a dramatic announcement in the Revier: "All those who are able to march should immediately return to their blocks, because we are leaving Auschwitz." Before I joined Anikó in our block, I had the presence of mind to enter the pharmacy of the Revier to help myself to some medicines. In a hurry, I grabbed two or three handfuls of small aspirin packets containing five tablets each, some rolls of paper bandage, and a small quantity of quinine, just because it was there. I sold the quinine after the liberation.

I ran to our block, where Anikó was waiting for me. It was vital not to lose each other in the confusion. The huge clothing storehouse in the basement of a block had either been broken into or the SS had opened it in order for us to get warmly dressed and take with us anything we could carry. We also rolled up a blanket each, and tied them with pieces of string that we found there. Unfortunately, there were no ready-made bags with straps, and we had no time to make even the most rudimentary rucksacks.

We were marched out of Auschwitz, and the Gates of Hell were left open. In this surging multitude of trudging women everyone was desperately struggling to get ahead of others, because trailing behind meant being shot. The icy road was strewn with corpses of men and women who had simply fallen and died, or had been shot. No one bothered to, or would have been able to, drag the bodies to the roadside, and they were trampled on, or stepped over if they were noticed in time. How could I ever forget the blue-eyed boy just before my feet?

On the way we heard that other earlier transports had received some provisions, but we did not receive anything after Thursday's small portion of bread, with maybe some jam or margarine. On the second day of the march we were already starving, and the green moldy bread that some peasants threw us in a village was manna from heaven.

Somehow in the crowd we drifted close to a middle-aged mother with a daughter about my age. The woman was my kind doctor from Udvarhely, Dr. Gizella Boehm. Wonder of wonders, she gave me and Anikó four sugar cubes. I think it saved our lives. Later we met once more, and she again gave us a few cubes of this precious concentrated energy. Dr. Boehm's gesture of supreme humanity toward strangers was probably a unique mitzvah (act of charity) on the Death March (the deadly march of the camps' inmates toward Germany just before the arrival of the Soviets). At long last, unable to drag our sore, blistered feet any further, we attained our most ardent short-term desire: a railway station with trains waiting for us.

Once we were packed into the trains, I would say that we were snowed-in standing sardines. Falling was impossible, although we could not feel our frozen feet, which had no strength to support us. Have you ever heard of human beings dying upright? You could have seen this in those death trains.

One evening we reached our destination—the most notorious women's concentration and extermination camp, Ravensbrück, not far from Berlin. (Of course, we had no idea where we had arrived.) All of us, half-frozen and dead on our feet, tumbled out of the railroad cars to face a routine selection. Anikó and I were alarmed, because she suffered from an abscess in her left hand caused by the string that had tied the blankets to her hand in the Death March. Would she pass the selection? Fortunately, this selection turned out to be fairly cursory.

Anikó's life-threatening abscess could not be left untreated. Somehow, she was admitted to the infirmary, and her hand was immediately operated on. Anikó remembers with gratitude the doctor and the nurse for the fair treatment she received. The operation, unbelievably, was performed under general anesthetic. Who understands why they didn't "put her to sleep"? Luckily, there was no logic at all in the death camps.

On February 16, we were shipped to Neustadt-Glewe. The roll call that preceded our transport became for Anikó and me one of the most frightful, dramatic hours of our camp life. Anikó was scheduled to have the bandage on her hand changed, because her wound was healing very slowly, probably owing to our starvation-level diet.

When we had to line up for the roll call, Anikó was not there. I was desperately trying to gain time by moving backward, to the left, behind the rows of five. After about half an hour of this nerve-racking "row-jumping," I saw Anikó appear at long last, running toward our column. Somehow we managed to fall in line and were earmarked for the transport to Neustadt-Glewe, which was to be our third and last concentration camp.

Neustadt-Glewe was not an extermination camp. It was a typical work camp established with the purpose of supplying workers to certain industrial enterprises. Unemployment was rampant in our camp, along with the concomitant starvation and the infestation of millions of lice, who must have been as starved as we were.

Eventually the harsh winter gave way to spring, and somehow, with the warmer rays of the sun, rays of hope started warming our hearts. Weak and weary as we were, some of us huddled together in a group on the bare floor of our room, telling recipes for favorite dishes and imagining elaborate menus for feasts, especially weddings to which we would invite one another. Bözsi from Beregszasz described a mouth-watering cheese dish with an outlandish Slovak name, *strapachka*. Less than a month later she was to prepare it for us in the town of Parchim, in one of the German family kitchens at our disposal on our way home.

In the early morning of May 2, 1945, at Neustadt-Glewe in Germany, precisely one year after the roundup of most Hungarian Jews into ghettos, we were free.

CHAPTER SIXTEEN

Women in the Forced-Labor Camps

Felicja Karay

The Nazis established fourteen factory-labor camps for Jews in the Radom district of Poland. The Skarżysko-Kamienna labor camp, which was in operation from April 1942 until August 1944, was the largest, oldest, and most important of these factory camps. I shall use it as my model in describing the fate of women in the labor camps because research on the Skarżysko-Kamienna camp has focused on the inmates' internal life,[1] and because men and women there coexisted in daily life, making it possible to examine a broad range of behavior patterns.

The Organization of the Camp

The state ammunition plants in the city of Skarżysko-Kamienna were built in 1927. With the German occupation, they were placed under the stewardship of the German munitions concern Hasag (Hugo Schneider Aktiengesellschaft, Hasag-Leipzig). To help meet wartime production needs, a Jewish camp was established on the plant premises. On October 15, 1942, the camp had 4,361 inmates, including 1,771 women.[2] There was a practical reason for the relatively high proportion of women (which was unusual in armament factories): Hasag paid the SS in Radom five zlotys per day for each male laborer but only four zlotys for each woman.[3]

All the Hasag factories in Skarżysko were divided into three *Werks* (sections), and the camp also had three divisions corresponding to the Werks. Each camp was a separate unit governed by three authorities: the German commander; the factory guard (*Werkschutz*), consisting of Ukrainians who were responsible for security, routine administration, and executions; and the Jewish internal administration (*Lagerverwaltung*), composed of the camp elder (*Lageraelteste*), the police force, and miscellaneous officials.

In each camp a three-echelon social structure corresponded to the three large transports that reached the camp. First, Jews from the ghettos of Radom were mobilized, starting in the summer of 1942. By late June 1943, this "Radom echelon" numbered 6,408 people, of whom about half were women.[4] That summer, approximately 2,000 men and women from the Majdanek concentration camp were added to the workforce. Because the letters *KL* were printed on their clothing, they were called *kaelnik* or *kaelanka*. Another 2,500 inmates arrived from the Płaszów camp in November 1943, forming the "Płaszów echelon." In all, roughly 25,000 Jews passed through the Skarżysko camp, and at least 20,000 of them are believed to have perished.[5]

A class hierarchy also emerged, headed by the "prominents," the leaders of the internal administration and their assistants. Below them were the "bourgeoisie," a handful of inmates who managed in various ways to smuggle valuables and money into the camp and to trade in them. Most inmates belonged to the "proletariat," who struggled to survive and to avoid descending to the bottom of the hierarchy, the "musselmen" (more accurately, *musselmänner*)— those who lost their will to live and looked like corpses.

For both male and female inmates, the chances of survival depended on such personal factors as age, health, and occupation. Level of education, cultural background, and social origin had little if any effect. The inmates' fates were, however, directly linked to their jobs and the statuses they had managed to acquire in the camp's class structure.

The three Werks differed in size, type of production, and the supervisors' attitude toward the Jewish prisoners. The Polish laborers who toiled with the Jews were residents of Skarżysko and surrounding towns and returned home at the end of the day. The Jews were marched from the camps to the factories and back again each day, escorted by the Jewish police and their assistants. Many Poles were appointed junior managers; thus they, together with *Volksdeutsche* (ethnic Germans who lived in Eastern Europe) and the few Germans, supervised the inmates' work. The Jewish police were in charge of doling out the soup at the noon recess, an extremely important function in view of the starvation in the camp.

Like the men, the women worked in two shifts, day and night, without adequate sanitary conditions and without work clothes. At first, they found it harder to adjust to the work than the men, many of whom had been skilled or unskilled laborers. It was difficult for a woman who had been a housewife, a seamstress, or a high school student to become, in a matter of days, a skilled worker who could operate a complicated machine. Several women eventually became experts; their testimonies provide an amazingly detailed description of their work.

Women were posted to various departments, including the most difficult, the *Granatenabteilung* (shell department). Here, a shell cleaner, for example, carried eighteen hundred shells, weighing nine pounds each, to the polishing machines in a ten-hour shift. When the women from the Płaszów transport arrived, the Polish workers warned them that they would not last more than a few months. To their good fortune, relates Zofia Horowicz, some decent people among the Poles promised to help.[6]

In Werk A, the largest, most women manufactured light ammunition for the infantry. The output expected of them was constantly being raised, and the assembly-line work demanded intense concentration.

Many women were employed in the departments that finished and inspected ammunition parts. Although this work was not arduous, anyone who earned the displeasure of the German women managers faced a bitter fate. Marianne Tietge was notorious for her blows and kicks to the genitals of men and women alike, and Dora Pawlowska was no better.[7]

Werk B turned out anti-aircraft ammunition. Here, two German overseers, Georg Hering and Wilhelm Leidig, were famous for their cruelty. When a large quantity of *schmelz* (defective pieces) built up, they sentenced the workers, men and women, to forty or sixty lashes on their naked torsos.

Women who, through bribery or "pull," obtained work in the kitchen, the flake mill, the vegetable patch, or the mess hall of the Werkschutz were much better off than the production workers, for their jobs enriched their diet and gave them an opportunity to pilfer food to sell in the camp. The women used various strategies to obtain these prized jobs. One woman torched the machine at which she worked and bribed her Polish supervisor with a bottle of vodka; to her joy, she was transferred to the flake mill, where a Volksdeutsche named Laskowski protected his workers.[8]

Werk C was the most infamous site in the entire Radom district. In the notorious "death department" (*Menschenmordende Abteilung*), underwater mines were packed with yellow picric acid powder, a substance that turned the workers into green-haired monsters with black hands. Next to the "Pikryna" was a production floor for land-based mines; its key chemical, TNT, gave the prisoners reddish-pink skin. Women in both departments were employed to weigh the powder and sort and pack the mines. And because mortality among the men was so high, women were also put to work at the presses.[9] In the department where the shell cases were filled, it was the women's task to stir the boiling TNT, with two seconds per stir, 1,800 stirs per hour, and 21,600 in a twelve-hour shift, all without sitting.[10]

A world away from these torture chambers was the most coveted workplace, the detonator department. This was easy labor, although detonators were known to explode. The director, Hermann Schmitz, treated the inmates very decently. When Eda Jewin was seriously injured and her sister killed in a detonation incident, Schmitz had Eda taken to the city hospital, and when she returned to the camp he secretly sent her parcels of food.[11] Notwithstanding his kindness, Schmitz personally surrounded himself with the most beautiful women.

All ethnic groups in the factory labor force—Germans, Ukrainians, Poles, Volksdeutsche—displayed rampant antisemitism and a wish to exploit the inmates to maximum advantage, as laborers and as individuals. In day-to-day life, however, treatment of Jews varied enormously. The Jews' most extensive day-to-day contact was with the Poles who worked in the factory. The Polish foremen in Section 58 of Werk C were notorious throughout the camp for their bestial cruelty.[12] Generally speaking, almost all the male former prisoners complain of beatings and extortion by the Poles, whereas the women express few grievances.

The factory, with all its complex problems, was only one arena in the struggle for survival. Living conditions in the camp, determined above all by Hasag's wish to save on production costs, affected the prisoners' fate no less. Conditions at the camps in Werks A and B were better than in Werk C, but only marginally. Officially the inmates in all three camps received, twice a day, three-quarters of a liter of watery soup with dried potato flakes, two hundred grams of bread baked partly with the same potato flakes, ersatz coffee, and occasionally a dollop of jam. Twice a week, a spoonful of sugar was added to the soup. On entering the camp, prisoners were stripped of personal valuables, including extra clothing and shoes. When their only set of clothing wore out, it was "replaced" with paper sacks; instead of shoes, the prisoners received wooden clogs. They were not given utensils, soap, or towels.

The first contingent of prisoners at Skarżysko, male and female, were housed on an abandoned production floor at Werk A known as Ekonomia, which had four-tier bunks but no mattresses or blankets. The barracks built subsequently were extremely overcrowded and infested with lice, fleas, and bedbugs. Nevertheless, they were more comfortable than Ekonomia, which as late as December 1942 still accommodated 1,316 women and 933 men.[13] The latrines and shower huts were also inadequate, and hot water was unheard of. Once a month, the prisoners were taken to a public bath in Werk A for a hot shower and disinfection of clothing.

Disease spread rapidly under such conditions. The lack of underwear made women especially susceptible to urinary-tract infections. Dysentery and foot sores were also common. Seasonal outbreaks of typhus claimed hundreds of lives. Although each Werk had its "clinic" (*Revier*) and medic, no medication was available, and the first doctors appeared only in 1943. Until the spring of 1943, selections were carried out twice a week in each camp, and all the ill and infirm were sent to Werk C, where they were murdered by the Werkschutz at the "shooting range" (*Schieástand*).

Sexual Harassment and Assault

The testimonies of prisoners contain several allusions to sexual harassment by overseers even though Germans were prohibited from *Rassenschande* (racial shame—that is, behavior beneath the dignity of one's race). The Germans, most of them young bachelors, attempted to quench their libido by exploiting the Polish women in the factory, although this was explicitly prohibited. Much more dangerous were attempts to approach Jewish women, which might be construed as Rassenschande. In all three Werks, however, there were rumors of "forbidden sexual liaisons" and the exploitation of Jewish women. The inmates in Fritz Schwinger's department at Werk A knew the identity of his lover but turned a blind eye because Schwinger was a decent person who helped his workers. At Werk B, factory manager Walter Glaue occasionally picked out a young woman in addition to his steady lover. When Bella Sperling was executed on charges of sabotage, rumor had it that Glaue had impregnated her and therefore wished to get rid of her.[14]

More conventional courtships also took place: the young German Porzig, for example, asked the beautiful Rena Cypres whether she would welcome him if he visited her after the war. The women could not tell whether Hermann Schmitz, the popular department head at Werk C, had a Jewish lover, but they forgave him his eccentricities. When a factory manager decided to distribute underwear to the female prisoners, Schmitz ordered "his girls" to lift their skirts in order to show what was lacking.[15]

The most famous tryst in the factory took place in the Werkzeugbau department (for instrument production). Everyone noticed that the foreman, Hugo Ruebesamen, tended to loiter excessively in the vicinity of the most beautiful Jewish woman in the department. The supervisor was informed, and he flayed the woman until she bled in an attempt to force her to admit that she had had sexual relations with Ruebesamen. When she would not, she was sent to the SS headquarters in Radom, from which she disappeared without a trace. Although Ruebesamen also refused to confess, he was sentenced to three months' imprisonment.[16]

Sex between Poles and Jews was forbidden, but several Poles "started up" with attractive young Jewish women. The testimonies do not indicate whether these seductions ended in intercourse, which would have been difficult to conceal under factory conditions, or in mere groping in dark corners. Gałczyński, supervisor of the garden at Werk B, would invite women to "work" with him in the greenhouses on cold winter days, and several of these women became pregnant. When he tried to seduce a married woman, her husband made sure that officials in high places became aware of it, and the amorous gardener was dismissed.[17]

Nevertheless, German commanders were reluctant to deprive themselves of any of life's pleasures, and in all three Werks, there were known cases of individual and collective rapes of Jewish women. Dozens of testimonies mention the Werkschutz commander Fritz Bartenschlager, who would sometimes attend selections in order to choose "escort girls." In October 1942, for example, five of these women were taken to a feast at his apartment, where they were ordered to serve the guests in the nude and were ultimately raped by the revelers. In January 1943, when Bartenschlager's visitors included SS district commander Herbert Boettcher and Franz Shippers, the SS commander of Radom, three women, including nineteen-year-old Gucia Milchman, who was renowned throughout the camp for her extraordinary beauty, were brutally raped and then murdered.[18]

Other commanders chose the most beautiful young women of each newly arrived transport as personal "housemaids." (Almost all these women were later killed.) When Paul Kiessling, camp commander at Werk C in 1942, tired of his "maid," he sent her to Hans Schneider, Werkschutz commander at Werk A. Schneider discovered that the woman was pregnant and dispatched her to the "shooting range."[19] Rank-and-file Ukrainian guards are not known to have taken part in this behavior, evidently because they were barred from the camp when off duty.[20]

Markowiczowa of Werk C

At the Skarżysko camp, in accordance with German policy, all internal administration officials were men. The sole exception was Fela Markowiczowa, camp commander at Werk C, who had attained her position on her own merit. She succeeded in developing relations with the factory management and the camp authorities and knew how to bribe Germans and Ukrainians to allow her free rein in administering the camp. The Hasag management was satisfied with this arrangement because Markowiczowa's heavy-handed regimen met their needs.

At Werk C, the "yellow kingdom," where dozens of people starved to death each day and scores were slaughtered in the nearby forest, the proud, intelligent, vigorous, and uninhibited Markowiczowa ruled with an iron fist. Indeed, her subjects called her "the queen" or "Katherine II."[21] Markowiczowa placed members of her family in key positions in the administration, organized a "royal court" in a family barrack known by the prisoners as the White House, and distributed all jobs in the camp for payment or by whim. She included several members of the intelligentsia in her "royal council" and was not averse to offering help to the camp writer, Mordchai Strigler. Her "royal guard" was composed of strapping young policemen, from whom the queen derived double benefit: the large sums of money that she charged for the positions and a supply of lovers. On the positive side, however, she not only allowed the prisoners to engage in cultural activities but actually supported them.

Markowiczowa hated women and appointed none to any position of importance. All of her police, their commanders, and those in charge of the bread storeroom, the clothing storeroom, and the prisoner registration office were men. The women had to make do with positions as overseers of a barrack or a room (*Blockaelteste, Stubenaelteste*) or as nurses at the infirmary; a few became supervisors of labor details.

Trade and Commerce

In order to live, prisoners were obliged to seek ways to become part of the economic life of the camp through labor, trade, and services. This activity went on in all Nazi camps.

In Skarżysko, the "Radom women" were the first to take up crafts. Although most of them were destitute, they had smuggled in all manner of small items that turned out be lifesavers—sewing needles and thread, knitting needles, scissors, mirrors, bowls, Primus stoves, clothing, even bedding. They obtained their raw material as the men did, by "organization"—that is, pilfering from the factory—thus risking the death penalty for "sabotage." Yarn and fabric were also brought in by Poles who ordered the finished products from the prisoners. To get the materials past control at the factory gates, it was necessary to bribe the Werkschutz men, who quickly learned that this was a good source of additional income.

Many men in the camp were skilled cobblers, tinsmiths, carpenters, and so on. Although the women had a narrower range of skills, they knew how to exploit their abilities. Seamstresses and knitters rarely lacked customers; a female prisoner would knit a sweater for a Polish boss or sew a shirt for a supervisor in exchange for bread. Some women made children's clothes or underwear from the rags handed out at the factory for use in cleaning the machines; others produced dolls that they sold to Polish workers at the factory.[22]

The women in the ammunition quality-inspection department unraveled the gloves they were given and used the yarn to knit lacy scarves and muffs, for which there were always buyers. There was also a "cosmetics" market; chalk (used to mark shelves) and machine oil were made into a special "cream" that served as both blush and lipstick. On several occasions the makeup saved exhausted women from death during selections.[23] Embroiderers also found work: when a German supervisor named Mierschowa discovered that Ala Neuhaus was a superb embroiderer, she released Neuhaus from her job at the machine so that she could spend most of her time embroidering for her.[24]

Even in the camps, women could not get by without a handbag in which to conceal a morsel of bread, a rag that served as a towel, a sliver of soap, a comb, a soup plate, a spoon. Ala Erder and her mother manufactured bags out of the jute-cloth aprons that were handed out at the factory. The aprons were hard to smuggle into the camp, but the risk was worth taking, for the bags, embroidered with colored threads extracted from rags, were easily sold to both Jews and Poles.[25]

Some women peddled their products at the factory and in the camps. Others, who had no special skills, sold small slices of bread, a handful of cigarettes, sugar cubes, or garlic cubes. Some women bought miscellaneous foodstuffs from the Poles and sold them to "cooks," who mixed them into the local broth, heated the result in cans over a bonfire, and sold it to all customers. Some obtained apple peels from the Poles, dried it, and made it into a "tea" that added flavor to a cup of boiling water.[26] Women who lacked the small amount of money needed to start a "business" would turn to the "services": washing and cooking for prominents, mending clothes, and cleaning the barracks.

Underground Activities

The subject of Jews' labor in ammunition factories leads into their role in sabotaging production. Such sabotage could be performed in three possible ways: reducing output, introducing defects, and stealing the product for the Polish partisans in the nearby forests. Women from the Płaszów transport, for example, damaged the anti-aircraft shells that they filled, by imprecision in threading. They were frequently beaten for this deliberate carelessness.[27]

It was possible to pilfer ammunition for the partisans only with the collaboration of the Poles. Ziuta Hartman and her Polish supervisor, together with several other inmates, organized the systematic transfer of "scrap"—crates of ammunition—to a cache in a forest.[28] At the Pikryna, the Polish foreman, Kopecki, persuaded Towa Kozak and a friend to steal cubes of TNT for the partisans. He threatened to "wring [the girls'] necks if they dared chirp."[29]

Many such escapades failed. Lola Mendelewicz, working for the infantry at Werk A, stole rounds of ammunition and gave them to her boyfriend, Edek, who passed them on to the partisans. When they decided to escape, they were both tracked down and executed.[30]

Women also played a significant role in organizing underground assistance from outside—the transfer and distribution of money donated by Jewish and Polish relief organizations in Warsaw. Starting in late 1943, these funds began to reach the camp in various clandestine ways. "Distribution committees" were set up at all three Werks.

Mutual Assistance

Like the men, the women sometimes fell victim to various disasters: loss of relatives, disease, work accidents, backbreaking labor, overseers' beatings, confiscation of goods and money by the Werkschutz, and so on. Often a change of workplace severed a protective relationship, and the arduous labor along with starvation dangerously weakened the inmate. Some women, like some men, descended to the musselman level and were chosen for death in the selections. On average, however, far fewer women than men met this fate.

In extreme cases, the last hope for survival was mutual assistance. Women expressed contrasting opinions on the availability of such aid. Roża Bauminger, a forty-year-old teacher, claimed that human interaction in the camps descended to the level of utter bestiality, survival of the fittest, and the abuse of the weaker by the stronger. But Frania Siegman, a genial young woman, described friendships and willingness to help.[31]

At Skarżysko, as in all Nazi camps, the desperate battle for life and death led to violence among all the prisoners, women included. The men were at least united by the traditional education they had received as children and their general command of Yiddish. This was not the case with the women. The Radom women were steeped in conservative tradition and Jewish folklore, and they spoke only Yiddish. The kaelniks were a more heterogeneous group, which included assimilated women, several nightclub stars from the big city, and Bund members who adhered to secular Yiddish culture. Most of the Płaszów contingent had secondary or higher education, spoke only Polish, and were totally assimilated. The veterans sarcastically termed them *Krakower inteligenz* (Kraków intelligentsia).

Relations between prominents and rank-and-file inmates were marked by undisguised hatred. Many testimonies recount violence by Jewish policemen against both classes. Most women supervisors of the barracks maintained tolerable relations with women prisoners and were not accused of brutality. At Werks A and C, however, several Jewish "nurses" were infamous not only for pilfering their patients' food rations and remaining belongings but also for euthanasia.[32]

Alongside these manifestations of hostility were many manifestations of mutual aid in the Skarżysko camp. It was usually confined to one echelon and administered by small cells. The basic mutual-aid cell was composed of survivors from the same family—a married couple, a mother and daughter, sisters and brothers. Single men and women first looked for *landsmannschaft* survivors—Jews from the same city—who sometimes helped one another. Although the authorities insisted that residential arrangements coincide with workplaces, former neighbors tried to share the same barracks. Thus, a Skarzysker barrack, a Szydlowcer barrack, and other locality-specific barracks emerged.[33]

Women inmates developed close relationships and devised new ways to help each other: either pairing by age, with the older looking after the younger, or forming "camp families" composed of four to five women who shared a shack, their labor, and their possessions. In some groups the oldest woman took several younger women under her wing.[34] In Werk C, youth groups coalesced along ideological or political lines—for instance, members of the Zionist youth movement Akiva supported each other, as did Bund members from Warsaw, who joined up with resident Bundists from small towns in the Radom district.[35]

Mutual assistance was especially important at times of illness. Any patient who survived the deadly typhus epidemic of the winter of 1943–1944, which claimed the lives of almost all the women of the Płaszów echelon, did so with others' assistance. The angels of mercy included Mrs. Carmel, who looked after her young comrades, and Drs. Wasserstein and Rotbalsam, who provided medical assistance. There were also nurses worthy of the name, male and female, such as Zosia and Szaweslajn, who on several occasions removed patients from the infirmary at the last moment, carrying them on their backs, and thus saved them from selection.[36]

Bunk Romances among Jewish Inmates

Romantic liaisons among the Jewish inmates were inevitable. Such couplings of *"kuzyns"* (cousins) became widespread in all three Werks. The Krakower inteligenz women at first rejected the advice of the experienced kaelniks that they find kuzyns if they did not wish to meet a quick death. These educated and assimilated young women regarded even the local prominents as "trash that rose to the surface in the tempest of the war and that would sink after the storm passed;"[37] they could not imagine having an affair with some miserable cobbler from the shtetl who did not even speak Polish. Their resistance, however, eroded with the ravages of time, disease, hard labor, and, above all, fear of famine. The best solution was to find a kuzyn from among the Płaszów men, especially those assigned to the local police.

In the spring of 1944, the prisoners' living conditions improved slightly, as Hasag came to realize that the prospects of obtaining new transports of Jews were nil and the survivors in the camp were too depleted to meet the requisite pace of output. Better nutrition and living conditions also revived social life. Now it was not only the prominents who sought a *kuzynka,* but also rank-and-file men. There were also reverse cases of women who had managed to obtain good positions or small amounts of money and could now choose their own lovers. Even some women who worked at Pikryna found kuzyns, despite their off-putting appearance.

Each couple had to solve technical problems; partitions made of paper sacks and old blankets were erected around the bunks, and the number of darkened corners in each barrack grew. The neighbors knew full well what was going on in the nearby bunk, and gossip spread. "Couplets," light ditties based on popular folk songs and well-known tunes in Polish and in Yiddish, immortalized various types of romances. For example:

> For soup, for soup
> For a piece of bread
> Girls will spread their . . .
> Just between you and me,
> They'll do it even
> When there's no need.[38]

This is not to say that the entire inmate population metamorphosed into kuzyns and kuzynkas. On the contrary, many single women and men remained abstinent. At first, they condemned "fornication in the shadow of death," but over time they became ambivalent—enraged by the couples' "shamelessness" but envious of their intimacy. Eventually all inmates became accustomed to the situation, and the voices of condemnation ceased.

Why did this phenomenon become an integral part of the camp experience? Many of the inmates were young, single, and in search of a soulmate or of the possibility of commingling; others sought material assistance; but most believed that life would be easier with a partner. The institution of kuzyns was an important manifestation of the will to survive. Several of these relationships turned into true love, leading to marriage after the war.

The inmates had no shortage of "ordinary" human problems. The parents of Marilka, for example, horrified by what might happen to their young, beautiful daughter in the "depraved" society of the camp, decided to marry Marilka and her fiancé in a ceremony that met the requirements of Jewish religious law. Rabbi Finkler of Werk A actually provided a *ketuba* (a Jewish marriage certificate). In her subsequent testimony, the bride described her "wedding dress": a skirt, a sweater, and a turban of sorts. One of the guests read the ketuba and conducted the ceremony. The rings were made of metal, and bottles of drink and some food were found.[39]

Some Jews reached the camp with their spouses, and in several cases, love triangles emerged, and the participants had to confront moral dilemmas. This situation, too, was immortalized in a ditty:

> Come, I have a secret to tell
> The "cousin" here don't go so well!
> They dance on two fronts in their life
> They have a "cousin" and a wife![40]

As "immorality" among the kaelniks soared, a growing number of prominents, including married ones, exploited the heightened demand for companions and chose kuzynkas for themselves. For the kuzynkas, pairing up was sometimes the only way they could avoid death and starvation, yet their spouses often experienced seething jealousy. The husband of a couple from the Majdanek transport, for example, was sent to the pikryn section of Werk C, where starvation and hard labor soon caused him to fall gravely ill. His wife, an attractive woman, chose to obtain food and money in the accepted manner to try to save her husband's life. Her husband, aware of the situation, refused to accept this assistance. Only by the miracle of last-minute help from friends did he survive and manage to transfer to another job. Even then, he was unable to forgive his wife for some time.

The "bunk romances" had their dangerous aspects. Although many women stopped menstruating under the afflictions of hard labor and malnutrition, impregnation was frequent. Pregnant women were singled out for death in every selection. Abortion was out of the question; although the camp had doctors, instruments and medications were unavailable. Some women managed to conceal their condition until the last minute by various ruses (for example, by wearing girdles or loose clothing). In one shocking case described by Towa Kozak, an unknown Jewish woman at the factory delivered her baby in the toilet; as soon as they were discovered, mother and child were murdered.

If women were in the camp when they went into labor, they were helped by their friends or the local doctor. Their babies, however, were taken from them immediately and, in most cases, abandoned in a distant shack until they died. The writer Mordchai Strigler, a prisoner who performed janitorial work in the camp, attests to having found corpses of babies under bunks and in garbage heaps. Dr. Wasserstein's testimony tells the tragic account of a baby who had been hurled into a container of corpses and could not be saved.[41]

Babies had no right to exist in the Skarżysko camp, but several children circulated in the three Werks. Boys and girls between the ages of twelve and fourteen were considered fit for work. In most cases, both the Poles and the Germans protected them. Bosses were also known to intervene: Zipfel, a German, saved twelve-year-old Frieda Ostojewski on the ground that "this child has a mother, and she must live."[42] In other cases, however, children were beaten for failing to meet work quotas or for suspected sabotage.

Evenings and Free Time

Days, weeks, and months passed. Upon returning "home" after work, the inmates experienced the most important and longed-for moment of their day:

the distribution of bread and a second portion of soup. They then had the whole evening at their disposal until curfew.

The women's regular rendezvous point was the laundry shack (*Waschraum*), where they could wash themselves and their clothes, consult, and gossip. Madzia, who had smuggled a gold chain into the camp in a sewing box with a false bottom, sought a goldsmith who could break the chain into small pieces that she could sell one by one. Maria, who had left some of her possessions with Polish acquaintances, was looking for a policeman's kuzynka who could deliver her letters to a Polish go-between in another section. Rena related excitedly that her bunk neighbor had changed kuzyns. Frequently, curses rang out against various supervisors and local prominents.

When the camp expanded in 1943, new barracks were built at the three Werks, each divided into three rooms (*Stube*) with a furnace in the middle. The forest supplied plentiful wood, and the furnace became a hub around which the women would gather: one in an attempt to heat her remaining soup in a tin can, another trying to dry her sole set of underwear. Some lucky person who had obtained a potato cut it into thin slices, spread it with garlic, and fried *pletzlech*, to her neighbors' great envy. Sometimes a policeman would rush in to restore order. Rivka dissociated herself from the general commotion and sat wrapped in the remnants of her blanket, shivering with fever. She was afraid to admit that she was ill lest she be transferred to the Revier, known to be the corridor to the afterworld. Her neighbor in the bottom bunk, carefully cloaked in bits of paper, had other worries: her kuzyn would visit her tonight, and her period had begun. Still, she had done well to collect a few rags in time.

Thus a typical evening passed, unless there was a selection or a sudden visit by members of the Werkschutz in search of contraband. On Fridays, the atmosphere in the camp was somewhat different. At Werk A, Rabbi Finkler's barrack became a place of congregation and prayer for any Jew who sought a little solace. At the other two Werks, too, the men tried to observe Jewish tradition and formed a prayer quorum in one of the barracks. The women sought to do the same in other ways: as twilight approached, candle stubs flickered here and there, the shouting and quarreling ceased, and peace descended. Each woman wished to be alone in a corner, to commune with herself, to weep for a lost father or mother, a husband posted to another camp, a sister who had recently succumbed to typhus, or a baby who had been plucked from her arms in the last *Aktion* (deportation). Maria recited a memoir she had written about her mother, lighting Sabbath candles in a home that no longer existed. The others listened in silence, tears streaming down their faces.

Later, the barracks filled again with noise and commotion. Acquaintances dropped in. A friend from the shack next door brought Rivka a can of soup. Couples hid in the darkened bunks. And in the evening, there was a surprise: a pair of wandering minstrels, *"der Zinger"* and his girlfriend Hanna, had come to give a performance. The fame of their fine voices had spread throughout Werk A; even the commanders would invite them to perform.[43] Such Yiddish songs as "Mein shtetele Belz" and "Mein yiddishe mameh" soothed the listeners' grieving hearts. At curfew, the barracks emptied of their guests. The women lay sleepless in the dark, when suddenly a lone clear voice burst into a well-known tune:

> There in the forest
> Not far from the town
> Behind bars and fences
> Barbed wire all round
> Oh, that is my prison
> Alone, no family near,
> And no one, when I die,
> To shed a tear.

A gloomy chorus took up the refrain:

> In Camp Skarżysko
> Ours is a very bitter lot!
> In Camp Skarżysko . . .
> My hands and my feet
> Tremble at the very thought
> Oh, that I had never
> Known Skarżysko at all.[44]

Thus the prisoners of Skarżysko began to seek release and solace. On some evenings young women would sing familiar tunes with themes of Jewish festivals and customs—the women's conventional way of preserving Jewish tradition. One of the men, Eliezer Lewin of Werk C, managed to arrange a

Passover seder for "religious functionaries."[45] For the women, communal worship was not a crucial need. Only the wives of the prominents could get a whiff of the festival atmosphere by preparing some suitable dish in accordance with tradition. For the others, the only way to celebrate a holiday was by singing or praying alone. One festival was felt throughout the camp: Yom Kippur. Many men and women, including secular Jews, fasted on this day, which became for them a day of mourning for their murdered relatives.

The attempts to preserve tradition relied on the initiative of the men, but camp literature originated with the women. It appeared spontaneously among the young women from the Radom echelon and then passed to the men. In all the barracks, lamentations, hymns, and ballads were composed and sung, at first only in Yiddish but then, after the women from the Płaszów camp arrived, in Polish as well. The idea of organizing an occasional observance to mark the beginning of the Sabbath arose. Although most of these celebrations did nothing to fill empty stomachs, talent was not lacking. In Werk C, the Akiva youth movement boasted the violinist and musicologist Mosze Imber, the author Maria Szechter, and the poet Rut Kornblum. Young Zionist activists, including the sisters Henryka (Henia) and Ilona Karmel (author of *The Estate of Memory*) and the Gottlieb brothers, coalesced around this core group.[46] Mosze Imber led communal singing in Yiddish and Hebrew and added Polish folk songs. Fela Szechter recited poems by Julian Tuwim, and her sister Mania added recitations of prose. When Henia Karmel was present, the audience benefited from her lovely verse in Polish:

> In Skarżysko woods,
> The echo bears
> My tormented song.
> And they sway, the trees
> To its musical beat
> As they sing along.
> And the trees there quake,
> They sigh as they shake
> Their tears uncontained,
> For to them alone
> Branches heavy with snow
> Have I willed my pain.[47]

Women affiliated with the two ideological groupings, Bund and Akiva, were the first to launch a *Kulturkampf* (a cultural conflict) of sorts, undoubtedly a manifestation of the lengthy standoff between these movements. One of the Bundists, Hedzia Ross, together with her husband, Henoch, had been active in Yiddish education and culture with the Zukunft youth movement. She spearheaded the campaign against Hebrew and Polish songs. The Bundist women brought to the camp their movement's anthem, "Di shvue," and the revolutionary songs of the Jewish proletariat from the alleys of Warsaw. One of these songs, "Ojf di kanonen," became the unofficial anthem of Werk C, and even the women from Kraków, who had not known a word of Yiddish upon their arrival, sang it lustily: "One day we'll meet at the cannons, and then the rifles shall speak with thunder!"[48]

The few literary works that have been preserved permit us to differentiate between the songs of the men and women. The main themes of the men's songs, which were mostly anonymous, were complaints about the hard labor, the killings, and the inmates' estrangement from their environment:

> Werk C, the very worst of all . . .
> At night we return exhausted and broken
> From dragging shells and pouring TNT . . .
> But there is nobody here who can help us!
> Thus we live and we die, alone and unknown . . .
> At backbreaking labor, in sunshine and rain
> There is no rest at all for the Jew working here!
> When, oh when will it end.[49]

The women's writing showed much greater diversity. Henia Karmel penned lyrical songs and macabre accounts of typhus patients covered with lice. Maria Szechter-Lewinger's memoirs provide hair-raising testimony of the horror of Pikryna. The poetry of Hela Brunnengraber (also referred to as Blumengraber) was characterized by yearnings for home and for her mother.[50] The genre in which women were most dominant and successful, however, was the couplet, ballads on current events that served the function of a daily newspaper. Scores of anonymous ballads were written, not only mocking the kuzynkas but ridiculing the prominents and criticizing such policemen as Dawid Bugajski of Werk C, who forcibly extorted ransom from the prisoners:

Here there is a businessman and also an official.
And here Eisenberg rules.
And the bandy-legged Bugajski
claims a double portion of contributions . . . [51]

The women also organized "concerts," as public performances in the camps were called. The young women from Majdanek began to put on small shows in their barracks, charging admission in the form of a portion of bread, a few zlotys, or some rags. Members of the bourgeoisie at Werk B were amazed and humbled to discover exceptional talent in song, recitation, and dance among their emaciated neighbors. The performers at Werk A included not only "der Zinger," Hayim Albert, and his girlfriend, but also Maryla Tyrmand, who was famous for her recitations.[52]

The most noteworthy concerts were those at Werk C, because Markowiczowa thirsted for entertainment and the German commander of the camp, Schulze, encouraged this activity. In the summer of 1944, a special platform was erected in the forest for two public concerts. Rows of benches were positioned before the platform for the German guests, and thousands of prisoners gathered on the grass to see and hear chorale and solo songs, the reading of a "camp journal" in a humorous vein, and dance. The high point was the performance of a mixed choir directed by Mosze Imber, which sang songs by Mordchai Gebirtig and other songs in Hebrew and Polish.[53] The prisoners' applause and shouts of joy were coupled with apprehension about the meaning of this liberal policy and the intentions of the camp authorities.

Evacuation

The day of reckoning came in late July 1944. The advancing Soviet forces halted at the Vistula, giving the Skarżysko management time to evacuate the factories and camps. A rumor spread of preparations for a selection. "Queen" Markowiczowa and her family fled from Werk C one night, and at least 250 inmates escaped through openings cut in the camp fence. The escapees included nearly all the Bund members, Hedzia and Henoch Ross, and most of the policemen. The openings, however, turned out to have been a German trap; nearly all the fugitives were murdered in the nearby forests by Germans, Werkschutz, and Poles.[54]

Before the evacuation, a selection took place in all three Werks. All inmates who were physically spent, most pikrynists, and all those who were ill were sent to their deaths, as were young men who had displeased the Germans for various reasons. Some women faced death with exceptional courage. At Werk A, where all the ill inmates were evacuated, young Dr. Greenberg refused to abandon her ailing mother and accompanied her to her death.[55] At Werk B, Linka Goldberg beseeched the German commander Haas to spare her mother's life, and he finally consented.[56] When Giza Leinkram saw her mother being taken to the trucks with the other victims, she chased her, and her mother barely managed to push her away at the last moment. At Werk C, the two Fortgang sisters and Dr. Mina Krenzler—young women whom the Germans had selected to join the transport of the living—chose to die with their mothers. When Dora Rozenblat was separated from her mother, she refused to abandon her and assaulted a policeman. The Werkschutz men, unable to separate them, shot both as the entire camp looked on.[57] Some of the 6,500 men and women inmates who remained alive were transferred to the Hasag factories in Częstochowa, Leipzig, and Buchenwald.

To assess the differences between the methods used by women in their struggle for survival and those used by men, I refer to the accounts of two workers at Pikryna. Izak Jakober, who was taken to Skarżysko in the Płaszów transport, was assigned to work at the presses. His team managed to meet the murderous daily quota of 1,650 cubes of pikryn only when encouraged by beatings administered by the Germans and Poles. They were constantly famished. Jakober had sold his clothes and shoes long before; by the time of this account, he clothed himself in paper sacks and almost never washed.

Pikrynist Towa Zilberberg arrived alone from Majdanek and therefore decided to form an alliance with her friend Pola. While sorting the cubes of TNT, she pilfered some of the finished product and mixed it with her own cubes to alleviate the burden of her quota. As time passed, she learned to avoid the beatings of her Polish supervisor. When another prisoner who worked right beside her died of exhaustion aggravated by starvation, Towa resolved to take every possible action to save herself. At each break, she rushed to the nearest building with water spigots in order to wash her face and to drink, a remedy that camp veterans had recommended as a way to keep the poison of Pikryna from entering her body. In the camp, she washed policemen's shirts in exchange for bread. She found an old sweater, unraveled it, and together with her comrade knitted a new one that they sold for bread. She learned how to cope with starvation: she cut her bread into thin slices, eating one in the evening and one in the morning before work. She concludes her account by saying, "We women had an advantage over the men because their living conditions were worse than ours. They were given the same food rations but worked much harder and needed more."[58]

At first glance, men and women seem to have used similar methods to survive. Both engaged in "organization," trade, crafts, and services. But men who ceased to wash and shave soon forfeited their human semblance and hastened their death. For women, such "female" traits as the ability to cope with hunger, a sober view of reality, a willingness to establish relations with others for mutual aid and support, a sense of responsibility for their immediate surroundings, and a willingness to compromise were of great utility. The women paid more attention to personal hygiene than the men; they kept their bodies and hair clean and mended their clothing. Even the women at Pikryna had some form of clothing and did not wear paper suits. Women knew how to weave string into a belt and adorn their shabby attire with a collar sewn from a rag. All this helped them maintain a human, even feminine, appearance. When Mordchai Strigler arrived from Majdanek, he was amazed at the attractive appearance of the women at Skarżysko and came to the conclusion that thinness became them.[59]

This advantage had major consequences on all levels. In general, it strengthened the women's will to cope with the material conditions and avoid personal deterioration. In the factory, their nearly normal appearance induced their overseers to give them more assistance, subject them to fewer beatings, and, most important, treat them more humanely. In daily life in the camp, women were more successful than men in preserving the vestiges of the reality they had known in their former lives. They used more "normal" tactics in their struggle for survival—sexual relations instead of beatings, services instead of informing, an attractive appearance instead of a position on the police force. Among the men, the struggle was much more brutal.

The conclusion seems clear that the policy of equality at the starting line—equal living conditions for men and women—gave women a clear advantage.

Further, in their struggle for survival, women were favored by their biological characteristics and adaptability.

Did the German authorities share this attitude? When Heinrich Himmler demanded that all surviving Jews be "evacuated" (in 1943), SS officer Wilhelm Krueger complained about the loss of skilled workers for military enterprises, especially the women: "The remaining Jews are those in the best physical condition, who are called 'Maccabis'; they are excellent workers. There are also female workers, and it transpires that they are physically much stronger than the men. Incidentally, this fact also became evident in the evacuation of the Warsaw Ghetto."[60]

Krueger's remarks about women are remarkably similar to the views expressed by camp prisoners. The conditions at Skarżysko, then, may have been not random but meticulously planned. The Hasag management knew from the beginning that an "equal starting line" policy would give women a greater likelihood of survival in view of several circumstances: enough living space to conduct social life, lack of restrictions on work during off-hours, unofficial consent to business dealings with the Poles (including smuggling of merchandise and food into the camp), the appointment of men to the internal camp administration, and finally, disregard of the existence of sexual relations among the prisoners.

For purposes of comparison, it is worth examining the theory of women's biological superiority in the context of the concentration camps. Rudolf Hoess, commander of Auschwitz, wrote in his memoirs that, according to facts in his possession from Auschwitz and other camps, the "natural" mortality was higher among Jews than among other prisoners in all localities. The main reason for this, he believed, was neither the living conditions nor hard labor but the psychological state created by the loss of families and all hope of rescue. Hoess adds: "Jewish women perished much more quickly than did the men, even though, as I know from experience, women are usually more resistant and stronger than men both psychologically and physically."

Was the main factor in the high mortality of women in Auschwitz their psychological condition, as Hoess postulates? Describing the methods invoked by Jews in Auschwitz adopted in their struggle to survive, he states: "Everything that I have said is also true of the women, with one difference: for the women, everything was a thousand times harder, much more depressing and injurious, because the living conditions in the women's camps were incomparably worse. The women were allocated smaller living space, the hygienic and sanitary conditions were greatly inferior . . . and when women reached the 'point of no return,' the end was not long in coming. Those living corpses that were still walking around were a terrifying sight."[61]

For Rudolf Hoess, it was convenient to attribute the death of women to psychological factors. But his own information leads us to the opposite conclusion: the German authorities in the camp subjected women to harsher living conditions than those of the men, and deprived them of their human and feminine visage by shaving their heads and making them wear uniforms. Consequently, returning to our question whether women were more likely to survive than men, the final determinants were neither subjective factors, nor biological superiority, nor "female" characteristics and skills, nor different methods used in the struggle for survival. The main determining factor, in fact the only one, was the policy of the Nazi regime. This conclusion is equally relevant in any discussion about the lives of women in the labor camps.

Notes

1. Felicja Karay, *Death Comes in Yellow: Skarżysko-Kamienna Slave Labor Camp* (Amsterdam: Harwood Academic Publishers, 1996).

2. Juden, Staerkemeldung am 15.10.1942, Hasag-Werke Skarżysko-Kamienna (hereafter: Staerkemeldung), Adam Rutkowski Collection, YV, 0-6/37-3.

3. Raul Hilberg, *The Destruction of the European Jews* (Chicago: Quadrangle, 1961), p. 336.

4. Hasag Werke Skarżysko-Kamienna, Betriebskarte, Bundesarchiv Koblenz (hereafter: BA), R 3/2040.

5. Skarżysko-Kamienna, forced-labor camp, *Encyclopedia of the Holocaust*, ed. Israel Gutman (New York: Macmillan, 1990), p. 1360.

6. Zofia Horowicz, testimony, YV, 0-16/1156.

7. Marianne Tietge, Urteil in Kamienna Prozess, YV, TR-10/7, p. 12; Hana Zajdenwerg, testimony, YV, 0-33/1820.

8. Luna Lipszyc, testimony, YV, 0-33/1844.

9. Maria Szechter, "Pikryna działa, Prasy." Dokumenty zbrodni i męczeństwa, Polish (Kraków: Żydowska Komisja Historyczna, 1945), pp. 45–48. Maria Szechter-Lewinger delivered a horrific account of her work at the press as part of a four-inmate team that had to manufacture 1,650 cubes of TNT in each shift.

10. Zahawa Sztok, testimony, YV, 0-33/1843.

11. Eda Jewin, testimony, YV, 0-33/1838.

12. Sala Fass, testimony, YV, 0-16/1352.

13. Staerkemeldungen, December 1942.

14. Henryk Greipner, testimony, YV, 0-33/1815; Rywka Lewin-Abramowicz, 0-33/1810.

15. Rina Cypres, testimony, YV, 0-33/1857.

16. Anklageschrift, Kamienna Prozess, YV, Tr-10/7, p. 28.

17. Giza Leinkram-Szmulewicz, testimony, YV, 0-33/1841.

18. Hayim Milchman, testimony, YV, M-1/E/1972/1973; Srul Najman, Akta w sprawie Franz Schippers, YV, JM/3786.

19. Lola Arlajtman-Rozenfeld, testimony, YV, 0-33/1806.

20. Luna Lipszyc, testimony.

21. Szraga Knobler, testimony, YV, 0-33/3674; Roza Bauminger, testimony, YV, 0-16/828.

22. Hana Zajdenwerg, testimony.

23. Ester Hendelsman-Kerzner, testimony, YV, 0-33/1826.

24. Ala Neuhaus, testimony, YV, 0–33/1833.

25. Ala Erder, testimony, YV, 0–33/1817.

26. Paulina Buchholz-Schneider, testimony, YV, 0-33/E/142-2-1.

27. Felicja Bannet, testimony, YV, 0-16/828; Malka Finkler-Granatstein, 0-3/3323.

28. Zivta Hartman, testimony, YV, 00-33/1851.

29. Towa Kozak, testimony, YV, 0-33/1828.

30. Fryde Mape-Zonszajn, *Pinkas Chmielnik* (Tel-Aviv, 1960), p. 847.

31. Roza Bauminger, *Przy pikrynie i trotylu: Obóz pracy przymusowej w Skarżysku-Kamiennej*, Polish (Kraków: Centralna Żydowska Komisja Historyczna, 1946), p. 43; Frania Siegman, testimony, YV, 0-3/2979.

32. Regina Finger, testimony, YV, 0-16/161; Anna Warmund, 0-33/1849.

33. Fela Blum, testimony, YV, 0-33/1839; Zahawa Kampinski, 0-33/1849.

34. Malka Cukerbrot-Hottner, testimony, YV, 0-33/1655.

35. Moshe Kligsberg, "Henoch Ross," in *Doyres Bundisten*, ed. J. S. Hertz, Yiddish (New York: Unser Zeit, 1956), vol. 3, pp. 412–415.

36. Henryk Greipner, testimony; Helena Zorska, YV, 0-33/1797.

37. Rina Taubenblat-Fradkin, testimony, YV, 0-16/249.

38. Taubenblat-Fradkin, ibid. Translated from the Hebrew by Sara Kitai. Original in Polish.

39. Maryla Liberman, testimony, YV, 0-3/1268.

40. Fela Blum, testimony. Translated from the Hebrew by Sara Kitai. Original in Polish.

41. Mordchai Strigler, *In di fabrikn fun toit*, Yiddish (Buenos Aires: Union Central Israelita Polaca en la Argentina, 1948); Adam Wasserstein, testimony, YV, 0-16/1043.

42. Fryda Ostojewski-Amit, testimony, YV, 0-33/2575.

43. Hannah Albert, testimony, YV, 0-33/1832.

44. Strigler, *In di fabrikn fun toit*, p. 408. Translated from the Yiddish by Sara Kitai.

45. Eliezer Lewin, testimony, YV, 0-19/9-2.

46. Ruth Kornbloom-Rosenberger, *Vow: Remembrances, 1939–1945*, Hebrew (Tel-Aviv: Sifriat Poalim, 1986), pp. 54–67.

47. The poems of Henryka and Ilona Karmel, Archive of the Jewish Historical Institute, Warsaw, file 246. Translated from the Hebrew by Sara Kitai. Original in Polish.

48. M. Strigler, *Werk "Ce,"* Yiddish (Buenos Aires: Union Central Israelita Polaca en la Argentina, 1950), pp. 206–209.

49. M. Strigler, *Goiroilos,* Yiddish (Buenos Aires: Union Central Israelita Polaca en la Argentina, 1952), vol. 2, p. 84. Translated from the Hebrew by Sara Kitai. Original in Yiddish.

50. Hela Brunnengraber (Blumengraber), "Mojej Matce," "Pieśń ujdzie cało," ed. Michał Borwicz (Kraków: Centralna Żydowska Komisja Historyczna, 1947), p. 273.

51. Esther Netzer, testimony, YV, 0-33/650. Translated from the Hebrew by Sara Kitai. Original in Polish.

52. Rina Potasz, testimony, YV, 0-33/1848; Awraham Lewkowicz, testimony, YV, 0-33/1816.

53. Felicja Szechter-Karay, testimony, YV, 0-33/1759; M. Strigler, *Goiroilos,* vol. 2, p. 60.

54. Strigler, *Goiroilos,* pp. 268–284.

55. Menasze Hollender, testimony, YV, 0-3/1012.

56. Irena Bronner, testimony, YV, 0-33/1851.

57. Roza Bauminger, *Przy pikrynie,* pp. 59–60.

58. Towa Zilberberg, *Mother, Your Prayer Has Been Answered* (Hebrew) (Bnei Brak: Hamahberet, 1994), pp. 208–232.

59. Strigler, *In di fabrikn fun toit.*

60. "Sicherheitslage im Generalgouvernement am 31 Mai 1943," Documenta Occupationis Teutonicae, VI, Hitlerowskie prawo okupacyjne w Polsce, Generalna Gubernia (Poznań, 1958), p. 609.

61. Wspomnienia Rudolfa Hoessa [memoirs of Rudolf Hoess], ed. Jan Sehn, Polish (Warsaw: Wydawnictwo Prawnicze, 1960), pp. 133–135.

CHAPTER SEVENTEEN

Women in Theresienstadt and the Family Camp in Birkenau

Ruth Bondy

Cyklon B did not differentiate between men and women; the same death swept them all away. Because the same fate awaited all Jews, I approached the writing of this chapter with grave reservations: why should I focus on women? Any division of the Holocaust and its sufferers according to gender seemed offensive to me. The issue of gender seemed to belong to another generation, another era. But I did not want the story of the women of Theresienstadt to be left out. So I undertook this task in the name of the women of Theresienstadt and began to examine, for myself, in what way the lives of women in the ghetto differed from the lives of men, and how one could explain this distinction, if explanation is possible.

The ghetto of Theresienstadt—Terezín, in Czech—represents a break as well as a continuation in the lives of the Jews of Czechoslovakia. In normal times the man had been the provider of the family: married women, even those who had learned a profession or a trade while single, were housewives or worked in the family business; very few were employed. The relatively high percentage of women who registered as having a vocation on or after their arrival at Terezín (40 percent) were products of the retraining courses organized by the Jewish communities as preparation for emigration or life in different conditions in the Protectorate after the German occupation of western Czechoslovakia in March 1939.[1] Some of the newcomers perhaps assumed that it was to their advantage to be thought to have a vocation, however scanty their knowledge.

During the two and a half years before they were sent to Terezín, both men and women underwent profound crises, but for opposite reasons. The men lost their jobs and with them their economic security and their status; compelled to be idle or to work in forced-labor squads, shoveling snow or building roads, they felt degraded. The women, by contrast, had to cope with a new and growing burden of work: most Jewish families in Prague had been middle class and had employed Czech household help. By the spring of 1939, Jews could no longer afford to employ "Aryans"—and were forbidden to do so in any case. Now the women of the house had to stoke the coal fires, wash the clothes, prepare the meals from the scarce rations available for Jews, and knit and sew clothes for the family by recycling old material.

It was even harder for the women to say goodbye to their homes and their lovingly cared-for furnishings. The leave-taking often took place in two stages: first the family moved into a single room in a flat shared with several other Jewish families; then, after October 1941, when the first transports left for the Lodz ghetto, came the drastic reduction of all possessions. Each person was allowed to take only fifty kilograms of food, clothing, and other goods, on the transport. In preparation for the unknown, the women baked rusks, fried flour in fat, boiled milk and sugar to paste, changed white sheets for colored, and endlessly weighted and pondered what was most important to take. Many, in disregard of the strict prohibition, gave some of their possessions for safekeeping to Aryan friends (or those who seemed to be friends); others purposely damaged or destroyed what was left behind. Yet, many a woman tidied her flat before leaving, out of habit and hope.[2]

The trauma of leaving home, with its beloved possessions, went deeper in married women and persisted in the ghetto: while sitting with other women, peeling potatoes or splitting mica, they would talk again and again about what they had had to leave behind.[3] Sometimes they held on to a remnant from the past—a pocket watch, an ivory brooch—as if it were a thread that would lead them back home. The women often tried to cling to such a souvenir even during further deportations, until they stood naked.[4]

Women, more than men, tried to convert their place on the three-tiered bunks into a surrogate home, by covering the mattress with a colored sheet, hanging photographs on the back wall, or laying a napkin on the plank that housed their possessions.⁵ Leaving the ghetto on the way to the forbidding East meant losing a home again.

The two transports of builders (*Aufbaukommando*), harboring the illusion that a ghetto on Czech soil would be an asylum until the end of the war, were supposed to prepare the place for the eighty thousand Jews trapped in the Protectorate after spring 1941, when all emigration ceased. The builders were all men—artisans, engineers, laborers—and many of them belonged to the Hechalutz movement, a Zionist youth organization that prepared candidates for immigration to Palestine. Jakob Edelstein, the former head of the Palestine office in Prague and an ardent Zionist, was chosen to be Elder of the Jews of the new ghetto.⁶ After some persuasion, he agreed to include four women in his staff of twenty-four: Pepi Steiff, his faithful secretary; the secretary of his deputy; Edith "Ditl" Orenstein, a lawyer who had been active in organizing illegal emigration to Palestine; and Dr. Ruth Hoffe, a physician.⁷ The last two were included not only for their professional knowledge but also because they were life partners of two male members of the staff.

All twelve members of the Judenrat of Theresienstadt during its three-and-a-half-year existence were men, as were the heads of the various departments—economy, transportation, health, youth care, and so on. Even the Hamburg barracks, where most of the women were housed, were headed by men.⁸ The only department headed by a woman was the *Frauenarbeitseinsatz,* the employment service for women, headed by Ditl Orenstein. The ghetto police, who were not cruel and hated as in other ghettos, was composed only of men who had served in the army.

Contrary to the promises of the Germans, the mass transports started arriving before the ghetto had been prepared for the absorption of the prisoners. On her arrival Ditl Orenstein found the women depressed, disorganized, and despairing about the terrible conditions—they were obliged to sleep, even in freezing winter, on the bare, wet floor, without heating or sanitary facilities. As if that were not enough, the German *Kommandatur* issued an order that women and children were to be housed apart from men. This pronouncement aroused tremendous anger and bitter disappointment in the women, who had believed that they would live with their families in a "Jewish city." They demanded to see the SS commander, in vain. They were locked in the barracks and forbidden to have any contact with the men. At first they refused to work.⁹

Eventually, after some persuasion by Ditl Orenstein and her aides, some women began to work voluntarily. Work eventually became a regular duty for all women between the ages of fourteen and sixty; only mothers of small children and the disabled were excluded. The new arrivals, men and women, worked in big units (*Hundertschaften*), doing manual work as needed, until they were given steady jobs.

The number of inhabitants of Theresienstadt changed every month, every week. Transports arrived and others left for the "the East"—a euphemism that was not yet known to mean destruction. But from May 1942, when the transports of old people started to pour in from Germany and Austria, until the liberation, the number of women in the ghetto always exceeded the number of men, because their longer life span meant that more old women arrived than men and because men were sent separately to so-called labor camps. On January 31, 1944 women comprised 60 percent of the ghetto inhabitants, and their average age was fifty years.[10]

The traditional division of labor continued in the ghetto: of the 11,000 women in the ghetto workforce (approximately 85 percent of the female population), 2,600 were employed in cleaning and related jobs;[11] more than 2,000 were nurses, nannies, or teachers of children; 1,300 did clerical work; and 2,200 worked in the central laundry, in sewing, repair, and other workshops, and in agriculture. In April 1942 about 1,000 women were sent to the forests of Křivoklát for six weeks to plant saplings. This was the only female labor unit to leave the ghetto, and it did so over the protests of some of the husbands. When the first order for women to work in the central carpentry shop was placed, the idea of women doing "men's jobs" was not well received, but two regular units—one for carrying planks, and one for constructing bunks—emerged. All the heavy manual jobs—loading, transporting, building, water and sewage engineering—were done by men.[12] When ghetto currency was introduced in May 1943, in preparation for the visit of the International Red Cross, the salaries of women were on average 30 percent lower than the salaries of men.[13] (The "money" had only nominal value; the real means of exchange were food and cigarettes.)

The division of labor between the sexes reflected not only the Jewish past but the German present: the SS command in Theresienstadt was composed of men; women held only clerical jobs. The only uniformed German women seen in the ghetto were the *berushky* (ladybirds, in ghetto parlance) who searched the women's rooms for such contraband as money, cigarettes, medicines, flashlights, or electric appliances. They came from the nearby town of Leitmeritz and were at the bottom of the German hierarchy. Some were even punished for stealing from the ghetto inmates.[14]

The Jewish "prominents," who included former government ministers of France, Czechoslovakia, and Saxony, retired high-ranking officers in the German and Austrian armies, and world-famous scientists, were allocated better living conditions, exempted from work, and, most important of all, usually protected from the transports to the East. Women were classified as prominents based mostly on the status of their men: thus the widow of SA-Obergruppenfuehrer; the widow of a commander of the Danish fleet; the mother of two illegitimate sons of Hohenzollern ancestry; and the granddaughter of Bleichenroeder, Bismarck's financial adviser, were *Prominenten,* as was Else Bernstein, a granddaughter of composer Franz Lizst, the mother-in-law of Gerhard Hauptmann's son, and a well-known writer in her own right.[15] But the prominence of Kafka and Freud was not enough in German eyes to save their sisters from death, the former in Theresienstadt, and the latter in the East.

Trude Neumann, the youngest daughter of Theodor Herzl, the founder of the Zionist movement, died in Theresienstadt on March 17, 1943. The notes she wrote to the leaders of the ghetto ("I, the youngest daughter of the deceased founder of Zionism, wish to inform the local Zionists of my arrival and ask for their help"), to the nurses ("Mrs. Neumann-Herzl cannot bear the dirty nightdress and bedding"), and to herself bear witness to the mental illness she suffered before coming to the ghetto and to her anguish there.[16] These slips of paper were saved by a nurse for the aged, Trude Groag, whose poems written in the ghetto express the sufferings of the sick, lonely, and terrified old women who came to "Bad Theresienstadt" believing that they were being sent to an old-age home. Helpless, hungry, and longing for their children far away, they died in the thousands.[17]

The Jews of the Protectorate came to the ghetto with their families, but only the leaders and the prominents had the privilege of living in a small room together with their kin. A kind of family life existed after June 1942, when the last Czech citizens were evacuated and the whole town became a ghetto; the inhabitants were free to move about in the streets and to visit each other at their living quarters in the barracks and evacuated houses. Families, couples, and friends used to meet during the few hours between the end of the work day and the beginning of the nightly curfew. (The curfew changed according to season and collective punishments but usually started at eight in the evening.) This daily meeting became for many the center of life.

According to a ruling published in the *Tagesbefehle* (the daily orders), women had to cut their hair short and men's hair could be no longer than three millimeters. But this order and another forbidding the use of lipstick were never seriously implemented.[18] Anyone who had managed to save such a precious possession as makeup used it sparingly, saving it for meetings with her beloved.[19] The women wore their own clothes brought from home, even when they became too big or shabby with time. As long as the women kept their mental and physical strength, they paid attention to their appearance. Alice Hansel-Haas, the energetic, elegant head of one of the cleaning units, worried after the removal of a cancerous breast about whether she could ever again wear a bathing suit and whether her husband would become reconciled to the change. Several days later her sister-in-law was wearing the tweed coat and shoulder bag of Mrs. Haas, whose worries had ceased forever.[20]

As in all concentration camps, most of the women in the ghetto stopped menstruating, at least for a time, because of undernourishment and mental shock; others suffered irregular periods. Contrary to the view that the cessation of menstruation led to depression and worries about future fertility, in my own experience and observation it was generally received with relief.[21] No sanitary napkins or cotton wool was available, and cotton napkins and folded pieces of linen absorbed poorly, chafed, and were hard to wash. But the disappearance of menstruation made it difficult to know when one was pregnant.[22]

At first, women who had arrived pregnant were allowed to give birth, but in July 1943 an order for compulsory abortion was issued. The parents had to agree to the abortion in writing.[23] The heads of the living quarters, the *Zimmeraelteste,* were asked to report any case of pregnancy known to them. Babies born henceforth were sent with their parents on the next transport to the East. "They kill babies in their mothers' womb," wrote Egon "Gonda" Redlich, the head of the youth department, in his diary.[24] After a Jewish obstetrician had saved the wife and newborn child of an SS from death, Gonda's wife, Gerti, and several other pregnant Jewish women were allowed to continue their pregnancies, and on March 16, 1944, Gerti bore a healthy son. When Gonda, his wife, and the baby were included in September 1944 in a transport to the East, they acquired a baby carriage for the journey, which took them straight to the gas chambers of Birkenau. Some pregnant women preferred to be sent to the East than agree to an abortion. About 230 babies were born in the ghetto of Theresienstadt; about 25 survived. (One of them, Dr. Michael Wiener, was chief of the medical corps of the Israeli army until 1994.)

Terezín had a home for babies and toddlers—mostly orphans and children brought to the ghetto without their parents. The ghetto also housed mothers who had been forced to leave their infants with their non-Jewish spouses. One such mother, Fisherova, managed, despite the insufficient nourishment, to nurse the weakest babies for almost two years, thus saving their lives.[25] In contrast, Gonda's diary tells of a nursing mother, suffering from an excess of milk, who preferred to give it to her husband than to a motherless infant.[26] The orphans were hungrier than children with mothers, for the mothers always managed somehow to supply their children with additional food, often at the expense of their own nourishment.[27]

Hundreds of young couples married hurriedly in October 1941, when the transports started, in the hope that being married would ensure their deportation together. In the ghetto legal marriage could not take place, but weddings were held according to Jewish rites. In addition, some unmarried couples registered as married, hoping to share a common fate: to stay together in the ghetto if one of them was protected from deportation by a job, or to leave together for the dreaded East.[28]

The list of professions and jobs shielded from deportation changed with the years: until September 1943, members of the AK transports, the builders of the ghetto, were exempted, and until 1944 working physicians and nurses were not included in the transports. A group of young women was saved by their work in agriculture. Also exempted were most of the women in the mica workshops, which prepared insulation materials for the war industry.[29]

Most girls and young women avoided speaking of food while hungry, but former housewives would "cook" for hours, telling each other how they used to prepare mushroom sauce with cream or debating the preferred number of eggs for dumplings. Some would even write down recipes, whose ingredients seemed like greetings from another world.[30] In addition to the memories, an entire cooking industry existed in Theresienstadt. The common kitchens in the barracks supplied a black fluid in the morning and a thin, grayish soup and two or three boiled potatoes, often rotten, at noon. The evening bread ration was distributed in the living quarters. All this saved the inhabitants of Theresienstadt from the maddening hunger that existed in the ghettos of Poland and ensured minimal nutrition for everybody, but the rations were not enough to give them a feeling of satiety. In the women's barracks and dormitories there were, in addition to the communal kitchens, "warming kitchens," stoves heated by coal, where the women were allowed to place small pots, mostly of soup made out of their dwindling food supplies brought from home, potatoes stolen during sorting or peeling, or stalks left in the vegetable gardens after the produce had been delivered to the German command. For birthdays, dark, bitter bread was soaked in black "coffee," with some sugar, margarine, and jam added; at least in its brown color, this concoction resembled chocolate cake.[31] A booklet written to mark the first year of existence of the Hamburg barracks announced proudly that its three warming kitchens could accommodate as many as eighteen hundred pots a day.[32]

Indeed, people were proud of the work they did for the common good, without the supervision of the SS, who were rarely seen inside the ghetto. When SS did appear, the male prisoners were obliged to show their respect by removing their caps, and the women by bowing.[33] In this matter, as in other circumstances, discipline was more stringent for men.

The sentences handed down by the law courts of the ghetto for theft, taking bribes, insults, and other internal offenses, along with the punishments given by the SS command for such offenses as smuggling goods into the ghetto, making contact with the outside world, or possessing money or cigarettes, were announced daily in the Tagesbefehl. The number and percentage of men punished far exceeded those of women (the ratio was about four men punished to one woman punished).[34] This inequality may have been a result of the leniency of the Czech gendarmes toward women who returned from the vegetable gardens with a cucumber or some spinach leaves smuggled in their clothing. Or perhaps men, especially those in the transport department, had more opportunity to steal or were more daring in defying the commands of the SS. (Stealing from such common property as the kitchen or the coal supplies was morally tolerated, in contrast to theft from other inmates, which was regarded as despicable.) Those sentenced by the SS to severe punishment were either brought to the Small Fortress, the nearby Gestapo prison, where most of the Jewish prisoners were tortured to death, or they were sent with the next transport to the East.[35]

Some Jewish men felt themselves superior to the Jewish women in coping with ghetto conditions. For example, Fritz Wohlgemut, head of the food distribution service (*Menagendienst*) in the Hamburg barracks, writes: "Women are not used to keeping discipline and therefore it is often up to the Menagendienst to educate them, to make it clear to the women that they cannot come to get their food whenever they like, but only when it is the turn of their room."[36] The men, however, were dependent on the women for comfort. The women's living space was usually the daily late-afternoon meeting place. The women prepared the additional food, if there was any, darned the men's torn stockings, repaired worn clothing, washed their linen and stockings (usually in cold water and without soap), and searched for fleas and lice.

Generally men, with the same rations, suffered more from hunger and women more from filth, bedbugs, and fleas, which became the eleventh plague of Terezín, because of the terrible overcrowding (as many as sixty thousand Jews lived in Terezín, where seven thousand people had lived before the war).[37] The bugs resisted all efforts to keep the room clean, to air the bedding, to disinfect. All the women's memoirs about ghetto Theresienstadt describe the war against dirt and insects. In the heat of summer, when the bedbugs on the bunks were especially agile, many women slept on the ground in the yards. In some rooms, the old women had to wash from head to toe every day, with each supervising the other, and the rooms were swept each morning. The bread was transported on former hearses, and brought in by workers with dirty hands and stained coats. Hedwig Ems, who arrived in Theresienstadt at the age of seventy-one, always wiped her ration of bread with a napkin, at least symbolically cleaning it.[38]

The underground in ghetto Theresienstadt, organized by Communists, Zionists, and Czech nationalists, was not equipped with weapons and never made practical preparations for an uprising. In its everyday activities—clandestine meetings, smuggling in the ghetto, illegal education of the children—the women were equal partners, although the men had more opportunities to work outside the ghetto and to make contact with the outside world.

The only women's organization active in the ghetto was WIZO, the Women's International Zionist Organization. On the initiative of Klara Caro, the wife of the rabbi of Koeln, about twenty women used to meet on Saturday afternoons after Caro's arrival in summer 1942, mainly to listen to lectures on Zionist topics. In time, the number of participants grew to two hundred.[39] The central personality among the ghetto women was Hannah Steiner, one of the founders of WIZO in Czechoslovakia and the former head of the emigration department of the Jewish community in Prague, who arrived in the ghetto in July 1943. A woman of energy and optimism, Steiner continued to hope that she and her husband, as owners of a certificate, would succeed in leaving for Palestine, until her death in Birkenau proved her wrong.[40]

According to Klara Caro, good and generous people grew more so in disastrous times, whereas small and petty ones became even smaller. Dozens of memoirs written by women attest to solidarity, mutual help, friendship, sacrifice, and togetherness even in the harshest conditions.[41] Others, however, claim the opposite: "One would assume that the common tragic destiny would lead to mutual help and to fair relations, but the opposite happens—not always. The overcrowding, the despair, the hunger, the diseases, the cold, the dying all around, make people bad, impatient, domineering."[42] Opinions also vary concerning relations between women from Germany and Czech women, who were better off in the ghetto. On one hand, there are complaints from the women from Germany about hard-hearted and arrogant behavior by the women of Czech origin. On the other, there is praise for their friendship and devoted care during sickness.[43] I dare to say that the solidarity of women outweighed the selfishness.

During the first months of the ghetto's existence, children aged twelve and under were housed with their mothers, but living with hundreds of women of all ages had a disturbing influence on them. Children's rooms were therefore established in the barracks, and after June 1942, when the last civilian population left Terezín, children's homes were established. The mothers were not forced to let their children move into the homes, but most of them were glad to do so, hoping—rightly, as experience proved—that it would be better for the children. In the homes the living conditions were easier even if the children were obliged to sleep, eat, learn, and play in the same room that had earlier served only as a classroom for five hours a day. The children received some additional food and some sort of education, and they had friends and company. Most of the children loved the homes, although some were lonely at night, and bedwetting was not uncommon. Because most of the mothers perished together with their children, I found no account of how the separation at night affected the mothers. Besides the daily encounter in the afternoon, some mothers found jobs in the homes so as to be near their children. Others looked for "lucrative" jobs (in agriculture, the kitchens, or the post office), where they could get their hands on some extra food for their children.

Some books about Theresienstadt, especially those published in the United States, suggest that the prisoners were preoccupied by sex.[44] At this point I allow myself to speak from experience, as one who came to the ghetto at the age of eighteen and lived for a year and a half with girls my own age. The undernourishment and the stresses of life weakened the sex drive considerably. Young couples longed most of all for physical closeness, for an embrace, for warmth, for comfort. Also, little or no privacy was available in the ghetto: a couple could lie together under a blanket on a bunk in a crowded, illuminated room, but the sex act, if it happened, had to be quick, quiet, in full clothing, and in unromantic circumstances.

Things were different for young men who were properly nourished, such as cooks, butchers, and bakers. Not only was their sex drive mostly intact, but they could afford a private corner and beautiful girls. In this respect the situation was similar to that in the outside world except that the valuable commodity was not gold, diamonds, or money but food. Even more important, holders of important jobs were allowed to shield their closest family and friends, up to thirty souls, from transports to the East until the autumn of 1944, when almost all of them, together with their families, were sent to the gas chambers. Paid prostitution was not needed; men of position could always find a lover, even if they were far from good-looking.[45] Lesbian relationships were extremely rare in the ghetto; most of the young women of my age, including me, had been brought up in puritanical homes and did not even know what the word *lesbian* meant.[46]

Sometimes marriages became stronger in the ghetto—perhaps in part because of the separate living quarters, which prevented everyday bickering and made the brief daily encounter a special occasion. (Gonda Redlich, however, describes in his diary the difficulty of living with his wife in a tiny, cramped room.)[47] The work that the women did, often in an area new to them, gave them self-assurance, so that relations between married couples became more equal or even reversed, with the women the provider and the strong one. But some marriages did not withstand the strain of ghetto life, and both women and men found new partners, until all were swept away by the transports.[48] Many people felt a thirst to squeeze as much as possible out of life, for as long as possible.

The undernourishment, the overcrowding, and the poor sanitary conditions made most ghetto inhabitants susceptible to a never-ending chain of maladies. The high number of deaths among the women—19,878 women out of a total of 32,647 deaths between November 24, 1941, and July 31, 1944—reflects the high representation of women in the population at large and in the ghetto. In general, sickness and death were equally common among men and women. The greater resilience of women was not yet as pronounced in Theresienstadt as it became in Auschwitz.

The suicide rate (171 men and 259 women committed suicide before July 1944) was higher in Terezín than in the surrounding population, but it was relatively small in view of the living conditions. In addition to an active form of suicide (by hanging oneself, taking poison, or leaping out a window), there was a passive one, simply losing the will to live. As long as there was hope that somebody might need them at the end of the war, the women clung to life.[49]

The constant dread that even this remnant of family life could come to an end in the form of a transport to the East, and the fear of separation forever, haunted the ghetto. The first reaction to the scheduled transport of somebody beloved (only parents with children under sixteen had the "privilege" of being sent with them) was to join voluntarily: sons and daughters with their parents, brothers with their sisters, lovers with each other.[50] The few left behind in the ghetto felt guilty and suffered pangs of conscience:

> Tomorrow five thousand shall leave
> and we stay behind, shamed and small . . . [51]

The Nazis exploited this family attachment cynically during the mass transports in autumn 1944: first they pretended to be sending four thousand able-bodied men to a new labor camp (which turned out to be Birkenau). On the day after their departure, the women were offered a chance to join voluntarily, to be reunited with their husbands and sons. Hundreds of women flocked to the Magedeburg barrack, the seat of the ghetto administration, to register. They and their children were brought straight to the gas chambers. Among the victims was the poet Ilse Weber, with her ten-year-old son. Fritzi Zucker, the wife of Otto Zucker (one of the central figures of the ghetto), was standing next to the train when the ghetto commander, Rahm, said to the SS escort: "This is Mrs. Zucker. It is your responsibility to see to it that she is in her husband's arms this evening."[52] At that time Otto Zucker was already ashes. Fritzi, who had worked in Terezín as housemother in a children's home, followed his fate. Similarly, Hedwig Eppstein, the wife of the second Elder of the Jews, who left the ghetto on October 28, 1944, in the last transport to be gassed in Auschwitz, was convinced that she was going to meet her husband.[53]

After seventeen thousand people left with the transports of autumn 1944, Theresienstadt was a city of women. The only men remaining were most of the prominents, all the Danish Jews, and others privileged in German eyes. The women took over the jobs previously done by men, including heavy manual work like unloading coal and potatoes.[54] In November 1944, the Germans ordered women and children to throw the ashes of all the dead of the ghetto (almost thirty thousand people), which had been kept in numbered urns, into the Eger River, to remove the damning evidence.

Women influenced the life of Theresienstadt by their mere existence, as wives, mothers, sisters, lovers, friends, and in jobs that helped others, such as nursing and child care. They also played an important part in cultural life. Because of the segregated living quarters, cultural activities were at first organized separately by men and women, out of the same need. But after June 1942 men and women worked together in the department of leisure (*Freizeitgestaltung*).

A group of professional painters, all men, had found refuge in the drawing room of the technical department, enabling them to paint secretly the realities of ghetto life. Women painters, such as Amalia Seckbach, Malvina Šalková, and Charlotta Burešová, painted mostly for themselves, without any expectation that their work would ever be recognized or even seen outside the ghetto. Vienna-born Friedl Dicker-Brandeis, who was an accomplished painter before coming to the ghetto, is today the best known of these artists, thanks to the painting lessons she gave in the children's home. Of the hundreds of children to whom painting brought hours of happiness, few remained alive, but approximately six thousand of their paintings were saved and bear witness to the vision of Friedl Dicker-Brandeis, whose life came to an end in Auschwitz at the age of forty-six.[55]

Women were an integral part of the rich cultural life of the ghetto, as opera and cabaret singers, actresses, directors, and musicians.[56] The rehearsals and performances, which took place in addition to the usual eight to ten working hours, required great physical strength, but they also added strength by providing an opportunity for the participants to forget the everyday realities, to work professionally, and to learn from a gifted conductor or a demanding director.

Men and women in Theresienstadt, youth and children, wrote poems or at least rhymes expressing the absurdities and sorrows and small pleasures of ghetto life. Hundreds of poems written by women—Gerty Spiess, Ilse Weber, Trude Groag, Else Dormitzer, Ilse Blumenthal-Weiss, Gertrud Kantorowitz[57]—were preserved. Even if some of them do not meet the highest literary standards, they all express the ability to identify with the suffering of others and the fear of what was yet to come. The poems eased the burdens and horrors of everyday life. Reciting and reading poems was a popular way of passing the long evenings after curfew. The strong impulse to leave a testimony to further generations is shown by an unknown woman who, while waiting to be admitted to the gas chambers, gave three poems to a Polish kapo, asking him to pass them to a prisoner in the men's camp.[58]

We have come now to the last chapter, the family camp B/2/b in Birkenau, where 17,500 inmates of Theresienstadt were sent between September 1943 and July 1944. This was the only Jewish family camp in the vast complex of Auschwitz-Birkenau. Although men and women lived in separate barracks, they could meet for a few minutes while walking the camp road to the latrines, or they could meet clandestinely for a moment in the barracks. Here, at Birkenau, only a day after their arrival, the differences between the sexes was already striking. The men, in hats with cut-off brims and in trousers and coats thrown to them at random—too short, too long, too wide, too small—looked like sad black storks. The women, also wearing garments that had been distributed to them at random, had somehow succeeded in only twenty-four hours in adjusting them to their bodies and sewing up the holes, using needles made out of wooden splinters and threads pulled out of the one blanket allocated to them.

Some of them learned to iron shirts with bricks heated in the stove.[59] They carried the heavy wooden soup barrels, three women on each side, for the privilege of scraping whatever stuck to the sides and bottom after distribution—most of it for their children, husbands, or brothers. In the same conditions, with the same scarce nourishment, they could bear hunger more easily, and deteriorated more slowly, than the men.[60]

Nobody knew for certain the reason for the family camp's existence—why there had been no selection on arrival (as in all the other transports), why the prisoners' hair was not shaved, why they were not taken outside for work. It was assumed that the special treatment was connected with the planned visit of an International Red Cross delegation in Theresienstadt and some other camp and that they would be kept alive until the end of the war. The SS even allowed Fredy Hirsch, a sports teacher from Aachen, to open a children's home in B/2/b. But exactly six months after their arrival, all 3,800 of those who had survived from the first transport (about 20 percent had died of cold, hunger, or disease) were gassed during one night, without any selection. Those who had arrived three months later knew that the same fate awaited them in June 1944. Because of the heavy bombing attacks on Germany by the Allies, the Nazis needed working hands, so a selection was held by Dr. Mengele and his helpers in the family camp in late June. Mothers of children were allowed to present themselves for selection. But after a six-month stay in Birkenau they knew that this meant leaving their children to face death alone. Only two of about six hundred mothers of young children appeared for selection; all the others decided to stay with their children to the end. Mothers of girls under the allowed age of sixteen tried to pass them off as older and were determined to stay with them if they failed.[61] Girls of the right age tried to spruce up their mothers to make them look younger and healthier so they would pass.[62] One young mother sedated her small baby and tried to smuggle him out wrapped in a bundle. But the baby's cry gave her away.[63]

I worked in the children's block, taking care of a group of five- and six-year-olds. Some of their mothers came to me before the selection to ask my advice—what would I do? I tried not to give them a straight answer: "How could I know? I don't have a child of my own." But after they persisted, I said: "I think if I had a small child I would stay with him." They nodded: their decision was the same; they just wanted my approval. For years the heavy burden of responsibility weighed on me: the mothers were young, they could have survived and begun new families. But after my daughter was born, I was reassured: I would not have left her alone when she most needed my embrace.

I finish where I began: most of the prisoners of Theresienstadt and of the family camp at Birkenau, both men and women, tried to stay humane to the end, united as human beings.

Notes

1. H. G. Adler, *Theresienstadt, 1941–1945*. (Tübingen: J. C. B. Mohr, 1960), p. 417.
2. Gerty Spiess, *Drei Jahre Theresienstadt* (Munich: Christian Kaiser, 1984), p. 38.
4. Svet, Františka Faktorová, p. 182.
5. Grete Salus, *Niemand, Nichts: Ein Jude.* (Darmstadt: Damstaedter Blaetter, 1981), p. 11.
6. Ruth Bondy, *Elder of the Jews* (New York: Grove Press, 1989), p. 245.
7. Interview with Edith Orenstein, 1979, Archive Ruth Bondy.
8. Bejt Terezin Archive (BTA), 85, Kibbutz Givat Chaim, Israel.
9. Edith Orenstein, Prague 1945, BTA, 8.
10. Adler, *Theresienstadt*, p. 417.
11. Kaethe Starke, *Der Fuehrer schenkt den Juden eine Stadt* (Berlin: Haude und Spencersche Buchhandlung, 1971), p. 47.
12. BTA, 85, chapter "Einsatz," pp. 4, 7.
13. Adler, *Theresienstadt*, p. 418.
14. Bondy, *Elder of the Jews*, p. 277.
15. Karel Lagus and Josef Polák, *Mešto za mřízemi* (Prague: Naše Vojsko, 1964), p. 85.
16. Zionist Central Archive H-25; Bondy, *Elder of the Jews*, pp. 300–302.
17. Trude Groag, *Lieder einer Krankenschwester* (Bejt Terezin, 1975).
18. Lagus and Polák, *Mešto za mřízemi*, p. 83.
19. Egon Redlich, *Theresienstadt Diary, 1942–1944*, BTA, 7/9/1943.
20. Starke, *Der Fuehrer schenkt den Juden eine Stadt*, p. 77.
21. Marlene E. Heimann, *Gender and Destiny: Women Writers and the Holocaust*. (Connecticut, 1986), p. 7.
22. Redlich, *Theresienstadt Diary*, BTA, 10/29/1942.
23. Lagus and Polák, *Mešto za mřízemi*, p. 217.
24. Redlich, *Theresienstadt Diary*, BTA, 11/24/1943.
25. Mariana Becková, BTA, 192, p. 1.
26. Redlich, *Theresienstadt Diary*, BTA, 2/9/1943.
27. Vera Hajková, BTA, p. 3.
28. Lagus and Polák, *Mešto za mřízemi*, p. 130.
29. Spiess, *Drei Jahre Theresienstadt*, p. 38.
30. Arnoštka Klein, BTA, 197, n. 9.
31. Kaethe Breslauer, Yad Vashem, 02/217.

32. BTA, 85.

33. Tagesbefehl 10/20/1942 and other dates, BTA.

34. This ratio is according to my count of verdicts in two hundred Tagesbefehl.

35. Bondy, *Elder of the Jews,* pp. 261–262.

36. BTA, 85.

37. Dr. Bertha Landré, BTA, 231.

38. Hewig Ems, BTA, 12, pp. 12, 20.

39. Klara Caro, Yad Vashem, 02/244, BTA, 435.

40. Bondy, *Elder of the Jews,* pp. 366–367.

41. Rose Weglein, BTA, 123.

42. Landré, BTA, p. 21.

43. Spiess, *Drei Jahre Theresienstadt,* p. 59.

44. E.g., George E. Berkley, *Hitler's Gift: The Story of Theresienstadt* (Boston: Branden, 1993).

45. Navah Shan, *I Wanted to Be an Actress* (Hebrew) (Tel Aviv: Kibbutz Meuchad, 1991), p. 41.

46. Tamar Hermann, "Theresienstadt Diary, 1944–1945" (Hebrew), in *Yalkut Moreshet* (November 1989), pp. 195–208.

47. Redlich, *Theresienstadt Diary,* BTA, 6/15/1943.

48. Ibid., 10/9/1942.

49. Ems, BTA, p. 2.

50. *Svět bez dimenzí,* Věra Hajková, p. 81.

51. Ilse Weber, *In deinen Mauern wohnt das Leid* (Gerlingen: Bleicher Verlag, 1911), p. 95.

52. Lagus and Polák, *Mešto za mřízemi,* p. 241.

53. Starke, *Der Fuehrer schenkt den Juden eine Stadt,* p. 151.

54. *Theresienstadt* (Hebrew) (Tel Aviv: MAPAJ, 1946), Ditl Orenstein, p. 61; Grete Wiener, p. 221.

55. Friedl Dicker-Brandeis, *1898–1944* (Státní Židovské Museum, Prague, 1988).

56. E.g., pianists: Alice Sommer-Herz, Edith Kraus-Steiner; singers: Heda Grab-Kernmeyer, Liesl Hofer, Anny Frey; actress: Váva Šan; dancer: Kamilla Rosenbaum; director: Irena Dodal.

57. Ludvík A. Václavek, *Deutsche Lyrik im Ghetto Theresienstadt* (Weimarer Beitraege, 1982), p. 25.

58. Oto Kraus and Erich Kulka, *Factory of Death* (Hebrew) (Yad Vashem, 1960), pp. 199.

59. M. Hermannová and H. Schuetzová, *Kdo chce budoucím něco mříci: Musí promluvit* (Prague: Svícen, 1994), p. 63.

60. Salus, *Niemand, Nichts,* p. 9; Avraham Ofir, BTA, 5/-B8.

61. Hermannová and H. Schuetzová, *Kdo chce budoucím něco mříci,* p. 22.

62. *Svět bez dimenzí,* Ela Fischerova, p. 18.

63. *Svět bez dimenzí,* Anna Hyndrakova, p. 143.

CHAPTER EIGHTEEN

Memoirs of Auschwitz Survivors
The Burden of Gender

Myrna Goldenberg

C oncentration camp memoirs have forged our consciousness of the Holocaust. The words of Elie Wiesel, Primo Levi, Paul Celan, Tadeusz Borowski, Abba Kovner, Aharon Appelfeld, Dan Pagis, Arnost Lustig, and Piotr Rawicz, the "chief witnesses," break the silence of the unspeakable and unimaginable.[1] Because these men are exceptional writers and because their testimonies are eloquent and compelling, their memoirs have been regarded as typical of "the" Jewish Holocaust experience.

Yet hundreds of memoirs written by women survivors document "different horrors within the same Hell."[2] Although all Jews were designated for extermination, the Nazis treated Jewish men and women differently, and women had different experiences.[3] To represent the Holocaust more fully, we must therefore examine the memoirs of women as well as those of men. The memoirs I draw on in this chapter emphasize women's strong concern for one another as well as their dependency on one another to withstand the barbarism of the camps; their adaptation of homemaking skills into coping skills; and the effects of their heightened physical vulnerability and fear of rape.

The authors of the three memoirs I consider in this chapter are survivors of Auschwitz-Birkenau: Sara Nomberg-Przytyk, Cecilie Klein, and Judith Isaacson. All three were bright and ambitious when the Nazis interrupted their lives. Two were unsuspecting. They represent different degrees of religious observance and assimilation as well as different levels of economic security and different professional aspirations and achievements. Before Birkenau they shared only the accident of their birth into Jewish families in the early twentieth century and their hope and expectation that they would live out their lives with a loving family and caring friends and colleagues.

In Sara Nomberg-Przytyk's memoir, *Auschwitz: True Tales from a Grotesque Land,* we trace the movement of a woman from isolation, depression, and detachment into a community of women prisoners who, like her, were politically active Communists before the war.[4] They gave her practical and moral support and a reason to live.

Nomberg-Przytyk was born in 1915 in Lublin to a well-known Hasidic family. A committed Communist, she was arrested in 1934 for her activism. When the Germans invaded Poland in September 1939, she fled to the East to escape. But she returned to her native country in 1941 and lived in the Bialystok ghetto. In August 1943, she was deported from the ghetto and transferred to Auschwitz-Birkenau. She observes that Birkenau was organized as a "devilish system in which the SS men and the [prisoner] functionaries were united by a chain of cruelty."[5]

After the humiliating process of being shaved, she felt so dehumanized, so alone and so deeply depressed, that she prepared a noose with which to hang herself. A political comrade from the Bialystok ghetto, however, found her and provided the bread, warm sweater, and boots that restored her physically; no less important, the other woman promised friendship. She fell asleep with "hope in [her] heart . . . and began to thaw from inner warmth."[6] During a selection, another comrade sneaked her into the safe group. Time and again, her political network rescued her from hard-labor *Kommandos* and selections. Her relative sense of security enabled her to observe the camp's system and to try to understand the "terrible logic" that governed the process, "as though there were some justification in killing the sick, the elderly, and the unattractive."[7]

Nomberg-Przytyk describes the prisoners she came to know, profiling each by indicating the degree of help and compassion that each of them displayed toward others. Her section of the camp contained many members of anti-fascist political organizations who strove to protect or ease the life of their comrades.[8] Assigned to work in the infirmary on a ruse, she felt safe and created a surrogate family with the infirmary cleaning woman, eighteen-year-old Magda, who became her "camp daughter" throughout the months in Birkenau and later, very briefly, in Ravensbrück.

Most of this memoir focuses on the strategies through which the women attempted to foil the Nazi plan for extermination. Nomberg-Przytyk describes how Dr. Josef Mengele smiled as he ordered the death of all newborns and their mothers. There is no place on earth for Jews, he explained, and "it would not be humanitarian to send a child to the ovens without permitting the mother to be there to witness the child's death."[9] The women conspired to deliver babies in silence and secrecy, in the barracks rather than the infirmary. And then, to save the mother's life, they would kill the baby immediately and tell the mother that it was stillborn. Such was the tragic and cruel necessity for the survival of pregnant women in the camps.

Nomberg-Przytyk contends that, despite the conditions, "there was room for hope and dreams." She tells of women whose dreams ennobled them and reports instances of nurturing and kindness in the Communist network and elsewhere. In the January 1945 transport from Auschwitz to Ravensbrück, Sara was nearly frozen to death and too sick to keep awake; a woman she did not know and never saw again begged her to accept a blanket and some dry crusts of bread. The donor's generosity saved Sara's life. In the next camp, she was alone again until she befriended Klara, and the two supported each other. Sara sold her winter coat to her block elder for a loaf of bread and margarine and shared her feast with Klara, who declared, "We ate the coat."[10] Together they awaited spring, the Americans, and freedom. The persistent theme of this memoir is the need for connectedness. We are left with the implicit admonition to develop and nurture relationships, to care for one another, and to take responsibility for one another, for in loneliness, there is no protection against violence and despair.[11]

In the second memoir, *Sentenced to Live,* Cecilie Klein follows the customary structure of the Holocaust survivor memoir, beginning with a description of near-idyllic family life in the pre-Nazi period.[12] Born in 1925, she was the youngest of an observant Jewish family with six children. They lived in Jasina, a scenic, colorful town of twelve thousand in the foothills of the Carpathian Mountains, where class distinctions were indicated by the number of times a week a family ate meat. When Cecilie was about six, antisemites set fire to "Jasina's largely Jewish business district," demolishing her parents' large, successful clothing store. Her father, "an intellectual who always seemed to have a book in his hand," then earned money by tutoring students. Until his death in 1934, he depended heavily on his Hasidic-bred wife to feed the family from the profits of her small grocery. Klein describes her short, plump mother as a saintly woman, whose deeds of charity instilled in her children a strong commitment to others.[13]

After March 15, 1939, when the Germans marched into Prague, Klein lived a nightmare. Her schooling ended abruptly at age fourteen when her teacher ordered the Jewish children out of the building. Because her father had been registered as a Polish citizen, Hungarian law classified the whole family as Poles and "aliens." Her mother and her sister Mina, three years her senior, were arrested. After their release, the three women fled to prevent re-arrest.

Because Klein felt responsible for her family, she decided to pass as a non-Jew to earn some money. She trained as a dental technician but never felt safe enough to stay in one laboratory and earn a secure spot. To support herself and her mother, she lived as a fugitive, moving from job to job and from place to place, ending up in Budapest. Learning a trade on the run, hiding her identity, feeling enormous isolation, and coping with increasing hunger, Klein reached womanhood and confided her feelings to her poetry and her diary. However often she "fell victim to the evil side" of human nature, she held fiercely to her belief that loyalty to her family was more important than her own safety.

During this period, she became engaged to Joe, the son of family friends. When the Nazis occupied Hungary in March 1944, she left Joe and his family in Budapest, where they had been promised a secure hiding place, to return to her mother and sister, now in Chust (Huszt). A month later, the Nazis forced the ten thousand Jewish inhabitants of Chust, including the Kleins, into a ghetto. Cecilie, her mother, and Mina and her small family experienced painful public humiliation, a prelude of what was to come. She recalls the SS and the Hungarian police and neighbors screaming curses and contemptuous epithets at them: "Cursed Jewish pigs, dogs, filthy Jews, old Jewish cow, scum of the earth, bloodsuckers, parasites who spread foul diseases, demons." Worse was to follow. Just before the Kleins were loaded into cattle cars, Cecilie writes, "We were marched off in groups to a brick factory near the station for a degrading body search. First we were ordered to strip naked, men and women together. Then the women and the girls were lined up on one side and were ordered to lie on our sides on a wooden table. While an SS officer gawked and jeered, a woman with a stick poked around our private parts. My burning cheeks betrayed my sense of shame and humiliation. I sobbed for my mother, subjected to this bestial invasion."[14] Even more humiliating and shocking to Cecilie was the behavior of citizens who had volunteered to witness the degradation of their Jewish neighbors. She vowed to survive, if only to confront them about their betrayal.

After a three-day ride in a cattle car, she and the other women arrived at Auschwitz, where they were required to stand naked on stools: "Five male prisoners appear alongside the stools, scissors in hand. . . . In seconds, the men cut off [the women's] hair, shave their heads, then their intimate parts. The cut hair around the stools was collected by three male prisoners."[15]

Of the Klein family, only Cecilie and Mina survived the initial selection process, and they intensified their familial relationship by becoming each other's "camp sister." Camp sisters accepted responsibility for each other's survival, by sharing food, risking punishments, encouraging each other, and providing physical care, even to the extent of keeping each other from going to the infirmary. After Mina learned that her infant son and her mother had been sent to the gas chamber, she was so despondent that she wanted to throw herself on the electrified barbed wire fences. But Cecilie's threats to kill herself with Mina stopped her: "She held herself back, out of love for my life, not hers. In this place of evil we became known as the Two Good Sisters."[16]

Cecilie lived for the purpose of keeping them both alive: "When Mina would tell me, 'Let's end our lives today,' I would persuade her to wait another day, pointing out that the day is almost over and our bread is about to be distributed. Another time I begged her to wait until it gets cold. 'Why end our lives on a sunny day.' . . . I discovered ways to force her to eat, and taught her to redden her cheeks by vigorously pinching them before each SS selection."[17] She alerted herself to be aware of any changes that indicated Mina's physical or mental weakening. Besides trading an "occasional slice of salami for a pat of soft margarine," which she forced down Mina's throat, she traded two pieces of bread for a better-fitting dress for Mina, one that made her "body look less emaciated, thereby improving her chances of passing the next selection."[18] Six months later, however, it was Cecilie who lost the will to survive. Then Mina reversed her role, pulling herself from her despair to care for her sister and thus gaining a reason to live. (Mina and Cecilie both survived the war, found their husband and fiancé, respectively, and forged new lives.)

Despicable camp conditions and sadistic camp staff do not dominate Klein's narrative. Indeed, they are mentioned only when they impinge on her ability to nurture her sister. The dominant issues are hunger, as in every Holocaust memoir, and caring for someone else—her sister—in order to give purpose to her own life in an otherwise meaningless setting. Their relationship helped both sisters maintain some human dignity.

The third memoir, *Seed of Sarah,* begins with the author's first encounter with antisemitism. Judith Isaacson was the only child of a secular, cultured family in Kaposvar, in Hungary's Lake Balaton region. At her gymnasium's anniversary celebration of the 1848 Hungarian Revolution, on March 15, 1938, just two days after the *Anschluss* (Germany's annexation of Austria), Judith's poetry recitation was interrupted by shouts of "Shut up, Jewess!" "Dirty Jew!" and "Away with the Kike!"[19]

Next came a series of laws that barred Jews from various jobs, set a maximum wage for all Jews, required them to wear the Star of David, confiscated their property, and confined them to a ghetto before finally deporting them. Yet, despite the hardships, Judith Isaacson's enthusiasm for life permeates her book. She describes mouthwatering food at family gatherings, her loving grandparents who owned a bakery and had fresh-baked rolls delivered to the house every morning, her doting uncles, her schoolmates with their teenage antics and romantic crushes, and her own ambitious plans to study comparative literature at the Sorbonne.

With the imposition of the First Jewish Law denying Jews equal citizenship, her father prepared for the worst, making plans for the family's emigration to Milwaukee, where his brother was on the faculty of Marquette University. He was, however, called to military service in September 1939. With no time to complete the arrangements, he left home in his fancy dress uniform, complete with insignia and sword, but with the Jews' canary yellow armband on his left sleeve. The family never saw him again. Hungarian soldiers interrupted the High Holiday services in 1940 to take Judith's uncles for work in a labor camp.

To Isaacson, the war meant two physical threats: fear of rape and the shortage of food. As a beautiful, vivacious teenager, she was troubled by persistent rumors of Jewish girls being sent to the front as prostitutes and then shot into open ditches. Food shortages troubled everyone who could not operate on the black market, but Judith's grandparents' lush garden alleviated some of the deprivation. On March 19, 1944, however, Hungarian Jews faced what for them had been unthinkable—orders for deportation.

Challenging Nazi edicts, Isaacson hid some family valuables, her school documents, and treasured photographs in the root cellar and gave her bicycle and typewriter to non-Jewish friends for safekeeping. But her indomitable spirit was shaken on July 2, 1944, during the first stage of deportation in her city, when she was forced to endure a humiliating body search ("Did they really think I would hide gold in my vagina?").[20] The next day, her nineteenth birthday, was spent in the municipal stables with the other six thousand Jews remaining in Kaposvar, all waiting to be loaded onto the cattle cars. Three and a half days in a cattle car packed with seventy-five people, with one bucket for drinking water and another for human waste, spawned nightmares of mass burials and rape. The transport arrived at Auschwitz amid the horror of a night sky emblazoned by flames and polluted by the stench of burning flesh.

Judith, along with her mother and Aunt Magda, passed the selection and entered Birkenau, where they were processed inhumanly through showers and shaves. Judith was one of five hundred women sent to the doorless, windowless, bunkless barrack known as Mexico because of its impossibly poor conditions. It was so crowded that the women could not even lie down on the dirt floor. They were given rags to wear, and large red crosses were painted across their backs to mark them as prisoners in an annihilation camp. "The women began to repair their dresses the first day. They borrowed a few pins they found in the dresses one from the other. They tore a piece of the long dresses and put it on the head to be nicer."[21] After a week of rejecting the putrid soup and rancid bread, hunger and thirst forced them to eat and drink what was provided. Trying to hold on to a thread of optimism, Judith recited poetry and hummed classical music in a feeble attempt to sustain her identity.

Isaacson was lucky because she was in Auschwitz for only three weeks. In July there was a large selection to decide the fate of the women in Judith's barrack—along with that of ten thousand to fourteen thousand other women. The women, including Judith, her mother, and her aunt Magda, were ordered to line up, nude, for a "medical" selection. The women were sent off "into three distinct herds. . . . The majority straight ahead, toward the freight train. The sick and worn hobbled left, toward a waiting truck. A select group of young girls steered right and marched off nude, in rows of five. . . . [I remembered] my uncle Imre's warnings: 'Risk your life to avoid a girls' transport.' I shuddered with a sudden insight into our options: Straight ahead—slave labor. To the left—death. To the right—mass rape at the Russian front."[22] Her mother was sent straight ahead, while Judith and her aunt were directed to the right, to the group with young girls. To this day, Isaacson is not sure whether it was the terror of rape that emboldened her, or the hope of staying with her mother, but she and Magda ran into the crowd with her mother, despite the pistols pointed at them. To the amazement of the Kapos and the other prisoners, they were not shot, and they remained together.

From Auschwitz, they were shipped to Hessisch Lichtenau, a small German town that housed a munitions factory that used Jews as slave labor. There, Isaacson was called a horse and was forced to drag wagons of shells from one place to another.[23] Lichtenau was a village of homes with trees outside and lace curtains inside. Although Isaacson had spent only three weeks at Auschwitz, she had forgotten "this other Europe, this other twentieth century."

In the munitions factory, she and her peers flirted with male workers and even planned escapes together, to no avail. Hyena, the "homeliest overseer," caught Isaacson off guard one day and accused her of daydreaming about men: "I can read your face. But dreaming is all that's left for you, bitch. After the war, you'll be transported to a desert island. No males—not even natives. Much use'll be your fancy looks, with snakes for company. Do you suppose the Americans will win the war? That would be your death sentence. We'll shoot you Jewish bitches before the Americans come—it's the Fuehrer's decree. Your fate is sealed either way: No men. No sex. No seed of Sarah."[24]

Judith, always preoccupied with food, formed partnerships with other prisoners and organized potato-stealing ventures until the potato barrels were taken indoors. To steal more efficiently, she "ripped a band from the hem of her striped dress, and sewed on a large pocket."[25] Starvation also led the women to raid the garbage and eat rotted vegetables. The risky food forays, however, had their humorous aspects; for example, her mother, while stealing cabbages, suddenly spied the Kommandant. She quickly stuffed the cabbages into her blouse, proudly parading her newly jutting breasts. Toward winter, as they were fed thicker soup and occasional pieces of meat, some of the women resumed menstruating, and their fantasies turned to thoughts of men. Sharing such dreams linked them to each other and to the future.

The women celebrated Chanukah with singing and extended exchanges of "fabulous recipes" from memory.[26] Isaacson also recalled a "lengthy discussion about *retes,* the incredible flaky Hungarian strudel. Marcsa liked it filled with peppered fried cabbage, but the rest of us preferred it sweet, with apples, sour cherries, or creamed cottage cheese." The women shared "dozens of ultra-rich recipes: mousses, *palacsintas, tortas*—everything topped with whipped cream or chocolate."[27] In the last weeks they were so hungry that "our whole amusement shortened to tell each other what kind of soups and meats and vegetables and cakes our mothers used to make. Nobody of us knows exactly how to make, but we found out and explained very seriously. I learned to cook at nights in the factory."[28] Finally, on April 20, 1945, she, her mother, and Magda reached Leipzig and liberation.

Sharing recipes and cooking techniques was not a trivial matter. It had a powerful psychological effect because it reflected a commitment to the future. That the recipes were usually related to the Sabbath and holidays assumed a future with a Jewish flavor. Moreover, the discussions about cooking recalled the women's former lives when they had status in their families and communities, and although those recollections brought their misery into sharp focus, they also brought the women some hope. Thus kitchen memories not only established a continuum between the past and the future, they also reminded the women of their strengths as nurturers, homemakers, and inventive cooks. Sharing memories reaffirmed their community, and sharing recipes in the context of planned starvation therefore had an ironic therapeutic effect, if only for the length of their discussions.

The three memoirs I have examined are linked by the reoccurrence of several themes: a preoccupation with hunger and obtaining food, the importance of social bonding, heightened fear of physical vulnerability and sex-specific humiliation, and reliance on prewar homemaking skills as coping strategies. Although men shared the preoccupation with hunger and food, the women's memoirs are unique in their emphasis on the other issues. For example, the three women I have discussed are explicit in describing the physical vulnerability that women felt—as mothers and as objects of potential sexual assault. "According to SS guidelines, every Jewish child automatically condemned his mother to death," both in the selections and in the routine workdays.[29] Any woman in the selection line holding a child, her own or someone else's, was sent to the gas chambers, but women who were in their early months of pregnancy and looked fit for slave labor escaped immediate death, and some managed to deliver in the camp. That is why many women physicians tried to save their poison for children born in the camp—to prevent both mother and child from being sent automatically to the gas chambers.[30]

All three women also discuss their shame and sexual humiliation; standing naked and being shaved and searched affected all three deeply. Klein suffered for her mother as well as herself. Isaacson was mortified. Nomberg-Przytyk cried, despite her contempt for the SS who were responsible for her humiliation. Similarly, the fear of rape caused great anxiety among the women. (Not surprisingly, it is rarely mentioned by men.) Although rape by the SS in the death camps was rare,[31] the women were terrorized by rumors or threats of rape—as is evident in both Isaacson's and Klein's memoirs. When Nazi soldiers occupied her family's apartment, Isaacson worried whether she would be able to "convince a German soldier not to rape" her, and when she prepared a rucksack for the transport to the resettlement area, unaware of her true destination, she told her mother that she feared rape more than death and wanted to take poison with her. A few days later, her uncle told her that he had witnessed a mass raping of Jewish girls who were buried alive in mass graves that they had dug.[32] Klein vividly portrays the tragedy of one of the girls in her barracks. While they waited for their clothes to be disinfected, all the women were nude and subjected to the soldiers' "lewd and cruel threats," but one young girl was singled out and taken to the officers' barracks to be returned two days later, "scarcely recognizable, incoherent, face and body swollen and bruised."[33]

The three memoirs I have discussed also illustrate the importance of connectedness, nurturance, and caregiving in women's memoirs. Social bonding, the formation of groups of two or more, encouraged the women to struggle to survive. These groups functioned as surrogate families that took on the responsibility of gathering food, "organizing" necessities, building hope, and sustaining life in any way possible.[34] In both Cecilie Klein's and Judith Isaacson's narratives, natural family bonds are intensified as sisters pledge to care for each other, whereas Sara Nomberg-Przytyk forms a surrogate family with her prewar political friends. When she finds herself alone again in the next camp, she adopts a camp sister to improve both their chances for survival.

Although political and family affiliations were the stimuli for these supportive relationships, virtually all women, as revealed in scores of memoirs, formed surrogate families because, as one German-Jewish survivor of Auschwitz explained, it was "the best way to survive. You needed others who helped you with food or clothing or just advice or sympathy to surmount all the hardship you encountered during all those many months and years of incarceration."[35] Lucie Adelsberger, for example, was adopted as a "camp mother" by two teenage girls who tried to provide her with clothes and food whenever they could. As she noted, "There were many families like this and everyone . . . felt responsible for one another, often putting their own lives in jeopardy by denying themselves the very morsel of bread they needed for their own survival." Even for those who did not survive, the "friendship and love of a camp family eased the horror of their miserable end."[36]

Such bonding was not exclusive to women, but it is difficult to find consistent evidence of men's caring about one another to the extent that women did. Elie Cohen found that comradeship was "occasional," if not rare, among men, and was conspicuous by its absence. Although he points out that nothing could ever guarantee survival in a death camp, "lone wolf" behavior could almost guarantee death.[37]

Women memoirists even used bonding imagery to narrate and to understand their experiences. For example, Giuliana Tedeschi's attitude toward survival is reflected in her metaphor: "Prison life [in Auschwitz-Birkenau] is like a piece of knitting whose stitches are strong as long as they remain woven together; but if the woolen strand breaks, the invisible stitch that comes undone slips off among the others and is lost."[38] The women often describe extraordinary caring of one woman for another, and they even recount the "feminization" of male prisoners, "men who had to learn to trust and share in the manner of women."[39] Men, many survivors assert, "had to learn behaviors that women already knew."[40]

Notes

1. David Patterson, *The Shriek of Silence: A Phenomenology of the Holocaust Novel* (Ithaca: Cornell University Press, 1992), 6.

2. Myrna Goldenberg, "Different Horrors, Same Hell," in *Thinking the Unthinkable: Human Meanings of the Holocaust,* ed. Roger Gottlieb (New York: Paulist Press, 1990),

150–166; see also Carol Rittner and John Roth, eds., *Different Voices* (New York: Paragon, 1993).

3. Sybil Milton, "Women and the Holocaust," in *When Biology Becomes Destiny*, ed. Renate Bridenthal, Atina Grossman, and Marion Kaplan (New York: Monthly Review Press, 1984), 298; Joan Ringelheim, "Women and the Holocaust: A Reconsideration of the Research," *Signs* 10, no. 4 (1985): 745; Marlene Heinemann, *Gender and Destiny: Women Writers of the Holocaust* (Westport, Conn.: Greenwood Press, 1986), 2–5.

4. Sara Nomberg-Przytyk, *Auschwitz: True Tales from a Grotesque Land* (Chapel Hill: University of North Carolina Press, 1985).

5. Ibid., 20–21.

6. Ibid., 24.

7. Ibid., 29.

8. Ibid., 38.

9. Ibid., 69.

10. Ibid., 98, 135–136, 144.

11. Ibid., 154.

12. Cecilie Klein, *Sentenced to Live* (New York: Holocaust Library, 1988).

13. Ibid., 8–10.

14. Ibid., 73.

15. Ibid., 79.

16. Ibid., 84.

17. Ibid., 81–82.

18. Ibid., 83–84.

19. Judith Magyar Isaacson, *Seed of Sarah: Memoirs of a Survivor* (Chicago: University of Illinois Press, 1990), 10.

20. Ibid., 55.

21. Ibid., 151.

22. Ibid., 85.

23. Ibid., 89.

24. Ibid., 108.

25. Ibid., 111.

26. Ibid., 103.

27. Ibid., 111.

28. Ibid., 152. See also Cara De Silva, ed., *In Memory's Kitchen: A Legacy from the Women of Terezín* (Northvale, N.J.: Jason Aronson, 1996).

29. Lucie Adelsberger, *Auschwitz: A Doctor's Story* (Boston: Northeastern University Press, 1995), 100.

30. Ibid., 101. See also Gisela Perl, *I Was a Doctor in Auschwitz* (1948; reprint Salem, N.H.: Ayer, 1984), 80–86; Olga Lengyel, *Five Chimneys* (New York: Ziff and Davis, 1947), 110–113.

31. Milton, "Women and the Holocaust," 20.

32. Isaacson, *Seed of Sarah*, 42, 47, 53.

33. Klein, *Sentenced to Live,* 85–86.

34. Israel Charny, ed., *Holding onto Humanity—The Message of Holocaust Survivors: The Shamai Davidson Papers* (New York: New York University Press, 1992), 131–136.

35. Lore Shelley, ed., *Auschwitz, the Nazi Civilization: Twenty-Three Women Prisoners' Accounts* (Lanham, Md.: University Press of America, 1992), 36.

36. Adelsberger, *Auschwitz,* 98–100.

37. Elie A. Cohen, *Human Behaviour in the Concentration Camps* (1954; reprint, London: Free Association Books, 1988), 182–183.

38. Giuliana Tedeschi, *There Is a Place on Earth: A Woman in Birkenau* (New York: Random House, 1992), 124.

39. Goldenberg, "Different Horrors, Same Hell," 151; Myrna Goldenberg, "Lessons Learned from Gentle Heroism: Women's Holocaust Narratives," *Annals of the American Academy of Political and Social Science* 548 (November 1996): 87.

40. Claudia Koonz, *Mothers in the Fatherland* (New York: St. Martin's Press, 1987), 381.

CHAPTER NINETEEN

The Split between Gender and the Holocaust

Joan Ringelheim

The strands are all there: to the memory nothing is ever lost.
Eudora Welty, One Writer's Beginnings

Human memory is a marvelous but fallacious instrument . . .
not only do [memories] tend to become erased as the years
go by, but often they change, or even grow, by incorporating
extraneous features.
Primo Levi, The Drowned and the Saved

At a conference on the Holocaust in 1979, I found myself in an informal discussion with Yael Danieli, Eva Fleischner, Henry Friedlander, Raul Hilberg, and Sybil Milton.[1] Danieli, a therapist who works with children of survivors, raised the question of why these children tend to fear that their mothers had been raped. She thought that this fear was widespread and that it might represent some reality.

Without apparent hesitation, those of my colleagues who responded claimed that the children were describing not actual incidents of abuse but rather fantasies induced by the media's sexualization of the Holocaust. No one quoted any research; no one referred to any documentation or studies of interviews of survivors, male or female. There was just an immediate and resounding denigration of the question, and the discussion ended. No other related issues were raised, and no other questions posed. No one discussed the relationships between women and children in the Holocaust. No one spoke about the possible connection between gender and survival. No one talked about German women as perpetrators or collaborators. No one discussed the structure of the women's camps, women as political prisoners, women in resistance, or the relationships between men and women, women and women, men and men. No concepts were readily available to shape such conversations; there was no historical road map. Feminist theory would have helped, but no one at that time was prepared to apply it to the Holocaust.

Also in 1979, I conducted the first interview for my research on women and the Holocaust (actually, my first interview ever), with a woman named Susan. She talked about the uses of sex in Theresienstadt, where "you survived as a woman through the [Jewish] male." She spoke of having rejected the advances of an SS man in Auschwitz-Birkenau and of having "dated" a Polish man from the men's camp.

In the summer of 1982, I was visiting Susan at home when she suddenly said, "I was raped in Auschwitz." She added that the incident was her fault and that she wasn't gang-raped. I began to counsel her. I tried to convince her that it wasn't her fault. I then said something like, "When you are ready to speak about this, perhaps in six months, I would like to hear about it." Not surprisingly, Susan didn't say anything more about the rape.

After talking with a friend who is a sociologist, I realized that not only did I not ask for the details of what had happened but I also made it impossible for Susan to continue. Yet, upon coming to this realization, I didn't run to the phone to ask her what had happened. Instead, I referred to this scenario repeatedly as a lesson about what not to do in an interview. Finally, a few years later, I decided to ask Susan to tell me her story.

Susan was twenty-one years old when she was deported to Auschwitz in 1943. She quickly became one of the "privileged prisoners." A Polish male prisoner, tall and blond, approached her one day and offered her some food—sardines, she recalled. She wanted attention, even affection—and of course, she was hungry. But she said that she was not looking for sex and never suspected his motives. He told her where and when to meet him; she went, and "he grabbed and raped me." She did eat the sardines, but she added that she was never caught in such a situation again. Her story, whatever else it means, is an indication that some Jewish women were sexually victimized even within concentration and extermination camps.

I believe that we avoid listening to stories we do not want to hear. Sometimes we avoid listening because we are afraid; sometimes we avoid listening because we don't understand the importance of what is being said. Without a place for a particular memory, without a conceptual framework, a possibly significant piece of information will not be pursued.

A few years after this meeting with Susan, I interviewed a Jewish survivor (let's call her Pauline) who told me that she had been molested by male relatives of the people who were hiding her. They threatened to denounce her if she said anything about it. Pauline, who was eleven or twelve years old when she was first hidden, took the threats seriously. She didn't tell the young Jewish woman who checked on her periodically. She didn't tell her twin sister. After the war, she didn't tell her husband or her daughter.

"This is the first time I ever admitted this," she remarked in 1984:

> [I was] . . . physically developed for my age. . . . Constantly afraid of men. . . . Men would try to touch me. I was even afraid of the family— the sons (as well as the cousins, uncles, brothers-in-law, and other male relatives of the family), because I was constantly [fondled] . . . [except] when the father was there. . . . I was afraid of strange older men . . . they would rub themselves [against me]. . . . It was more than just [touching]. . . . This happened even on trains. We used to travel. We were very packed in. And men would . . . you know, I can still smell it. It was a tremendous fear . . . but somehow it didn't affect my [sex life later]. . . .
>
> Boys were romantically pleasant. But you know older men. I didn't imagine it. . . . They were rubbing me and pushing themselves [on me]. . . . I was scared. They were drunk, you know, the Poles. . . . They would expose themselves in front of me. . . . I remember I was always . . . afraid that I am going to be raped. . . . [The] first time I was scared to say no. Felt guilty. It was [a] very complicated situation. I tried to stay out of situations when I saw that I [was] alone with any of those sons. I would rather not . . . come in. . . . I would try to look if the parents [were] there; if any of my girlfriends were . . . there. All

kinds of situations when I went to [my] girlfriend's house and [her] father would be alone and he would try something. [I] didn't run away, didn't scream. Didn't put attention to myself, . . . I was scared. Very scared.

I can still feel the fear. . . . Sometimes I think it was equally as frightening as the Germans. It became within me a tremendous . . . I [didn't] know how [to deal with it] . . . what to do with it. I had nobody to talk [to] about it. Nobody to turn to. . . .

You see, [with] a boyfriend I was in control or I felt that I [was]. But here I was a hopeless victim . . . and it's different when you are liked; sex is different when you like someone. But when you are put upon, you hate it, it's awful.

[But] I have nobody to complain to. Everything has to be wonderful, because that's what they want to hear. . . . I am happy, everything is fine, I'm alive. They took me from hell. Have to be grateful. I felt guilty always. Somehow I was [guilty]; really thought that maybe, something about me . . . even a child feels it's his fault if an adult does something. [Their touching me and rubbing themselves against me] went on for a year.

After telling me of this situation, she asked a question:

In respect of what happened, [what we] suffered and saw—the humiliation in the ghetto, seeing our relatives dying and taken away [as well as] my friends, . . . then seeing the ghetto . . . burn and seeing people jumping out and burned—is this [molestation] important? It is only important to me at the moment. It is past, gone. . . . What I want to say is that it is not the most important part of my life. When the war was over . . . this fear disappeared.

Although Pauline minimized the significance of the specifically female aspects of her Holocaust experience, the pain and shame in her words and tone of voice were unmistakable.

Pauline had decided to talk with me when she found out that I was doing research on women and the Holocaust. She knew that her story would interest me; she also knew that her situation explained the special complications that hiding could hold for girls or women during the Holocaust. But she also wondered whether her molestation was important. Was this part of her story also a part of the Holocaust story? Although Pauline recognized her experiences as different from men's, she did not know how or where to locate them in the history of the Holocaust. Her memory was split between traditional versions of Holocaust history and her own experience.

This split is not surprising, as most researchers—whether writing about hiding, escaping, passing, the ghettos, the camps, or the resistance—have minimized or ignored issues of sexual vulnerability and assaults against women, let alone more complex issues having to do with gender and the Holocaust. Consequently, the split between genocide and gender-specific trauma exists not only in the memories of witnesses but also in the historical reconstruction by scholars. A line divides what is considered peculiar or specific to women from what has been designated as the proper collective memory of, or narrative about, the Holocaust. The connection between genocide and gender has been difficult to conceive for some; for others, it has been difficult to construct. Pauline, for example, found this connection difficult to integrate into her Holocaust story.

The "final solution" to the Jewish question called for the death of every woman, man, and child defined as a Jew. Neither geography, nationality, class, professional or economic status, nor gender would permit escape for very long. The logical conclusion is that every Jew was equally a victim of the Holocaust. It is not surprising, then, that most perspectives on the Holocaust have been gender-neutral or seemed to erase gender as a category of analysis. And it is no wonder that any emphasis on gender can seem irrelevant or even irreverent.

Then again, there was something unusual in the intention to kill every woman and child along with every male from a targeted community. The Nazis' "final solution" was one of the first such events in history that did not treat the female population primarily as spoils of war but instead explicitly sentenced women and children to death. Consequently, without some focus on gender, it is impossible to understand the victimization of women in its many forms, including the killing operations.

Such erasure of gender may make it impossible even to see women as victims. Legitimation for targeting Jewish men was plentiful in Nazi antisemitic and racist propaganda and, more to the point, in Nazi policy. The decision to kill every Jew did not seem to require special justification to kill Jewish men. They were already identified as dangerous. This was not so for Jewish women and children. Heinrich Himmler's words speak to this need for justification

and legitimation: "We came to the question: what about the women and children? I have decided to find a clear solution here too. In fact I did not regard
myself as justified in exterminating the men—let us say killing them or having
them killed—while letting avengers in the shape of children . . . grow up. The
difficult decision had to be taken to make this people disappear from the face
of the earth."[2] Jewish women, then, were connected to the "race struggle" of
National Socialism because they carried the next generation of Jews.

If we consider the circumstances of Jewish women and children during
the Holocaust, it seems impossible not to give gender serious attention. To return to Pauline for a moment: because most non-Jewish men in Europe during
this period were not circumcised, Jewish women and young girls could hide
more easily than Jewish men or boys. This may mean that more female Jews
were saved in hiding—another not insignificant consequence of biology. At the
same time, we cannot ignore the particular vulnerability and victimization of
these women and girls in these situations. Pauline's story may not be typical.
But if Anne Frank's diary remains the paradigm of hiding, we will never know,
because it will be assumed that danger lurked only when Germans located
those in hiding.

Some might argue that rape, abortion, sexual exploitation, and pregnancy
are always potentially part of a woman's life and that the ubiquity of these experiences means that they can have no relationship to an event that has been
described as unique. Others feel that discussions of sexuality desecrate the
memory of the dead or the living or the Holocaust itself. While these positions
are understandable, the fact remains that the victimization of Jewish men during the Holocaust did not usually include their sexual exploitation.

It has been difficult to confront the fact that Jewish women were victims
as Jewish women, not only because some Jewish men exploited Jewish women,
but also because Jewish men could not protect women and children from the
Nazis. In other words, it has been too difficult to contemplate the extent to
which gender counted in the exploitation and murder of Jewish women, and
the extent to which the sexism of Nazi ideology and the sexism of the Jewish
community met in a tragic and involuntary alliance. Men could and did op-
press women sexually, and women were aware of that possibility. "Male memory can confront women as victims, but cannot confront male oppression,"
Irene Eber, a scholar and survivor, told me in a conversation in 1987. She continued: "The same may be true for women survivors. They can see themselves

as Nazi victims, but not as victims of Jewish men or even Nazi men, except perhaps as non-female victims."

To ignore the plight of Jewish women is to ignore more than half of the Jewish population who were deported or murdered. Because of this omission, it is difficult either to ask about or to deal with such side effects of Nazi persecution as the sexual abuse described by Pauline.

In the 1990s similar questions were raised, and to some extent answered, with respect to the war fought in the former Yugoslavia. It is clear that women in Bosnia have been specifically targeted as women and that rape has been part of the genocidal strategy of "ethnic cleansing." When we think about this war, we visualize male and female victims differently because of the way gender functioned in this context. At the moment the image is indelible. And yet, this is an image that we cannot seem to form about the Holocaust. Although sex does not fully define or describe a woman's struggle, it is the most obvious place to begin if one wants to investigate women's experiences. If the obvious is avoided, it is easy to turn away from the more obscure or more complicated issues of women's experiences during this period—such as the different roles and functions of Jewish women and men in the ghettos with respect to work, housing, and food; the differences in the male and female death rates in the ghettos; the differences in the structure of the women's and men's camp in Auschwitz-Birkenau; and the different roles and functions of German women and men in the mobile killing operations.

One would think that the importance of the study of gender during the Holocaust would be widely accepted today. Unfortunately, however, that is not true. Let me mention a few examples.[3] In December 1993 the Research Institute of the United States Holocaust Memorial Museum held its opening conference, a four-day event with eighteen panels and eighty participants, sixteen of them women. The panels had such titles as "Antisemitism and Racism as Factors in Nazi Ideology," "The Politics of Racial Health and Science," "Multiple Voices: Ideology, Exclusion, and Coercion," and "The Place of Survivors." Lectures addressed the persecution of the disabled, homosexual men, and blacks; the "ordinary men" who became murderers; and the rescuers, the churches, the bystanders. But not one lecture concerned women or gender. When this omission was questioned, the answer sheepishly offered was, "We forgot." This answer was given even though panels on the issue of gender were proposed to the planning committee.

Furthermore, the Permanent Exhibition of the United States Holocaust Memorial Museum contains no conceptualization of women during the Holocaust. In brief segments of the exhibition, one can ponder the roles of Freemasons, Roma and Sinti (Gypsies), homosexuals, Jehovah's Witnesses, and political prisoners, but not women. In an otherwise problematic piece on the museum in *Ms.*, Andrea Dworkin wrote: "In the museum, the story of women is missing. Women are conceptually invisible: in the design of the permanent exhibition, by which I mean its purpose, its fundamental meaning; in its conception of the Jewish people. Antisemites do not ignore the specific meaning or presence of women, nor how to stigmatize or physically hurt women as such, nor do those who commit genocide forget that to destroy a people, one must destroy the women. So how can this museum, dedicated to memory, forget to say what happened to Jewish women?"[4]

Does this mean that we do not see women in the exhibition? Absolutely not. Women are everywhere: in photos of German civilians; in a segment on propaganda showing the film director Leni Riefenstahl; in the representation of books burned; in the segments on refugees, exiles, Anne Frank. Documentary footage and photos show women in the ghettos, as victims of massacres, and as rescuers and resistors. In addition, women are certainly represented in the film of eyewitness testimonies shown at the end of the exhibition, and in the "Voices from Auschwitz" audio theater on the third floor. Women also played an important role on the Permanent Exhibition team, of which I was a member.

When the preceding argument (that women were everywhere in the museum) was presented to me by my colleagues at the museum, I answered with the following:

> There are groups in the United States Holocaust Memorial Museum's Permanent Exhibition whose victimization cannot compare even numerically with the particular victimization of women, yet there is no sentence to this effect anywhere in the P.E. [Permanent Exhibition]. It is not a question of using gender as the defining characteristic of the P.E., but rather indicating somewhere, where appropriate (e.g., Arrival at Auschwitz), that women were victimized in particular ways. The P.E. says that children and the elderly were gassed upon arrival. That is hardly accurate—women and children made up

a significant population in these first selections, often 60–70% of those gassed. Such a sentence would not have been difficult to add, nor would it have changed the P.E. very much. But it would have been important. Gender may not define the Holocaust, but it is not trivial either. Certainly it is not less significant than Roma and Sinti [Gypsies], homosexuals, political prisoners, etc.—and of course all of these groups include women. I had argued against a "women's room" which had been proposed for the P.E., because the lives and deaths and sufferings of women are too integrated into the entire picture to segregate their experiences. We integrate photos, footage, voices, testimony; however, we don't integrate a conception [about women].

One can say there is an implicit conception in the museum that women, whether Jewish or non-Jewish victims, whether perpetrators, bystanders, rescuers, or collaborators, do not constitute a group like Jews, Russian male POWs, Gypsies, Jehovah's Witnesses, homosexual men, and so on. Because Jewish women, when victimized, were targeted as a subgroup of the larger group of Jews, they were not considered a class of victims by the museum. Yet women turned out to be dangerous to the Nazis specifically in their difference from men: in their ability to carry the race. The question remains: Is gender a category like Jews, Gypsies, and so on, or a subcategory like the Jewish Councils?

Whatever the answer, some conceptualization of gender is needed. I think that most members of the Permanent Exhibition team believed (and still do) that since Jewish women were persecuted and killed because they were Jewish, there is no need to say anything specific about their persecution and murder. The view of the museum bears some resemblance to the views expressed by Cynthia Ozick in a letter written to me in 1982. She responded to a query about a conference on women and the Holocaust as follows:

> I think you are asking the wrong question. Not simply the wrong question in the sense of not having found the right one; I think you are asking a morally wrong question, a question that leads us still further down the road of eradicating Jews from history. You are—I hope inadvertently—joining up with the likes of [the Revisionists] who [say] that if it happened to Jews it never happened. You insist that it

didn't happen to "just Jews." It happened to women, and it is only a detail that the women were Jewish. It is not a detail. It is everything, the whole story. . . . The Holocaust happened to victims who were not seen as men, women, or children, but *as Jews.*

At the end of her article, Dworkin writes, "Because the museum did not pay attention to women as a distinct constituency with distinct experience, what women cannot bear to remember will die with them; what happened will die with them."[5] Dworkin gives the museum both too much power and too little credit. The Permanent Exhibition is not the entire museum. Women's experiences are being represented in its Oral History Department and Archives, in more than 190 oral history projects on the Holocaust around the world, and in many published and unpublished memoirs, and so on. Yet Dworkin's warning should be heeded.

I think that these contemporary examples point to the general reluctance to explore the questions about gender, including sexual exploitation amid the other horrors of the Holocaust—whether because it is thought to be trivial in comparison with genocide per se or because it is thought to be banal, or because it is too close to what we know in everyday life.

The Holocaust is defined by death. In this domain of death, it is crude if not obscene to avoid talking about gender. The death rates in certain ghettos have been broken down by sex, as have some ghetto deportation lists and some Einsatzgruppen reports identifying the sex of those murdered. And yet, in the mid-1890s, when I began to research death and survival rates, no historical or sociological analyses of the documents had been conducted from the point of view of gender.

Talk about sex or sexual exploitation may be too intimate for some; talk about genocide of Jewish women and children, too frightening. If we look at the experiences specific to women, however, we must include the sexual, and we must eventually come to the death and killing rates.

To the Nazis, Jewish women were not simply Jews; they were Jewish women, and they were treated accordingly in the system of annihilation. Research suggests that more Jewish women were deported than Jewish men, and more women than men were selected for death in the extermination camps.[6] Jewish men did not stand in line for Jewish women when it came to the killing operations; Jewish women stood in their own lines and were killed as Jewish women. Nor can Jewish men stand in for Jewish women as we try to understand their everyday life during the Holocaust, with its terror, loss, escape, hope, humor, friendships, love, work, starvation, beatings, rape, abortions, and killings. Jewish women and men experienced unrelieved suffering during the Holocaust, but Jewish women carried the burdens of sexual victimization, pregnancy, abortion, childbirth, killing of newborn babies in the camps to save the mothers, care of children, and many decisions about separation from children. For Jewish women the Holocaust produced a set of experiences, responses, and memories that do not always parallel those of Jewish men. As Pauline said: "Everything else is the same. But there are certain things that are different." If in the gas chambers or before the firing squads all Jews seemed alike to the Nazis, the path to this end was not always the same for women and men. The end—namely, annihilation or death—does not describe or explain the process.

Notes

1. The views expressed in this paper are solely my own and do not necessarily reflect the views of the United States Holocaust Memorial Museum.
2. Bradley F. Smith and Agnes F. Peterson (eds.), *Heinrich Himmler: Geheimreden 1933 bis 1945* (Frankfurt: Propylaen, 1974).
3. One example is the chapter by Lawrence Langer in this book, which asserts that there is nothing to be gained from using gender as a category for analysis in the study of the Holocaust. Langer implicitly argues against a feminist position and feminist proponents that he never identifies. Langer assumes that a feminist perspective would only conclude that women survived better than men or that women's support groups were stronger than men's, etc. Consequently, he reduces a study about gender to a form of competition. This is simply wrong. He ignores the complexity and diversity of feminist scholarship on the Holocaust as well as the actuality of women's and men's lives during the Holocaust.
4. Andrea Dworkin, "The Unremembered: Searching for Women at the Holocaust Memorial Museum," *Ms. Magazine* (November–December 1994), p. 54.
5. Ibid., p. 58.
6. See Joan Ringelheim, "Women and the Holocaust: A Reconsideration of Research," in *Different Voices: Women and the Holocaust,* ed. Carol Rittner and John K. Roth (New York: Paragon House, 1993); Mary Lowenthal Felstiner, *To Paint Her Life: Charlotte Solomon in the Nazi Era* (New York: HarperCollins, 1994); and Raul Hilberg, "Men and Women," in *Perpetrators Victims Bystanders* (New York: Aaron Asher Books/HarperCollins, 1992).

CHAPTER TWENTY

Gendered Suffering?
Women in Holocaust Testimonies

Lawrence L. Langer

I f the world of the German labor camps, concentration camps, and death camps has taught us anything, it is that abnormal living conditions prompt unpredictable responses. Listening to the voices of women who survived those domains reminds us of the severely diminished role that gendered behavior played during those cruel years. Even when we hear stories about mutual support among women in the camps, the full context of these narratives shows us how seldom such alliances made any difference in the long-range effects of the ordeal for those who outlived it. Because it can never be segregated from the murder of the many, the survival of the few cannot be used as a measure of why some women survived and others did not.

Let me begin with the written monologue of Mado from Charlotte Delbo's trilogy *Auschwitz and After,* which appeared in full English translation only in 1995. Delbo, a non-Jew, was arrested for underground activity and sent to Auschwitz in January 1943, together with 230 other French women. Only 49 returned. Delbo visited many of them after the war, and in one of her volumes she explored the damaging effects that their interlude in the camp had on their subsequent lives. Mado, one of these survivors, reveals a neglected consequence of the camp experience, which I call the "missed destiny of dying." In our haste to celebrate renewal, we are inclined to ignore the scar that intimate contact with the death of her women friends and supporters has left on the memory and feeling of the witness.

Mado begins: "It seems to me I'm not alive. Since all are dead, it seems impossible I shouldn't be also. All dead. Mounette, Viva, Sylviane, Rosie, all the others, all the others. How could those stronger and more determined than I be dead, and I remain alive? Can one come out of there alive? No. It wasn't possible."[1] Delbo then invites us to unravel the tapestry of paradoxes that Mado weaves around the belief that she is "living without being alive"—a talking corpse. This idea recurs often enough in our encounter with the voices and faces of other women survivors to force us to admit it into our colloquy about the Holocaust. Its fate there, however, will depend on whether we let it fester or pledge to explore the sources and echoes of its taint.

Mado does not exalt her own survival, or the aid from her friends that helped to make it possible; instead, she mourns the death of others: "One morning, when it was still pitch dark, I woke up to the sound of roll call. Next to me, Angèle Mercier did not move. I did not shake her. Did not feel her. Without even looking at her I knew she was dead. She was the first to die next to me." Mado then gives us a lucid and honest appraisal of what it means for her to be among "those who came back": "I do what one does in life, but I know very well that this isn't life, because I know the difference between before and after." She tries to explain what she means by this: "All the efforts we made to prevent our destruction, preserve our identity, keep our former being, all these efforts could only be put to use over there [*là-bas*]. When we returned, this hard kernel we had forged at the core of our hearts, believing it to be solid since it had been won through boundless striving, melted, dissolved. Nothing left. My life started over there. Before there was nothing. I no longer have what I had over there, what I had before, what I was before. Everything has been wrenched from me. What's left? Nothing. Death."[2]

In other words, the immediate threats of Auschwitz led to the creation of a community among Mado and her fellow deportees that may have sustained some of them as memories of their lives prior to the camp faded and vanished. But that community, she says, is gone now, most of its members victims who did not return. Mado refuses to delude herself about the rupture that prevents her past from gliding into a fruitful future: "This superhuman will we summoned from our depths in order to return abandoned us as soon as we came back. Our stock was exhausted. We came back, but why? We wanted this struggle, these deaths not to have been in vain. Isn't it awful to think that Mounette died for nothing, that Viva died for nothing? Did they die so that I, you, a few others might return?"[3] She knows that this question should be answered in the negative, even as she clutches at the opposite possibility in futile hope of minimal consolation.

The experience of staying alive in the camps cannot be separated from the experience of dying in the camps. The clear line that in normal times divides life from death disappeared there, and memory is unable to restore it. Mado is married and has a son, but her family is unable to help her forget. It's not a matter of forgetting, she insists. You don't choose memories; memories choose you. And because of that, she cannot embrace her roles as wife and mother. Love has become a gesture, not a source of fulfillment. She can't tell this to her husband, because then he would realize that "all his caring hasn't alleviated the pain." Mado's concluding words give shape to the idea that one can outlive a deathcamp without having survived it: "People believe memories grow vague, are erased by time, since nothing endures against the passage of time. That's the difference; time does not pass over me, over us. It doesn't erase anything, doesn't undo it. I'm not alive. I died in Auschwitz but no one knows it."[4]

Is Mado's story exceptional? Judging from the testimonies I have seen, I would have to conclude that numerous other women who outlived the atrocity also inhabit two worlds, the world of then and the world of now. One biological feature of their gender, the capacity to bear children, has had a singular impact on their efforts to confront their ordeal, an impact that they could not and cannot share with male inmates. The phenomenon of maternity continues to haunt them with the memory and anticipation of a special suffering that lacks any redeeming balance. When Charlotte Delbo went to visit one of her Auschwitz companions in a lying-in hospital in Paris after the war, her friend complained that her newborn infant brought her no joy; all she could think about was the children in Auschwitz being sent to their death in the gas chambers. Like Mado, this woman has not escaped the taint of memory that has frustrated her bid to reclaim her role as mother.

Because this dilemma seems gender-specific, let us pursue it for a moment. In her testimony, Holocaust survivor Sally H. recalls the march to the train that would carry most of her family to their death in Auschwitz. Her most vivid memory is of a young girl among the deportees who was in an advanced stage of pregnancy:

People did get married in the ghetto. People think that the ghetto was just, you know, closed in—they were getting married, because people had hope things would go on. And there was that, my mother's, a friend's daughter. She was eighteen years old, Rachel Goldfarb. I have to mention names, they're not here. She got married, and she got pregnant, became pregnant. And when we had the, when they took us out of the city we didn't have a train, there were no trains, to walk to the trains . . . I don't know the mileage to Garbatka. And I always remember Rachel, she had a very big stomach, I was eleven and a half, close to twelve. So at the time, you don't think about things like this. She was pregnant, and she was very big. It was very hot, it was the second day of Succoth, it happened to be very hot. And she was wearing a trenchcoat and her father's shoes. Isn't that something? I can't forget it. And my mother, her mother, her father, and some other women were walking around her, made a circle around her, because— I don't know—either she would deliver the baby soon, or they didn't want the SS to see her. I don't know. And she never complained, she never asked for water or anything.

Years and years later when I had my own children, all of a sudden she came to mind. I mean all that time it was just like everything else, but when I became pregnant, all of a sudden Rachel's face was always in front of me. What happened to her. Because when we walked to the trains, there again like I said before, if you would be here that minute and not there, I wouldn't be here now. We were at the train station, and there must have been thousands of people sitting and waiting for the train.[5]

Because Sally H. and her sister, together with about a dozen other young girls, were randomly chosen by the SS to go to a nearby farm to work in the fields, she was not there when the others were deported that night, although she remembers hearing their screams. She and her sister were subsequently shipped to Skarżysko, and they were still alive when the war ended. Her parents did not return but, together with the pregnant Rachel, were gassed in Auschwitz.

Like Mado, Sally H. cannot simply celebrate the birth of her own child because in her imagination she associates it with the doom of Rachel and her unborn infant. She suffers from what I call a tainted memory, and neither the passage of time nor an unwilled amnesia can erase it. There may be a valid text about small communities of women who survived through mutual support or some strength of gender, but it exists within a darker subtext emerging in these testimonies. To valorize the one while disregarding the other is little more than an effort to replace truth with myth.

Yet witnesses are often reluctant to forgo the option of a dignified gendered response. This reluctance can result in a clash between texts and subtexts that frequently remains unnoticed as the auditor engages in what we might call selective listening, in search of proof for a particular point of view. A classic example is the testimony of Joly Z., who lost all her family in Auschwitz except her mother, with whom she remained despite a transfer to Hamburg and then Bergen-Belsen, where they were liberated by the British in April 1945. She insists that the mutual support between mother and daughter enabled both to survive, and she ends with a little homily about the duty of asserting moral responsibility in the camps no matter what the conditions.

Embedded in her testimony, however, is a subtext, what I call a durational moment, that challenges her main text and reminds us how complex is the task of judging gendered behavior when painful circumstances like the following deprive one of the freedom to enact moral responsibility:

> JOLY Z.: There was a pregnant woman among us. She must have been in a very early pregnancy when she got in the camp. Beautiful woman. I remember her eyes always shining. Maybe the very fact that she had a life within herself gave her this extra energy and hope, to want to survive. But the time had come and she had to deliver, and in the washroom they prepared a bed for her, and I was assisting . . .
>
> INTERVIEWER: In Auschwitz?
>
> JOLY Z.: No, this was not in Auschwitz, this was already in Hamburg. And I was assistant to the doctor there, and that was a prisoner doctor. And I prepared the little box with some soft rags for the baby. And in the other room I heard suddenly the cry of the baby. I never saw or remembered before a newborn baby. And I was waiting for the baby with the little box in my hands. And then a tall SS man brought out the baby holding him or her upside down. And put it under the sink,

and opened the water, and he said, "Here you go little Moses, down the stream." And drowned the little baby.

INTERVIEWER: What did you do?

JOLY Z.: For a long time, for a long time, it was very difficult to have hope after that.[6]

Compassion plays a negligible role here. The ritual of childbirth may be defined by the witness's expectations, based on her innocent sense of what should happen, but the outcome is decided by the SS, who sees both mother and child, and the witness too, as victims of a specific doom, not agents of their own fate. When giving birth and killing at the same time became the rule rather than the exception for the cruel directors of this bizarre drama, its "actresses" were victimized by events beyond their control that mocked their efforts to create for themselves a gendered part.

Indeed, in some instances, women were forced to *reject* what they regarded as one of their natural roles, as a result of their ordeals in the camps. Consider the testimony of Arina B. She was married in the Warsaw ghetto in 1941. The following year, she and her husband were deported to Treblinka, but on the journey he managed to tear the wire grate from the window, help her out, and leap after her. Others who tried to get out were shot, but they managed to escape. They lived for a while with local farmers, then returned to Warsaw to stay on the Aryan side, but were finally drawn back within the ghetto's walls by a desire to visit her parents and his brother. Subsequently, she was sent to Majdanek, and then to Auschwitz. Her narrative moment begins:

> The worst—you know, the worst part of my being in concentration camp, my nine months' pregnancy. I was pregnant when I came to camp. In the beginning I didn't know that I'm pregnant, nobody knew. But when I find out . . . it's hard to understand what I went through. Especially the last days, when the child was pushing to go out, and I was afraid I'm gonna make on the—you know how we call the beds, you know the bunk beds, and they're gonna beat me up. And I was so afraid because I got twenty-one [lashes] in Majdanek. And all the time my body was, you know, blue, my whole body was blue. I was afraid of beating because I didn't want to be crippled. I said to myself, if something—let them shoot me, you know, to finish

my life, because it was very hard to live, very hard. Many times I was thinking to go on the wire, you touch it and just finish, but in the back of my head was "Who gonna tell the world what happen?" Always the same thing. . . .

And when I came back one time from the outside, I got terrible pains, and we had midwife in the barracks, and she heard the way, you know, and she said to me, come out on the oven. You know, in the barrack was a great oven going through. I went out to the oven, and the baby was born. And she said, "You have a boy." And she took away the boy, and till today I don't know where is the boy. I beg her, I hear crying, and I beg her to give me the baby. I'm very, I said, "I don't want to live, I want to die with my baby, give me my baby. I don't have any, you know, I said I lost my, you know, strength and everything, I can't fight any more, I want to die." And she look at me, and she sit down, and she beg me to quiet up, and she said: "You're so beautiful. You're gonna find your husband. You're gonna have children, still children." I still remember the words what she told me. I said, "I can't live any more. I want to die. And till now I don't know where's my baby."[7]

How shall we read this narrative? That in the camps, women helped each other to survive? My earlier mention of the role that the "missed destiny of death" plays in the memories of witnesses receives concrete expression here. In the chaotic scheme of values created for their victims by the Germans, a birth moment is a death moment, and a mother's ambition is to leave her life to join her murdered infant. In the dialogue between hope and despair that we have just heard, nothing remains to praise. Whose spirit can the midwife's soothing words gladden?

But Arina B.'s story doesn't end here. She continues:

I was lucky. I find my husband after the war. I didn't know for three months if he's alive, but I count on two people—my sister and my husband. And they're alive . . . I find my husband. And finally we made home in Marburg an der Lahn in Germany. And I was so afraid to have a child; he wants family. And I said: "For what? Again gonna happen, again gonna kill our children?" I was so afraid always. And I got my son. I was pregnant with second child and I didn't want it. I was afraid again. And I said to my husband, "I don't want to have a child any more. I hate to be in Germany; I hate all the Germans. I can't stand these stones, covered with blood, everything is in blood." And I was so . . . if he was thinking to have a baby, I was angry at him. And I said, "Fine, I'm going to look how to get rid of it, the baby." And I went, I got rid.[8]

The chronological text of Arina B.'s story has a happy ending, as her midwife in Auschwitz proves to have been a subtle prophet. Six years after coming to the United States, Arina B. had another child, and she now salutes with pleasure her two beautiful children and four grandchildren. But almost in the same breath, she furnishes a durational subtext, unwittingly internalizing her own image of stones covered in blood: "I'm like stone," she reports, "sometimes I feel I'm stone—inside, you know."[9] We are left with a complex portrait of a woman who has survived an unspeakable ordeal to pursue a normal life while simultaneously abnormal death continues to pursue her. Although her previous "homes" include Majdanek, Auschwitz, and Ravensbrück, she has adapted far better than Charlotte Delbo's Mado; however, we must still face the dilemma of defining vitality for a witness who calls herself a woman of stone.

The testimony of Shari B. gives us a vivid glimpse into how circumstances could curtail the independent spirit of a young girl between her seventeenth and eighteenth year, a spirit that under normal conditions would certainly have flourished with a decided feminist flair. Arrested by the Gestapo while living in Bratislava with false papers, she is interrogated and beaten at night and during the day forced to clean out the police officials' offices. One afternoon, she approaches a window on the second floor and is wondering whether to jump out when an officer enters and says, "Are you thinking of jumping? I can put you out of your misery right now, if you want." He aims a pistol at her head, and she remembers thinking, "If I faint, they will surely kill me," so she tells herself: "This moment will pass. This moment will pass." Finally, he puts the gun away, saying, "I don't want to cause a mess in the office. They're going to shoot you like all of the Jews anyway."[10]

Eventually, she is deported to Theresienstadt. Her determination not to let the Germans kill her is further tested on the journey, when she tries to climb through the small window of her boxcar. The other people in the car pull her back, arguing, "If you escape, they'll come and shoot us." A fracas ensues among the prisoners, and Shari B. remembers turning to them and crying, "You are old; you are all old and have lived your life already, but I am young and want to go on living." Fear is a powerful deterrent to community spirit, however, and the illusion that one woman's survival can be isolated from the potential death of innumerable others can be maintained only by ignoring the inroads that German terror made on the individual will.

In spite of her inner resolve to resist, in Theresienstadt Shari B. is reduced to the demeaning state of utter vulnerability, a situation that many of her gender report as worse than the threat of death. She and the other women in her barrack are lying around naked when some SS men start walking through the room. She weeps as she speaks: "We were dehumanized. This was our most humiliating moment and I hated them that they should be able to walk around and see us naked." But there was nothing she could do. The episode is seared on her memory, as she relives it still engulfed by hatred and shame.

This is bad enough, but in Shari B.'s narrative we have an instance of how her ordeal lingers on in the response of her son. She and her husband had left Czechoslovakia and come to the United States after the war, but he died young of lung cancer, leaving her with two small children to raise herself:

> Once I read a report that children of Holocaust victims are affected, and I asked them [her children], "How do you feel about this? Do you feel you are affected?" And they said, "Mommy, how can you ask such a question? Of course we are affected!" And I said, "But you know, I never really told you anything as long as you were little." And they said, "Yes, but do you think we didn't know every time someone spoke about Germans or so on, you always had a comment?"
>
> And then I recalled an incident that happened. My son went to school, he was about six and a half or seven, and at school they must have told him about the Holocaust. And he came home, and he raised his hand and said, "Heil Hitler!" And I did not say anything, but I said, "You know, Robbie, don't ever say that." And he became very serious, and he didn't ask me why not. He went to the bathroom, and wouldn't come out for quite a while, and . . . So I would knock, and said, "Now, what are you doing there? Come out, please." And he came out, and his hand was bleeding, and so I said, "How did you

hurt it, what happened?" And he said, "I scratched it out, so I should never say it again."

So I don't know. I didn't tell him anything. I felt I never really spoke to them while they were little, yet I must have conveyed something.

Holocaust testimony is not a series of links in a chain whose pattern of connections can be easily traced, but a cycle of sparks erupting unpredictably from a darkened landscape, teasing the imagination toward illumination without ever offering it the steady ray of stable insight. My final fragment of women's witnessing probes how Edith P., who, as she says, has a wonderful family but no past, strives to merge her memories of Auschwitz into her present life. In the course of her meditation, she accents for us the delicate balance between gender and human identity, and the tension between personal and cultural origins of the self, that surface in so many of these oral narratives:

> I just want to say, I've been liberated thirty five years, going to be this month—April fourteenth [1980]. And as I get older, and my children are all self-sufficient and no longer at home, and I am not busy being a mother and a wife, and I can be myself—I have given a great deal of thought how I should conduct myself vis-à-vis the Germans, how I should feel. Should I hate them? Should I despise them? . . . I don't know; I never found the answer. . . . But sometimes I wish in my darkest hours that they would feel what we feel sometimes, when you are uprooted, and bring up children—I'm talking as a mother and a wife—and there is nobody to share your sorrow or your great happiness. Nobody to call up and say something good happened to me today: I have given birth to a beautiful daughter; or she got all "A"s; she got into a good college. I mostly remember when holidays come, I have tried to preserve the holidays as I saw it at home, transfer it to my own children. We have beautiful Passovers like I saw it at home. But the spirit is not there. It's beautiful, my friends tell me, when I invite them, that it's beautiful, it's very spiritual. But I know it's not the same. I . . . I . . . there's something missing. I want to share it with someone who knows me really . . . [11]

"I am no longer busy being a mother, a wife, and I can be myself"—under other circumstances, we might applaud this as a triumphant liberation of the pure feminine spirit from more traditional and, for some, confining activities. But how can we say that in this case? Edith P.'s Holocaust experience has undermined the rhetoric of renewal and self-discovery. The subtext of her life and her testimony is not a quest for release but an admission of irreplaceable loss. What she calls her absent past is permanently present *inside* the woman who is utterly alone at a Passover seder despite the company of her husband, her children, and her friends.

The curtailed potential of her stillborn life as a sister and a daughter, or her incomplete life as a wife and mother, because she is cut off together with her husband and children from the family she cannot share with them, leaves her a legacy of internal loneliness that nothing can reverse. But if we substitute for these gendered terms the more generic ones of parent and child, we move Edith P. and the other women I have been discussing into a human orbit that unites them through a kind of regret that cannot be sorted by sex. To be sure, pregnancy and childbirth are biologically unique experiences, and we have heard how they have been endured under unbearable conditions. But if we examine the following brief, complex moment of testimony, involving not only a wife, husband, and infant but also the daughter of the witness by a second marriage, we may glimpse the danger of overstating the importance of a biologically unique experience. The family is awaiting deportation, and the witness records the feeling of utter helplessness that seized so many victims at moments like these:

> This was summer. Outside there was a bench. So we sat on the bench, my wife holding the kid [their infant child] in her arms. In my head, what to think first of. You want to do something, and you know you're in a corner. You can't do *anything*. And when somebody asks me now, "Why didn't you fight?" I ask them, "How would *you* fight in such a situation?" My wife holds a child, a child stretches out [its] arms to me, and I look at him, and she says, "Hold him in [your] arms, you don't know how long more you'll be able to hold him. . . . " [The witness sobs with remembered grief, as his daughter from his second marriage, who is sitting next to him on the

couch, puts a consoling arm around her father and leans her head on his shoulder.] Me, a man, crying.[12]

Exactly like Edith P., Victor C. might protest, "I have a family, but no past," and could we reasonably argue that there is a gendered difference between the two expressions of anguish? The origins of humiliation were often dissimilar for men and women, because womanhood and manhood were threatened in various ways. But the ultimate sense of loss unites former victims in a violated world beyond gender. Victor C. clings to his daughter in the present, but the subtext of his life is the moment when, as the member of an earlier family, he was separated from his wife, his child, his mother, and his grandmother, all of whom were shipped to Auschwitz and gassed. Shall we celebrate the fact that because he was a man, and able to work, his life was saved? I think that he, a man crying, would not agree.

In the testimonies I have studied, I have found little evidence that mothers behaved or survived better than fathers, or that mutual support between sisters, when possible, prevailed more than between brothers. We do have more accounts of sisters staying together than brothers, but that is probably because brothers were more often separated by the nature of the work they were deemed able to do. This is an example of situational accident, not gender-driven choice. In all instances, solicitude alternated with frustration or despair, as the challenge of staying alive under brutal conditions tested human resources beyond the limits of decency—although we hardly need to mention that the victims shared no blame for their plight.

As for the ability to bear suffering, given the unspeakable sorrow with which all victims were burdened, it seems to me that nothing could be crueler or more callous than the attempt to dredge up from this landscape of universal destruction a mythology of comparative endurance that awards favor to one group of individuals over another. The pain of loss and the relief of survival remain entwined in the memory of those lucky enough to have outlived the atrocities. All efforts to find a rule of hierarchy in that darkness, whether based on gender or will, spirit or hope, reflect only our own need to plant a life-sustaining seed in the barren soil that conceals the remnants of two-thirds of European Jewry. The sooner we abandon this design, the quicker we will learn to face such chaos with unshielded eyes.

Notes

1. Charlotte Delbo, *Auschwitz and After,* trans. Rosette C. Lamont (New Haven: Yale University Press, 1995), p. 257.

2. Ibid., pp. 258, 259.

3. Ibid., p. 260.

4. Ibid., p. 267.

5. Tape T-1154, testimony of Sally H., Fortunoff Video Archive for Holocaust Testimony at Yale University (hereafter Fortunoff Video Archive).

6. Tape T-220, testimony of Joly Z., Fortunoff Video Archive.

7. Tape T-2045, testimony of Arina B., Fortunoff Video Archive.

8. Ibid.

9. Ibid.

10. Tape T-66, testimony of Shari B., Fortunoff Video Archive. All quotations from Shari B. are from this source.

11. Tape T-107, testimony of Edith P., Fortunoff Video Archive.

12. Tape T-192, testimony of Viktor C., Fortunoff Video Archive.

CHAPTER TWENTY-ONE

Women in Holocaust Literature
Engendering Trauma Memory

Sara R. Horowitz

T he image remains vivid in the retelling: a twenty-two-year-old woman, visibly pregnant, bicycling to the hospital to deliver her first baby. Now, almost a half-century later, as Itka Frajman Zygmuntowicz relates to me the circumstances surrounding the birth of her firstborn, the memory calls forth the same amalgam of emotions: joy and sorrow, hope and loss, future and past.[1]

Eleven days after her nineteenth birthday in April 1945, the Swedish Red Cross brought Itka Frajman to Lund, Sweden. By then she had survived one ghetto and three camps. In October 1941, the Frajman family had been forced from their home in Ciechanow, Poland, a small town about fifty-five miles north of Warsaw, into the Nowe-Miasto Ghetto. The following year, after the liquidation of the ghetto in November 1942, they were transported to Auschwitz. In January 1945, Itka was moved from Auschwitz in a forced six-day march to Ravensbrück. One month later, she was taken to a third camp, Malchow, also in Germany, where she remained until the liberation. She was the only member of her family to survive. A year after her arrival in Sweden, she met Rachmil Zygmuntowicz, also a Holocaust survivor. One month later, they married. Early in 1948, she became pregnant.

Early one Friday morning in her ninth month of pregnancy, she experienced an unsettling event. "My water bag broke," she recounts. "But I didn't know then what that meant, what was happening to me." Alone at home, she consulted a neighbor, also a camp survivor. The neighbor, too, was at a loss and suggested that the pregnant woman ask her doctor. So on October 2,

1948, Itka Frajman Zygmuntowicz mounted upon her bicycle and pedaled down the streets of Boras, Sweden, to the hospital. Less than twenty-four hours later, she gave birth to her first son.

Decades later, she tells this story with a mixture of amusement and horror. "I had no idea I was endangering my life and my unborn child." She explains, "I was thirteen when Poland was first occupied, nineteen at liberation. I spent my teenage years in camps. I didn't see a normal pregnancy carried to term in a normal situation. I didn't know what you were supposed to do. I didn't know it wasn't a good idea to get on a bicycle." She pauses for a moment, then adds: "And I had no one to tell me this, to advise me, because my mother was killed in Auschwitz."

On Friday afternoon, with the baby not yet born, a friend warned Zygmuntowicz's husband, "The baby's not going to live." Such cases, the friend told him, where the water breaks too soon and the baby is not born immediately, do not auger well. But at one in the morning on Saturday, October 3, 1948, Zygmuntowicz gave birth to a healthy son. Soon after, her husband stepped into the hospital room where she lay recuperating. She recalls him standing with his hands behind his back, looking sad. He didn't speak. His sorrow puzzled her. "I said to him, 'You know, we have a son,' and he broke down crying." Only then did he offer her the flowers he had hidden behind his back. "Because he didn't know if we had a baby or if the baby died." Later she added, "My son was born the same year as the State of Israel."

I begin my discussion about women in the Shoah (the Hebrew word for the Holocaust) by sharing this story about a particular survivor—a woman who, over the course of time and memories, has become a friend—for several reasons. First, to make clear that my point of departure and return is always the testimonies of survivors. Only the careful attentiveness to their voices authorizes my own in this area. Second, the story makes clear that the atrocity and trauma of the Nazi genocide did not end with liberation of the camps but continues to color what happens later. Third, and perhaps most pertinent for our purposes, this story illustrates that Jewish women survivors experienced, and reflect back upon, the war both as Jews and as women.

As Zygmuntowicz recounts it, the birth of their first child marked the young couple's emotional investment in the future. Having survived the war bereft of family, Zygmuntowicz begins to rebuild a family. Linking this personal event with the founding of the State of Israel, too, represents a triumph over the forces of death that had all but eradicated Eastern European Jewish life. At the same time, the memory carries the shadings of bereavement. With the retelling of the birth also comes the retelling of absences—of the death of Zygmuntowicz's mother, who would have indoctrinated her into adult womanhood, and of the loss of her own teenage years to Nazi atrocity. These losses and their connection with her own crucial ignorance suggest a gender-based wounding, a shattering of something innate and important to her sense of her own womanhood. This idea of gender wounding emerges in literary texts by women—and, differently, in works by men. Embedded in Zygmuntowicz's memory of childbirth are a series of near losses: her own alarm at her water breaking, her dangerous ride to the hospital, her husband's fear that they have lost the baby so late in the pregnancy, and his tears that are of joy but also of sorrow. Thus each time she speaks of birth, she speaks also of death, or of destruction.

Why examine Shoah narrative from the perspective of gender? One might argue that the Nazi program of genocide was predicated not upon gender but upon "race." At the same time, however, women's testimonies reveal distinctly different patterns of experience and reflection from those of men. In recalling and grappling with memories of personal and collective loss, trauma, and displacement, and in reconstructing a sense of meaning and ethics, women may remember differently from men—or they may remember different things. Missing from male versions of survival are experiences unique to women, such as menarche, menstruation, and pregnancy in the concentration camps; the strategies some women devised to endure and survive; the ways other women met their deaths; the subsequent effect on women survivors in family, friendship, and civic relations; and the way women reconstruct shattered paradigms of meaning in the face of cultural and personal displacement. In addition, examining the ways the atrocity of the Shoah affected women or men, in specific terms—in their roles as mothers, fathers, wives, husbands, daughters, sons, lovers, friends, workers, homemakers—reveals to us something of the trauma they continue to bear.

In discussing women in Shoah literature as a fulcrum to understanding the gender implications of trauma, I shall explore three areas: the way women are figured in texts by men, the way women's experiences and remembrances are represented in narratives by women, and the significance of gender as a perspective for understanding Shoah literature, generally.

In many Holocaust narratives by men, women are portrayed as peripheral, helpless, and fragile; as morally deficient; or as erotic in their victimization. In Art Spiegelman's *Maus*,[2] for example, the story of the artist's parents, Vladek and Anja Spiegelman, both concentration camp survivors, is conveyed through a combination of Vladek's words (as told to Art in a series of taped conversations spanning several years) and Art's graphics.[3] Vladek's stories, whether of events before, during, or after the war, consistently depict Anja as a sensitive, loving, and emotionally fragile woman who survives thanks to her husband's enterprising shrewdness and pragmatism. By the time Art began collecting material for his book, Anja had been dead for several years. Her suicide is one of the few segments of Spiegelman's book that shows human rather than animal characters. The suicide sequence depicts a younger Art as doubly victimized— first by his mother's smothering love, then by her guilt-inflicting suicide. "You *murdered* me, Mommy, and you left me here to take the rap!!!" is his closing speech.[4]

Intermittently, Art searches for his mother's diaries, to know "what she went through while . . . apart" from Vladek. Vladek repeatedly reassures Art that his narrative suffices to tell both of their stories: "I can tell you. . . . She went through the same what me: TERRIBLE!" Only at the end of the volume does Vladek reveal that after Anja's death, in an attempt to "make order" with his memories, he burned her notebooks and no longer recalls what she had written.

Anja's missing diaries exemplify the marginality of women's experience in constructing a master narrative of the Nazi genocide. Vladek burns the notebooks not out of malice but in response to his own pain, and then he subsumes her memories within his own. In the absence of her own words (written, Vladek explains, in the hope that someday her son "will be interested by this"), Anja's story is recoverable only through the reconstruction of Vladek's and Art's memories. In Art's recollection, Anja's love smothers and her suicide wounds, and in Vladek's recollection Anja appears weak and dependent. In many other male Holocaust narratives, women are presented as helpless victims (although the men were no less helpless), as absent loved ones (although the men, too, were absent), and as needing rescue (although the men, too, needed rescue).

Vladek's narration skirts moments of failure and loss. In *Maus II,* his testimony ends with memory of the reunion with his beloved Anja, soon after liberation. "We were both very happy, and lived happy, happy ever after," he tells his son, then asks Art to stop the tape recorder. Deliberately cut off at that moment is everything that happens next—Anja's suicide, Vladek's own incessant nightmares, recurrent thoughts of their murdered son, Richieu. How would Anja narrate her story of atrocity and survival? How would her diaries depict her life in the camps, her marriage with Vladek, her memories, her losses, her motherhood?

Vladek's recollections reflect his own memories of his own experiences and his own inner life. The episodes he selects to recount—and those that memory selects for him—are shaped by his ongoing struggle to master a horrific past. However faithful he endeavors to remain to this past, his narrative of its events cannot possibly recount Anja's inner life. Nor can he speak with certainty of her experiences while they were apart. Vladek ventriloquizes Anja unselfconsciously, creating dialogue, motive, inner thought, and feelings. Yet Spiegelman's portrayal of his parents' survival hints to us that Vladek's version of Anja may contain significant lacunae. The comic strip intimates that Anja was more than the emotionally frail spouse Vladek portrays. Unlike her husband, whose survival efforts were directed only toward his family, Anja served as a translator and courier for a resistance group (without her husband's knowledge). Her participation in this dangerous work implies that Anja was not so devoid of resources and courage as Vladek's recollections suggest. And Vladek's failure to save his child, Richieu, from Nazi murder quietly stands against his compilation of daring gambits and studied cleverness that, in his narrative, effect his and Anja's survival.

Vladek's tellings repeatedly cast himself and his wife in exaggerated gender roles—the brave and resourceful man, the fearful and dependent woman. Perhaps his strong insistence on Anja's utter dependence marks an attempt to compensate for his failure to accomplish what, as a father, he most desperately wished to accomplish. The trauma of actual helplessness as a father, then, is countered by the memory of heroic performance as a husband.

The rarity of women's voices is striking in the contemporary discourse about the Holocaust. Not that women survivors have failed to produce diaries, memoirs, journals, novels, vignettes. Women wrote in ghettos and in hiding, as Rachel Auerbach's essays attest;[5] some even managed to do so in Nazi slave labor camps.[6] Women continue to publish their reflections in many languages. Many women leave records of their experiences, in the form of letters, manuscripts prepared for their families, and oral or videotaped testimony, such as those gathered under the aegis of the Fortunoff Video Archive for Holocaust Testimonies at Yale University. Nevertheless, works by women survivors are cited less frequently in scholarly studies, women's experiences are rarely central to the presentation of a "typical" Holocaust story, and significant works by women soon fall out of print, becoming unavailable for classroom use. How we think about and how we teach the Holocaust has been based predominantly on the testimony—written and oral—of male survivors. As one survivor remarked to me during an interview about her Holocaust-based work of fiction, "No one has yet written the history of women in the Shoah."[7]

The few studies on women and the Holocaust, primarily by historians, take one of two approaches. The first approach asserts the equality of men and women—as victims, as resistance fighters, as sufferers, and as survivors of Nazi atrocity.[8] In this view, the events of the Holocaust undermine sexism. The second approach seeks to distinguish women's lives and deaths from those of men, and to bring into view uniquely female experiences.[9] These works tend to focus on pregnancy, menstruation, prostitution, and rape.

Both these approaches yield valuable insights, and the concomitant research adds to the important store of knowledge about women during the Shoah. But, when posed antithetically, each approach skews the discussion, thereby misrepresenting the actual experiences of women victims and the recollections of women survivors. The first produces a unified (unisex) version of the Holocaust, which unintentionally ends up occluding experiences particular to women. In this version, women are seen as identical to men, with the universe of the concentration camp functioning as a great equalizer. The second inadvertently reproduces the marginalization of women, by presenting their experiences almost exclusively in terms of sexuality. In this version, women are seen as particularly vulnerable—biologically vulnerable—to Nazi brutality and, at the same time, as predominantly "bonding" and "nurturing" even in face of extreme atrocity. All women become "mothers," regardless of actual circumstance.[10] Treating women as a more or less unified group with similar behavioral characteristics ignores important differences in cultural background, social class, age, economic standing, level of education, religious observance, and political orientation—differences that, like gender, contribute to the way victims responded to their circumstances. In addition, both versions tend to present an idealized portrait of women's behavior—strong (like men) or nurturing (like women)—which erases the actual experiences of women and, to an extent, domesticates the events of the Holocaust. And yet, the breakdown of values and resistance, whether spiritual, physical, or psychological, is one index of Nazi brutality.

Between these poles, I pursue a different tactic, suggested not by any theoretical stance a priori but by the reflections of women survivors.[11] Itka Zygmuntowicz, for example, writes of her liberation at the end of the war:

> All on earth that I loved and held sacred I lost in the Holocaust, including nearly six precious years of my life. All on earth that I had left after liberation from Malchow, Germany, was my skeletal body minus all my hair, minus my monthly cycle, a tattered concentration camp shift dress without undergarments, a pair of beaten up unmatched wooden clogs, plus my "badge of honor," a large blue number 25673 that the Nazis tattooed on my left forearm on the day of my initiation to Auschwitz inferno. I was homeless, stateless, penniless, jobless, orphaned, and bereaved. . . . I had no marketable skills. . . . Jewish homes, Jewish families, and Jewish communities were destroyed. I was a displaced person, a stranger; alive, but with no home to live in. I had no one to love me, to miss me, to comfort me or to guide me.[12]

Zygmuntowicz's references to the cessation of menses and her lack of undergarments point to particular ways the Holocaust affected her as a woman, a subject she elaborates elsewhere. At the same time, her bereavement and displacement, the tattoo and wooden shoes, all identify her as an object of the genocidal practices aimed equally at Jewish men and Jewish women. The bringing together of both sets of details—one particular to women, one relevant to all Jewish inhabitants of the camps—implies that survivors' reflections are inevitably gendered, and also that gender does not constitute the totality of one's experience.

Following Zygmuntowicz's lead, I would like first to place the texts of women within the more broad-based conversation of Holocaust discourse. How do (and how did) different women reflect upon, recollect, and interpret their experiences of Nazi atrocity? For one thing, women's testimonies reveal the precariousness of childbirth during the Holocaust. In the ghettos, hard physical labor, scarce food and medical supplies, and the threat of roundups or selections made pregnancy a life-threatening event for the mother, the baby, and the community. In the camps, the consequences of pregnancy were even worse: visibly pregnant women and women with small children were selected for immediate killing.

Pregnancy comes to mean different things in different accounts. It may serve as evidence of the special vulnerability of women, or of the predominance of the life force. The way a pregnant mother grapples with her condition, the response of other women, and the treatment she receives from the Nazis, make pregnancy testify to the strength or the fragility of the intimate bonds that tie human lives together.

The related tropes of pregnancy and motherhood have led later scholars to focus on one of two distinct forms of narrative: those of atrocity and those of heroism. In narratives of atrocity, pregnancy and motherhood render women especially vulnerable to Nazi brutality. By contrast, in narratives of heroism they provide an arena for resistance against genocide.

Central to narratives of heroism is the portrayal of women conspiring against the genocidal will of the Nazis in order to save a newborn or a child. The accounts often focus on a secret pregnancy, with a baby born healthy and either hidden with its mother or smuggled to safety. These narratives valorize not only the protective agency of women but also motherhood itself. The mother's determination to carry to term at the risk of her own life proves powerful enough to prevail over the forces of death. Because the mother's success requires the help of others, individual pregnancy is seen as evidence of the nurturing bonds that connect women. And by drawing attention to "happy endings"—the few babies saved, the few pregnant women protected—such stories create a feeling of optimism in face of a destruction that we know, historically, was almost completely achieved.

By contrast, in narratives of atrocity, the mother is not strong enough to keep the baby alive. The fetus may be aborted, the infant stillborn or killed soon after birth. In some instances, Jewish women kill the baby to preserve their own or the mother's life; in other cases, the Nazis kill the child, often together with the mother. These narratives reverse the conventional symbol of pregnancy as hope and regeneration. Instead, birth becomes synonymous with death. The overwhelming magnitude of the genocidal forces renders resistance futile. Narratives of atrocity convey the immeasurable losses that women suffered, their powerlessness, and their lack of meaningful choices.

When writing about women in the Holocaust, scholars tend to emphasize one or the other of these two types of narratives. Such selectivity, while elucidating an aspect of life and death under Nazi rule, leads to partial interpretations of women's behavior. In the actual testimonies of women survivors, the strands of these two narratives are often intermeshed. In a single remembrance, narratives of heroism and of atrocity may oppose and undercut one another. Anna K., for example, found herself pregnant at Buchenwald.[13] Eventually, the rumor that a woman was pregnant circulated throughout the camp. An SS officer lined up all six thousand women in the camp and announced, "Whoever is pregnant is going to be hanged to show you all that it's not right." Although Anna K.'s identity was revealed, she was saved from death by the liberation of Buchenwald. After giving birth, Anna K., uncertain of her husband's survival, was sent to Switzerland with her baby daughter. Her husband eventually made his way to Switzerland, and the family began life anew in the United States.

One is tempted to read Anna K.'s testimony as a narrative of heroics exemplifying "biological resistance." In Anna K.'s remembrance—and in her husband's—her pregnancy and the birth of her daughter give hope to her husband in his own struggle. At the same time, however, Anna K.'s story contains more somber undertones. She recollects hearing about other women in the camp, pregnant "ahead of me," whose destiny, darkly hinted at, remains undisclosed. Were it not for the timely Allied victory, Anna K.'s pregnancy would have sealed her death.

Similarly, in Sara Nomberg-Przytyk's memoir, "Esther's First Born," the nineteen-year-old Esther regards her pregnancy as a guarantor of the future and a healing balm against the bereavements she has suffered.[14] "I want to give birth to this baby. It's my first baby. It moves. It kicks me. It will probably be a son. My husband is not here anymore. That's his son" (p. 68). Against the backdrop of Esther's joyous anticipation, Nomberg-Przytyk's narrator struggles to save other women from the lethal consequences of pregnancy in Auschwitz. We learn that the doctor delivers women in their own blocks rather than in the infirmary in order to keep the pregnancy and birth secret, thus preserving the mother's life. "Our procedure now is to kill the baby after birth in such a way that the woman doesn't know about it" (p. 69). In the grotesque situation of the death camp, murder can be life-giving. The doctor tells Nomberg-Przytyk, "I want so much for the babies to be born dead, but out of spite they are born healthy" (p. 69).

Throughout the narrative, Esther remains confident that she will survive with her baby. "I am sure that when Mengele sees it he will let me raise it in the camp. It is going to be a beauty because my husband was very handsome" (p. 70). Momentarily, the narrative suggests, that Esther's gambit will triumph. The baby is born healthy and—uncannily—mother and child are not sent immediately to their death. But inevitably, Mengele ultimately selects Esther and her firstborn for death.

Ilona Karmel explores these complexities further in her novel, *An Estate of Memory*, which focuses on one woman's pregnancy in a slave labor camp.[15] Forming a "makeshift family," three women protect a pregnant fourth, provide food from their own inadequate rations, deliver the baby in secret, and arrange to smuggle it from the camp to safety. To them, the survival of the baby girl symbolizes triumph over the machinery of death. "So the child, carried like a parcel out of the camp, kept growing, until it was big enough to take upon itself the burden of their longing for a proof, for the sign that out 'in the Freedom' they still mattered" (p. 277). At the same time, the moral victory is undercut by a counternarrative about another baby born in the camp and left to starve. The Nazi doctor orders, "The child should be laid in cotton wool . . . the child should not be fed anything, not even water" (p. 255). Moved by compassion, women feed the infant sugar water, at great personal risk. These feedings only prolong the baby's agony. This brutal story, part of the oral history transmitted among the camp women, serves as a touchstone to Nazi cruelty. It also undermines the sense of heroic possibilities asserted by the rescue of the baby girl. The chasm between "normal" life and atrocity is made concrete by the differences in what pregnancy connotes in the camps and in memory of life before the war. Karmel's novel contrasts one woman's prewar "longing for a child" (p. 166) with another's sense of her unborn baby as "a tormentor who sucked her strength, snatched every crumb away" (p. 242).

But Karmel does not use pregnancy only to illustrate the biological vulnerability or endurance or nurturing capacity of women. The joint effort to protect the pregnancy becomes a fulcrum upon which to explore moral dilemmas of survival. The familial bond among women remains tentative and fragile against the assault of Nazi atrocity. Fighting to retain moral agency under dehumanizing conditions, the women forge a code of ethics: acting on behalf of the group is altruistic, while defending one's own well-being is selfish. The women fight aggressively to preserve their makeshift families. But as circumstances grow more intolerable, the group ethic unravels. One woman wonders, "What is it? Anything done for someone else is a sacrifice, a noble deed; but try to do the same thing for yourself and the sacrifice becomes a disgrace. Why? I too am someone; I've no contract for survival" (p. 342).

In her two stories "The Shawl" and "Rosa," Cynthia Ozick explores the protective capacity of motherhood, and the fragmentation of the survivor who could not, ultimately, do the work of mothering.[16] When women cannot feed and shelter their children, and protect them from pain and from death, maternal love itself becomes an instrument of torture. Rosa remains forever a bereaved mother, the absence of her daughter, Magda, the only steady presence in her life. In "Rosa," then, Ozick uses the unbearable memory of witnessing the death of one's child to explore not only the issue of truncated mothering during the Shoah but survivor trauma generally.

As the writings of Sara Nomberg-Przytyk, Ilona Karmel, Ida Fink, and other survivors indicate, women writers do not simply provide raw material for contemporary researchers to analyze. Women have themselves been interpreters and analyzers of their own experiences, using the space of their writing to think through the complexities of the Shoah for its survivors and for others. Their writing expands our cognitive and psychological understanding of the Holocaust, using narratives of victimization and survival to meditate on the problematics of memory, testimony, and trauma.

In thinking about women's representations of the Shoah, we must not fall into the practice of viewing women only as objects of a particular subset of genocidal practices connected to their biological functions. Because these experiences, so particular to women, are most blatantly missing from male accounts, our strongest temptation may be to retrieve and elaborate these effaced narratives, as I have done here—reconstructing, as it were, Anja Spiegelman's lost diaries. Although this effort enables us to discuss women's unique experiences, limiting our discussion in this way would—ironically—serve to reinscribe male experience as normative for the development of a master narrative, and would relegate women to the category of the mother, or the victim of sexual abuse. Our task, however, is to examine women not only as objects of particular abuses, as developers of particular survival strategies, or even as thinkers about their own experiences. We must examine the place of gender in accounts of men as well as those of women.

Just as Nazi atrocity attacked Jewish women both as Jews and as women, it also attacked Jewish men both as Jews and as men. Often, Nazi brutality took the form of attacks on male biology, on the secondary sex characteristics that made Jewish men publicly recognizable as Jewish men: beards and earlocks. Like women, men were forced to endure the public exposure and shaving of their genital hair. Circumcision made Jewish men easily identifiable and, hence, particularly vulnerable. Jewish men hiding in the Aryan world under false papers were in constant danger of betrayal by their "Jewish genitalia." Shoah literature by men—both memoir and fiction—refers explicitly and repeatedly to these facets of genocide, which are the focus of the sardonically titled chapter "The Tool and the Art of Comparison," in Piotr Rawicz's *Blood from the Sky*.[17] In this novel, the narrator fears that his circumcision will betray his Jewishness. The film *Europa, Europa* depicts Solomon Perl's fear of two levels of exposure—of his nakedness and his Jewishness—when he hides under an assumed identity in an elite school for Hitler Youth.

These specifically male fears, humiliations, and torments are embedded more subtly and pervasively in particular tropes or figures of speech that emerge in men's Shoah writing. I have written elsewhere, for example, about the trope of the wounded tongue in the works of Piotr Rawicz, Elie Wiesel, Elias Canetti, and H. Leivick, and its significance for male trauma memory in post-Shoah writing. In these texts of twentieth-century Jewish trauma and displacement, the wounded tongue figures ambivalently as marking and obliterating maleness. As such, it represents displaced circumcision and displaced castration.

Antisemitic ideology feminizes Jewish men, depicting them as both more and less than "real" men, and genitally other as women are genitally other. In other ways, too, men experienced an assault on their sense of manhood. On a behavioral level, men found themselves unable to fulfill the traditional role of protectors of their wives and families, which damaged their capacity to function as men. The Nazi genocide destabilized the boundaries of the self, unmaking the gendered self. In men's writing, the memory of the Shoah inserts itself in the relationship between fathers and sons. These traumas of victimization and survival, experienced as gender woundings, testify to the fragmentation at the extremity of suffering.

Notes

1. Itka Frajman Zygumtowicz, interviews, June 27, 1989, and November 5, 1996.

2. Art Spiegelman, *Maus* (New York: Pantheon Books, 1988).

3. Sections of this discussion of *Maus,* and the discussion of pregnancy in the camps, appeared in a different form in Sara R. Horowitz, "Memory and Testimony in Women Survivors of Nazi Genocide," in *Women of the Word: Jewish Women and Jewish Writing,* ed. Judith Baskin (Detroit: Wayne State, 1994), pp. 258–82.

4. The suicide sequence was originally published in Art Spiegelman, "Prisoner on the Hell Planet," *Short Order Comix,* no. 1 (1973), and was interpolated into the text of *Maus.*

5. See, for example, Rachel Auerbach, "Yizkor, 1943," trans. Leonard Wolf, reprinted in *The Literature of Destruction,* ed. David G. Roskies (Philadelphia: Jewish Publication Society, 1988), pp. 459–464.

6. For example, two sisters—Ilona Karmel and Henia Karmel-Wolfe—wrote poetry on the backs of pilfered work reports while in a slave labor camp. Some of these poems were collected and published in the original Polish in *Spiew za Drutami* (Song behind the wire) (New York: Polish Jewish Press, 1947).

7. Irene Eber, interview, February 4, 1992.

8. For example, in *The Theme of Nazi Concentration Camps in French Literature* (Hague: Mouton, 1972), Cynthia Haft asserts that "the camp system grants complete equality to men and women" (p. 121).

9. For example, Marlene E. Heinemann, *Gender and Destiny: Woman Writers and the Holocaust* (Westport, Conn.: Greenwood Press, 1986).

10. Heinemann, for example, sets up "three categories of mothers," including "mothers and women above age forty-five" (*Gender and Destiny,* p. 22), a category that inexplicably subsumes all women under the heading of mother.

11. Cultural studies and postmodernist theory teach us that each of us reads texts with cultural and ideological assumptions that frame our interpretation. I do not naively claim here to exclude myself from this understanding of reading practices; rather, I wish to indi-

cate that I have allowed the texts I have read to interrogate theory, to serve in some fashion as a test case for some theoretical positions within feminism.

12. Itka Frajman Zygmuntowicz, with Sara Horowitz, "Survival and Memory," in *Four Centuries of Jewish Women's Spirituality: A Sourcebook*, ed. Ellen M. Umansky and Dianne Ashton (Boston: Beacon Press, 1992), p. 290.

13. Testimony of Anna K., Fortunoff Video Archive for Holocaust Testimonies, Yale University (hereafter FVA), tape T-1115.

14. Sara Nomberg-Przytyk, *Auschwitz: True Tales from a Grotesque Land,* trans. Roslyn Hirsch (Chapel Hill: University of North Carolina Press, 1985).

15. Ilona Karmel, *An Estate of Memory* (Boston: Houghton Mifflin, 1969; reprint, New York: Feminist Press, 1986).

16. Cynthia Ozick, *The Shawl* (New York: Knopf, 1989).

17. Piotr Rawicz, *Blood from the Sky,* trans. Peter Wiles (New York: Harcourt, Brace and World, 1964).

Contributors

Gershon Bacon is a senior lecturer in the Department of Jewish History of Bar Ilan University, where he holds the Rabbi Samson Raphael Hirsch Chair in Modern Jewish History. He is the author of *The Politics of Tradition: Agudat Yisrael in Poland, 1916–1939* (1996) and the co-author, with Gershon D. Hundert, of *The Jews in Poland and Russia: Bibliographical Essays* (1984). His latest book, entitled *From Poland to Eastern Europe: The Jews of Eastern Europe, 1722–1914,* is in press.

Yehuda Bauer is Professor of History at the Hebrew University in Jerusalem, where he holds the Machover Chair for European History. He is also the chair of the International Research Institute in Yad Vashem. Among his many well-known books on the Holocaust are *Flight and Rescue: Brichah* (1970); *American Jewry and the Holocaust: The American Jewish Joint Distribution Committee, 1939–1945* (1981); *Out of the Ashes: The Impact of American Jews on Post-Holocaust European Jewry* (1989); and *The Holocaust in Historical Perspective* (1978). His most recent book is *Jews for Sale? Nazi Jewish Negotiation, 1933–1945* (1994).

Daniel Blatman is a lecturer on the faculty of the Avraham Harman Institute of Contemporary Jewry at the Hebrew University, Jerusalem. He is the author of *For Our Freedom and Yours: The Jewish Labor Bund in Poland, 1930–1949* (published in Hebrew in 1996; an English edition is forthcoming).

Gisela Bock is Professor of History at the Free University of Berlin, where she holds the Chair in Western European history. She is the author of *Zwangssterilisation im Nationalsozialismus: Studien zur Rassenpolitik und Frauenpolitik* (1986); co-author, with Pat Thane, of *Maternity and Gender Policies: Women and the Rise of the European Welfare State, 1880–1950* (1991); and the editor of *Rassenpolitik und Geschlechterpolitik im Nationalsozialismus* (1993).

Ruth Bondy is a survivor of Theresienstadt, Auschwitz-Birkenau, and Bergen-Belsen. She is a journalist and writer and a longtime member of the editorial board of Israel's *Davar* newspaper. Famous for her biographies of Enzo Sireni (*The Emissary*, 1977) and Jackob Edelstein (*The Elder of the Jews: Jackob Edelstein of Theresienstadt*, 1989), she is also the author of *The Israelis: Profile of a People* (1969). Her autobiography, entitled *Whole Fracture*, was published in Hebrew in 1997.

Liza Chapnik is a Holocaust survivor who took an active part in the underground movement in Grodno, Poland, and then in Bialystok. In April 1944 she was appointed the chairman of the Bialystok antifascist organization by Kastus Kalinovski of the Soviet Partisan Brigade. After World War II she and her family moved to Moscow. She received her Ph.D. from the Moscow Pedagogical Institute of Foreign Languages in 1952 and joined the faculty there. In December 1991 she and her family left the former Soviet Union and emigrated to Israel.

Ida Fink is one of the most well known writers on Jewish experiences during the Holocaust. Her collection of short stories, *A Scrap of Time and Other Stories* (1989), originally published in Polish in 1983, has been translated into many languages and won the Anne Frank prize in Amsterdam and the Moravia prize in Rome. She is also the author of the novel *The Journey* (published in the United States in 1992). Parts of her most recent book, *Traces*, appeared in *The New Yorker* in 1997.

Myrna Goldenberg is a professor of English at Montgomery College in Rockville, Maryland, and director of its Humanities Institute. She also teaches at the University of Maryland and Johns Hopkins University. Her published works include "Different Horror, Same Hell: Women Remembering the Holocaust," in *Thinking the Unthinkable*, ed. Roger Gottlieb (1990); and "Testimony, Narrative, Nightmare: The Experience of Jewish Women in the Holocaust," in *Active Voices: Women and Jewish Culture*, ed. Maurie Sacks (1995). She also wrote the preface and notes for *The Beautiful Days of My Youth*, a Holocaust memoir by Anna Novac (1997).

Sara R. Horowitz is director of the Jewish Studies Program and an associate professor of English literature in the Honors Program at the University of Delaware. She has published many articles on Holocaust literature and women Holocaust survivors. She is the author of *Voicing the Void: Muteness and Memory in Holocaust Fiction* (1997). She is also a founding co-editor of *Kerem: A Journal of Creative Explorations in Judaism*.

Paula E. Hyman is the Lucy Moses Professor of Modern Jewish History and Chair of the Program in Judaic Studies at Yale University. She is the author of *From Dreyfus to Vichy: The Remaking of French Jewry, 1906–1939* (1979); *The Emancipation of the Jews of Alsace: Acculturation and Tradition in the Nineteenth Century* (1991); and *Gender and Assimilation in Modern Jewish History* (1995). She is also the co-editor of the forthcoming *Encyclopedia of Jewish Women.*

Marion Kaplan is a professor of history at Queens College of the City University of New York. She is the author of *The Making of the Jewish Middle Class: Women, Family and Identity in Imperial Germany* (1991) and the forthcoming book *Jewish Life in Nazi Germany: Dignity and Despair.*

Felicja Karay is a survivor of the Holocaust in Poland. She was in three camps at Płaszów, Skarżysko-Kamienna, and Leipzig. She immigrated to Israel in 1950 and received her Ph.D. from Tel Aviv University. She is the author of *Death Comes in Yellow: Skarżysko-Kamienna Slave Labor Camp* (1996), which won the Jacob Buchman Foundation memorial prize. She is currently a researcher at the Diaspora Research Institute at Tel Aviv University and gives seminars organized by the Ministry of Education and Yad Vashem on teaching the Holocaust. Her latest book is entitled *Rackets and Rhymes: the Hasag-Leipzig Slave Labor Camp for Women* (forthcoming in Hebrew).

Bronka Klibanski is a survivor of the Holocaust. During World War II she was an active member of Dror and the Zionist resistance movement in Grodno and Bialystok. She was a courier for the underground and also fought with the partisans in the forests. After the war she emigrated to Israel, where she worked at Yad Vashem as a researcher. She is the author of *The Archive of Abraham Silberschein* (Hebrew, 1984) and *The Collection of Testimonies, Diaries and Memoirs in the Yad Vashem Archives* (1990). She also edited and published the papers of Mordechai Tenenbaum.

Lawrence L. Langer is Alumnae Chair Professor of English Emeritus at Simmons College in Boston. His books include *Holocaust Testimonies: The Ruins of Memory* (1991), which won the National Book Critics' Circle Award for Criticism and was chosen as one of the "ten best books of the year" by the *New York Times Book Review* editors; *Admitting the Holocaust: Collected Essays* (1995); and *Art from the Ashes: A Holocaust Anthology* (1995). His most recent book is *Pre-Empting the Holocaust and Other Essays* (1998).

Dalia Ofer is the Max and Rita Haber Professor for Holocaust Studies and Eastern Europe at the Avraham Harman Institute of Contemporary Jewry of the Hebrew University of Jerusalem. She is also the academic chair of the Vidal Sassoon International Center for Research on Antisemitism. She is the author of *Escaping the Holocaust: Illegal Immigration to the Land of Israel, 1939–1944* (1991); and the co-author, with Hannah Weinner, of *Dead End Journey: The Kladova Sabac Affair* (1996).

Renée Poznanski is a professor in the Department of History of Ben Gurion University in Israel. She is the author of *Etre juif en France pendant la seconde guerre mondiale* [Being a Jew in France during the Second World War] (1994; forthcoming in English).

Joan Ringelheim is director of the Department of Education and the Department of Oral History at the United States Holocaust Memorial Museum in Washington, D.C. As part of her pioneering work on women in the Holocaust, she edited the proceedings of a conference on women and the Holocaust in 1983 and wrote an article entitled "Women and the Holocaust: A Reconsideration of Research," which first appeared in *Signs* in 1985. More recently, she has written "Deportations, Death and Survival: Nazi Ghetto Policies against Jewish Women and Jewish Men in Occupied Poland," in *Nach Osten: Verdeckte Spurent nationalsozialistischer Verbrechen,* ed. Theresa Wobbe (1992).

Nechama Tec is a professor of sociology at the University of Connecticut in Stamford. She is the author of six books and numerous articles about compassion, resistance to evil, and the rescue of Jews during World War II, including *When Light Pierced the Darkness* (1987); *In the Lion's Den: The Life of Oswald Rufeisen* (1990); and *Defiance: The Bielski Partisan* (1993), which won several prizes, including the 1994 Anne Frank prize. She is also a Holocaust survivor, and her autobiographical book, *Dry Tears* (1982), tells the story of her family's passing in Poland.

Michal Unger is finishing her Ph.D. dissertation, "The Internal Life of the Lodz Ghetto, 1940–1944," under the supervision of Professor Yisrael Gutman at the Hebrew University of Jerusalem. She was the curator, scientific adviser, and editor of the catalogue for the exhibition "The Last Ghetto: Life in the Lodz Ghetto, 1940–1944." She is the author of several articles on the Holocaust and is also the editor of Joseph Zelikowiec's *Ba Yamim Ha Noraim Ha'Hem* [In Those Nightmarish Days] (1994).

Lidia Rosenfeld Vago is a Holocaust survivor from Transylvania, Romania. She and her sister lived through Auschwitz, the Death March, and the Ravensbrück and Neustadt-Glewe concentration camps. They returned to Transylvania, where Lidia married Bela Vago (then a student of history, later a well-known professor and Holocaust scholar). She graduated from V. Babes University in Cluj, Transylvania. After emigrating to Israel in 1958, she taught in high schools until her retirement in 1984. She has devoted the years since then to several Holocaust-related projects.

Lenore J. Weitzman is Clarence J. Robinson Professor of Sociology and Law at George Mason University in Fairfax, Virginia. She is the author of four books, including *Sex-Role Socialization* (1979), *The Marriage Contract* (1981), and *The Divorce Revolution: The Unexpected Social and Economic Consequences for Women and Children in America* (1985), which won several awards, including the Distinguished Contribution to Scholarship Award from the American Sociological Association. Before her recent move to Virginia she taught at Stanford and Harvard universities and was awarded Harvard's *Phi Beta Kappa* teaching award.

Index